The Silent Cry

THE SILENT CRY

Mysticism and Resistance

⇒>◆<⇐

DOROTHEE SOELLE

Translated by Barbara and Martin Rumscheidt

Fortress Press
MINNEAPOLIS

Library of Congress Cataloging-in-Publication Data

Sölle, Dorothee.
    [Mystik und Widerstand. English]
    The silent cry : mysticism and resistance / Dorothee Soelle.
        p. cm.
    Includes bibliographical references and index.
    ISBN 0-8006-3266-4 (alk. paper)
    1. Mysticism. I. Title

    BL625 .S61513 2001
    291.4'22--dc21   00-067713

Manufactured in the U.S.A.   AF 1-3266
05   04   03   02   01   1   2   3   4   5   6   7   8   9   10

For Fulbert

Nourished by your words of encouragement and contestation
this book grew
and would not have been written
without your reminding me
every dark day
of the light
in whose light we shall come to see

O deeply buried treasure, how wilt thou be unearthed?
O elevated nobility, who can reach thee?
O rushing fountain, who can drain thee dry?
O luminous radiance, power that breaks forth,
hiddenness laid bare, security that is hidden,
assuring confidence, harmonious stillness in all things,
manifold good in the silence of concord,
thou silent cry, no one can find thee
who knows not how to let thee go.

From an anonymous letter of the fifteenth century

In lumine tuo videbimus lumen.
(In thy light we will see light.)

Psalm 36:9

CONTENTS

INTRODUCTION

Why, when God's world is so big,
did you fall asleep in a prison
of all places?
RUMI

FOR MANY YEARS I have been drawn to and borne by mystical experience and mystical consciousness. Within the complex phenomenon of religion, they appear to be central. All living religion represents a unity of three elements that, in the language of the great Catholic lay theologian Friedrich von Huegel (1852–1925), we may call the institutional, the intellectual, and the mystical (see chapter 3). The historical-institutional element addresses itself to mind and memory; in Christianity it is the "Petrine" dimension. The analytical-speculative element is aligned with reason and the apostle Paul. The third element, the intuitive-emotional one, directs itself to the will and the action of love. It represents the Johannine dimension. The representatives of all three elements tend to declare themselves to be absolute and to denigrate the others as marginal; however, without reciprocal relationships among the three elements, religion does not stay alive. Reciprocity between institutional, intellectual, and mystical elements of religion may take the form of polarization, or the exchange may be dialectical.

What enticed me to the lifelong attempt to *think* God was neither the church, which I experienced more as a stepmother, nor the intellectual adventure of post-Enlightenment theology. I am neither professionally anchored nor personally at home in the two institutions of religion—the church and academic theology. It is the mystical element that will not let go of me. In a preliminary way, I can simply say that what I want to live, understand, and make known is the love *for* God. And that seems to be in little demand in those two institutions. At best, what Protestant theology and preaching articulate in what they designate as "gospel" can be summed up as follows: God loves, protects, renews, and saves *us*. One rarely hears that this process can be truly experienced only when such love, like every genuine love, is mutual. That humans love, protect, renew, and save *God* sounds to most people like megalomania or even madness. But the madness of this love is exactly what mystics live on.

What drew me to mysticism was the dream of finding a form of spirituality that I was missing in German Protestantism. What I was seeking had to be less dogmatic, less cerebral and encased in words, and less centered on men. It had to be related to experience in a twofold sense of the word: how love for God came about and what consequences it has for life. I was not looking for what Thomas Müntzer refers to as "made-up, fictitious faith," that is, something that is fine for the head and keeps the institution functioning. Instead, I searched for the mystical element of faith—in the Bible and other sacred writings, in the history of the church, but also in the everyday experience of lived union with God or the divinity. The distinction between the ground of being perceived in personal terms, or, in transpersonal terms, need not concern us here. For are "mindfulness" or "pure attentiveness" of Buddhist tradition not other words for what the Abrahamic traditions call "love for God"?

Often an expression like "longing for God"—which could be a different rendering of "mysticism"—evokes embarrassment; yet, tradition declares that our greatest perfection is to need God. But it is precisely that longing that is taken to be a kind of misguided indulgence, an emotional excess. In recent years, when two of my friends converted to Roman Catholicism, I could not approve. In the first place, the denominational divisions of the sixteenth century are no longer substantive for me. Second, in the Roman institution—with its unrelenting "nyet" to women, to a humane sexuality, and to intellectual freedom—I only find in double measure the coldness from which both my friends were fleeing. But what these two women were seeking they found, above all, in the liturgy of the Catholic Church. The experience of mysticism made them feel at home. That is what I am looking for, too, and that is what this book is about.

The history of mysticism is a history of the love for God. I cannot conceive of this without political and praxis-oriented actualization that is directed toward the world. At the beginning of the seventies, I wrote *Death by Bread Alone (Die Hinreise)*, a book with autobiographical undertones. Many of my friends on the political and Christian left became worried. "Dorothee is leaving," I heard them say in Holland, "will she ever return?" But that was not my worry; what I was particularly trying to do was to hold together what Roger Schütz, the founder of the Protestant monastic community in Taizé, calls "*lutte et contemplation*" (struggle and contemplation). I did not want to travel on two distinct pathways. What in the late sixties we named "politicization of conscience," at the time of the political evensong of Cologne, has in the meantime become widely generalized. More and more Christians and post-Christians understand the connection between setting out and then coming back again (*Hinreise* and *Rückreise*). They need both.

There has been very little examination of the relationship between mystical experience and social and political behavior. Social-historical enquiry always recedes—especially in today's mysticism boom—in favor of a "perennial philosophy" (to borrow the name of Aldous Huxley's famous anthology), a way of thinking that is outside time. It looks at God and the soul alone, without any social analysis. To say the least, such an approach is an abridgment. What interests me is how mystics in different ages related to their society and how they behaved in it. Was the demeanor of flight from the world, separation, and solitude adequate for mysticism? Were there not also other forms of expressing mystical consciousness to be found in the life of communities as well as individuals? Did mystics not have a different relation, communally and individually, to the "world," to the whole of society, both in practice and in theory? The prison, of all places, in which we have fallen asleep (Rumi)—is this what we are supposed to regard as the world's eternal condition, unaffected by real history?

My questioning is focused on social reality. This means that for the sake of what is within, I seek to erase the distinction between a mystical *internal* and a political *external*. Everything that is within needs to be externalized so it doesn't spoil, like the manna in the desert that was hoarded for future consumption. There is no experience of God that can be so privatized that it becomes and remains the property of one owner, the privilege of a person of leisure, the esoteric domain of the initiated. In my search for concepts that depict the possibilities open to mystics of their relation to the world, I find a series of different options. They lie between withdrawal from the world and the transformation of the world through revolution. But whether it be withdrawal, renunciation, disagreement, divergence, dissent, reform, resistance, rebellion, or revolution, in all of these forms there is a No! to the world as it exists now. The reformer Teresa of Avila; the Beguines of Flanders, who created their own new forms of life; Thomas Müntzer, the revolutionary leader of peasants; and Daniel Berrigan, the Jesuit destroyer of weapons of mass destruction—all of them lived their mysticism in the repudiation of the values that ruled in their worlds. For those who want the world to remain as it is have already acceded to its self-destruction and, consequently, betrayed the love of God and its restlessness before the status quo.

During the years in which this book came into being, I tested and experimented with it in seminars in New York, Hamburg, and Basel, and with people elsewhere. After some initial hesitation, I decided upon the concept of "resistance" as my focal orientation. Later perhaps, in a different time, it might be possible to write a book on "mysticism and revolution." But for us who live in the transition to the third millennium of the common era, however, "resistance" seems to be the formulation that is more accurate and closer to reality.

For me, as a citizen of a rich, industrialized country, "resistance" has become in recent years more and more important as an expression of political culture. It is as if in this word I could express best what common life really means, even though I know very well that most often, for people who are just learning to walk, it is like a shoe that is too big. The word contains the memory of the European resistance against Nazism, Fascism, Stalinism, and the human rights violations in the sphere where power was exercised by Socialist regimes. It also contains the memory of the dead, such as Sophie Scholl and Dietrich Bonhoeffer, who in their protests and battles gave up their lives.

"*Résistez*" is a battle cry that persecuted Huguenots scratched on the wall in the tower of Aigues-Mortes. I do not want to be separated from them and the many others all over the world, who in seemingly hopeless situations practiced the madness of the No! from a different love of life. What I can do in the context of the rich world is minute and without risk in comparison with the great traditions of *Résistance*. The issue is not to venerate heroes but together to offer resistance, actively and deliberately and in very diverse situations, against becoming habituated to death, something that is one of the spiritual foundations of the culture of the First World. It is us, indeed, who find ourselves "asleep in a prison / of all places," even though God's world is "big" and the recognition of the other bigness invites even us into other ways of living.

With the word "mysticism," I try in a two-fold sense to name a process in which I find myself: the discovery of traditions of mysticism and their appropriation. To make something one's own also means to re-collect it in the sense of internalizing it. When I read how mystics thought, dreamed, spoke, and lived, my own life looks more and more mystical and amazing to me. It is as if I were growing other ears, a third eye, wings of the morning. I understand myself better because I learn from these "brothers and sisters of the free spirit" a language that brings my own experiences closer to me and lets them shine. Of course, my own deprivation also becomes more clear, for the prison can be named only by someone who calls me to come out of it.

The Greek word for "reading" means to have renewed cognition, to re-cognize. To read texts of mysticism is to have renewed cognition of one's self, of a being that is buried under rubble. Thus, the discovery of the mystical tradition also sets free one's own forgotten experience. For that reason, there is little I can do with the modesty of some scholars of mysticism. They steadfastly understand themselves as nonmystics, as persons who have not experienced anything and are only delivering secondhand goods—as if mysticism could occupy one just like any other business. I look for something among mystics that I, a prisoner in the huge machine, do not receive. It's not my wish to admire the mystics, but to let them re-collect me so that daily I see the inner light as clearly as possible, for it is hidden also within me.

But if I need both, the inner light of being at one with every living thing and the resistance against the machine of death, how do I get them together? What does the "and" in the subtitle of this book mean, mysticism and resistance? Does resistance truly grow from mystical experience? Or do mystical experience and certainty grow from the solidarity of resistance? Are there not enough mystics who have turned their backs on the world, who politically are totally resigned and swallowed up by their own narcissism? Is their mysticism then not deep enough, their poverty not poor enough, and their connectedness not secure enough? Perhaps "grow from" is not the correct way to put it. It might imply that mystical, unmediated nearness of God has to find a sort of ethical application focused on humans. That would still be a fatal conceptual separation of ethics and religion.

To overcome that separation more and more is the aim of this book. If it is true that God is love, then the separation of religion and ethics—or, in the technical terminology of the academy, the separation of systematic theology and social ethics—is dangerous as well as detrimental to both sides. It is self-destructive for religion and ethics because it empties religion, reducing its basis for experiencing the world. It turns ethics into arbitrary arrangements of individual tribes and hordes.

The "and" between mysticism and resistance must be understood more radically, and that is precisely where the difficulties arise. For one cannot think what one does not do. You cannot perceive or observe God's love by looking at others. "The observer sees nothing." I can see God's love only when I become part of it myself. Thus, some of the fundamental weaknesses of this book, apart from the writer's personal ones, are weaknesses of our political-intellectual culture. Our religiously grounded resistance is still so weak, so experientially impoverished, so little practiced that we can hardly think it.

The title of this book is an address to God that is taken from an anonymous letter from the late Middle Ages, presumably from a pastor to a penitent in difficulties and distress (see chapter 5). "My child, be patient and leave off because God will not be torn from the ground of your heart. O deep treasure, how wilt thou be unearthed?" This is followed by a series of addresses to God that, as often happens in the language of German mysticism, do not use the traditional personal metaphors like Father, King, Most High, but new, nonpersonal ones like treasure, fountain, radiance, or "security that is hidden" in order to name the deity. In that sequence of metaphors is found the paradoxical expression "the silent cry" that has fixed itself in my mind for years now. It is a mystical name for God, whose divine power is not grounded in domination and commandment. It is a name that everyone can use, everyone who misses the "silent cry" that has often become inaudible among us. May the one who also cries in us help us all to learn to hear the cry in the foundations of the world.

I. WHAT IS MYSTICISM?

1. WE ARE ALL MYSTICS

If all human beings were lovers, the distinction
would disappear between mystic and non-mystic.
NOVALIS

Mysticism of Childhood

I DO NOT WISH to begin with a definition of mysticism but with one of the many narratives of experience that carry this book. It is an authentic testimony from a culture not our own but of the indigenous peoples of North America. Black Elk (1863–1950) was a hunter, warrior, healer, and chief, and one of the last great seers of his nation, the Oglala Sioux. As an old, nearly blind man, he told his life story to a white friend, John J. Neidthardt, who reproduced the text as faithfully as possible. Black Elk remembers the time when he was four and five years old and first heard voices.

I know it was before I played with bows and arrows and rode a horse, and I was out playing alone when I heard them. It was like somebody calling me, and I thought it was my mother, but there was nobody there. This happened more than once, and always made me afraid, so that I ran home.

It was when I was five years old that my Grandfather made me a bow and some arrows. The grass was young and I was on horseback. A thunderstorm was coming from where the sun goes down, and just as I was riding into the woods along a creek, there was a kingbird sitting on a limb. This was not a dream, it happened. And I was going to shoot at the kingbird with the bow my Grandfather made, when the bird spoke and said, "The clouds all over are one-sided." Perhaps it meant that all the clouds were looking at me. And then it said: "Listen! A voice is calling you!" Then I looked up at the clouds, and two men were coming there, headfirst like arrows slanting down; as they came they sang a sacred song and the thunder was like drumming. I will sing it for you. The song and the drumming were like this:
"Behold, a sacred voice is calling you;
All over the sky a sacred voice is calling."
I sat there gazing at them, and they were coming from the place where the giant marsh lives (North). But when they were very close to me, they wheeled about toward where the sun goes down, and sud-

denly they were gone. When they were gone, the rain came with a big wind and roaring. I did not tell this vision to anyone. I liked to think about it, but I was afraid to tell it.[1]

The child, not yet named Black Elk at that time, has an original experience of the other reality. He experiences it without any doubts or uncertainty, in that objectivity that issues in a complete giving over of oneself to what is being experienced. He is outside himself, hears a bird speak, sees two men gliding from the clouds, hears a voice, and learns a new song.

This mystical experience is embedded in native culture that has rituals for entering into visions. *Hanbletsheyapi* (a cry for a vision) is a kind of prayer that is at the center of native religiosity and is even more important than the rites of purification in the sweat lodge or the use of the peace pipe. Such crying for the sake of a vision is also simply called "lamenting" in the sense of a religious self-expression. "In the old days, all of us, men and women, we begged for it all the time."[2] Through lamenting or calling, people prepare themselves ritually for a vision. "There are many reasons for going to a lonely mountain top to 'lament.' Some receive a vision when they are very young and when they do not expect it. Then they go to 'lament' that they might understand it better. We 'lament' when we wish to make ourselves brave for a great ordeal such as the Sun Dance. Some people 'lament' in order to ask some great favor of the Great Spirit, such as curing a sick relative. We also "lament" as an act of thanksgiving for some gift from the Great Spirit. But perhaps the most important reason for lamenting is that it helps us to realize our oneness with all things and with Wakan-Tanka who is the source of all things."[3]

The culture of indigenous peoples allows someone with "a confused soul" to call forth the Great Spirit's help through a vision. The individual steps of such a search are ritually ordered: a visit to the holy man, choosing how many days to fast and lament, finding helpers who will climb the mountain with the lamenter, determining the place where the purification lodge is to be built, following established rules, and finally, sending the companions away. Fasting and keeping watch enhance the readiness of the one who seeks a vision. The shouts resound again and again: "Grandfather, I am sending a voice! To the Heavens of the universe, I am sending a voice that my people may live."[4]

The vision heals the disquieted individual human being but is, of course, tied into the myth of the whole people and its ritual. "Without community, the vision consumes you."⁵ Those who see visions do not pray for themselves but call out repeatedly, "Protect my people!" They remain in an ongoing and intensive attentiveness focused on the divine presence.

The vision of the child, who later was to lead the resistance against the overwhelmingly greater white power to preserve an alternate way of living, is to be understood against the background of the religious culture of a people. The questions to be put to a text like that of Black Elk are not: Who has seen such a vision? What sort of special people are they? What typifies their psyche? Questions like these are still those of an examining curiosity that works with an elitist perception of mystical experience. The questions that we who are white, nonnative, and orphan-like in relation to nature, have to learn to ask are these: Which culture works with such experiences? And which culture destroys them? Native culture has a high regard for dreams that grows with an educational process for taking dreams seriously. Among the first questions a native mother asks her child in the morning is: what did you dream? When I heard this for the first time I felt ashamed because I used to ask my children only: Did you do your mathematics homework? Do you have your lunch? The experiences of other cultures may not be immediately helpful to us, but they do at least make us aware of the deficits of our own culture.

I try to democratize mystical experience, that is, not to understand it as an elitist affair of a few select people, but—as Ernst Bloch puts it in the famous concluding sentence of *The Principle of Hope*—as "something that shines into the childhood of all and in which no one has yet been: homeland."⁶ I want to remind us of the buried mysticism of childhood. There are for many of us—I almost want to say for every one of us—moments of heightened experience in childhood in which we are grasped by a remarkable, seemingly unshakable certainty. Mystics of the various ages have called upon this buried experience. For example, Thomas Müntzer speaks of a high "amazement"; the word means being frightened as well as amazed. The amazement, according to his own testimony, set in when he was a child, six or seven years old.

The American mystic and Quaker John Woolman (1720–1772) tells of how he came to know "the workings of God's love" even before he concluded the seventh year of his life. "I remember, while my companions went to play by the way, I went forward out of sight; and sitting down, I read the twenty-second chapter of the Revelations [sic]: 'He showed me a river of water, clear as crystal, proceeding out of the Throne of God and the Lamb, etc.' And in reading it my mind was drawn to seek after that pure habitation which I then believed God had prepared for his servants. The place where I sat and the sweetness that attended my mind remains fresh in my memory."[7] The Quaker tradition is very apparent in this text. The six-year-old child experiences something of God's presence. Such certainty does not derive from the authority of a book, dogma, or priest. The highly charged moment gives the child a deep sense of unity without mediation: God is here. The pure river of living water flows also for me. Here and now, I am united with the great life, with the whole of life. I am a part of the whole and indestructible; the inner light shines also for me.

It is said of Ramakrishna (1836–1886) that even as a boy he would be in ecstasy when he saw white cranes flying before the dark clouds of a thunderstorm. He became one with what he experienced. When we start digging up the buried mysticism of childhood, the feeling of oneness and of being overcome arises anew. Memory clings to little, insignificant details. "As if it were yesterday" we say in such moments and tie together the place, time of day, and season of the year with a specific experience of overwhelming joy and happiness, of being alive or of longing, and the pain of having to part.

One more comparable experience is drawn from the circle of our own culture. Sitting in an orchard with her baby sister next to her, a nine-year-old girl experiences something that in her later retelling she refers to in a nearly defensive manner as "the thing." Her language is awkward and almost deliberately toned down. She draws upon religious instruction but exactly this literary weakness points out the authenticity and, at the same time, the universality of such experiences. "Suddenly the thing happened, and, as everybody knows, it cannot be described in words. The Bible phrase, I saw the heavens open, seems as good as any if not taken literally. I remember saying to myself, in awe and rapture, So it is like this; now I know what heaven is like, now I know what they mean in Church. The words of the 23rd Psalm came into my head and I began repeating them: He leadeth me beside the still waters. Soon it faded and I was alone in the meadow with the baby and the brook and the sweet-smelling lime trees. But though it passed and only the earthly beauty remained, I was filled with great gladness. I had seen the far distances."[8]

Our habit of leaving childhood behind us as quickly as possible thoroughly uproots such childhood experiences for people of our culture. We then label those experiences as craziness or silliness and then hide or trivialize them in terms of our "nothing but . . ." formulae. Such experiences are explained away as an overactive imagination, indigestion, overexcitement, and the like. By banishing them from our children, we destroy them within ourselves at the same moment.

The trivialization of life is perhaps the strongest antimystical force among us. Some people are literally obsessed by the compulsion to trivialize everything. What an allegedly correct way of thinking, censorship, falsifying history, and suppression was supposed to achieve in the former countries of the Eastern Bloc is accomplished in our system by the trivialization that gently lulls us. One can try to think, feel, experience, and communicate everything, but the moment such expressions see the light of day, they are robbed of their significance and meaning and are thrown on the dump. They have no cash value in relation to the currency that dominates our culture. "It amounts to nothing" expresses exactly the reality of this domination; it is of no value because it does not pay.

Let me give an example. In the early eighties, young people in the former German Democratic Republic had the "Swords into Plowshares" badges ripped off their jackets and sweaters. Such violent measures are unthinkable in the free West. The desired conformist behavior is achieved among us without physical violence and heavy-handedness. Badges, buttons, ideas, and feelings drop off by themselves. An individual can cherish them but they mean nothing. The relevance of any expression of life now depends on what it can yield in the exchange of the currency of power and money. Everything else is trivialized away. Perhaps there is no weapon that has been used as perversely and effectively against the otherness of children and women's conscientization than this creeping trivialization of experiences and feelings that are considered pointless for the struggle for survival. The trivialization of women exists as an ongoing malevolent belittling: whatever is consistently and without opposition declared to be irrelevant—like so much that women experience, feel, and come to know—loses its language; perhaps it may echo for a while within a person, but it creates no response.

For mystical consciousness, it is essential that everything internal become external and be made visible. A dream wants to be told, the "inner light" wants to shine, the vision has to be shared. In many indigenous cultures in North America, names originate in visions. But in our world, the machines of trivialization work so must faster than we do: dreams are the concern of one's psychotherapist and ideas of a different life belong to the private sphere. Such dreams and ideas are therefore of no consequence and the inner light is rationalized away. It is so easy to douse the inner light of a human being. And we busily assist in doing just that as we learn to make the world's efficiency our own. We cut ourselves off from our own experiences by looking upon them as irrelevant and not worth talking about or, what is no less cynical, not communicable at all. We are losing dreams, those of the night and those of the day, and increasingly we lose the visions of our life.

Thomas Merton (1915–1968) was a mystic and a man who fought in the resistance against the Vietnam War. He said that "if you want to know me, don't ask where I live, what I like to eat, how I part my hair; rather, ask me what I live for, in every detail, and ask me what in my view prevents me from living fully for the thing I really want to live for."[9]

Are Mystics Completely Different?

The attempt to democratize mysticism made here faces a number of objections. They have nothing to do with how things are rationalized away by flattening them out; instead, they arise from the opposite, from an exaggerated reverence. The argument is as follows: we ordinary nonmystics have nothing to do with sanctification, ecstasy, submersion, or the other extraordinary dimensions of the soul's mystical being. For in the imagination of normality, this extraordinary dimension withdraws not only from rational discourse but also from permissible religious communication as it is carried on in the ecclesial institutions established for that purpose. Admittedly, every religion has its mystical component but only in a form that is manageable and capable of keeping the fire under control.

But those potentialities that can be actualized at any time should not misdirect us into conceiving of mystical consciousness in an extremely restricted sense. Mystical experience should not be limited to the spiritual zenith of contemplation, as was done at times in the language of the Middle Ages. John of the Cross (1542–1591) declares quite explicitly that God does not reserve this high calling of contemplation for particular souls. "On the contrary, He is willing that all should embrace it. But He finds few who permit Him to work such sublime things for them."[10]

Mystical elements are also present in ordinary forms of religious, pantheistic, or aesthetic experience. Often, religious feeling—in the broadest sense of the word—rises above the substantive content of experience, and the hidden, nonrational, often subconscious aspects become more expressive and powerful than those that have been made known. As normal consciousness expands, hidden powers are released so that truth may be unveiled. The experience of divine presence no longer happens through the mediation of doctrine, sacred text, or sacrament. Time stands still in the presence of the mystical now.

Experiences of this kind abound, whether they are articulated in theistic or nontheistic terms. The numerous examples of such simple, "lowly" mysticism that I cite in this book are in every way meant to encourage us to take our own experiences seriously, to save and to frame them like an important photograph. These primary, immediate experiences make me suspicious about the division made by those who busy themselves with mysticism. They divide people into those who have firsthand visions and auditions and those who traffic in secondhand goods. People who bring no more than a sympathetic openness to mystical experience, who attend to it with innermost participation, and who allow themselves to become enthusiastic are then able, through diligent study, to immerse and engage themselves. Such people are also part of the sisterly, brotherly circle of the friends of God. Why should the people who listened to Meister Eckhart in Cologne, Erfurt, or Strasbourg not have been guided and transformed by the inner light even when specific and demonstrable experience was not forthcoming at that moment?

The Romantic poet Novalis (1772–1801) takes up the vision of Joachim of Floris (d. 1202) and with him sings the praises of the community of the *commystes* (the fellow mystics) beyond the ages.

> You shall make known the final age
> that is to be a thousand years,
> find being in extravagance and
> with Jacob Böhme shall converse.

It is quite beside the point to ask of such a text: did you experience this yourself? The authenticity of a witness goes beyond biographical inquiry. The customary distinctions between mystics and nonmystics are ruled out in the face of the claim that we are all mystics in the sense of a demand on life that cannot be relinquished. Mystical thinking itself contradicts that distinction of scholars.

But the attempt to delimit genuine mysticism *(Mystik)* from mysticality *(Mystizismus)* also does not get us much further (see chapter 3). It is as if language resisted ultraunambiguity and unwarranted clarity. In terms of the history of language, the noun "mysticism" is of fairly recent origin. It appeared in German about two centuries ago in connection with the great Romantic discoveries within the history of religion. Jacob Böhme, too, was discovered at that time as a mystic, and the adept appropriated his name as a kind of code word.

The Latin *mysticus* (full of mystery) has been in much longer use. For example, the "litany of Loreto"(1531), from the Italian pilgrim-church of Loreto, uses the word in an address to the Mother of God: Mary is praised as *rosa mystica* (mysterious rose). The linguistic root of the word lies in the Greek verb *myo:* I close my lips or my eyes, which refers to the rituals of initiates into mystery cults. In subsequent Western tradition, not much has remained of this root in the Greek mystery cults that started with the mystical theology of Dionysius the Areopagite, a Syrian monk of the late fifth and early sixth centuries C.E. What does remain is the basic assumption that a mystic is someone who has particular experiences that bring about altered states of consciousness deriving from the encounter with the other, the divine reality.

In nontheistic religions, this altered state is generally referred to as "illumination," while theistic religions speak of it as the union of the soul with God *(unio mystica).* This union of the divine-within and the divine-without occurs in the spark of the soul. There is a fusion of the divine that resides in every human being's soul with the divine, who is absolute being and the ground of all that is. This ground (called *Brahman* in Sanskrit) and the individual breathing soul *(Atman)* are one. *Atman* is *Brahman.* The famous saying of the Vedas: *tat tvam asi* (that thou art) sums up a basic experience common to all mysticism.

The following discourse of the Muslim mystic Bayezid Bistami (ninth century) has been passed on: "Bayezid was asked what the ninth heaven is. 'I am the ninth heaven,' he answered. 'And the throne that rests thereon?' 'I am that too,' he said. When the questioner continued asking, he said, 'I am the tablet, I am the stylus. I am Abraham, Moses, Jesus. I am Gabriel, Michael, Israfil. Whoever comes into true being is dissolved in God, is God.'[11] In his anthology on mysticism entitled *The Perennial Philosophy,* first published in 1944, Aldous Huxley speaks of the three gates into mysticism. "We can begin either at the bottom, with practice and morality; or at the top, with a consideration of metaphysical truths; or, finally, in the middle, at the focal point where mind and matter, action and thought have their meeting place in human psychology."[12]

The lower gate is the one preferred by teachers who rigorously focus on practice. Huxley's example here is Gautama Buddha who has no use for speculation. Buddha's most important concern is to extinguish the hidden flames of desire, bitterness, and delusion. Currently, many groups within the New Age movement seek to gain entrance through this lower gate by means of practices that enhance concentration. Yoga, disciplined diet, breathing techniques, and physical and spiritual exercises are all forms of the altered way of life that focus on mystical composure and ultimately illumination.

According to Huxley, philosophers, theologians, and those who are given to speculative thought enter by the upper gate. There is growing evidence today of a new philosophy of the metaphysical that, inspired by postmodern natural science, feels its way toward a kind of idealism.

In this book, I am primarily concerned with those who seek entrance through the middle gate. Huxley views these people as "exponents of spiritual religion." He includes India's contemplatives and the Sufis of Islam and, from the Christian tradition, the mystics of the late Middle Ages, the left wing of the Reformation, and the original Quakers.

My preference for this middle gate and, above all, but not exclusively, for its Christian representatives, is by no means a denigration of the two other entrances. Rather, I want to focus on a way by which mystical experience appears to be possible for and accessible to all human beings. It is my purpose to bring back the experience of the unknown life as something that was stolen from us before we were even born. I do not want to submit absolutely to the fateful coercion of modernity that Max Weber referred to as the "disenchanting of the world" and, correspondingly, elevate science to the level of a totalitarian deity next to which we are to have no other gods. By means of the experiences of the middle gate, possibilities of another life may become visible.

Mystical Sensibility

In principle, mystical experiences are no different than those promised and celebrated in many religions. Mystical experiences are neither above nor below those heightened experiences described in religious language as being made whole, liberation, the peace of God, coming home, and redemption. The difference lies only in *how* mysticism deals with these experiences. Mysticism lifts such experiences out of the abstractness of religious doctrine and frees them for feeling, experience, and certainty.

Walter Hilton (d. 1395) distinguished between three stages in the experience of grace that makes us new. People reach the first stage by faith alone and the second by faith in God and the imagination of the humanity of Jesus. In the third stage, the soul beholds the divinity that is united with the humanity of Christ. "This is the best, highest, and most perfect degree of love, and it is not attained by the soul until it is reformed in feeling."[13] The grace that makes us new is the same on every stage, but the people who perceive it only "by faith" cannot feel and taste it. Church doctrine is satisfied when it is accepted by faith whereas the mystic claims to experience grace by what Hilton calls "feeling." Those who live only by faith's acceptance have not yet experienced existentially what it is all about.

In this self-imposed modesty, which has ecclesial sanction and imposes a prohibition on the mystical self, there lurks perhaps one of the difficulties central to modern Protestantism. Its defensive stance toward the emotions turns the enormously fetishized "faith" into a nonexistential category; that is, into something essentially made-up, "fictional, contrived" (*Ertichtet*) as Müntzer said against Martin Luther, that brings forth no life and of necessity petrifies in conventionality. The repulsion of experience, as well as the fear of engaging it, represents a kind of spiritual suicide that at the turn of this century continues to cause church membership to decline.

There is a directness of experience in which people can say: "God came to see me," or "I saw the light at the end of the tunnel," or "this thing happened to me at such and such a time." I do not want to set such experience apart from what in the arrogance of scholarly language is sometimes called pious affection. Mystics are quite ordinary people: shoemakers, nannies, dyers of wool, home-care workers, or physicists. The God experienced in mysticism is not one of the *beati possedentes* (those who belong to the blessed adept). As the Flemish mystic Jan Ruysbroeck (1293–1381) put it, God is "common," that is to say, accessible to everyone. Ruysbroeck talks about the "outpouring, mild mutuality of the divine nature" and about the human being who "is amazed at God's mutuality." God "belongs to all creatures in common." "God is there for everyone, with all the gifts divine. The angels are there for everyone."[14]

If that is true, the rigorous distinctions between direct experience, as happens in vision, audition, or stigmatization, and mediated experience of innermost assuredness, cannot be the last word. Mediation, intermediate steps, and interactions between the religious genius or guru and the ordinary person who also desires to taste God are necessary for our thinking. To know that "the angels are there for everyone" serves the purposes of God.

A thinker who teaches such steps is the American philosopher and psychologist William James (1842–1910), the brother of the writer Henry James. In a letter, dated April 17, 1904, to a colleague who was not a believer, he gives an account of his relation to mysticism in his typical form as a skeptical observer of himself and of others' experiences.

> I have no living sense of a commerce with God. I envy those who have, for I know the addition of such a sense would help me immensely. The Divine, for my *active* life, is limited to abstract concepts which, as ideals, interest and determine me, but do so but faintly, in comparison with what a feeling of God might effect, if I had one. . . . Now, although I am so devoid of *Gottesbewusstsein* [sense of God] in the directer and stronger sense, yet there is *something in me* which *makes response* when I hear utterances made from that lead by others. I recognize the deeper voice. Something tells me, *'thither lies truth'* . . . I have grown so out of Christianity that entanglement therewith on the part of a mystical utterance has to be abstracted from and overcome, before I can listen. Call this, if you like, my mystical *germ*. It is a very common germ.[15]

This "common germ" appears also in James's 1902 lectures on *The Varieties of Religious Experience*. Here we meet an incorruptible, scientifically trained psychologist of religion whose own observations push him ever beyond the self-imposed bounds of skeptical rationality. I have learned extraordinarily much from this book; it is a collection of materials that can be regarded almost as a textbook on the middle way. Next to the elaborate testimonies of the great speculative mystics, there are testimonies also of miners and itinerant preachers, ordinary women and men of high society, alcoholics and hysterics. Another fascinating element in James's book is its openness to a view that is alert to contradictions—which is the perspective of an involved observer. It is indeed apparent that he is rooted in nineteenth-century philosophy and its individualistic constriction and pre-Freudian interpretation; yet, the way he deals with his own skepticism increases my respect for his work, over the self-assured areligiosity that prevails today.

The clearest expression of James's mediation between elevated and everyday mystical experience is the development of a sensibility for mystical happening that can be ours when we allow the testimonies to touch us. Next to the timeless moments, the "now" of Meister Eckhart or others drunk with God, there are more common, everyday transcending experiences that allow us to speak about the "mystical germ" or "mystical sensibility." I begin with the best-known example: what happens in love, when people give themselves wholly and without reserve to another human being, deserves to be called mystical.

Novalis asks, "What is mysticism, what has to be approached and dealt with mystically (in the manner of mystery)?" He answers somewhat surprisingly with the combinations of the concepts of "religion, love, nature and state." At a later time, I shall address the critique of false mystification (see chapter 3). In the interest of democratizing the concept of mysticism, I refer once again here to generally human experiences such as giving oneself to someone or something that is not one's "I." Such a self-giving is precisely the I that is experienced as a prison much too narrow and small for the reality of the You. Before I knew you, lovers say to each other, I was blind and deaf and did not know the language of flowers and birds; I lived without living. Some of the essential features of such mystical overwhelmingness are a feeling of being one with all that lives, an immersion or diving into a hitherto unknown whole, a cessation of the ego and a simultaneous discovery of the real self, amazement, and an intensive, unfathomable joy. These dimensions are often described as basic mystical experiences.

Medieval mysticism often grounds this mystical sensibility in the theology of creation. Because the soul comes from God and is created by God, it cannot satisfy itself with anything less than the experience of God. All other peace fails to bring peace. In a dialogue between the soul and God, Mechthild von Magdeburg (1212–1277) speaks about the dissatisfaction of the mystical experience. "Since God no longer wanted to be in himself, he made the soul and gave himself to her out of great love. Of what are you made, soul, that you rise so high over all creatures, and mingle with the Holy Trinity and yet remain wholly in yourself?—You have spoken of my origin, now I tell it to you truly: I was made in that place from love, therefore no creature can satisfy me according to my noble nature, and no creature can unlock me, except love alone."[16] William James identifies four characteristics of the experience of mystical assurance:

- the loss of all worry; the sense that all is ultimately well with one; the peace, the harmony and the willingness to be, even though the outer conditions should remain the same;
- the sense of perceiving truths not known before that make life's mysteries lucid;
- the objective change that the world seems to undergo, making it seem "new" and never having been seen that way before;
- the ecstasy of happiness.[17]

Quite simplemindedly, a convert relates the following about the experience of his moment of certitude. "The very heavens seemed to open and pour down rays of light and glory. Not for a moment only, but all day and night, floods of light and glory seemed to pour through my soul, and oh, how I was changed, and everything became new. My horses and hogs and even everybody seemed changed."[18] One might well object that this transformation of horses and pigs is trivial. But this really shows that such basic experience is not tied to the level of formal education, to class, or maturity of a person. Mystical sensibility even in such a form has to be accorded full reality. God's gifts cannot be separated from their giver. All things take on "the hues of God" and God's gifts are not entities in themselves but point to the giver. Meister Eckhart (1260–1328) says: "God never gives, nor did He ever give a gift, merely that man might have it and be content with it. No, all gifts which He ever gave in heaven or on earth, He gave with one sole purpose—to make one single gift: Himself. With all His gifts He desires only to prepare us for the one gift, which is Himself."[19]

One objection to the democratizing concept of mystical sensibility might be that what we are dealing with here are mere gifts of this or that delight, power, self-affirmation; but in no way are we dealing with God. Nevertheless, the separation of giver and gift is untenable. Such is the inextinguishable radiance of those gifts that it holds within itself, which is what Eckhart called "the preparation for the one gift." In the experience of amazement, of knowing oneself to be one and feeling oneself unseparated, God's self is already entering into us. The experience of being given and receiving a gift is one, not two. As if the gifts first gave themselves and only then, on a higher plain, the giver.

If we acknowledge this basic aspect of being overwhelmed by a gift, then faith in God—or a Jamesian memory-like religiosity—is not a precondition for experience. Mystical sensibility has theistic, atheistic, and pantheistic forms. A woman who did not know whether God existed once asked a Buddhist monk if the Buddha believed in God. The monk replied: "He didn't speak of God, which is different. If a man realizes God and is among other men who do not, it is useless to speak about Him for they would not understand. It is better to indicate how they can come to know Him themselves. Man must discover God and his true Self or Ego by following the Path of Enlightenment."[20] Instruction cannot begin with God but must connect to people's experience. And one of the central experiences—I call them "mystic sensibilities"—is that the self's seclusion is broken open. We are not merely the ones we know or believe ourselves to be. We all can leave ourselves; we are all able to be different and to immerse and transcend ourselves.

"I Am What I Do": C. S. Lewis

Here, I take up the spiritual autobiography of the English writer C. S. Lewis (1898–1963). A literary scholar, early science-fiction writer, and author of the children's classic *The Chronicles of Narnia*, Lewis converted to Christianity and became a popular and humorous apologist of religion. "The first is itself the memory of a memory. As I stood beside a flowering currant bush on a summer day there suddenly arose within me without warning, and as if from a depth not of years but of centuries, the memory of that earlier morning at the Old House. . . . It is difficult to find words strong enough for the sensation which came over me; Milton's "enormous bliss" of Eden . . . comes somewhere near it. It was a sensation, of course, of desire; but desire for what? . . . before I knew what I desired, the desire itself was gone, the whole glimpse withdrawn, the world turned commonplace again, or only stirred by a longing for the longing that had just ceased. It had taken only a moment of time; and in a certain sense everything else that had ever happened to me was insignificant in comparison."[21] Lewis had been a professor in Cambridge for many years when, at age 58, he wrote *Surprised by Joy*. His text is an extraordinary mixture of two narrative styles. The highly reflective and the reluctantly direct expressions create tension. On one side is the meticulously observant, carefully instructing professor who is well trained in self-examination, maintaining an awareness of the time, assessing his own self with irony, and keeping his distance. On the other is a man who has experienced being most profoundly grasped and who tries to express what God does to him. He names place and time with great precision but immediately blurs the borders of time; he speaks of the "memory of a memory." His style is filled with numerous literary illusions to classical literature, rare Greek terms, and citations such as "without warning" from *The Cloud of Unknowing* (chapter 4), which provide irony and distance. One hears a great scholar speaking here from an almost Olympian height. What happened to him in mystical experience he addresses only with hesitation, extreme reluctance, and even sarcastic amusement.

> The odd thing was that before God closed in on me, I was in fact offered what now appears a moment of wholly free choice. In a sense, I was going up Headington Hill on the top of a bus. Without words and (I think) almost without images, a fact about myself was some-how present to me. I became aware that I was holding something at bay, or shutting something out. Or, if you like, that I was wearing some stiff clothing, like corsets, or even a suit of armour, as if I were a lobster. I felt myself being, there and then, given a free choice. I could open the door or keep it shut; I could unbuckle the armour or keep it on. Neither choice was presented as a duty; no threat or prom-ise was attached to either, though I know that to open the door or to take off the corset meant the incalculable. The choice appeared to be momentous but it was also strangely unemotional. I was moved by no desire or fears. In a sense I was not moved by anything. I chose to open, unbuckle, to loosen the rein. I say "I chose," yet it did not really seem possible to do the opposite. On the other hand, I was aware of no motives. You could argue that I was not a free agent, but I am more inclined to think that this came nearer to being a perfectly free act than most that I have ever done. Necessity may not be the opposite of free-dom, and perhaps a man is most free when, instead of producing motives, he could only say "I am what I do."
>
> Then came the repercussion on the imaginative level. I felt as if I were a man of snow at long last beginning to melt. The melting was starting in my back—drip-drip and presently trickle-trickle. I rather disliked the feeling.[22]

The event itself, what he calls the "odd thing," is depicted chiefly in terms of images. Yet, they too are not drawn in poetic certitude but are relativized and taken back through terms such as "a kind of," "I could say," "I think," "one might say." Nevertheless, the images assert themselves in spite of Lewis's relativizing phrases. A texture emerges that renders the experience itself more clearly, at least for the skeptical consciousness, than purely poetic language can. The I that speaks here is said to be frozen, armed, dead: it is compared to a lobster in its shell, to a man in stiff clothing, or a knight in armor. Finally, it appears as a snowman. The world of this encapsulated I is ordinary and boring, orderly and void of anything sensational. In such normality of existence, God is not present or known. In the cited text, God is mentioned only in a temporal subordinate clause: "Before God closed in on me." It is as if God had to be kept hidden as much as possible. The experience of the commonplace world, of triviality, and of being dead is then named in philosophical language as "necessity" and set over against "freedom." What happens for only a brief moment is liberation of the ordered boredom of the commonplace for mystery. Every cover, form, role, and frigidity that normally kept the I under control falls away. The I is free. The lobster's armor breaks into pieces, the snowman melts, and the true self emerges in a fleeting moment, leaving behind the "longing for the longing." Freedom and necessity become one; choosing the way and being chosen are the same and the experience gathers itself in the sentence "I am what I do."

In the *Tao-te Ching*, Lao-tzu (sixth century B.C.E.) says that the immersion into the Tao is free of desire. As long as we still desire, wait, and yearn, union is not complete. Rather, union must flow freely from ego-lessness and not be commanded by the will. Obedience given under the order of another power is not the deepest experience of God; being one is. The medieval mystics celebrated the departure from the self. *Gang uz dir selbst uz* (go out of yourself), they would say, also using "coming out" phrases to refer to the old I being left behind. This is how they depict the way out of being caught up in the world and escaping the trivial. In Lewis, "I am what I do" signifies mystical union. The congruence of being and doing and being-with-oneself is an experience of ecstasy, of being outside oneself. But, inasmuch as that experience is lived through the well-known feeling of melting away, that ecstasy is taken back in the ironic remark, "I rather disliked the feeling."

In this text of an old Cambridge professor, the play between mystological distance and mystical affect helps make visible the mystical sensibility of those locked up in different snowmen and lobsters. "I am what I do": a simple and grandiose sentence, a definition of the mystical experience of wholeness. For when are we what we do? When do we succeed in reconciling freedom and necessity, in balancing gravity and grace, as Simone Weil (1909–1943) puts it? Being what we do—why is that so impossible?

Lewis describes as accurately as possible the choice he faces in this moment. It is a completely free choice, without duty, threat, or promise, without desires or fears that might be attached to one or the other option of the choice before him. What this man of learning describes comes very close indeed to what Meister Eckhart calls acting *sunder warumbe* (without a why and wherefore). Nothing conditions or determines the decision to open oneself, to remove the corset, or unbuckle the armor. Lewis's manner of characterizing this "perfectly free act" shows how he understands unfreedom, or the prison in which we have fallen asleep. When can we say that we *are* what we do?

I remember a stroll with a friend of my youth. We sat down in the woods and wanted to kiss each other. A small piece of wood was poking me from below, but I dared not say anything. I did not want to break the magic of the moment; my confidence was too weak. Our relationship, even though I did not know it at the time, was rather superficial; we were trying each other out. Perhaps I believed that the little stick would just dissolve by itself. And while I dared not stand up and find another place, the spell was long broken—and I *was not* what I was doing. I kissed not because I wanted to kiss but to hold on to the magic spell.

The mystic Heinrich Seuse (ca. 1295–1366) reports how once, when he was immersed in deep contemplation, a woman came to the cloister gate, wanting to speak with him. But he had her sent away, not wanting to be disturbed in his contemplation. Of course, it was shattered, and with the woman, who had left sadly, God had also left. Upon realizing this, he ran after her for hours through the barren countryside.

This situation where we are not quite what we do, where we kiss, drink, work, laugh, or meditate only with part of ourselves, is the most normal of situations. We are not wholly present in what we experience; we are still watching ourselves, and we do not attain the self-forgetfulness of being one. We do not play as a child can play; rather, we observe ourselves. Our doing—for example, earning a living—is often smaller than we are. It does not express our riches, strengths, and our longings. Instead, it gets us stuck in a kind of lifeless self-satisfaction that resembles a lobster's armor. We cannot be what we do in the office, the household, the factory; we have become so estranged from ourselves that this being one can at best be postponed to the weekend or vacations.

In order to be what we do we need a different attentiveness, a different intensity, a different immersion into what we do holistically, without dividedness. But we do know this rare condition when being and doing becomes one. "I am all ears" is a lovely saying that expresses the concentration of our strengths. When am I all eyes, all mouth, all hands, all body, all soul? The mystic's answer to that question is curious, for it combines being one with the I stepping out from its present limits, with ecstasy.

2. ECSTASY

Take all away from me
But leave me ecstasy
And I am richer then
Than all my fellow-men

EMILY DICKINSON

Stepping Out and Immersing Oneself

MYSTICAL EXPERIENCE happens when the I steps forth from its self-imposed and imagined limits. The I leaves the everyday world and, at the same time, leaves itself as the being defined by that world. When Emily Dickinson (1830–1886) says, "Take all away from me / But leave me ecstasy," the I itself is also included in the word "all." There is an enthusiasm that makes us richer than all that can be owned. Ecstasy is an expression of the uttermost freedom from what determines our lives. However, it is a freedom that many look upon as rage or mania, or as being outside or beside oneself.

Plato discussed ecstatic passion in the *Phaedrus*. At the beginning of that dialogue, Socrates criticizes eros in the manner of the Sophists, as a dangerous delusion and as contrary to reason. But then Socrates takes back this rationalistic rebuke and ascribes a completely different role to rage, mania, and being outside or beside oneself. He says that the greatest goods are given to us through a madness that itself is granted us through divine favor. If you take away their holy rage and their madness, the prophetess of Delphi and the priestesses of Dodona accomplish merely paltry results or none at all. Socrates discerns this productive ecstasy, this divine "rage," or "divinely granted madness" in four areas. Ecstasy is at work in prophecy, therapy, poetry, and love. Plato includes rage and being outside or beside oneself in the actions of mysticism and, as elsewhere in his thought, judges the older stage of culture, with its piety and reserve, to be contrary to the sophist-enlightened world of the present. Instead of handing these conditions over to the ridicule and mockery of the know-it-all, Plato takes them up and abolishes them—in the Hegelian sense of *aufheben* (abolish): *tollere* (to remove), *conservare* (to preserve), and *elevare* (to raise up).

27

This means that the possessed—those who are drunk with God, as they are spoken of in other mystical traditions—are richer than those who remain in possession of their strengths and riches and, hence, are possessed with themselves. It is no coincidence that Emily Dickinson relates the possessedness of ecstasy and the question of property and wealth. The ability to enter into ecstasy has a connection to mystical sensibility, for without that ability the vast array of humanity's expression and rituals, known as religion, cannot be understood. "Civil religion," with its scanty, bourgeois manifestations that look ever so normal to us, does not even preserve the memory of this stepping out from oneself. What does that mean? The spouse of Jonathan Edwards (1703–1758), the preacher of the Great Awakening in New England, speaks of "the sweetest night I ever had in my life."

> I seemed to myself to perceive a glow of divine love coming down from the heart of Christ in heaven into my heart in a constant stream, like a stream or pencil of sweet light, . . . so that there seemed to be a constant flowing and reflowing of heavenly love, and I appeared to myself to float or swim, in the bright, sweet beams of the sun. . . . I think that what I felt each minute was worth more than all the outward comfort and pleasure which I had enjoyed in my whole life put together. It was pleasure, without the least sting, or any interruption. It was a sweetness, which my soul was lost in; it seemed to be all that my feeble frame could sustain. . . . The glory of God seemed to overcome me and swallow me up, and every conceivable suffering, and everything that was terrible to my nature, seemed to shrink to nothing before it.[1]

Written in the emotional and wordy genre of eighteenth-century edification literature, this account describes an ecstatic experience of God: a taking-leave of one's senses, but of the sort that has been described countless times as a hitherto unknown condition of blessedness. That experience is identified—in the above account as "the heart of Christ in heaven"—with names that are historically marked by tradition and the spiritual world. But the basic experience of being one, free from fear, of complete blessedness, and of stepping out from oneself is very similar and unmistakable in the most diverse of testimonies. Whether someone believes in God or assumes the existence of a higher being seems irrelevant in the face of a real experience of "swimming" in God. An answer to such questions adds little or nothing to the experience.

Spiritual freedom occurs when we become aware of our limits through leaving them behind. Mystical ecstasy means to discover the limiting of the spirit and to cross over the imposed limits. Only in seeing again do I know that I was blind; that I was squatting in a prison becomes apparent only when the prison door opens. It is not the self that is stepped over and left behind, but the torpid I that has fallen asleep in the prison. Lived immanence is not what is left behind for the sake of a fantastic transcendence; rather, a new relation of transcendence and immanence is sought after wherein immanence is no longer too dense, too sealed up, and beyond reproducing itself in a trivial round. It is to be an immanence that opens itself to transcendence and takes part in it. But how is that to happen without exiting from the familiar, without un-becoming or dying off?

An autobiography from the close of the nineteenth century tells the following story.

> One brilliant Sunday morning, my wife and boys went to the Unitarian Chapel in Macclesfield. I felt it impossible to accompany them— as though to leave the sunshine on the hills, and go down to there to the chapel, would be for the time an act of spiritual suicide. . . . For nearly an hour I walked along the road to the 'Cat and Fiddle,' and then returned. On the way back, suddenly, without warning, I felt I was in Heaven—an inward state of peace and joy and assurance indescribably intense, accompanied with a sense of being bathed in a warm glow of light, . . . a feeling of having passed beyond the body though the scene around me stood out more clearly and as if nearer to me than before, by reason of the illumination in the midst of which I seemed to be placed. This deep emotion lasted, though with decreasing strength, until I reached home, and for some time after, only gradually passing away.[2]

The speaker here is trained in examining the self and having a sense of time; his reflection has entered into his speech but, comparable to the process Socrates follows in Plato's text, he has not let it take complete control. He creates an open space for himself and moves away from the open space that is assigned to him from the outside, from domesticated ecstasy. "Spiritual suicide" is what he calls the concession of the ecstasy permitted under the rule of modern reason. For the speaker, the gifts of precise observation and critical distance from himself do not exclude mystical experience. On the contrary, they relativize the absoluteness of the worldview of science. It is precisely the scientific integrity of many modern witnesses of such experiences of God that makes their testimony believable. It is as if they quite unexpectedly came upon the simple question of Rumi, one of the greatest Muslim mystics, whom we have already cited: "Why, when God's world is so big, / did you fall asleep in a prison / of all places?"

Commotion and Unity: Martin Buber

Why did we fall asleep in a prison without noticing it? The Jewish philosopher of religion Martin Buber (1878–1965) published a collection of mystical texts under the title *Ecstatic Confessions*. I consider the introduction to that book to be a noteworthy document not only of German Expressionism, the language of which swirls in this text, but also of modern, if not postmodern, mystical search. Later, Buber decided to distance himself from mysticism and to criticize himself for his earlier engagement of it. This decision will be discussed further on in connection with "community" as an orienting concept (see chapter 9).

One of Buber's texts is titled "Ecstasy and Confession," published in 1909.

> The commotion of our human life, which lets in everything, all the light and all the music, all the mad tricks of thought and all the variations of pain, the fullness of memory and the fullness of expectation, is closed only to *one* thing: unity. Every gaze is secretly crowded with a thousand blinking glances that do not want to be its siblings; every pure, beautiful astonishment is confused by a thousand memories; and even the quietest suffering is mixed with the hissing of a thousand questions. This commotion is sumptuous and stingy, it heaps up abundance and refuses encompassment; it builds a vortex of objects and a vortex of feelings, from whirl-wall to whirl-wall, things flying at each other and over each other, and lets us pass through, all the length of this way of ours, without unity. The commotion lets me have things and the ideas that go with them, only not unity of world or of I: it is all the same. I, the world, we—no, I the world am what is moved out of reach, what cannot be grasped, what cannot be experienced. I give the bundle a name and say "world" to it, but the name is not a unity that is experienced. I give the bundle a subject and say "I" to it, but the subject is not a unity that is experienced. Name and subject belong to the commotion, and mine is the hand that reaches out—into empty space.[3]

Buber juxtaposes two basic concepts: commotion and oneness. The "commotion of our human life" is characterized in such terms as fullness, abundance, vortex, bundle, world. It is the bewildering diversity and beauty of this visible world, its objects, ideas, and feelings. Interpreted in the language of tradition, it is flesh, not spirit; it is the material, visible world of the created and not the invisible world of the creator. This commotion lets us have things but closes itself to unity.

Interpreted in the terminology of postmodernity, this commotion is the radical pluralism of what rushes over us and takes control of us without any prearranged priorities. It is the bewildering force of the unlimited abundance of gratification and possibility. The I of that text looks to me like a rural child exposed for the first time to the glitz and profusion of excess of an urban megamall. But this I does not just gladly go with the flow of this extravaganza of consumerism; something is missing. From the text's very first sentence onward, what is lacking is expressed in helpless, repeated stammering: unity. In positing and naming unity, the world does not attain it, nor is the subject able to create the unity it seeks. Both the world and the I are subjected to the commotion. No matter how colorful, multifaceted, spacious, and enticing its presentation, it remains closed. The I that cannot be at home in the created world stretches out its hand—"into empty space."

A mystical text indeed! Mystical is the experience of the world as a locked-up prison, glitz and profusion notwithstanding. Mystical is the search for the unknown in the midst of abundance. And mystical is the lostness that overcomes the I without unity that is experienced. In *Being and Time* (1927), Martin Heidegger describes the world as "disposability." That concept corresponds here to what Buber calls "the commotion." Is there anything that is not available for disposal, that cannot be categorized as "at hand?" Is there a way out of the commotion, in which we have things and they control us, in which we are objects even when we feel like subjects who, indeed, touch, examine, and choose "everything"? Mystical also, and in every sense of religious tradition, is the picture of "the hand stretched out—into empty space." It is as if this stretched-out hand was the only sign of stepping out, of detaching oneself, of freedom and of "going out of yourself" *(gang uz dir selbst uz);* the only evidence of the destruction of this I ensnared in the commotion.

> But that is the divine meaning of human life: that the commotion is, after all, only the outside of an unknown Inward which is the most living thing of all; and that this Inward can withhold the experience of itself from knowledge, which is a daughter of the commotion, but not from the vibrant and self-liberating soul. The soul that has tensed

itself utterly to burst through the commotion and escape from it is the
soul that receives the grace of unity. Whether the soul meets a loved
human being or a wild landscape of heaped-up stones—from this
human being, this heap of stones, grace catches fire, and the soul no
longer experiences some particular around which a thousand other
particulars are buzzing, not the pressure of a hand or the look of the
rocks; rather it experiences unity, the world: itself. All its powers come
into play, all its powers unified and felt as one, and there in the midst
of the powers lives and radiates the beloved human being, the con-
templated stone: the soul experiences the unity of the I, and in this
unity the unity of I and world; no longer a "content," but what is infinitely more than any content.[4]

Where do we really belong? Where are we at home? Our text
comes from Jewish tradition that distinguishes the visible world from
the invisible deity, but we cannot just leave it at that. How do we get
out of the commotion? That is the question that has to be answered
before *the* question—where do we belong?

COMMOTION	ONENESS
visible world	invisible deity
"this" world of created things	creator
multiplicity	unity
ownership and domination	serenity, the inner ground
objectivity and subjectivity	the soul's union with God
creatureliness	being beyond disposition
death	birth

STEPPING OUT

the way out
cutting oneself off
denying oneself
letting go of oneself
abandoning
coming to naught
ecstasy

Over against the outwardness of the commotion, Buber sets the
inwardness of the soul. Over against rational cognition, which he
called a "daughter of the commotion," he sets the event of mystical
experience. The writer of that text calmly presupposes that human
life has divine meaning; he does not debate it, perhaps because his

hand has already reached out—into empty space, as seen from the world's vantage point. The inward is called "soul" and what it is capable of is said to be both revolutionary: "to burst through the commotion" and regressive: "to escape from the commotion." What is meant by unity becomes more apparent only at this point; experiencing it is not far removed from what William James referred to as "mystical sensibility." Buber now calls the source of unity "grace" and interprets it by means of the notion of the wholeness of all powers, by their coming together rather than their dispersal. The feeling of boundlessness takes the place of the restrictedness in which the commotion ensnares us. The unity experienced causes us to be more and more independent, more and more "released" (ledig)—as the German mystics would also call this emptiness—from the conditions of the outward world. "But there is an experience which grows in the soul itself, without contact and without restraint, in naked oneness. It comes into being and completes itself beyond the commotion, free of the other, inaccessible to the other. It needs no nourishment, and no poison can touch it. The soul which stands in it stands in itself, has itself, experiences itself—boundlessly. It experiences itself as a unity, no longer because it has surrendered itself wholly to a thing of the world, but because it has submerged itself entirely in itself, has plunged down to the very ground of itself, is kernel and husk, sun and eye, carouser and drink, at once. This most inward of all experiences is what the Greeks call ek-stasis, a stepping-out."[5]

The way inward is pushed onward—almost violently in such expressions as "without contact," "free of the other," and "inaccessible." It is a way that is separated more and more from the actual and mediating experiences of the heap of stones or the loved human being. The mythical concept of nakedness emerges. I try to make sense of it by referring to a contemporary of mine, the Latin American bishop and mystic Pedro Casaldáliga (see chapter 15). In an interview, he said that faith was "disrobing" itself more and more to him. More and more, faith was shedding the wrappings of tradition, the nostalgia of childhood, and assuaging assurances; and consolations were less and less important. The soul's "naked oneness" seeks an analogous experience. To plunge down to the very ground or to submerge oneself becomes one with stepping out. Buber's text comes to its culmination in "God's highest gift." The linguistic paradox is that it is precisely in this stepping out that ecstasy is said to be "the most inward" of all.

Rabi'a and Sufi Mysticism

The prison where we sleep away our lives becomes visible only in and through the experience of stepping out. Perhaps no religion has articulated the ecstasy of being outside-of-oneself as passionately, wildly, and daringly as did the Sufis, the mystics of Islam. Their name, from the Arabic *suf* (wool), points to their origin in East Persian asceticism; Sufis wore the woolen garment of asceticism and poverty. They arose in the Islamic world in the eighth century. In Persian and Turkish, they are generally referred to as dervishes. They are itinerants who spend their lives in prayer. One may think of them as descendants of early Christian Desert Fathers, as well as precursors of the orders of mendicants of the High Middle Ages. Sufism signifies that one owns nothing and is possessed by nothing.

The name has also been associated with the word *safi* (pure), which may be related to ritual ablution and liberation from all egotism. Even though opposed by Islamic orthodoxy, Sufis understood themselves to be deeply rooted in faith. They acknowledged Islamic law, which has to be lived in believing (*iman*) in the oneness of God. "The Qur'ān speaks of '*islam*' as the exclusive and utter devotion of the believers to the will of God, and an unconditional acceptance of the commandments. '*Iman*' is the inward aspect of faith while '*ihsan*' signifies the uprightness, the virtue of 'venerating God as if one were looking upon God.'"[6] The triad of *islam, iman,* and *ihsan* are to be regarded as the foundation also of Sufi piety.

There is an account of Bayezid Bistami's (d. ca. 874 C.E.) visit to Mecca and the sanctuary of the Kaaba. "When I came the first time to the house, I saw the house; when I came the second time to the house, I saw the lord of the house. The third time, I saw neither the house, nor the lord of it. That is to say, I was lost in God. I no longer knew anything. If I had seen anything at all, it would have been God. . . ."[7] Becoming lost in God is another way of speaking of ecstasy and of being freed from the prison in which we have fallen asleep. It signify less flight from the world than being superior to it, independent from the visible, free from what the senses perceive and experience. Tradition ascribes the following to Rumi: "What is Sufism? He said: 'to find joy in the heart when the time of sorrow comes.'"[8]

One of the most important figures of early Sufi mysticism was a woman, Rabi'a al-Adawiya, the saint from Basra (ca. 713–801 C.E.) Her contemporaries praised her as "the one wrapped in a special veil, the one set afire by longing and love, bewildered by nearness and fervor, the one lost in union with God, accepted by men, she, the second immaculate Mary. . . ."[9] According to Annemarie Schimmel's reports, to this day, a particularly pious woman is spoken of as a "second Rabi'a." Muslim women who also understand themselves to be feminists, such as the Bangladeshi human rights activist, Sartaz Aziz, claim Rabi'a as one who offers a nonpatriarchal spirituality. Here is a tradition that has survived its own self-inflicted damage!

We do not know very much about Rabi'a's life; in the few known facts, the language is clear in relation to the central institutions that have to do with property and sexuality. Rabi'a was a freed slave who lived in abject poverty. When people tried to persuade her to seek help from relatives in order to ease her poverty, she told them: "I would be ashamed to ask for the things of this world from the one to whom the world belongs. How then could I ask for them of those to whom they do not belong?" To the proposition that she get married, she reacted in a similar manner. The dialogue with a spiritual leader that has been handed on reflects the contrast between the normative institution of marriage and the mystical independence of a woman: "My being is long since bound in matrimony. That is why I say my being is extinguished in me and has revived in him [God]. And since that time I live in his power; indeed I am nothing but he. Whoever would have me for a bride must ask not my consent, but his." Hassan asked her how she had raised herself to this level. She said, "By losing in him all that I had found." When he inquired further, "By what method do you come to know him?" she answered, "Oh, Hassan! You know by a certain method, but I know without a method."[10]

She once walked along a street in Basra, holding a torch in one hand and a pail of water in the other. Asked why, she replied, "I want to put fire to paradise and pour water over hell so that these two veils disappear and it becomes plain who venerates God for love and not for fear of hell or hope for paradise."[11] She would be a "miserable hireling" were she to serve God out of fear of hell and a "bad servant" were she to do this from a desire for paradise. "I have only served God, because I love and desire God." We owe Rabi'a some of the most beautiful mystical love poems of all times.

> With two loves I have loved You
> With a love that is selfish
> And a love that is worthy of You:

In the love that is selfish
I busy myself with You
And others exclude.

In the love that is worthy of You
You raise the veil
That I may see.

Yet not to me is the praise in this or that,
But, in that and this, is the praise to You.[12]

The topic of disinterested, noncalculating, and purposeless love for the sake of love is central to mysticism as such. To love God, not because of powerful institutions, or even because God commands it, but to do so in an act of unencumbered freedom, is the very source of mystical relation. To love God is all the reason there needs to be. That Rabi'a loves God means that she has freed herself from the institutions, the images, the traditional roles of women, and the rituals of religion; she "is what she does." She expects no reward but lives in the pure presence of the joy that no longer requires an object by which to live.

The orthodoxies that have been handed down to us in the monotheistic religions called for obedience to the commanding God. They threatened with punishment and enticed with rewards—images of hell and heaven resting on that authority. In technologically advanced centers of the world, authoritarian religious systems are in sharp decline. Mystical perceptions and approaches to God, however, are entirely different: "God, if I worship Thee in fear of hell, burn me in hell. And if I worship Thee in hope of Paradise, exclude me from Paradise; but if I worship Thee for Thine own sake, withhold not Thine everlasting Beauty."[13] Mysticism may be regarded as the antiauthoritarian religion per se. In it, the commanding lord becomes the beloved; what is to come later becomes the now; and naked or even enlightened self-interest that is oriented by reward and punishment becomes mystical freedom.

Rabi'a once went on a pilgrimage to Mecca. When she saw the Kaaba, to which she had come to offer her worship, she said: "I need the lord of the Kaaba; what good is the Kaaba to me? I have come so close to him that his saying 'whoever draws closer to me by an inch, I draw closer to him by a yard' applies to me. What have I to do with the Kaaba?"[14] Rabi'a introduced the element of "disinterested love" into the severe teaching of the early ascetics and, in so doing, transformed Sufism into genuine mysticism. She established love for the sake of love as the center of Sufi mysticism, and in every age Sufis have repeated her well-known prayer, "O my Lord, in this world, whatever you have decreed to be for me, give it to your enemies; and whatever part of the world to come you wish to give to me, give it to your friends—you are enough for me."[15]

Mansur al-Hallaj: *Agnus Dei Mohamedanus*

That God alone is enough is asserted in the most diverse forms of mysticism, as Teresa of Avila (1515–1582 C.E.) says, *Solo Dios-basta.* This gives voice to an absolute insatiability, for nothing on earth can satisfy the seeking. At the same time, it expresses a coming to rest in God, a coming home of the homeless being that cannot find its way in the commotion. A Sufi once pointed to his garments and said, "There is nothing in that cloak except Allah."

One of the greatest mystics of Islam is Mansur al-Hallaj (al-Husayn ibn Mansur Hallaj) (858–922 C.E.). With a passion unknown before him, he spoke of the distance that union with God sometimes hurls a human being into, a distance from ideas, conceptions, linguistic formulation, images, and ways of experiencing the deity. Every idea we have of God fails God. Indeed, each idea produces a false familiarity with the divine, a humble haughtiness that lurks behind piety. In order to overcome this distance of domesticated religiosity, al-Hallaj, more radically than others, chooses to use a puzzling form of contracted speech, daring paradoxes, and contradictions of established, traditional teaching. For example, he warns against one of the basic religious duties of every Islam believer: confessing the oneness of God. "Do not let yourself be deceived by God and do not despair of God. Do not desire God's love and do not rest content with not loving God. Do not speak about God in order to provide confirmation of God, nor be inclined to deny God. And beware of confessing the oneness of God!"[16]

The outward dimension of religious law, according to al-Hallaj, is unbelief concealed—a paradox of formulation. To perceive clearly what only the unbeliever takes to be an object of perception is the essence of unbelief! The gulf between theology (as the rational knowledge of God) and mysticism (the experience of God) has rarely been made so visible in mystical language as it has in Sufism.

One of the pillars of Sufism is *dhikr* (the earnest), which is the urgent focusing on God through repeated utterances of God's name. As eating and drinking keeps us alive, *dhikr* sustains us spiritually, a kind of metaphysical recollection that draws us back from forgetting God. There are cleansers that restore luster to all things; according to Sufi masters, the recollection of God restores the heart's luster. The presence of God is already in people and it is *dhikr* that brings it back.

> Never the sun rises and never it sets
> Without my mind striving after You,
> Never do I sit down to speak with people
> Without You being my last word.
> I drink no cup of water thirstily
> Without finding your image in the glass.
> No breath do I take,
> be it in sadness or joy,
> That does not join itself to the thought of You.[17]

Dhikr (literally meaning repetition or invocation) is a ritual recollection of God, which most often occurs in conjunction with a series of breathing techniques and body movements. The forgetful creature practices recollecting God. The Byzantine Church used the term "theomneny" for this practice of calling on the name of God, which could also be done in silence. Masters encouraged their pupils "to teach the nightingale of the tongue: *dhikr*," which could "be learned from a living master or otherwise from Khidr, the mysterious leader of pilgrims; no matter what, it must be a genuine imitation" that can be traced back to the Prophet himself or even to the angel who inspired him. One master charged his pupil, "Make the effort to repeat for one whole day, 'O Allah! O Allah! O Allah!'"[18]

In Sufism, the condition of ecstasy is practiced in a teacher-student relationship. By pondering individual suras of the Qur'ān, by continuously uttering the name of God, through specific breathing techniques and movements, in dance, or meditative listening to texts, the pupil reaches in four different steps culminating in the state of passing away or extinguishing, the mystical dying. This fourth and final step of ecstasy cannot be attained on one's own; as a persevering and an abiding in love, it is given by God. Orthodox Islam never recognized this fourth step and never conceded it to the Sufis. They themselves did not describe it, probably in order to avoid quarrel. Al-Hallaj is characterized by his consciousness in the reality of union; all actions were coordinated, done on a voluntary basis, and governed by his radiant intelligence.

One of the foundations of the lives of Sufis are words attributed to the prophet Muhammad, "Die before you die." Al-Hallaj sought his own death. His words, "Save me from God," was a demand of the pious to kill him; it depicts this transition into a mysticism of death. Small wonder that his boldness was regarded as blasphemy. In his thinking, love is more than and different from obedience. Love is made real through suffering. One of al-Hallaj's decisive declarations is "Suffering is He Himself, whereas happiness comes from Him."[19] Here, love differentiates between the gift ("from Him") and the Giver ("He Himself"); God's gifts of happiness, for which it is easy to be grateful, are not an expression of inward union. When these gifts are missing, people feel forsaken by God. But genuine relatedness to God does not attach itself to health or fame, fortune or success, neither in this nor in a subsequent world. Genuine relatedness liberates and in this sense teaches "to die before we die." Asked the way to God, al-Hallaj replied, "Pull back both your feet, and you will be with him—one foot from out of this life, and the other foot from out of the other life."[20]

In a certain sense that is exactly what Mansur al-Hallaj did and it led to his martyrdom. After years of imprisonment and everchanging trials, he was condemned to death. But his dying did not separate him from his ecstasy; he transformed ecstasy into a mysticism of death. His texts and his demeanor mirror a uniquely serene freedom that is perhaps most beautifully expressed in these words: "Whoever seeks God sits in the shadow of his penitence, but whomsoever God seeks sits in the shadow of his innocence."[21]

This statement contains a profound critique of those leftovers of piety that remain among us as well. They often sit "in the shadow of penitence" of self-accusation and feelings of guilt in the face of the world's situations. What is to be learned from al-Hallaj goes beyond this Protestant search for God; it goes into the consciousness of being sought by God and to be like a child that sits in the "shadow of innocence." The inner connection with Jesus' word is apparent, "Unless you become like a child, you will not enter the kingdom of heaven" (Matt 18:3). It is not the penitent children who seek the parents; rather, the happy children know that they are being sought, expected, and accepted in the shadow of innocence. "Whoever seeks God runs ahead of his revelations, but whomever God seeks has revelations that overtake his running."[22]

The reports of al-Hallaj's conflicts with the leading religious and political circles of Baghdad show traces of that inner certainty of oneness with God that made al-Hallaj a martyr of Islam. Shiites and Sunnites alike regarded him as someone dangerous. The first conflict arose when al-Hallaj sought to have the political rights of the Prophet's family recognized, whereupon he was flogged. Later he supported a friend who, through his office as chamberlain, tried to introduce improvements in the administration and more equitable taxation. After his final pilgrimage to Mecca, he concerned himself almost solely with the laborers in Baghdad's working-class district. He lived among them and earned his livelihood from carding cotton, the trade he had learned. He soon came to be called "the cotton-carder of the innermost heart." He also accepted the invitations of rich landowners and took part in the debates and discussions of scholars in the mosques.

It was among the common people that he achieved his primary success. He was known as "the God-possessed." No other Sufi was opposed as a sorcerer and revolutionary and admired as the purest mystic of the love of God as much as he. Behind the second trial, the one that resulted in his death sentence, were the financial specula-tions of Vizier Hamid. Al-Hallaj's followers protested against the religious accusations as well as against this kind of economic policy. The process against al-Hallaj was marked by intrigue and bribery. His ability to inspire the population was enormous and, in his oppo-nents' eyes, terrifying. His speech was at one and the same time spontaneous and well thought out, dialectical and exciting, a kind of jubilant, clamorous ecstasy.

Instead of blind imitation and obedience in relation to religious obligations, he taught passionate, overflowing love as the heart of the divine being. Such love was for him the mystery of creation. He used the word *ishg* to denote this love; even moderate Sufis in his day held it to be dangerous if not altogether illicit. But it is precisely such love that prompts the butterfly to fly into an open flame. The butterfly is not content with the light of the candle, with its warmth; it throws itself completely into the flame.

Goethe took up this image in his poem "Selige Sehnsucht" (blessed yearning) in his *Divan.* "The living that yearns for fiery death I will praise." Al-Hallaj's contemporaries—Goethe called them the "masses" that "readily turn to mockery"—found the image intol-erable, just as much as the famous expression *Ana 'l-Haqq*, which has been translated as "I am absolute truth" or "I am God." *Haqq* is one of the ninety-nine names of God in the Qur'ān. And as in the well-known mystical statement of the Upanishads that Atman (the soul, breath) is Brahman (the divine), here, too, the copula "is" is not a logical denotation of identity but, rather, a mystical identification.

A Sufi story tells of this mystical truth of *Ana 'l-Haqq* as follows: "The lover knocks at the door of the Beloved. 'Who is there?' asks the Beloved. 'It is I,' replies the lover. 'This house will not hold Me and thee,' comes the reply. The lover goes away and weeps and prays in solitude. After a long time he returns and knocks again. The Voice asks, 'Who is there?' 'It is Thou.' Immediately the door opens; lover and Beloved are face to face at last."[23] Like the sayings of Jesus in the Gospel of John concerning himself, al-Hallaj's expression *Ana 'l-Haqq* was intended to elicit confrontation. Countless poets of later times turned it into a familiar and honored term. Centuries later, Rumi wrote the following in his Masnavi epic, "People imagine that it is a presumptuous claim, whereas it is really a presumptuous claim to say *Ana 'l-'abd*, 'I am the slave of God'; The man who says 'I am the slave of God' affirms two existences: his own and God's, but he that says *Ana 'l-Haqq*, 'I am God,' has made himself non-existent and has given himself up and says, 'I am God,' i.e., 'I am naught, He is all: there is no being but God's.' This is the extreme of humility and self-abasement."[24] His most famous expression cost al-Hallaj his life. "When Hallaj was in prison, a dervish asked him, 'what is love?' He said, 'You will see it today and you will see it tomorrow and the day after.' On that day, they killed him; the next day, they burned his body and on the third day they scattered his ashes in the wind."[25]

Al-Hallaj was executed on March 26, 922 C.E. Contemporaries report what happened on his way to the cross: "On the way to his execution he danced, flinging his hands about like a high-spirited stallion, though laden with sixteen chains. They said, 'What sort of going is this?' He answered, 'Am I not going to my place of sacrifice?' Thereupon he uttered a loud cry and sang these verses:

> Never would I wish my friend to be accused of cruelty.
> He handed me what he drinks himself, as a host to his guest.
> But as the cup went round he called for the block and the sword.
> So it fares with him who drinks wine with the dragon in the heat of the
> summer."[26]

Mansur al-Hallaj was tortured, maimed, and hanged or crucified; early the next day, he was beheaded and, finally, burned. His ashes were scattered in the Tigris. A hundred years after his execution, people still waited at the banks of the Tigris for al-Hallaj's return. And to this day, poets and songwriters hail him as if he were among us. The renowned orientalist Annemarie Schimmel tells about a trip to a remote region in the Pakistani province of Sind in 1961 where she heard a folksong with the following refrain, "Ask lovers what is love's condition. If you don't believe me, ask them that are like Mansur."[27] Again and again, there sounded the call, "Ask them that are like Mansur" in the cool breeze of evening and faded away over the desert.

We Have Not Been Created for Small Things

> Once the Creator had a dream. He dreamt that only he knew the secret of the universe. What was to happen, were he to die? This worried and troubled him. He awoke and decided to create man and woman. And then he made a further decision: to throw away the keys to the universe. So that now every man and every woman has to create the world anew.

This orally transmitted Sufi story talks of the dignity of the human being, of the greatness in each, and the ability to step out of the self and create what was hitherto unknown and unnamed. "We are all mystics" is a mystical assertion inasmuch as it grounds the dignity of humans for being in the likeness of God. The greatest sin of humans is to forget that we are royal children. "Rabbi Bunam said to his disciples: Everyone must have two pockets, so that he can reach into the one or the other, according to his needs. In the right pocket are to be the words: 'For my sake was the world created,' and in his left: 'I am earth and ashes.'"[28]

These two pockets depict accurately the precariousness of the mystic consciousness in monotheistic religions. The first phrase is Talmudic (Sanhedrin 37) and refers to the greatness, the nobility of the human being; the second, alluding to Gen 18:27, refers to our transitoriness. The orthodoxies of the diverse denominations insist on the second assertion and emphasize the weakness and misery of human life and its dependency on God. Against such a pessimistic anthropology, mystics have always celebrated the greatness of the created soul in its capacity for love. Rumi hails our existence before creation.

> Ere there was a garden and vine and grape in the world
> Our soul was intoxicated with immortal wine.
> In the Baghdad of Eternity we proudly were proclaiming,
> "I am God."[29]

As Meister Eckhart puts it, we have "not been created for small things." "That we do not coerce God to do our bidding is due to the paucity of two things in us: humility that comes from the bottom of the heart and impetuous desire. I swear by my life: God is able to do everything in his divine power; what God cannot do is to deny himself to those humans who do possess those two things. Therefore, do not let trifles confuse you, for you have indeed not been created for small things."[30] Mysticism takes up the traditional teachings of the creation of the universe, of woman and man being in the likeness of God and of the participation of the created in the process of creation. But, as Rudolf Otto sums up Meister Eckhart, doctrines become "thoughts set aflame" and "exaltedness of self."[31] Religious knowledge turns into indestructible certitude; the back and forth between "humility" and "impetuous desire," between the right and left pockets into which we may reach, turns into a new unity.

As the experience of oneness with God, mysticism is the radical substantiation of the dignity of the human being. The different traditions give it varied expression; it ranges from the everyday language of the Hasidim about two pockets to the erotic hymns to God written by a Greek monk, Symeon the New Theologian (ca. 970–1040 C.E.). And yet, the basic experience of the dignity, greatness, beauty, and joy of the human being is the same. "I am loved by him who is not in this world. And amid this cell I see him who is outside this world. I sit upon my bed, and abide outside the world. Yet I see him who is eternal and yet born, and speak with him and dare to say: I love, for he loves me. I feed on contemplation; I clothe myself in it; united with him I transcend the heavens. And that all this is true and certain, I know."[32] Symeon declares this same assurance with the help of one of Paul's images of Christ. "We are limbs of Christ; Christ is our limb[s]. And my hand, the hand of the poorest creature, is Christ; and my foot is Christ; and I, the poorest creature, am the hand and foot of Christ. I move my hand, so does Christ, for he, in entirety is my hand: You must understand that the Godhead is undivided. I move my foot—it shines as he does. Say not that I blaspheme, but confirm this and adore Christ, who has made you so. For you too, if you will, can become his limb."[33] The impression that this is blasphemous is not all that far-fetched. To sober observers, the mystic's praise of the human being's greatness often seems to be megalomania, egocentric conceit, self-deification. How does the monk Symeon, alluding to the biblical verse that God's word is "a lamp unto my feet," claim that God's foot shines? How does the thirteenth-century German mystic, Mechthild von Magdeburg, ask herself, "Of what are you made, soul, that you rise so high over all creatures, and mingle with the Holy Trinity and yet remain wholly in yourself?"[34]

What appears to be arrogance and intrusion is connected with the basic experience of ecstasy. Of that experience, Buber says that it "is originally an entering into God, *enthusiasmos* (enthusiasm), . . . being filled with the god. Forms of this notion are the eating of the god; inhalation of the divine fire-breath; loving union with the god (this basic form remained characteristic of all later mysticism); being rebegotten, reborn through the god; ascent of the soul to the god, into the god."[35]

All of these images are desires for and experiences of union and have a sexual-ecstatic dimension. But it is not enough to reduce them to the sex drive or to trivialize them as compensation for lives that have not been lived out. They are not egomaniacal because they assert that all humans have the ability for God. According to Johann Gottfried Herder, nothing great has ever come into being without this *enthusiasmos*. Without mysticism, the image of the human being deteriorates into that of a consuming and producing machine that neither needs nor is capable of God. Mysticism differs from orthodoxy in that it heralds the capability of humans for God; it differs from our rationalistic orthodoxies of science in that it holds fast to the notion that we need God. The other, without whom we cannot picture ourselves, grounds us in dependency and reliance on the many others. Commonality with these others makes for and sustains life. The highest perfection of human beings remains that they are in need of God.

3. DEFINITIONS, METHODS, DELIMITATIONS

Only they who have added to it find the substance.
JOHANN WOLFGANG VON GOETHE

From the Hermeneutic of Suspicion
to a Hermeneutic of Hunger

ACCORDING TO a famous scholastic definition, mysticism is *cognitio Dei experimentalis* (the knowledge of God through and from experience). What is meant here is the knowledge of God that, instead of being obtained from instruction, tradition, books, and doctrines, comes from one's own life. In terms of this medieval definition, two possible ways of understanding God may be distinguished. There is the ordered way, dogmatically legitimated and hierarchically directed, and the extraordinary one, resting on experiment and experience, which is incapable of being fully institutionalized. That definition represents a concession to the preecclesiastical and the extraecclesiastical reality of religious experience.

It is a complex relationship that exists between religion and mysticism, between the hierarchical forms of organized religion and ecstatic individuals or visionary groups setting out on their own. Still, generally speaking, there are two observations we can make here. First, mystics have very rarely separated themselves from existing historical religions; without externally changing a single letter, they understood the meaning of these religions more deeply. They did not deny revelation but appropriated it differently. Second, conflict was part and parcel of the case: confrontation has to come between too much love for God and the institution that is concerned with regularity and order. Jesus and the temple aristocracy of Jerusalem; Muhammad and the upper echelon in Mecca that had made fortunes from the sanctuary of the Kaaba; Mansur al-Hallaj and the financial speculations of Vizier Hamid in Baghdad; Hildegard von Bingen and the ecclesiastical governors of Mainz who wanted to forbid her to bury an excommunicated nobleman in consecrated ground; Teresa of Avila and the misogynist board of censors who spoiled part of her writings, making them illegible; Jacob Böhme and his orthodox

Lutheran superintendent in Görlitz; and up to Teilhard de Chardin under forms of censorship imposed by the Curia; and Leonardo Boff under the Polish pope; all testify to such inevitability. Mysticism and organized religion are related like spirit to power.

The definition of mysticism as a perception of God drawn from experience originates with Thomas Aquinas and Bonaventure. It has the dimensions of independence from hierarchy, which in practical terms means that it is women-friendly. A certain zone of freedom is accorded it. Next to the ordered way to God that is laid out by the institution of the church, the teaching authority of the office, and the scriptures administered by that office, there is an additional access to God that cannot be channeled but is, instead, experimental and tolerated at the margins of the institution. It is no coincidence that this margin was the place preferred by women, who were barred access to the centers of sacred power. Here women perceive God in unmediated ways, transcending the bounds of rational perception. At the same time, it is a perception that also changes the already known world of feelings, steeping them in a different light. Here, they begin to search for their own language. Mysticism is a women's matter, albeit not exclusively, but predominantly so in Christianity. It was the opponents of mystical thought who saw this most clearly; when they could not ignore great mystical thinkers, they liked to stress how "masculine" those thinkers had been!

By interpreting this classic definition of mysticism in this way, I move away, hermeneutically speaking, from feminism's basic interpretation of Christianity as an unbroken patriarchal tradition of oppression. I enter into a space where the contradiction to the spirit of androcentrism and men's domination becomes visible. As *cognitio Dei experimentalis*, mysticism is such a place not only because women have again and again occupied it, but also because the religiosity of mysticism, its "substance," seeks to overcome the basic presuppositions of patriarchal thinking: power and dominance over "the other," be it the other sex, other nature, or other races and civilizations. In order to grasp this, I need a hermeneutic, a mode of understanding that goes beyond the critical hermeneutic of suspicion.

The hermeneutic of suspicion is a form of ideological critique. This hermeneutic begins by suspecting every text, every tradition, in terms of its legitimizing role in promoting the domination of the particular tradition. Paul Ricoeur speaks of the three "masters of suspicion" who determine the critique of religion—figures with whom every serious approach to religion after the Enlightenment has to engage. Karl Marx called religion "the opiate of the people," Friedrich Nietzsche referred to it as "Platonism for the people," and for Sigmund Freud it was "collective neurosis." The women's movement has appropriated this critique and has decisively deepened it; the movement itself is a "master of suspicion," understanding religion as the self-transfiguration of patriarchy.

The hermeneutic of suspicion has won its place through struggle and has in the past twenty years become commonplace, at least in post-Jewish and post-Christian culture. Today, women can know that all biblical texts are formulated in androcentric language and thereby transmit patriarchal social structures, whether they want to or not. Suspicion is an element that critical consciousness cannot relinquish. But is it enough to enable women and men to put new questions to religious tradition and to give expression to their experience by means of the tradition's language of suffering and hope? Must not another hermeneutic be articulated in a world where hope itself is exiled, where it has, so to speak, no work permit among us? Is suspicion our only lens? Is critical consciousness the only consciousness we have? And is the self-attestation of negativity all we can accomplish?

An example may illustrate my unease. In feminist discussion there is often a critique of religion's fixation on transcendence, including ecstasy, which is said to be just another attempt by patriarchal culture to abandon the body. "Ex-stase (standing outside) is another strategy to escape the body."[1] Here, religion is suspect, as one of the most effective instruments for keeping the body, sensuousness, and women under the suppression of the mind and the male. This suspicion is extended to include mystical feeling and the experience of ecstasy. Does religion not instill denial of and hostility toward the body? And does this not then serve the interest of strategies of social control of women?

Such a totalizing suspicion overlooks the reality of oppression and liberation both. The mystical ecstasy of losing oneself does not dismiss the body as an ill-functioning machine; rather, it sets the body free for a different and new self-expression. With equal justification one could speak of drunkenness as a flight from the body, or of the ecstatic dance, or the mania of which Plato speaks. If there is anything one flees from here it is torpor, monotony, ordinariness, and the trivialities everyone expects. What is left behind in being-outside-of-oneself is not the body but the body's instrumentalization as a tool for work or as a sex-object; its inconspicuousness is lifted in gestures of being-outside-of-itself. Sufis danced at funerals, tearing their clothes from their bodies in order to welcome the messengers of God; they laughed loudly in the face of the gallows and, like Rabi'a, went into the streets carrying water and fire.

In order to understand this ecstasy, to comprehend the mystical element in religion, we have to go beyond the hermeneutic of suspicion. Suspicion is appropriate wherever religion exercises unrestricted, total power over the life of women. In our situation, one in which organized religion appears to be negligible, to say the least, and irrelevant for the majority of people, our inquiry needs a different point of departure. Rather than asking what political domination religious power uses to consolidate its own power, we need to ask what it is that women and men are looking for in their cry for a different spirituality. I try to depict a hermeneutic of hunger.

In so doing I adopt what can be learned from the liberation theology of the Third World. The hermeneutics of the poor is one of hunger for bread and liberation. The Bible is read as the answer to what oppression, illness, lack of education, and apathy inflict on human beings. It is not suspicion that turns people away from the church; it is hunger that drives them to seek help wherever their dignity and their right to have a life are being respected.

But I also pursue what happens in the First World because of a hunger that is no less life-threatening. It has been described often enough, this hunger for spirituality, this search for meaning, or this bottomless emptiness into which consumerism plunges people. Depression and isolation transport women and men into a kind of spiritual anorexia where any kind of nourishment is nauseating. Suspicion can no longer release such people from the constraints of tradition; what drives them on is a yearning to live a different kind of life. The reason for going off to search, often in traditions that are alien rather than one's own, lies in the catastrophe of spiritual hunger in which the rich live.

This is where the hermeneutic of hunger differs from that of suspicion and of postmodern aestheticization. An aestheticization of mysticism often occurs where the social ego denies itself and, in a greedy hankering after experience that is reminiscent of late medieval crazes for the miraculous, falls in line with the trend that is making the social values of communal life disappear. There is an anaesthetizing longing for "pure religion" that incorporates mystical elements and appropriates them for the individual. Here, the inner light does not render reality more translucent, but only the ego that finds itself enjoyable in that light. Søren Kierkegaard adequately critiqued this stance in the "aesthetic stage" as a flight, as an escapism. Real hunger is different. The search for the edible bread of mysticism is not spurred on by dabbling, sniffing now at this and now at that religious tradition. Rather, that search grows with every new defeat of God, with every further destruction of the earth and its inhabitants. It learns to listen to the "silent cry."

Pluralism of Methods and Contextuality

One of the results of the hermeneutic of hunger is that diverse methods of approach exist side by side. For the study of mysticism, comparative study of religion is indispensable. The diversity of religious experience has an inner unity, namely the mystical core that expresses itself in such images as rebirth, unification, drunkenness, heavenly marriage, and many others. Principles such as "I am what I do" *(tat tvam asi)* or Meister Eckhart's *sunder warumbe* (acting without a why and wherefore) are basic formulae that facilitate comparison and assist in discovering what in the multiplicity is held in common, without however erasing the differences.

At the end of the method spectrum, opposite to the comparative study of religion, is sociohistorical inquiry. I use it in order to understand how in particular situations mysticism meant liberation or, at least, made resistance possible. Under what social conditions did people live out their mystical experiences? What were the prevailing norms and rules of their time and place? How was the relation of men and women defined and in what images was their relation to hierarchy and education depicted? What did the reality of women and children look like? The greatest sin, according to a Hasidic saying, is to forget that we are royal daughters and sons; only when I fully understand the conditions that marked the lives of Eastern European Jews can I identify with the depth and power of this saying from the culture of the shtetl.

It is precisely in the reception of mysticism that an approach that abstracts from social reality is very dangerous. I recall the characteristic of religion noted by Baron von Hügel, mentioned earlier. Drawing upon old traditions from Russian Orthodoxy, he distinguished between the three elements of institution, intellectuality, and mysticism, embodied in Christianity in the figures of Peter, Paul, and John. The interplay of those three elements is necessary, but it is currently deeply impeded in the still-Christian culture of the rich world. In simple terms, Peter and his followers rule in the Roman Catholic Church, Paul and his people rule in Protestantism, while the mystical element is pushed aside and remains invisible in both. Mysticism is without home—and yet is needed and sought after by many.

Years ago a First Nation shaman told me about college students who in the summer months come by the hundreds to the reservations in order to experience sweat lodges and ritual dancing. He called them spiritual orphans. Indeed, their spiritual hunger has to be taken seriously but not the "fast food" with which they seek to satisfy their hunger. If I understand the New Age movement correctly, its adherents believe that they can do without "Peter" and the institution. They misunderstand the significance of tradition and attachment. Many of them change gurus, groups, and rituals often—first precious stones, then deep breathing! The absence of the "Petrine" element leads to an all-too-heavy emphasis on the quality of experiences offered by a religious group.

But the "Pauline" element is also lacking almost completely. Many who belong to these sects reject on principle all intellectual clarity, the process of thinking through contradictions, or affinities to racist ideologies. For example, every kind of critique of reincarnation, a doctrine—spoken of as "the law of karma"—that often serves to burden people with guilt for their hopeless social situation, just glances off the union of guru, group, and ritual. What results is a dependency that flees from reality and that has nothing to do anymore with true mysticism. An insular small-group mentality, which revolves only around itself, aids and abets depoliticization and destruction of solidarity with others, particularly the weaker ones.

The inner and the outer, however, belong together, contrary to the highly overestimated notions of esotericism; everything inward desires to externalize itself. The orientation toward praxis that manifests itself in one's lifestyle and in how one relates to central social issues belongs to the heart of the mystical *gang uz dir selbst uz* (go outside of yourself). And questions about serfdom and division of labor, slavery, sexual behavior, war and paying taxes, armaments, and the idea of science were as central then as they are today for this going outside oneself. That is why I believe it to be methodologically necessary to include not merely the approaches of the study of religion, literary criticism, and intellectual history. In the pluralism of methods it is essential that sociohistorical contextuality not be overlooked.

My work is not that of a historian; rather, I pursue a theological interest that resists a certain neutrality of academic or scientific perception. In the interest of an alternate praxis of life, I want to know what mysticism means in different religions and at different times. The hermeneutic of hunger is in search of nourishment. It is a matter of course that mysticism cannot be judged on the basis of confessional points of view. An ecumenical outlook that incorporates sects as much as so-called unbelievers is indispensable for mystical consciousness. The pluralism of language and confession does not effect the unity of the fundamental experience.

In the most diverse religions, but also outside them, mysticism appears as experience and common movement. Speaking in terms of an image, I picture the religions of the world in a circle with the center as the mystery of the world, the deity. The adherents of those diverse religions are drawn by this X at the heart of the world and give it names such as Allah, Great Mother, the Eternal, Nirvana, and the Unsearchable. But giving a name and forming a tradition is not the decisive issue; rather, it is how far the pilgrims advance on the way from the periphery of the circle toward its center. How close is the unutterable X to us? That is the crucial question. We approach the center of the circle in that the distances between the various points of departures on the periphery become ever smaller the closer we come to the center. And so, the differences between the individual religious approaches also become less important: in the heart of God they have disappeared altogether. The more we persist in fixed positions of confessional orthodoxy, or in what Meister Eckhart calls modes (*Weisen*, or, in Latin, *modi*), the farther we are from others who do not belong to the community of religious language—as well as from the center. In terms of the image of movement from various points of departure on the periphery toward the center, tolerance increases with genuine piety. Fundamentalism, the extreme fixation on specific conceptions, rituals, and forms of conduct, is a massive and frequently violent denial of the mystical core. In this sense, fundamentalism is not the fruit of every religion but a matter that belongs to the periphery and the extreme opposite of mysticism.

Tolerance, however, does not wish to reside in the innermost sphere alone nor consecrate indifference toward external realities and circumstances. The hermeneutic of hunger elicits inquiry not only into the testimonies of mystical wisdom and ecstasy but also into their context. Contextuality is a counterweight to a rambling pluralism of methods; it connects us back to the real actuality of the witnesses and protects our relation to the mysticism we have come to see against a false worldlessness. Contextuality brings together the relation between others' mystical experience and one's own search, as well as the others' and one's own praxis.

Can it also help out with the difficult question of how genuine and false mysticism are to be distinguished? How are the mysticism of life and mysticism of death different? After all, a drunken murderer may also declare, "I am what I do."

The Distinction between Genuine and False Mysticism

Demarcation is a difficult but, at the same, irremissible task. The word "mysticism" alone calls for it. In common language, to refer to something as "mystical" connotes abnormality, incomprehension, puzzlement, and nonsense. Occult pseudoknowledge is said to be mysticism. Phenomena such as spiritism, parapsychology, astrology, tarot, pansophy, alchemy, or magic are lumped together in today's New Age boom under the umbrella of mysticism. Some students of mysticism try to escape this conceptual entanglement by distinguishing between a positive and a negative sense of mysticism. English has only the one word, expressing both those senses while, for example, German can make this distinction by speaking of the positive sense in the word *Mystik* and of the negative sense in the word *Mystizismus*. Correspondingly, German speaks of the *Mystiker*, a positive denotation, and of the *Mystizist*, a negative one. The latter is someone who casts amorous glances on genuine mysticism or flirts with it without ever risking her or his ego. "The *Mystiker* are foolhardy, the *Mystizisten* circumspect. The *Mystiker* seek immediacy, even if it costs them their life. The *Mystizisten* find everything immediate interesting. The *Mystiker* become fools or the enlightened. Any transformation is basically abhorrent to *Mystizisten*."[2] But even such an attempt seems, in my view, not to move us forward. It helps little to distinguish between immediate, genuine mysticism and mediated mystical entities that one has made one's own through learning, reading, and appropriation, or mediated mystical states produced by means of drugs, alcohol, or chloroform, which William James has impressively described.

But in this discourse, immediacy of experience is given a kind of transfiguration; it is as if this immediacy were wholly other as such because it comes from above. There is a deification of immediacy that precisely fosters the quiet side of mysticism, which turns its back on the world and has no mind for politics. By contrast, it was exactly the masters of contemplation who were always quite certain that God is not one who metes out privilege. They also knew that we are beings of language who live in the house of language, which means that every immediacy is mediated. The more this insight is lost in one's own experience of being grasped, the more dangerous those aspects of which one is not conscious become. By mediated I mean what is preformed through education, tradition, language, and the domain of images or, as in the now normative mediation of the world through technology, what they exclude, prohibit, and define as an aberration or psychic malady.

The internal difficulty of fixing the boundary between genuine and false mysticism becomes manifest only when a mysticism comes into view that is in itself negative, death-seeking, and aggressive. Such a mysticism became most clearly visible in the history of the twentieth century. In embracing its traditions of nationalism, militarism, and nature-romanticism, German fascism spawned a very peculiar mysticism. The Nazis not only seized upon many traditions of German mysticism from Meister Eckhart to Jacob Böhme, they also had their own revelations and sacred writings, rituals and consecrated places; they had the cults of blood and soil, fire and wind, martyrs, gurus, and the *Führer*. The criteria of what constitutes mystical experience are applicable to them. Nazi-mysticism, too, may be ranked with what William James lists as the criteria of mystical experience.

I refer back to two characteristics James mentions in his categorization (see chapter 1). He stresses the ineffability of the feelings the quality and value of which cannot be explained to someone who has not had those specific feelings. It is precisely this argument that I heard again and again in many conversations with Nazi devotees, "You did not experience it and you cannot understand it." Another characteristic of altered states of consciousness is their "noetic quality," that is, a perception and an insight into the depths of truth that discursive intelligence cannot plumb.[3] It is this perception of race and peoplehood, nobility of the soul and the German forest, the depth of German music and the uniqueness of German heroic death, that have sharpened my hearing.

Phenomena of this kind nourish a highly necessary hermeneutic of suspicion. The sincerity of adherents and their readiness to take risks do not suffice as criteria for the demarcation of genuine from false mysticism. The basis for the needed distinction between the spirits must be something else. This basis is an ethics that orients itself by the right the biologically inferior have to life, or, to put it in more current terms, the right of the economically expendable. As something directly religious, mystical experience goes beyond ethical demands but never in such a way that it suspends or negates the foundations of an ethic that rests in the affirmation that we are all creatures. Hence, mystical experience could not claim, in flights of self-imposed sovereignty, to judge who is worthy of living and who is not, which is what Nazi-mysticism claimed, as is quite evident. Contrary to an Aryan mystical affectedness, the criteria for genuine mysticism are those of ethics. They are generalizable; universality is not only a dream. God is indeed "common to all creatures," as Ruysbroeck puts it (see chapter 1). Whatever destroys this basic experience, as is done in racist, classist, and patriarchal systems of domination, or in mystical ego-mania, suspends this commonness of God and, hence, also destroys the very writing of ontology and ethics that genuine mysticism searches for and lives out.

Jewish mysticism interprets the fulfillment of every commandment as a *unio mystica* (mystical union) between a human being and God. That my will can become identical with the will of God is an expression of this unity. In very simple language, an English church hymn gives voice to this relation of God's breath and the breathing ego in the mystical union of both.

Breathe on me, Breath of God, fill me with life anew,
That I may love what Thou dost love and do what Thou wouldst do.[4]

This mysticism presupposes that it is possible to be of one will with God, "until with Thee I will one will." The mysticism of *Volk* (nation) and race that Nazism heralded presupposes a different ontology that had nothing to do with "the common good." Particularity proclaims itself as universality and hierarchy must set out to eliminate all anarchistic elements. The *unio* of this mysticism—union with the *Führer*'s will—may be an unmediated one and subjectively genuine. This is a negative mystical ideology that replaces exactly what we may know of God, namely, that God desires fullness of life for all, with a particular idol of power and dominance or with the idol of the victors.

4. FINDING ANOTHER LANGUAGE

⇒•⇐

Speaks the soul, then—alas!—the soul speaks no more.

FRIEDRICH SCHILLER

The Cloud of Unknowing and the Cloud of Forgetting

IN A SEMINAR on mysticism that I teach, we always begin with a brief meditation. I criticized one group who had fobbed off on us some music that, as far as I was concerned, was shallow and then had left us alone with our thoughts and feelings. One student objected to my criticism, saying, "Why? Feeling is something you always do alone." I found that to be an unbearable statement because it expressed hopelessness and a deep mistrust of the very possibility of sharing feelings with others.

When Jesus had fed the five thousand, they all felt the reign of God closer at hand, I countered. Disbelief and despair retreated. There were shared feelings of oneness, hope, and solidarity. Still, the objection of the student, born in despair over the possibilities of our language, remained. The student attached it to what Buber refers to as "the commotion of life," the bundle of external experiences, of the cognition of the "whirl-wall of feelings and objects." Language mirrors that commotion; it is incapable of communicating the experience of oneness. *Cognitio Dei experimentalis* (experience of God not mediated by books or doctrines) is not provided for in ordinary language. What cannot be observed also cannot be communicated. As in an image of the Sufi mystic Rumi, words are merely dust on the mirror we call experience, a kind of dust that the broom of "tongue" creates.

All mystics have had to suffer from this dust of words. They can describe in images but never name *tel quel* (exactly as it was) what happened to them. If it is true that all human beings are capable of ecstasy and can experience mystical moments of wholeness, then all human beings also share the helplessness of the language that we commonly use. How can we make ourselves understood about something that does not represent the objective reality that surrounds us? Can one explain the fragrance of a rose to a person who has no sense

55

of smell? Or convey to someone who is not in love the condition of being in love or the intoxication with God to someone sober?

Nearly all mystics give voice to the problems of the inadequacy of language. That which lifts us out of time and place, the experience of the "now" lifted above time as well as the awareness of how transient mystical moments really are, just cannot be grasped.

> [God] is pure Nothingness.
> He is not now, not here.
> I reach for Him
> and see Him disappear.[1]

In this verse, Angelus Silesius (1624–1677) plays with the German words *greifen* (to grasp) and *Begriff* (concept), hence, conceptualized. Literary scholars speak of the *topos* of the unspeakable, but this form of helplessness is more than a literary device. It is a basic experience that language is too small, too narrow, too dusty, too unexpressive, and too misleading to give word to the mystic condition. How could God be named? By necessity, are not all names too small? Is it not an altogether false assumption, not to say arrogant vainglory, to put into language that which is neither one thing or another? And if the self-negation of the one speaking belongs to the heart of this experience, how can they who are sick with the yearning to submerge and lose themselves completely even acquire speech? Most mystics knew: whatever is said about the deity is untrue. Their positions on this basic question oscillated between an acknowledged helplessness of language—sometimes bemoaned in an abundance of words in the sense of the topos of the unspeakable—and a radical despairing thereof. A Franciscan mystic in Italy, Angela of Foligno (1248–1309), calls her own highly precise descriptions of what she had experienced "blasphemies!"[2]

How can one take the Word (that uncomprehended, ungrasped *logos),* and "fling down the Word as fodder for the words," as Buber similarly expresses his loathing for trivialization? He names the contradiction "between the inner experience . . . and the commotion out of which they ascend, only to fall back into it again and again . . . the contradiction between ecstasy, which does not go into memory, and the desire to save it for a memory, in the image, in speech, in confession."[3]

In every mystical sensitivity there lives something that struggles against the ordinary and refuses to be put on the same level with it.

Such negation of everyday reality with its "nothing-but" trivialities and its definitions of life under the category of "business-as-usual" is not quite resistance against violent reality, even though it can function subversively to nurture this resistance. The fact that what ultimately concerns us, what Paul Tillich called the "mystical a priori" and in which, according to him, idealistic as well as naturalistic concepts of theology are rooted, should not be utterable, only nourishes our mistrust of language as such and isolates us. This is what the student in the seminar mentioned earlier rightly felt.

Yet no one can ever really settle for ineffability. Working on the impossible cannot be given up and the soul cannot renounce speaking of it. Nothing incites speakers to talk as much as ineffability. In a variation on Schiller's statement above, one might say, "if the soul is silent, then—alas!—the soul is silent no more." It is readily apparent that nothing makes speech so flat, so mindless, so banal, as the talk show axiom that language is at the disposal of any and everything. On the boundary and not in the interior is where language develops.

A classic example of Western mystical tradition concerning the impossible possibility of speaking is *The Cloud of Unknowing*. This practical introduction to contemplation was composed by an unknown fourteenth-century English priest, who may have been a Carthusian monk. It is a mystagogical work that addresses the individual needs of the seeker on whom the text persistently focuses. As a method of instruction, it has close affinity with Zen.

It seems to me that "cloud of unknowing" is a more profound metaphor for what scholarship calls the topos of ineffability. The metaphor goes back to Dionysius the Areopagite, the mysterious monk who possibly lived in Syria around the turn of the sixth and seventh century C.E. He spoke of the cloud of unknowing in connection with the cloud that covered Mount Sinai when Moses ascended it in order to receive the tables of the law from God (Exod 24:12-18).

This tradition of "negative" or apophatic theology also governs the writer of *The Cloud of Unknowing*. "When I say 'darkness,' I mean a privation of knowing . . . which is between you and your God. . . . If ever you come to this cloud, and live and work in it, as I bid you, just as this cloud of unknowing is above you, between you and your God, in the same way you must put beneath you a cloud of forgetting, between you and all the creatures that have ever been made."[4] The basic idea is that we take our place between two clouds. The first and lower one is the cloud we are to spread over everything while we are in the phase of immersing ourselves. This is the cloud of forgetting. Sensations, problems, and thoughts are to fall from us like ballast. "A simple awareness of anything under God, which forces itself upon your will and consciousness, puts you further away from God than you would be if it did not exist; it hinders you and makes you less able to feel, by experience, the fruit of his love."[5] The cloud of forgetting, to be spread out like a cover, is perhaps similar to what Jesus repeatedly expressed in the words, "do not be anxious." What to eat? What to wear? The cares and anxieties of everyday toils and troubles belong, together with our endeavors to understand them, under the cloud of forgetting. That cloud is not a luxury for people without material cares; on the contrary, it makes it possible for the poor to find joy in life, music, laughter. Without the cloud of forgetting, which always and above all is one of self-forgetting, we remain in bondage to heteronomy, to the rule over our lives by powers such as hunger, cold, age, and illness. The cloud of forgetting is an element of freedom; it liberates and allows us to approach openly the cloud of unknowing. Our longing, seeking, and sensing enters into the second cloud. It is possible to sense the inner stirring of love in the dusk of the cloud of unknowing.[6]

What does that mean for the language of the unspeakable? Mystical stammering has its origin at the point where the two clouds intersect. It has to spread the cloud of forgetting over the existing and already known language and then it may enter into the cloud of unknowing as Moses "entered the cloud" (Exod 24:18). "Then perhaps . . . he will show you some of his secrets, of which man may or cannot speak. Then you shall feel your affection all aflame with the fire of his love, far more than I know how to tell you or may or wish to at this time. For I dare not take it upon me to speak with my blabbing fleshly tongue of the work that belongs to God alone; and, to put it briefly, even though I dared so to speak I would not wish to."[7] Spanish mystic John of the Cross (see chapter 8) tells with greater passion of this sober wisdom of the mystagogical guide of the soul. That we cannot comprehend or grasp God is given as a gift of grace precisely to those who "see sharply" and "feel deeply." "These souls are herein somewhat like the saints in heaven, where they who know Him most perfectly perceive most clearly that He is infinitely incomprehensible; for those who have the less clear vision do not perceive so clearly as do these others how greatly He transcends their vision."[8] Thus, the more people enter into the cloud of unknowing the clearer it becomes, both that God is incomprehensible and that conventional language fails us.

The author of the *Cloud* puts the matter in his dry style as follows: "For no matter how spiritual a thing may be in itself, yet when we come to speak of it, since speech is a bodily exercise performed with the tongue, which is an instrument of the body, it is necessary that bodily metaphors be used [as these words, up or down, in or out, behind or before, on one side or on the other]. But should it on that account be interpreted and understood bodily? No, spiritually."[9] It is true that in the traditions of the West this contrast is frequently drawn between material or physical and spiritual, but it fails to explain what the real difficulty of mysticism is. The cloud of forgetting in relation to this world and its constraints must become more dense and more powerful than what is suggested by the two-story image of this world and the next. The prison that we fell asleep in is papered and furnished with language. The cultural interior of the prison cannot be simply left behind because language has long taken root in us as an instrument of domination. In order to liberate and renew ourselves, we need far more than the change of perspective from matter to spirit that tradition has so often embraced in a naive Platonic fashion. We need a new language in order to plunge into the cloud of unknowing.

Sunder Warumbe: Without a Why or Wherefore

Given its exuberance, enchantment, and immediacy, mystical sensibility can only sound ridiculous in conventional language. The *cognitio Dei experimentalis,* the "unity" that Buber speaks of in contrast to "commotion," cannot be mediated by books, authorities, or institutions precisely because language itself is part of multiplicity, commotion, and confusion and reflects them. For that reason language is in the service of purpose, calculation, and domination even if they who use language resist it. Why is our language so helpless? Why can we not share in communicating what we need the most?

I have learned much about this matter from Meister Eckhart. His concept *sunder warumbe* is for me an indispensable expression of mystical existence; it also introduces a different existential quality into the understanding of language. Preaching in German on the text of 1 John 4:9 *in hoc apparuit caritas Dei in nobis* (in this the love of God was made manifest among us) he spoke as follows:

> For this innermost reason you should perform all of your deeds without whys and wherefores. I say in truth, as long as you perform your

deeds for the sake of the kingdom of heaven or God or your eternal salvation, in other words for an external reason, things are not truly well with you. You may be well accepted, but it is certainly not the best way. For verily, if someone imagines that they will receive more in warmth, devotion, sweet rapture, and in the special grace of God than by the hearth or in a stable, all you are doing is taking God, placing a coat around his head, and pushing him under a bench. Because the person who seeks for God in a particular way, takes that way and misses God. But the person who seeks for God without a way will find Him, as He is, in Himself; and such a son lives with the Son and He is life itself. The person who for a thousand years asks the question of life, "Why do you live?" could provide the answer, the only answer, "I live because I am alive." The reason for this is that life is lived for its own sake and emanates from its own sources; hence it is lived entirely without whys or wherefores, because it lives for itself.[10]

This "without a why or a wherefore" that we should live in, that life itself lives in, what does it mean? It is the absence of all purpose, all calculation, every *quid pro quo,* every tit for tat, all domination that makes life itself its servant. Wherever we are torn between being and doing, feeling and acting, we no longer live *sunder warumbe.* Instead, we measure expenditure and success, calculate probability and benefit, or else obey fears we do not understand. I say this with a view to the goal-centered rationality that pervades our highly technologized world. Such a rationality prohibits any form of existence for which there is no purpose: we eat certain foods in order to lose weight, we take dancing lessons in order to keep fit, and we pray in order to facilitate specific wish fulfillment by God. The rose has ceased to bloom "without a why" or "because she blooms"; in the market-oriented world we inhabit, the rose in bloom is like every other object, an article of saleable merchandise. Meister Eckhart uses an amusing comparison to critique such calculating religion. "But many people want to look upon God with the eyes with which they look upon a cow; they want to love God the way they love a cow that you love because it gives you milk and cheese. This is how people behave who want to love God because of external wealth or inner comfort; but they do not love God properly: rather, they love their self interest."[11]

The *sunder warumbe* lies at the root of all mystical love of God. It is another form of expressing what C. S. Lewis summed up in his "I am what I do" (see chapter 1). *Sunder warumbe* also helps resolve the immense difficulties in mystical language between what cannot be put into words and muteness. For our relationship to language is really not much better than those who love God the way they love a cow. Our language is part of our life in the world of purposes and intentions. I say something in order to achieve or to receive something. I confront objects and make use of them. I am still in what Meister Eckhart called the spirit of the merchandisers, the mercantilism of the *do ut des,* which means I give a promise in order to receive something in return, using language in the spirit of utilitarian reification. Were I to take the spirit of unity seriously, the experience that neither sense-experience nor reason can permeate and search, I would not speak in order to appropriate something. Language would not then be a means to win the world for myself. It would rather celebrate joy and lament pain. It would not aim at something that I can conquer but instead aim to gather me in the now.

Mysticism's basic idea about what language can do—and what it cannot do adequately but also cannot relinquish under any circumstances—is oriented towards pure praise. While praise may have its reasons—and mingles with thanksgiving in the language of liturgy—in reality it always has the character of the *sunder warumbe.* For example, in praising the moon as it rises, in praising someone who is loved or, indeed, in praising the source of all good, the ego that is possessed by goals and that craves dominance vanishes. It has stepped out of itself. It has scuttled itself.

The spirit of the merchandisers has been let go, as is what Eckhart calls *Eigenschaft* (what is one's own): characteristic features, idiosyncrasies, and singularity, as well as love of self and egoism. That we may live without *Eigenschaft* in that sense is almost beyond comprehension and yet, at the same time, it is an expression of the most profound freedom that we can attain. We become free when, no longer wed *(ledig)* to fears and constraints, we are in God's presence "without a why or a wherefore."

For Meister Eckhart, all authentic deeds are those that emulate the original act of creation. They are deeds that spring from life and love. In this sense they are without a why and wherefore. Creation is not conformed to the cause-and-effect context to which we in our daily lives have conformed ourselves. For what purpose should God have created giraffes, wonderful stones that nobody sees, and also creatures like me? The mystical spirituality of creation articulates a relationship to the world that is in principle different from that which the instrumentalization of life imposes on us. "God, too, loves us without a why or wherefore. . . . But love has no why, no reason. If

I had a friend and loved him because good things and everything I desire might happen to me, then I would love, not my friend, but myself. I should love my friend for his own goodness and his own virtue and for the sake of all that he is in himself."[12] When our deeds emulate the original act of creation, then our language, too, has to be without a why and wherefore. Love, just like the rose, has no why. "She blooms because she blooms."[13]

If the words "I love you" mean I would like to sleep with you or I want you to marry me, then it remains in the domain of purpose. When "I love you" means that your physical measurements are ideal or you have a great job, then we remain in the realm of reason, which is destructive to love. Purposes and reasons differentiate me and my motivation, separating the person who speaks from her or his language. Then I cannot "be what I do." The language of this world, from which the mystics distance themselves with such passion, is articulated in terms of a hierarchical order and excludes authentic unity. Egoism, rationality of purposes, and hierarchical order are mirrored in our ordinary language. Linguistically, we take our bearings from distinctions, from *genus* and *differentia specifica,* and use them to classify things. We turn ourselves into rulers of the world and use language as an instrument of reification. We make the world our own and look upon it as our property.

Nowhere is this more apparent than in the current bioethical debate in which the distinction between inventing and discovering is dropped. The biogenetic codes that have been discovered are made the private property of those who own the world. The endeavor to patent everything perfects the power of control over what once used to be called "creation" and today is designated as genetic material. In such a perspective, the *sunder warumbe* does not exist nor anything that cannot be controlled, dissected, used, owned, and further utilized. But it is precisely this mystical knowledge of a different freedom, a freedom from the "why" that enables people to offer resistance. "If you should question truthful persons who act for their own reasons, 'why do you do what you do?' they should respond properly and say no more than 'I act because I act.' "[14]

A Language without Dominance

A language free of purpose and control—is there such a thing at all? The biblical creation narrative tells of God bringing animals and birds to Adam so that God might see what Adam would name them (Gen 2:19). Here man controls the natural world. Does the woman also belong to that sphere of control? One may debate the interpretation of the man's joyful shout, "This at last is the bone of my bones and flesh of my flesh!" (Gen 2:23). Is it the language of mystical praise, *sunder warumbe?* Or is it that of appropriation? Whatever the case, it is not until after the expulsion from paradise and after the curse God places on the serpent, the man, and the woman that Adam gives his helpmate the name Eve, the mother of all living things (Gen 3:20). The relationship of dominance is established in the act of naming. It happens only after the curse of patriarchy was uttered and the entry into the reality of the life and world of the ancient Near East was accomplished. It happens with enmity between humans and their environment, with fruitless toil on the field, and with the subjugation of one, made in God's image, under another also made in that image.

All mysticism is part of the endeavor to escape from this fate of language that serves the exercise of power, control, and possession. Traditional Western theology has most often defined the authentic relationship of believers to God as "obedience." This presupposes the separation between the one who commands and the one who obeys. How could creator and creature be united in oneness? Mystical theology has sought to depict a different unity or union than that which is based on dominance and, in so doing, has always appealed to biblical passages. "For from him and through him and to him are all things" (Rom 11:36) is a verse, much loved by Goethe, which expresses in hymn form the sought-after union. This fundamental idea of union appears in different words in the following verses from John: "that they may all be one; even as thou, Father, art in me, and I in thee, . . . that they may be one even as we are one, I in them and thou in me, that they may become perfectly one, so that the world may believe that thou has sent me" (John 17:21-22). All dualistic discourse of lord and servant, speaking and listening, and free and slave is left behind here; instead, a language is sought that is nonimperialistic and anarchistic (as the repeated use of "in" and "one" indicates). This basic quandary of language of domination versus language of oneness is precisely what mystics suffered from. They kept silent and hid themselves for fear of exclusion and persecution, or they harmed themselves through flight into the extremely private. They separated themselves from the tradition that in many places actually does grant more space than their orthodox interpreters can admit.

Such space, however, is not what is available in stringent philosophical or scholastic conceptuality. It is found in the capacity of poetic language for expressiveness, its freedom to narrate rather than philosophize, and its many linguistic resources for making meaning audible, palpable, palatable, resounding, and resisting definition. What I have in mind are the stylistic resources of rhetorical traditions that are employed in most of the texts of Western and Near Eastern mysticism; for example, frequent repetition, use of the comparison, hyperbole, negation, antithesis, and paradox. I refer to the great mystical poet and creator of language of the Middles Ages, Mechthild von Magdeburg, who was a Beguine, and her work *The Flowing Light of the Godhead*. In this work, she uses various but quite independent literary forms such as prayers, reflections, short aphorisms, conversations, and narrative pieces. Everything is told spontaneously, with extraordinary directness and vitality. The work includes everything that, as an untutored woman of the lower nobility, she had experienced and suffered in relation to God, from the "burning mountain" to the "bottomless well"—everything over a period of thirty-one years beginning in her twelfth year, according to her own testimony. Mechthild's language has often been hailed as particularly independent (the medieval word for that is *ledig*, not tied to something or someone).

[O]ur salvation has become a bridegroom. The bride is intoxicated with gazing on the noble face. In the greatest strength she comes out of herself, and in the greatest blindness she sees with the greatest clarity. In the greatest clarity she is dead and alive at the same time. The longer she is dead, the more merrily she lives. The more merrily she lives, the more she learns. The smaller she becomes, the more abundance she receives. The richer she becomes, the poorer she is. The deeper she dwells, the broader she is. The more imperious she is, the deeper her wounds become. The higher she rages, the more loving God is toward her. The higher she soars, the nearer she comes to the Godhead, the more beautifully she shines with the reflection of the Godhead. The more she works, the more softly she rests. The more she comprehends, the stiller her silence. . . . Ah, whither is our Savior-bridegroom being conveyed in the jubilation of the holy Trinity? Since God no longer wanted to be in himself, he made the soul and gave himself to her out of great love. Of what are you made, soul, that you rise so high over all creatures, and mingle with the holy Trinity and yet remain wholly in yourself?—You have spoken of my origin, now I tell it to you truly: I was made in that place from love, therefore no creature can satisfy me according to my noble nature, and no creature can unlock me, except love alone.[15]

This cataract of words breaks loose without ifs or buts, without whys or wherefores, a cascade of metaphors that accelerates in speed and in the passion of speech. The repetitious constructions of "the more . . . the more" rush onward with their paradoxical accentuations, and yet the text ends in a peculiar silence. It is a language of daring passion that has left behind the terms of time and space, reason and purpose, power and impotence. It is a language of first-order amazement, a mystical praise of creation and of the bridegroom-creator who "no longer wanted to be in himself." Here is the fulfillment of the prayer of Teresa of Avila: "Lord, give me other words."

The *Via Negativa,* the Way of Negation

In the tradition of mysticism, there are linguistic elements that are clearly indispensable and occur in the most diverse cultures. I address three highly notable forms of mystical language: negation, paradox, and silence.

The stylistic figure of negation belongs to the experience that is inexpressible in words. It is not this, it is not that, it is not what you already know or have seen or what someone told you before. "No eye has ever seen, no ear has ever heard such joy" is a line of Bach's chorale, *Wachet auf, ruft uns die Stimme.* The writer of that text, Philipp Nicolai (1556–1608), incorporates into that verse, after those negations, an ancient shout of jubilation "io io"—otherwise not known in Protestant hymnody—and thereby melds the language of the cloud of unknowing with a language in which the articulated word no longer has to be present: *Des sind wir froh / io io / Ewig in dulci jubilo* (of that we are glad / io io / forevermore in dulci jubilo).

What cannot be named positively can either be left in silence or must be named negatively. The Upanishads state that the self *(Atman)* "is to be described by 'No! No!' only, . . . Who so calls the Absolute anything in particular, or says that it is *this,* seems implicitly to shut it off from being *that*—it is as if he lessened it."[16] The negation of the "this" in the interest of the absoluteness of the absolute is the response to this danger: there is a knowing through unknowing.

A well-known text of Jalal al-din Rumi (see chapter 2) from *The Divan* illustrates both the concern that the absolute be denigrated and the power of knowing through unknowing. "What is to be done, O Moslems? For I do not recognize myself. I am neither Christian, nor Jew, nor Parsi, nor Moslem. I am not of the East, nor of the West, nor of the land, nor of the sea; I am not of Nature's workshop, nor of the circling heavens. I am not of earth, nor of water, nor of air, nor of fire; I am not of the Heavenly City, nor of the dust, nor of existence, nor of entity. I am not of this world, nor of the next, nor of Paradise, nor of Hell; I am not of Adam, nor of Eve, nor of Eden or Eden's angels. My place is the Placeless, my trace is the Traceless; 'Tis neither body nor soul, for I belong to the soul of the Beloved. I have put duality away, I have seen that the two worlds are one."[17]

In one of his sermons, Meister Eckhart uses the image of a ship. "Whoever can say the most of God speaks the most in the negative. This can be illustrated with the example of a ship. Were I a shipowner and gave a ship to someone who has never seen one, I would say that it is neither of stone nor of straw. That way I would have told him something about that ship."[18] This way of negation (*apophasis* in Greek, *negatio* in Latin) entered Christian mysticism with Dionysius the Areopagite and has become part of its tradition through a long process of historical impact. In the Areopagite's treatise on the heavenly hierarchy (*De caelesti hierarchia* 2, 3) he states concisely that in connection with the divine, negations (*apophaseis*) are true and affirmations (*kataphaseis*) insufficient. This view gave rise to the apophatic tradition. Mystical theology cannot rest contentedly with what is already known and with what has been already, but insufficiently, named. It distinguishes itself from the lower level of sensate knowledge and its "symbolic theology" where, for example, God is called Father. It also distinguishes itself from the middle level of rationality that in reflection speaks of the first cause and proceeds by means of affirmation, kataphatically. The ways of knowing that go beyond the rational have their place in apophatic and mystical theology. It is doubtful, however, whether there can be a radical *via negativa* or whether the mystics' language must always be complemented by the way of affirmation—on account of its contextual embeddedness and linguistic preformation that is becoming more and more apparent today.[19] Apophatic and kataphatic tradition, the true and the insufficient, actually devour each other and remain interdependent. Indeed, all three levels of symbolic, reflexive, and mystical theological-poetic language impoverish themselves when they shut themselves off from one another.

In his mystical theology, Dionysius teaches everything that God is not, clearly delineating himself from both biblical as well as doctrinal statements. "It has no power, it is not power, nor is it light. It does not live nor is it life. It is not a substance, nor is it eternity or time. It cannot be grasped by the understanding since it is neither knowledge nor truth. It is not kingship. It is not wisdom. It is neither one nor oneness, divinity. . . ."[20] Here, Dionysius refers to the quality of divinized humans, which belongs to the domain of relativity. In his radically apophatic manner of speaking, Dionysius also rejects such concepts as goodness or light because, as he maintained, God is utterly beyond everything and above everything and everyone.

The radical nature of this language leads into an abstract negation that denies the possibility of conceptual knowledge. This unknowing does not arise from ignorance; it comes to be after knowledge. It creates an unusual dynamic that forever seeks new concepts, words, and images and then discards them as inadequate. Not only is this so in Dionysius but also in the extensive circle of those whom he influenced and who, in turn, set their mark on the whole of medieval mysticism.

There is a moving story about such discarding of concepts that involves Thomas Aquinas, the greatest theologian of the Middle Ages. Shortly before his death in 1273, he had a mystical experience during the celebration of the Mass. The experience took away his speech. "Something was revealed to me that made what I have written and taught of no account," he said. He then stopped teaching and dictating. On his death bed, he interpreted the Song of Songs to the Cistercians who gathered around him. His demeanor was described as "negative theology lived out."[21]

At any rate, there is in the way of negation a progressive dynamic that uses prefixes such as "un," prepositions such as "over" and "beyond," and formulae such as "more than," "higher than," and "on the far side of." This dynamic expresses linguistically the presence of negative theology. In Greek, constructions with the prefix "hyper," and in Latin "super," have found their way into the vocabulary of mysticism in such absurd-sounding words like "super-eternal" or "super-being." The flowering of German mysticism in the twelfth and thirteenth centuries saw the creation of words with the prefixes "un," "über," or "ent," and the suffixes "heit," "keit," or "ung," producing a field of mystical words. This makes the conceptuality of philosophy and theology look more like a prison to escape from than a means of clarification!

Let me exemplify this knowing through unknowing and, at the same time, point to the path that leads from mystical theology to practical spirituality. The story of the Good Samaritan (Luke 10) can be interpreted mystically in such a way that the question of the knowledge of God becomes its focus. The priest and the Levite, who walk past the man who fell among robbers and was seriously hurt, are pious God-fearing persons. They "know" God and the law of God. They have God the same way that the one who knows has that which is known. They know what God wants them to be and do. They also know where God is to be found, in the scriptures and the cult of the temple. For them, God is mediated through the existing institutions. They have their God—one who is not to be found on the road between Jerusalem and Jericho. What is wrong with this knowledge of God? The problem is not the knowledge of the Torah or the knowledge of the temple. (It is absurd to read an anti-Judaistic meaning into a story of the Jew Jesus, since it could just as well have come from Hillel or another Jewish teacher.) What is false is a knowledge of God that does not allow for any unknowing or any negative theology. Because both actors know that God is "this," they do not see "that." Hence the Good Samaritan is the antifundamentalist story par excellence.

"And so I ask God to rid me of God," Meister Eckhart says. The God who is known and familiar is too small for him. To know God like another object of our cognition means to turn God into something that is usable, at our disposal. There are many places in mystical piety where the call is heard to leave God for God's sake. The priest and the Levite in the Lucan narrative could have heard it. In this sense, they could have learned to leave behind the object of God they were familiar with, in order to find the God who has assumed the form of a poor beaten-up man. To leave God for the sake of God means to relinquish a figure of God, a way of God, a mode or manner of speaking of God.

To give an example typical of our culture, this would mean letting go of the God of childhood, the God of our "home and native land," or the God of one's own family. The fundamentalistic defiance in which the God of childhood is clung to in as literalist a way as possible often gets in the way of living experience. The process of letting go would be a process of annihilation of the self that has evolved, a process that is necessary in order to know God in the unknown. To leave the ego or the I fits consistently into the apophatic tradition. That and nothing else is what the Samaritan is doing in the gospel narrative, and the mystical theologian from Nazareth is recounting nothing different.

The Paradox

Images, comparisons, and parables are found on every level of religious discourse. But its only mystical language with its attempt to stay close to "lived religion" that time and time again attains to "a glowing, explosive language in contrast to the 'cold' language of theology."[22]

An excellent stylistic medium that explosive language uses is the oxymoron, a deliberate fusing of two contradictory or mutually exclusive concepts into a new unity. One thinks of such expressions as "darklight," "sadjoyous" (Friedrich Hölderlin), "bittersweet," "eloquent silence," "filled emptiness," or "acquired dispossession." The coincidence of substantive or logical contradictions, *(coincidentia oppositorum)* comes about when in a single statement words are juxtaposed with each other that are insufficient on their own. This creates the paradox, which is an unexpected assertion that goes counter to general opinion or common knowledge. In terms of philosophy of language, the paradox is an attempt to approach from two opposite directions a factor that cannot be perceived or understood. Other than in dialectics, no synthesis results here nor a reconciliation of polarities. The opposition remains unmediated and cannot be resolved in language. Dionysius's phrase about the "darkness that outshines all resplendence" is a prime example of paradoxical language. Other bold word images are "whispering silence," "fertile desert," "soundless tone," and "silent cry." With the unserviceable means of a logical language that operates chronologically, such images seek to name mystical experiences. In the introduction to *Ecstatic Confessions*, Martin Buber speaks of "the language, which the commotion once laboriously created to be its messenger and handmaiden, and which, since the beginning of its existence, desires eternally the one impossible thing: to set its foot on the neck of the commotion and to become all poem—truths, purity, poem."[23] Paradox is the clearest expression of this desire and this struggle. Buber cites Meister Eckhart, "There I heard without sound, there I saw without light, there I smelled without movement, there I tasted that which was not, there I felt what did not exist. Then my heart became bottomless, my soul loveless, my mind formless and my nature without essence."[24]

In this form of discourse I am not interested in "prescriptive grammatical rules"—such as ineffability and paradox—that permit the identification of experience as mystical.[25] What interests me is the collision of conventional knowledge and its language, including that of science, which is and remains the "messenger and handmaiden" of that knowledge, on the one hand, with the mystical experience that is oriented toward a changed reality, on the other. I wish to proceed neither proscriptively nor merely descriptively. The debate over mystical language has referred to retrospective interpretations that follow the experience, the reflexive interpretations that accompany the experience, and the interwoven linguistic interpretations that precede and form the experience.[26] In his 1978 essay, "Language and Mystical Awareness," Frederick Streng dealt with the "soteriological expectations" to which that other language gives rise. "Another function of language found in mystical language is just as important. It is to evoke a change in the attitudes and mechanisms of apprehension within the mystically adept."[27] The adept themselves are changed in their suffering under the domination of conventional language and in their longing for transformation.

A song of the contemporary Dutch base-community movement contains this stanza:

> The desert shall bloom, it shall laugh and rejoice,
> Water shall run and it shall glisten,
> The thirsty come and drink
> The desert shall drink and it shall bloom.

This is the traditional mystical image of the desert; it is also very fine paradoxical language inasmuch as it has become movement and verb rather than being a simple paradoxical juxtaposition of an adjective with a subject. There is a poem, originating in the circle around Meister Eckhart and passed on anonymously, in which paradox also comes in the form of verbs:

> O my soul, go out; God, come in!
> When I flee from you, you come to me.
> When I lose myself, I find you. . . .[28]

Fleeing and coming, losing and finding become one process.

Silence

The third specific element of all mystical languages is silence, which is speaking coming to an end and producing at the same time an expanse of silence. In terms of day-to-day experience, two kinds of silence may be distinguished. One is a dull, listless, apathetic silence, a wordlessness arising from poverty, such as exists in cultures of poverty or between people who have nothing to say to one another. But besides this prediscourse silence, there is also a postdiscourse silence that arises from an abundance that transcends language as a means of communication. This silence after speaking does make use of words but only in order to leave them behind. The sought-after mediation is no longer needed; its instrument is laid aside—more accurately, it falls from one's hands because, in the place of mediation, there has emerged a union that no longer requires language as a tool. Being silent together is a higher degree of being together and of oneness. Just as listening to music can bring people together more than words, so too can the spoken—or written—word come closer to its limit, to silence, and fall silent freely or by necessity. Paradox and apophatic discourse are indicative of this "silence arising from abundance." Being cast out of this form of silence is a bitter experience because we then find ourselves thrown back into the apathetic silence of prediscourse and left all alone.

The authenticity of mystical texts arises from its proximity to the boundary between speech and speechlessness. In the best of cases, such texts are able to create an expanse of quiet, a time of silence. The eminent Rhenish prophet Hildegard von Bingen (1099–1179), writing to Wibert de Gembloux, a monk who had offered to be her secretary, recounts her peculiar audiovisual experiences, which she describes most soberly, setting herself apart from the "unconsciousness of ecstasy": "But from my childhood, since before I grew strong in bones and nerves and veins, I have constantly beheld this vision in my soul until the present time, when I am more than seventy years old. And my soul ascends in this vision, as God wills, to the height of the firmament. . . . The light I see is not local; it is far, far brighter than the cloud that carries the sun. And I cannot see depth or length or breadth in it. And it is called for me that shadow of the living light. And as sun, moon, and stars are reflected in the water, so in this light the images of the writings and the speech and the forces and many works of [humans] shine forth to me."[29] Hildegard provides exact information about this "shadow of the living light" and everything she sees and hears in it. "And what I write in the vision, I see and hear, and set down no other words than those I hear, and in unpolished language I bring them forth, just as I hear them in the vision. For in this vision I am not taught to write as the philosophers write.

And the words in the vision are not like the words that sound from the mouths of human beings, but like a vibrating flame and like a cloud moving in pure air."[30] The "shadow of the living light," in which the audiovisual experiences assume form and color, sound and language, can be named. In a great variety of artistic and scientific forms, Hildegard has communicated what she saw in "the shadow of the light."

But in her self-interpretation, composed in her old age, she goes one more step, the step into silence. "In the light . . . I sometimes and not often see another light which is called for me the living light, and when and in what manner I see this, I do not know how to say. And when I gaze on it, all sadness and all need are snatched away from me, so that then I have the manner of a little girl and not of an old woman."[31] The living and ineffable light withdraws from language. It is experienced in the transformation of body and soul that it effects. In its sober, self-examining precision, this letter also—if read correctly—creates a place of quiet and a time of silence. I assume that within a mystical, or sometimes even a poetic, text there arises time and time again this possibility of not only naming or calling for silence but of producing it, so that a reader allows the book to drop as she reflects on it, or a speaker of the text speaks with the silence, or a listener can sink into it. Silence is not only called up, it occurs.

In the sparse rigor of a poem written "For Nelly Sachs, Friend, Poet, in Admiration," Ingeborg Bachmann (1926–1973) attained the language and the silence of mysticism. Her text begins, "You words, arise, follow me!" All features of mystical speaking, of the *via negativa*, of paradox come together in a silence that is exhorted and becomes real.

> Let be, I say, let be.
> Into the highest ear
> whisper, I say, nothing,
> don't collapse into death,
> let be, and follow me, not mild
> nor bitter,
> nor comforting,
> without consolation
> without significance,
> and thus without symbols—
>
> Most of all not this: the image
> cobwebbed with dust, the empty rumble

of syllables, dying words.
Not a syllable,
you words! [32]

All religions, particularly the nontheistic ones, have practiced silence
and sought it out. Buddhism especially lives in silent contemplation;
here silence is more prayer than words can ever be. Christians of the
Orthodox traditions enter into ceremonial silence "in order to give
God the word." Quakers begin their worship assemblies with a
lengthy silence. And in the liturgical renewal of Roman Catholicism
after Vatican II, the view became accepted that speaking must be
rooted in silence. In philosophical terms, Ludwig Wittgenstein—
going far beyond the famous concluding sentence of his *Tractatus*—
made this observation concerning mystical experience: "There is
something that is inexpressible. Not as a result of a syllogism, but as
that which shows itself. It shows itself as source, not in the sense of
causality, but as transparency of the utterable toward a meaning that
simply lies on the other side of the utterable, outside the world." [33]
    The Wisdom of Solomon speaks of this source of silence as fol-
lows: "All things were lying in peace and silence, and night in her
swift course was half spent, when thy almighty Word leapt from thy
royal throne in heaven" (18:14 NEB). John of the Cross took up this
text from the Apocrypha, related it to Christ as the one Word and
then back into the silence of the beginning. "The Father uttered one
Word: that Word is His Son, and He utters Him for ever in everlasting silence; and in silence the soul has to hear it." [34] Redemption
through the logos signifies the soul's hearing and that is participation
in creation.
    "Don't speak!" is an often repeated admonition found in the most
diverse traditions of mysticism. At its most basic level, it calls for a
preparation, a becoming silent so that a voice other than one's own
may be heard. But the admonition goes much beyond this practice. In
mystical silence, as Rumi often calls it, there is a phase in which the
mystics so leave themselves behind that it is no longer they who
speak their prayer but God in them. The experience of infused prayer
testifies to a silence in which God is as active as the human being.
"Unknown to him, his prayer ascended. . . . Since he has left himself,
it is God who speaks his prayer with whom is both prayer and fulfillment." [35] In this sense, silence prepares for the prayer infused by
God *(oratorio infusa)*. Rumi counsels: "Do not speak, so that thou
mayst hear from the speakers what cannot be uttered or described.

Do not speak, so that the Spirit may speak for thee: in the ark of Noah leave off swimming."[36] What is this flood from which the mystic is to get away? It is the flood of words. The ascetic dimension in the exercise of silence is an act of purification, abstinence, becoming free from a habit. In his *Ecstatic Confessions*, Martin Buber lifts up silence as what protects against "the commotion." He cites the Great Magical Codex of Paris in which the mystic who is approaching the highest initiation is being admonished. "But you will see how the gods turn their gaze upon you and come against you by storm. You, however, shall at once lay your forefinger upon your mouth and say: 'Silence, Silence, Silence—*symbolon* of the living, everlasting God— protect me, Silence!'"[37] Buber regards silence as "our *symbolon* which protects us from the gods and angels of the commotion, our guard against its aberrations, our purification against its impurity. We ensilence the experience, and it is a star that travels along its path. We speak it, and it is thrown down under the tread of the market. When we are quiet to the Lord, he makes his dwelling with us; we say Lord, Lord, and we have lost him."[38]

Silence has a double meaning as part of the mystical experience; on the one hand, silence is the ascetic practice of preparation, a kind of fasting from words. On the other, it is the self-expression of the living light. Religious orders and monastic communities built the practice of silence and silent periods into their rules. Some distinguish three grades of attaining quiet: the silence of the mouth, the silence of the mind, and the silence of the will. They based themselves on biblical verses such as "the fruit of righteousness be quietness" (Isa 32:17 NEB) where the word "quietness" also refers to "peace." Luther translated the verse as follows, "Righteousness will yield eternal quietness and certainty." The crucial clause of the Carmelite rules also derives from Isaiah: "In quietness and in trust shall be your strength" (Isa 30:15).

Teresa of Avila, who in 1970 was the first woman to be accorded the title of "teacher of the church" by the pope, introduced two hours of silent prayer daily as the most important reform in her small newly founded convents. This silent or "inner" meditation was contested in the world of the Counter-Reformation. For the church authorities, the oral communal prayer in the words of the church's tradition and shaped by its doctrinal knowledge was beyond questioning. That people might pray without moving their lips and without murmuring words appeared strange, even threatening. Ignatius of Loyola, no less, was eyed with mistrust by the Inquisition authorities on account of this "inward praying," which they suspected to be subjectivity and heresy, precisely because of the emotional intensity known to be involved.

In addition to this general suspicion of heresy lodged against the Brothers and Sisters of the Free Spirit and the Alumbrados *(Illuminati)*, there also prevailed—as was frequently the case in connection with mystical movements—the sexist ideology that asserted the mental and spiritual inferiority of women. The University of Salamanca was dominated by the school of thought that asserted a woman was by her very nature incapable of silent meditation. Her emotional disposition makes her prone to being easily driven into heresy. For that reason, inward, genuinely spiritual prayer should be left exclusively to the man and to his intellectual lucidity. An erudite theologian could advance upwards on the theological ladder of concepts and deductions to genuinely spiritual prayer. Women, who grew up without Latin and often without the skill of reading, would do better to heed the admonitions of clerics and remain within the traditions of oral prayer. They were allowed obedience, but mysticism and the way to the Inner Citadel—the path that Teresa herself showed and lived—were prohibited.

Like her pupil John of the Cross, Teresa endured the conflict between traditionally established norms of discourse and the personal experience of silence. After an extensive struggle she secured a legitimate place for her new endeavor. Christian spirituality gained a new depth in the course of the sixteenth century in these alternate forms of prayer. Eventually the Church of Rome recognized this. The subjectivization that the religious authorities feared occurred in both silence and discourse. Yet the stronger counterforce against mere ego gratification lay precisely in the wordless immersion in which all the soul's powers became silent. In such silence the I relinquished all that is its own. And all believers, not only male clerics, are called to this way of inward prayer.

The language of mysticism includes in itself a silence that learns to listen and risks being submerged in the dark night of the soul. In Teresa's lifework of reform, this silence is contextualized within the social resistance that worked for the liberation of women from restriction, tutelage, and mindlessness. In clinging undeterred to her praxis, Teresa showed how a different language could present a different freedom.

Mysticism is not only for especially graced and elect individuals. Women especially did not transfigure their solitude in an elitist manner; they lamented it. Very often, they could not tell of God's presence; instead, they were ridiculed or accused when they spoke of God being present. I sense a similar difficulty in the most important religious movement of our time, the movement for peace, justice, and the integrity of creation. The political powerlessness of those who take part in the conciliar process is so great that their language is not understood: God without weapons is a laughingstock.

When young people maintain "vigils of silence for peace" in the shopping malls of our cities, in the very places where the golden calf is venerated, they make God visible simply by standing in those places. In silence they speak of God's presence. In these new forms of piety, which openly acknowledge and own their lack of power and do not hide inside churches, there is a mystical kernel. It is a silence that follows after information, analysis, and knowledge. It is public and whoever practices this silence must count on being abused. Such silence is evident in the daily defeats God endures that give rise to accounts like this: "my family won't have anything of this; the papers once again failed to report a single word about our action; I am all alone in my workplace and ostracized." And yet, the silence speaks of God's presence. In silence, God is *presente,* as actualized in this Spanish term of liberation theology.

5. THE JOURNEY

Self-knowledge teaches us whence we come, where we are
and whither we go. We come from God and are in exile.
And because the force of our love seeks after God, we
are conscious of this exile.

JAN VAN RUYSBROECK

Ladders to Heaven and Stations on Earth

THE QUANDARY OF mystical language did not always issue in
silence. On the contrary, it often led to attempts to articulate the
journey toward mystical experience with as much accuracy and differentiation as possible, in terms of steps, degrees, and stations. Paths
and trails were laid out, and mountains and valleys named and
described. The biblical image for the soul's ascent to God is Jacob's
ladder extending into heaven; in a dream Jacob sees the angels
ascending and descending (Gen 28:12). The "ladder to paradise"
(Johannes Climacus), the "pilgrimage of the soul to God" (Bonaventure), and the "ladder to perfection" (Walter Hilton) all signal how
much an itinerary is needed. Often it is a meticulously ordered ascetic path of purification and graduated immersion that leads to ecstasy
as the realization of mystic union.

The Sufis distinguished between three forms of the journey. First,
there is the "journey to God," which begins when one awakens from
ordinary sleep with the awareness of exile. Second, there is the "journey in God," which can begin only after the human ego has been
extinguished in self-annihilation. Third, there is the "journey through
God," which is the journey or search that God has begun and caused
and without which the human search is unthinkable. All three journeys are interlinked within each other.

The ninth-century Sufi mystic Bayezid Bistami is said to have
declared, "For thirty years I went in search of God, and when at the
end of that time I opened my eyes, I discovered that it was he who
had been looking for me."[1] This is how the theme of the journey,
traveled in stages, is presented in mystical paradox. In the midst of an
onerous search, Symeon the New Theologian, also on the journey,
"suddenly" discovered "that he was in myself, and in the center of

77

my heart he appeared like the light of a sun, round as a circle."[2] The following words of Bayezid are related: "For twelve years at a stretch I was the smith of my own being. I laid it on the hearth of asceticism, heated it red-hot in the fire of ordeals, set it out on the anvil of fear, and pounded it with the hammer of admonition. Thus I made it into a mirror that served me to gaze at myself for five years, during which I never ceased to dissolve the rust from this mirror by acts of piety and devotion."[3]

The rust is made up of the forgetfulness of God in which humans live as if in exile. They are no longer able to mirror God the way Adam, whom Sufis call "the first Sufi," could still do before the fall. Those on the journey are en route toward their primordial Adamic condition. The way back into the oneness of paradise and the seven heavens is described in seven steps of an ascending line: the world of nature is Adam's heaven; the world of forms is Noah's heaven; the world of spiritual perception is the heaven of Abraham; the world of imagination is the heaven of Moses; the world beyond forms is David's heaven; the divine nature is the heaven of Jesus, or of the Jesus hidden in the human being; and the seventh heaven is Muhammad's, which is also seen to be the divine being or the hidden Muhammad-dimension of every human being.

One of the great Persian mystics, Ferid Ed-Din Attar (d. ca. 1220 C.E.), describes the seven valleys in his epic *The Conference of the Birds*. Many religions depict the soul as a bird. Turks today still use the expression "the soul-bird has flown away" when they want to express that someone has died.[4] Attar calls the first transition point the "valley of seeking" in which all obstacles are removed so that the light of heaven may enter. "Huddled like a child in the lap of its mother, gather yourself in yourself, immersed in blood. Do not leave your inwardness in order to get yourself to the outer world. If you need victual, nourish yourself on blood. Blood alone nourishes the child in its mother's womb; and it comes from the warmth of inwardness. . . ."[5] When one compares this postpartum image to the corresponding language of Christianity, and how it puts *purgatio*—often interpreted only ascetically as self-purification—at the beginning of the journey, one cannot help noticing the gentler, preconscious desire-embracing tone in the treatment of the ego.

Attar's second transition point is the "valley of love"; it has no boundaries and mystical life (called *illuminatio* in Neoplatonic Christianity) begins in this valley. "To love, one must have no mental reservations; one must be prepared to throw a hundred worlds into the fire; one must know neither belief nor unbelief, harbor neither doubt nor confidence. Upon this way there is no difference between good and evil; where there is love, good and evil have vanished. . . ."[6] In the next valley, the valley of knowledge, the mystic enters into true contemplation, the soul takes part in God and God is seen in all things. "The wanderer will see the almond within the shell."[7] Pantheistic knowledge does not come at the end of the way, which still presents difficulty and consternation, but it is an important element made apparent in this valley.

Then come the valleys of self-sufficiency, pure unity, and consternation; in these valleys the mystical wanderer becomes the "prey of gloom and groaning."[8] Bitter lament and cries of woe accompany the wanderer up to the seventh valley of "dissolution and annihilation, beyond which you cannot go. You will feel yourself drawn on, yet you will be unable to progress further; a single drop of water will be like a sea to you."[9] This final valley celebrates a mysticism of death similar to what we have already encountered in al-Hallaj (see chapter 2). "Throw everything you have into the fire, even your shoes. When you have nothing more, think not even of a shroud and throw yourself naked into the fire."[10] Thus the merciless coercion of death and its bitterness is transformed into mystical freedom.

What does the recital of the different transition points mean? Are they not one of the many attempts to incorporate mystical experience into the language of traditional religiosity? Does mystical experience allow itself to be subjected to a method? Is there a practicable path that can be identified and then be pointed out to others? Is the "inner light" something to be taught? The answers to such questions reveal the differences between mystagogues and mystics. Mystagogues know of a *methodus mystica*; in their view, mystical experience cannot be learned or taught, but preparing for it can. They mark the paths and list possible steps to be taken on the way that leads out of the exile mentioned by the great Flemish mystic Jan van Ruysbroeck (1293–1381) cited above. Many mystics, irrespective of whether they represent the immediacy of "mysticism of experience" or the philosophically reflected "mysticism of essence," are considerably more reticent in this respect. Neither the Beguines, who were marked by mystical sensibility, nor their great preacher, Meister Eckhart, relied on a precise method.

Johannes Tauler (1300–1361) speaks simply of two kinds of seeking. The first consists of "external practice of good works" like humility, gentleness, and quietness. The second goes "much beyond the former and consists in human beings entering into their own innermost place, their ground. Only that way do they seek God in the sense of the biblical word of the reign of God that is within you."[11]

One may also interpret the necessary distinctions between people in the different stages with the help of typologies that may even invite someone to enter upon a possible journey. In *The Sparkling Stone*, Jan van Ruysbroeck distinguishes between four types of human beings, in ascending order: the hirelings, the faithful servants, the secret friends, and the hidden sons of God. The *hirelings* are

> those who love themselves so inordinately that they will not serve God save for their own profit and because of their own reward. These dwell in bondage and in their own selfhood . . . .
>
> The *faithful servants* are those who serve God in the outward and active life. . . . They . . . have, in some degree, subdued the dictates of self, but they have not yet learned to turn wholly inward. Consequently they are divided in heart, unstable in mind, and easily swayed by joy and grief in temporal things. Though . . . the faithful servant . . . may live according to the commandments of God, inwardly he abides in darkness. He lives more in the world of senses than of the spirit.
>
> The *secret friends* are those who have conquered self and entered on the inward life, which is for them "an upward stirring exercise of love." They have not as yet, however, become fully inward men. They possess their inwardness . . . as an *attribute*. And though . . . they feel united with God, yet in their union, they always feel a difference and otherness between God and themselves. For the simple passing into the Bare and Wayless they do not know and love; and therefore their highest inward life ever remains in Reason and Ways.
>
> How great is the difference between the secret friend and the *hidden son*. For the friend makes only loving, living, and measured ascents towards God. But the son presses on to lose his own life upon the summits in that simplicity which knoweth not itself. [Only when] we and all our selfhood die in God do we become his hidden sons.[12]

The doctrine of stages or steps tries to order, name, and delimit what cannot be ordered, named, and delimited. This variance remains even because the destination of the journey is hailed in hymn and conjured and touched for a brief moment but never with finality. It is always greater than those who speak of it. The Irish itinerant monk Columba (ca. 543–615) once said, "If your soul thirsts for the divine spring of which I now want to tell you, do not suppress that thirst. Drink but do not be filled."

Purification, Illumination, Union:
The Three Ways of Classic Mysticism

In the West, mystical ascent has most often been presented in terms of the model of the three ways that Dionysius, in the tradition of Neoplatonism, called *purgatio, illuminatio,* and *unio* (see *De caelesti hierarchia,* chapter three and elsewhere). Purification, illumination, and union (or perfection) are basic experiences on the way of mysticism. The classic triad begins with the purification or purging of the ego. To halt and to turn back, to fast, to keep awake and be silent, and to discipline the self (that may go as far as self-castigation) are said to serve the knowledge of self. Those who have "fallen asleep" in the prison of the I (Rumi), and those who are no longer aware of the "exile" in which we live (Ruysbroeck) are in need of exercises in such purification that help the self to come to a stop. According to Bonaventura, exercises of that kind are, first, the meditations that give peace to the soul and, second, prayer that illumines the soul, letting her see the light of wisdom. But only inner reflection, contemplation, opens up access to God.[13]

The asceticism of *purgatio* calms the restlessness of many desires; in this sense, it may be understood also as a manner of becoming empty *(ledig)* or free. It is said of a Zen master that one day he received a visit from a professor who wanted to learn something about Zen. The master poured his guests a cup of tea and kept on pouring when the cup was already overflowing. The professor saw it and finally could no longer keep quiet. "The cup is overflowing; you can't pour anymore into it!" The master replied, "Like this cup, you are brimming over with your own ideas and speculations. How am I to teach you Zen when you don't even empty your cup?"

Perhaps this understanding of purification as being emptied of cares, ideas, and purposes is more comprehensible to us than the preparation for the beginning of the journey that in the West is more focused on asceticism. Both share the exercise of letting go or of coming to rest through becoming empty. Giving up one's own will and being in possession of oneself not only means material renunciation but also voluntary poverty that forgoes being possessed of understanding and knowledge. Medieval mystics thought of *purgatio* as the restoration of the soul's God-likeness: the mirror can reflect once again when it is being cleansed.

In his *Vernünftige Einführung des äusseren Menschen in die Innerlichkeit* (Sensible Induction of the Outward Being into

Inwardness), Heinrich Seuse (1293/1303–1366) speaks of the journey. He writes that "A human being of acquiescence needs to be un-formed *(entbildet)* from the image of the creature, con-formed *(bildet)* to Christ and re-formed *(überbildet)* in the deity."[14] The concept of "un-forming" is to be found already in Eckhart[15] and signifies to come free of the constraint to mirror nothing but created things, the "this and that." Every spiritual education *(Erziehung)* begins with drawing away from something *(Entziehung)*.

The second step on the road of mysticism, illumination, is oriented here toward the Christ who forms us. Illumination is also often depicted as transformation. Christ illumines and forms the human being who has been "un-formed" from the creaturely, who has become empty and independent from life's external exigencies. The individual steps overlap; the renunciation of the things of the senses carries on also in illumination, as does the death of egocentric living, inasmuch as the purification of perception continues. The windows of the soul must be kept open so that the light of the new reality may stream in and completely enlighten and change the soul.

It is essential to point out that the phases of mystical life are not the accomplishments of an ascetically schooled ego. They are gifts of grace and it is expected that people will make use of them. These gifts are connected with knowledge, but one that comes more from receiving than from determining. Knowing and being known are one in mysticism—the opposite of modern patriarchal traditions of thought where objects said to be passive are taken hold of. This other, non-dominating kind of thinking is manifest also in a seeking that is actually a being found or in the understanding that the soul's "ascent" is none other than God's "descent." Transcendence and descendence belong together.

The union of the soul with God, sometimes called *perfectio* or deification, or *theosis* in Greek, is a matter of utterly overwhelming blessing. Bernard of Clairvaux (1090–1153) notes soberly that the lower grades of mystical life occur perhaps more frequently but that fulfillment takes place at rare moments and for a brief time. Deification means the utter annihilation of the old and known self. "But at times the inner human steps beyond reason and is torn from the self: this is the soul's escape."[16]

A pupil of St. Francis, Aegidius of Assisi (d. 1262), put it in a highly paradoxical manner: "I know a man who saw God so clearly that he lost all faith."[17] Ruysbroeck calls this final step "image-less freedom." About the "oneness of being itself" he says "people must move back from this as well as from everything that lives in God, for here there is nothing but an eternal repose in a pleasurable embrace of lovingly sinking away. . . . This is sombre stillness in which all who love are lost."[18] One may argue as to whether this escape into "imageless freedom" happens in a gradual ascent or a sudden tearing away. All who try to speak about it are agreed that this loss of self is an inexpressible bliss.

One of the most beautiful texts of German mystagogy is an anonymous letter from the fifteenth century that contains the words that form the title of this book. The writer instructs a searching young person, addressed as child, in the mystical path of "letting go." This text does not speak to the individual stations of the journey but, in its basic assertion, contains the three classic elements of purification, illumination, and unification. "Learn to deny God for the sake of God—the hidden God for the sake of the unveiled God. Be willing to lose a copper coin so that you may find a golden one. Pour out water so that you may draw wine instead. Creation itself is not so great that it can rob you of God or even of the slightest grace unless you yourself will it." Letting go, being separated from things, and being acquiescent is much more than being above it all. What Eckhart means, as well as the text just cited, is a three-fold letting go that is related to the world, the ego, and God. To let the world go means to bid farewell to possessions, money, and goods, everything that serves to secure life but too easily turns itself into life's lord. To let go of the ego does not only mean to put behind career, success, and respect but also one's feelings and moods, especially the depressing ones.

These two forms of calm are presupposed in the letter: it begins with the third, the truly mystical form, the one that relates to the soul. "Learn to let go of God!" What this means is to let go of the known God who appears in a specific manner, the God with whom we are as acquainted with as with pennies and water at our disposal. The God of Scripture and tradition has been hidden from the beginning. Here, that God is let go in favor of the unveiled, naked, and nameless God. The way depicted here looks like this: "If to avoid is what you seek, learn to suffer; if you wish to enjoy honey, let not the bee's sting dismay you. If you want to catch fish, learn to wade in the water. If you want to see Jesus on the shore, learn beforehand to sink in the sea! And if you should see the heavens crash and the stars fall, you will not be amazed. Not even God can take Godself from you unless you will it; how much less the creation! Listen, behold, suffer and be silent! Deny yourself in broad daylight; behold with reason; learn with wisdom; suffer with joy; rejoice with longing; yearn with patience; complain to no one."[19] The central assertion here is that "not even God can take Godself from you unless you will it." The experience of being one with God is stronger than one's own fear or depression and stronger than all authority based on hierarchy or custom; it is lumped together and named "the creation" in this text. The unveiled God, who still lives behind the hidden and inexpressible God, becomes one with the humans who have denied themselves "in broad daylight." The letter does not speak out of the search for the way; rather it comes really from God's nearness in "the stillness in all things." God is named in a paradox that is without equal. "Thou silent cry, no one can find you who knows not how to let you go." In the call to being acquiescent *(Gelassenheit),* the final sentence of the letter's message reconnects with how it began. "Learn to deny God for the sake of God," it says, as if in an act of pastoral consolation. The consolation admonishes: "Let go of yourself, my child, and thank God who has given you such a dwelling place." And so, letting go of the self (or the *via purgativa*) is at one here with letting go of God (or the *via unitiva*).

This text goes beyond many attempts to name with the help of the traditional stages of mysticism what the real subject is. There is nothing here of the ascetic-dualistic aspect that puts purification at the beginning as a condition and reaches the freedom of letting go of God only after the soul has been purged. The fact that Meister Eckhart and many other friends of God did not involve themselves in that mode of mysticism raises questions that—in the interests of a mystic spirituality sought after in our days—touch upon the beginning and conclusion of the journey. Much may be learned about the beginning of the relation between God and humans and about the union with God to be lived without withdrawing from the world, from someone who, at the time of the Reformation, lived out a political mysticism and died from it.

Traces of a Different Journey: Thomas Müntzer

Known as the "theologian of the revolution"[20] and Luther's opponent in the Peasants' War, Thomas Müntzer is deeply rooted in mystic tradition. Those who see in him only the heretic, the incessantly hounded man, and the fanatical agitator know only part of his story, just as the side of Marxism that is blind to religion does in its own way. In order to understand Müntzer's resistance not only against the crumbling world of the old church but also against the Reformation's alliance with feudalism, one has to go back to his mysticism. Without it, he would have integrated himself nicely into the Wittenberg form of theology and piety. Against that form, he, as a mystic, developed an understanding of the "crucified truth." Without giving it systematic structure, he portrayed in it a doctrine of stations of sorts that Walter Nigg has analyzed.[21]

Müntzer calls the first step in preparing for God "wonderment": amazement and fright begin when the eternal Word comes into the human heart. "And this wonderment at whether it really is God's Word or not begins to happen when one is a child of six or seven years of age."[22] Such wonderment is "inescapable," and in its immediacy it is close to the amazement Plato characterizes as the beginning of philosophy.

Such amazement is a basic religious and, at the same time, aesthetic experience of creation as the original blessing that every creature participates in. At the origin of all religion there is amazement and wonderment, asking us to take time to halt and to contemplate. Müntzer's interest in Gregorian chant and his attempt, rejected by Luther, to integrate it into the German mass, may perhaps be understood as a manifestation of his mystical love for wonderment.

But the search for the good beginning that can be found or produced again also has a political dimension. The reality of the original blessing that rests upon creation was again and again invoked in the late Middle Ages against inequality and oppression. From the English Peasants' War and John Ball's speech at Blackheath to the men in Wat Tyler's Rebellion in 1381, the word of the original equality of all human beings came to Germany: "When Adam delved and Eve span who was then the gentleman?" Müntzer exposes the "broth of profiteering, the thievery and robbery" of the lords and rulers who "make all creatures their possession. The fish in the water, the birds in the air, plants on the earth—everything must be theirs."[23] What is creation, given as a gift to all human beings and put at their disposal, has become private property. In connection with "wonderment," Müntzer quotes from Deuteronomy: "But the word is very near you; it is in your mouth and in your heart" (30:14 RSV). He speaks of the word's progress that takes its rise from the "abyss of the soul": "Now you ask perhaps, how does it come into the heart? The answer is that it comes down from God above in utter wonderment."[24] This inward word, heard through God's revelation the abyss of the soul, speaks to human beings without mediation, even without the Bible. Thomas Müntzer initially admired Luther. It is said that Luther had recommended him to a parish in Zwickau, but then Müntzer opposed Luther in the understanding of Scripture. Müntzer's view of the living Word of God as being "so very close to you"—and which constitutes the first step of mystical cognition *(cognitio experimentalis)*—represents a break with Luther's appeal for *sola scriptura,* (the Scriptures alone) as the basic principle of the Reformation puts it. What in the controversy over indulgences had served well in fighting the financial manipulations of the Church of Rome's authorities, namely this basic principle and its critical force, soon came to serve the consolidation of a new clerical domination. What came into being was a hardening of those interests that prohibit an unmediated lay piety, especially when it comes from below. In mystical amazement, wherein the Spirit of God speaks to the untutored and illiterate, in wonderment, there is an element of critique that needs to be directed at the theologians trained in the Scriptures.

In the course of the short time that it took Müntzer to ally himself with the movement of rebellious peasants, his own anticlericalism developed. Is it not the clerics, he asks, who hold people back from experiencing God without mediation in "the abyss of the soul?" Is it not Luther, who calls wretched women and men *Schwarmgeister* (enthusiasts who got carried away) and who won't hear of it that "people speak or read the word 'Spirit?'"[25]

Müntzer holds that God's revelation is not completed. He mocks with a derisive phrase what he calls *Bibel, Babel, Bubel* (Babylonic Bible babble) and says of Luther's faith that it is *erdichtet* (fictitious and ideological). "In short, there is no alternative: People have to smash such stolen, fictitious faith in Christ into rubble but at the cost of very great suffering of heart and painful sadness but also through unspeakable wonderment."[26]

Wonderment is what people experience and suffer when God addresses them. Skillfully criticizing what Luther did not intend but what his teaching in fact turned into, Müntzer said that clerics "lock up the Bible, saying that God is not allowed to speak to human beings personally."[27] Mystical wonderment and radical amazement alone set mystical spirituality apart from orthodox Lutheran faith.

The second step is what Müntzer calls *Entgröbung* (a process that turns us back from the rough ways we have made our own). This is a radicalized form of the *via purgativa,* more a self-mortification in which we may come free from "being glued to the world." This process is that of mystic seclusion, wherein one "separates oneself from every diversion." Müntzer was a master in expressing himself in a sharp tongue, using wit and nastiness; in his radical terminology, *Entgröbung* includes eradicating also the weeds, thistles, and thorns that grow in the heart. We are "God's acre" that has to "suffer the sharp plowshare of God." "Who so has not borne the night knows not what God can do," or "first, hell has to be suffered."[28]

This stage is where the breakthrough happens from unbelief to belief or, as Müntzer puts it, from the "honey-sweet" Christ of the carnal world to the "bitter" Christ, that is, to discipleship in the ongoing suffering of Christ. At this point the separation from Luther is beyond mending. Müntzer interprets Luther's doctrine of justification as a faith void of suffering, a faith that does not want to walk with Christ on the road that leads into suffering. Müntzer claims that Christ, after all, has already done all that is necessary for us. This "sweet" Christ is a poison because in such a claim the human being wants to "be like God" without being "like Christ."[29] A Christianity that is free of suffering leaves suffering to others. In the era of the Nazis in Germany, Bonhoeffer made a comparable critique of the church when he charged it with peddling "cheap grace."[30]

The contrast between Müntzer and Luther is based in Müntzer's mystical piety of suffering. Purification includes for him that people become free from fear. For the sake of the fear of God, they are to let go of the fear of creatures that rules in all of us since the fall. The worst fear of creatures is the fear of the authorities wherein people are kept dependent. Imprisoned in it, people cannot fear God. They remain locked in worries for their naked existence and lose their relationship to God over their fear of humans. "But the fear of God must be pure of all fear of humans or creatures whatsoever."[31] At the end of April 1525, shortly before the battle of Frankenhausen, Müntzer wrote a manifesto addressed to the miners of Mansfeld. It concludes with these words, "As long as they are alive, it will not be possible that you will be rid of the fear of humans; you cannot be told anything of God as long as they rule over you."[32]

Müntzer calls the third step the "long while" *(lange Weile)*; he refers to a freedom from the constraints of time, from rushing after whatever diverts us at any moment. This freedom is one free of desires, a genuine acquiescence. The term "long while" becomes more comprehensible when one takes into consideration the social conditions of the peasants, artisans, and miners among whom

Müntzer was working. It was not the false renunciation forced upon these simple people who can be neither "un-formed" nor "conformed" *(entbildet, bildet)* in the everydayness of their virtual slavery and impoverishment that Müntzer envisaged in this praxis of mysticism. What he tried to do was precisely to get away from the "short while" of distracting diversion in order "to tell something of God." "For that is why so few people know of the Spirit's initiating movement. Indeed, they ridicule it for they have not tasted the long while." The "long while" is an expression of freedom for it is only in another time that people will be truly "Christlike," namely in the "while" in and "through which alone God's work is known."[33] It is the calm in the very midst of impetuous passion; it is the assurance in which Müntzer, at age thirty-five, went to his death.

That Müntzer's journey was different may also be seen from the symbols that were part of his life. There is the heart, shown in his coat of arms, signaling the "passionate *(hitzig)* heart" of the mystic who participates in the suffering of Christ. Then there is the sword of Gideon, on which Müntzer called and which caused a friend to speak of him as the "persecutor of injustice." Most importantly, there is the rainbow, which adorned the flag under which the rebellion of Muehlhausen was fought. Six thousand bewildered, fleeing peasants were butchered in 1525; their alleged might claimed only six victims in the ranks of the attacking army of the rulers.

Being Amazed, Letting Go, Resisting: Outline of a Mystical Journey for Today

In this concluding section of a general introduction to mystical thinking, I try to name stations of the way of mysticism for people on the journey today. In this attempt I have been stimulated by the works of Matthew Fox who, particularly in his new reading of Meister Eckhart, depicts quite early in human history the mystical way of creation spirituality.[34]

Fox's way and that of traditional mysticism differ in two aspects. The first is where the way of mysticism is said to begin. In the understanding of mysticism inherited from the Neoplatonists Proclus and Plotinus, purging or purification are always the first step. The beginning of mystical piety is not the beauty and goodness of creation but the fall of human beings from paradise. That this loaded word "fall" does not appear in the Hebraic narrative of the expulsion from paradise seems not to be known. Instead, in this context, marked strongly by Augustine, there is little talk of creation, of the cosmos, and its original goodness. But does this not place the mystical journey at far too late a point in the course of the Christian history of redemption? One of the basic questions Fox asks again and again is whether we ought not refer first of all to the blessing of the beginning, that is, not to original sin but to original blessing? And is it not exactly mystical experience that points us to creation and the good beginning?

The second difference in comparison to the Western tradition of mysticism has to do with the vision of union with God. I agree with Fox on the matter of the *via unitiva*. He defines the goal of the journey differently in this stage; it is more world-related. The goal is creativity and compassion. Creativity presupposes union with the Creator, whose power lives in the oneness with us. Today we understand creativity not only as the transformation of an individual soul but of the world as a whole, in which humans could live together. To speak of this *via transformativa* means to embed the mystical project in the context of our life, which is marked by the catastrophe of economic and ecological exploitation.

For me, mysticism and transformation are indissolubly interconnected. Without economic and ecological justice (known as ecojustice) and without God's preferential love for the poor and for this planet, the love for God and the longing for oneness seem to me to be an atomistic illusion. The spark of the soul acquired in private experience may, indeed, serve the search for *gnosis* (knowledge) in the widest sense of the word, but it can do no more. A genuine mystical journey has a much larger goal than to teach us positive thinking and to put to sleep our capacity to be critical and to suffer.

As in the journeys of former times, the stages of today's journey flow one into the other. The three stages are as follows: to be amazed, to let go, and to resist. The first step taken on the way of mysticism is amazement. I relate an experience by way of example: When my oldest son was learning to read numbers, he stood still one day in front of a house's number plate and did not move an inch. When I wanted to move him on with my "come on!" he said, "Look, Mummy, what a wonderful 537!" Naturally, I had never seen it. He spoke the number slowly, tasting it in a mood of discovery. He was submerged in happiness. I think that every discovery of the world plunges us into jubilation, a radical amazement that tears apart the veil of triviality. Nothing is to be taken for granted, least of all beauty!

The first step of this mystical way is a *via positiva,* and it occurs in the primordial image of the rose that blooms in God. The jubilation of my five-year-old responds to the experience of "radical amazement," as Abraham Heschel (1907–1972) calls this origin of our being-in-relation.[35] Without this overwhelming amazement in the face of what encounters us in nature and in history's experiences of liberation, without beauty experienced even on a busy street and made visible in a blue-and-white number plate on the wall of a house, there is no mystical way that can lead to union. To be amazed means to behold the world and, like God after the sixth day of creation, to be able to say again or for the first time, "Look! How very good it all is!"

But it is not enough to describe this amazement as an experience of bliss alone. Amazement also has its bleak side of terror and hopelessness that renders one mute. The ancient Greeks already defended themselves against this bleakness by an injunction against adoring things; Horace summed it up in his motto *nihil admirari* (admire nothing). But this prohibition, with the help of which scientific thinking once was supposed to banish the fear of fear, has succeeded in banishing the demons together with all the angels. Gone is the sensation of paralyzing fright together with the ability to be marvelously amazed. Those who seek to leave behind the terrifying, sinister side of wonderment, the side that renders us dumb, take on, through rational superiority, the role of those who own the world. In my view, to be able to own and to be amazed are mutually exclusive. "What would it help someone, if he gained the whole world but damaged his soul?" (Matt 16:26, in Luther's German translation).

The soul needs amazement, the repeated liberation from customs, viewpoints, and convictions, which, like layers of fat that make us untouchable and insensitive, accumulate around us. What appears obvious is that we need to be touched by the spirit of life and that without amazement and enthusiasm nothing new can begin. Goethe's friend Herder said that "without enthusiasm nothing great and good ever came to be in this world. Those who were said to be 'enthusiasts' have rendered humankind the most useful services." This is exactly the point where the Christian religion—in a world that makes it possible for us human beings, through science, to create cosmic consciousness while, at the same time, through technology, also to undo creation—must learn anew from its own origin in the tradition of Judaism.

What this means in relation to where the journey takes its beginning is that we do not set out as those who seek but as those who have been found. The goodness we experience is there already long before. In an ontological and not necessarily a chronological sense, before the prayers of those who feel abandoned and banished there is the praise without which they would not perceive themselves as banished ones. This ability for wonderment brings about consenting to one's being here, being today, being now. "Being here is magnificent" (Rainer Maria Rilke). Like every form of ecstasy, this ability implies a self-forgetfulness that, as if by magic, lifts us out of ordinary self-forgetfulness and its corresponding triviality.

Amazement or wonderment is a way of praising God, even if God's name is not mentioned. In amazement, whether we know it or not, we join ourselves to the heavens "who declare the glory of the Eternal One" (Ps 19:1). "The beginning of our happiness lies in the understanding that life without wonder is not worth living."[36] Such an understanding of the wonder of being is not dependent on whether the origin of creation is conceived of in personal terms, as in the Abrahamic religions, or in nonpersonal ones. Radical amazement does not have to atrophy as scientific knowledge increases and better explains what is; on the contrary, such amazement grows in the finest scientific minds who frequently feel attracted to mysticism.

Can amazement, the radical wonderment of the child, be learned again? Whatever the badly misused word "meditation" means, it embraces a form of stopping and tarrying wherein individuals or communities intentionally set aside for themselves times and places other than the ordinary ones. Listening, being still, at rest, contemplating, and praying are all there to make room for amazement. "Hear this, O Job, stop and consider the wondrous works of God" (Job 37:14). The unknown name of the mystical rose reminds us of our own amazed blissfulness.

The practice of amazement is also a beginning in leaving oneself; it is a different freedom from one's own fears. In amazement we detrivialize ourselves and enter the second stage of the mystical journey, that of letting go. If to praise God is the first prompting of the journey, then to miss God is another unavoidable dimension of it. The more profound the amazed blissfulness of the *sunder warumbe* (the utter absence of any why or wherefore), the darker the night of the soul *(via negativa)*. The tradition that most often places this way of purification at the beginning and points out ever new ways of asceticism, renunciation, and escape from desires also teaches to discern how far one is from the true life in God.

Letting go begins with simple questions: What do I perceive? What do I keep away from myself? What do I choose? We need a bit of "un-forming" or liberation before we, in the language of Seuse, can be "con-formed" to Christ or transformed. In the world ruled by the media, this "un-forming" has yet a wholly other status than it had in the rural and monastic world of the Middle Ages when life was so much less subject to diversions. For us who today know a hitherto-undreamed abundance of available consumer goods and artificially manufactured new needs, this stage of the journey plays a different role than it does in the cultures of want. We associate rituals of purification and fasting most frequently with such puritanical "giving-up" performances alleged to be necessary in the development of industrial labor morality. In postindustrial consumer society, this ethics works less and less. Our letting go is related above all to our growing dependency on consumerism. We need purification *(purgatio)*, both in the coercive mechanisms of consumption and in the addictions of the everyday working world.

The more we let go of our false desires and needs, the more we make room for amazement in day-to-day life. We also come closer to what ancient mysticism called "being apart," which is living out concretely one's farewell to the customs and norms of one's culture. Precisely the fact that our mysticism begins not with banishment but with amazement is what makes the horror about the destruction of wonder so radical. Our relation to the basic realities of ownership, violence, and the self is changing. In this turning away from our rough ways *(Entgröbung)*, the road becomes increasingly narrower. Companions and friends take their leave and the initial amazement clouds over. The symbol of the first stage of mysticism's path is the rose, that of the second stage is the dark night.

To miss God is a form of tradition called "suffering from God." To become more and more empty means not only to jettison unnecessary ballast but also to become more lonely. Given the destruction of nature that marks our context, it becomes more and more difficult to turn back to certain forms of our relationship to and with nature and to the original amazement. Mystical spirituality of creation will very likely move deeper and deeper into the dark night of being delivered into the hands of the principalities and powers that dominate us. For it is not only the poor man from Nazareth who is tortured together with his brothers and sisters on the cross, it is also our mother earth herself.

The horizon of ecological catastrophe is the backdrop before which today's road of the mystical journey has to be considered. To praise God *and* to miss nothing so much as God leads to a "life in God" that the tradition called the *via unitiva*. To become one with what was intended in creation has the shape of *cocreation;* to live in God means to take an active part in the ongoing creation.

The third stage leads into a healing that is at the same time resistance. The two belong together in our situation. Salvation means that humans live in compassion and justice cocreatively; in being healed (saved) they experience also that they can heal (save). In a manner comparable to how Jesus' disciples understood themselves to be "healed healers," so every way of union is one that continues onward and radiates outward. Being-at-one is not individualistic self-realization but moves beyond that to change death-oriented reality. Being-at-one shares itself and realizes itself in the ways of resistance. Perhaps the most powerful symbol of this mystical oneness is the rainbow, which is the sign of the creation that does not perish but continues to live in sowing and harvesting, day and night, summer and winter, birth and death.

BEING AMAZED	LETTING GO	HEALING / RESISTING
via positiva	*via negativa*	*via transformativa*
radical amazement	being apart	changing the world
bliss	letting go of possession, violence and ego	compassion and justice
praising God	missing God	living in God
the rose	the "dark night"	the rainbow

II. PLACES OF MYSTICAL EXPERIENCE

6. NATURE

To see a world in a grain of sand
And a heaven in a wild flower,
Hold infinity in the palm of your hand
And eternity in an hour.

WILLIAM BLAKE

Places and Placelessness

WHERE DO PEOPLE experience mystical oneness, breakthrough, or wholeness? Where and when and under what circumstances does it happen that they move from feeling banished into a different state of consciousness—and in that different oneness they can let go of their atomistic separateness? Are there particular situations or events that bring about the experience of ecstasy and oneness? Is the desert such a place? Is the premonition of one's death such an event? Or is it the gathering of people who in silence do no more than wait upon the Lord? Is there really something called a place of mystical experience? Where are we to look for it? Or is this a false question?

God can "close in on me," as C. S. Lewis puts it, on a summer day beside a flowering current bush, but just as well in a prison cell, or even in a lecture hall. We have neither the right nor even the possibility to limit the number of places of mystical experience. To remain faithful to the road without roads means to consider every place, even churches, suitable for God and, with Rumi, to know that "placelessness" is the mystical "place" (see also chapter 4 above).

And yet, we are surrounded by a cloud of witnesses. There is a mystical tradition, teaching and communicating itself, that excludes nothing and no one. We need not begin at point zero. In the second part of this book, seeking to name a variety of places for mystical experiences, I pursue my aim of democratizing mysticism without trivializing it. Those places are to be as accessible as possible. If God is "what is of all the most communicable," as Meister Eckhart mentions,[1] then the domain of God's self-communication is not in extreme behavior, such as self-flagellation, esoteric rituals, or drug scenes. In the interest of democratization, I have decided to work with the places that are given naturally rather than created artificially. Such accessible places are nature, eroticism, suffering, communion, and joy. I recognize the arbitrariness that belongs to every selection; it is not my intent to exclude other places such as work, sports, or, of all things, music.

It is in nature, the place without which we would not be at all, that the experience of becoming one is documented perhaps most often and most diversely. I begin with an experience that the Swiss writer Otto F. Walter (1928–1994) recounted in an interview. When asked by his interviewer, Karl-Josef Kuschel, whether he went through a phase of atheistic critique of religion, he replied:

> I do not believe that I am an atheist. Let me tell you of an experience I had. I was nineteen years old at the time, I guess. I was travelling by train to Lucerne; it was afternoon, the light and moving shadows were signaling a thunderstorm, sun and shadow played on the fields. I was alone in the car, I opened the window and just stared in amazement at this landscape. I was completely overcome and could have shouted for joy. I wept and had the feeling: This is God. That is what lives and what ought to be. It was an image of peace and of harmony of everything with everything. I had the feeling that I was part of it; I felt the rhythmic movements of recurrence in their infinite multiformity within me. It was a mystical, a kind of pantheistic experience, that is, the experience of God in nature. When I am asked to speak on the level of theory about religion and God, it is that experience that rises up unforgettably before my eyes. It has prevented me from intellectually coming to the point where nothing is left of God. Mystics have called such an experience of the divine "the little spark."[2]

There are innumerable testimonies of nature mysticism of this kind. I shall try once again to interpret them in terms of a "mystical journey for today" (see chapter 5). Here, to be amazed means to be overcome, to break forth in shouts of joy, or to weep. The experience of the other of nature is unforeseeable; it can be neither arranged nor chosen. Only in retrospect can it be denied or pushed aside. Eugène Ionesco provides an interesting example of this. Looking back on a mystical experience in his youth, he acknowledges experiencing "intensity, presence, light" wherein heaven seemed "to be much closer to me, almost within reach of my hand." What he denies is that all this had any relevance for his subsequent life. He knowingly dismissed the experience. "I can say that since then I have done without heaven and have the impression that heaven has let me drop out. Deeper and deeper I threw myself into life, lecherously, gluttonously.

. . . All these desires that seek to be met are things that are supposed to make up for what I lost one day, even though I know well enough that they cannot make up for it."[3]

The original experience, transcending the domain of the individual's self that is seen to be autonomous, participates in the letting go of what is known and, hence, already named. The ego lets go of itself and submerges itself into a *cognitio experimentalis* (an experiential cognition). As Otto Walter said, "I had the feeling: This is God." It is no accident that, in naming the other, whatever is taken for granted politically, socially, and culturally disappears and the "image of peace and of harmony of everything with everything" suddenly arises. And here is the critical distance to given reality that Walter makes a central theme in his later book. Somewhat helplessly the author speaks of God with a new name: "what ought to be." It was something that he discovered from the play of light and shadow on the fields.

In premystical terminology, we are all part of nature, at once dependent on and opposed to it. Even today, on occasion we feel threatened by it, and we use it as a means for survival. Yet, in every culture there are experiences of nature that leave behind this realm of fear, purpose, and use and turn the calculating observer into someone overwhelmed in amazement: "Pigs eat acorns, but neither consider the sun that gave them life, nor the influence of the heavens by which they were nourished, nor the very root of the tree from whence they came."[4] One may well criticize this sentence of priest, poet, and mystic Thomas Traherne (1634–1673) as all too anthropocentric. I would rather direct that criticism, however, at the world of consumerism, a world that is incapable of pausing and pondering what it uses, a world that is regarded as normative. Instead of making use of the world and all that is in it, ordinary, normal mystics begin with halting praise of it. Again and again, the observer turns into lover, flowing together with the beloved. In the solitude of the Trappist monastery, Thomas Merton listens to the rain and meditates. "The night became very dark. The rain surrounded the whole cabin with its virginal myth, a whole world of meaning, of secrecy, of silence, of rumor. Think of it: all that speech pouring down, selling nothing, judging nobody, drenching the thick mulch of dead leaves, soaking the trees, filling the gullies and crannies of the wood with water, washing out to places where men have stripped the hillside! What a thing it is to sit absolutely alone, in the forest, at night, cherished by this wonderful, unintelligible, perfectly innocent speech, the most comforting speech in the world, the talk that rain makes by itself. . . ."[5] At the beginning of the mystical journey, amazement happens in the rain, or next to an almond branch in bloom, or in view of "starry heaven above me." In whatever situation, it happens in and with the other of nature.

Particularly in classical Christian mysticism, this "in" and "with" is brought together with the metaphors of teaching and reading, book and school, master and teachers. Here, creation is not regarded as material and is not subjected to human domination. Creation is the book that God wrote. To read in it means to put amazement and cognition together. Bernard of Clairvaux testifies that whatever he knows of divine things and Holy Scriptures he learned in woods and fields. "I have had no other masters than the beeches and the oaks."[6]

Julian of Norwich (ca. 1343–1416) writes, "Also in this he showed me a little thing, the quality of an hazel-nut in the palm of my hand" so that she might recognize "the Maker, the Keeper, the Lover."[7] As a teacher, nature does not explain in words but in pointing out makes for visibility. "George Fox said, 'I was come up to the state of Adam in which he was before he fell. The creation was opened to me; and it was showed me, how all things had their names given to them, according to their nature and virtue.' "[8] Nature herself "speaks" and people read the praise of God on her lips. In an artful catachresis, Handel, bringing together a number of incompatible images, puts "hearing" God's Word and "seeing" springtime into this aria.

Meine Seele hört im Sehen	(My soul hears in seeing
wie den Schöpfer zu erhöhen	how to exalt the Creator,
alles jauchzet, alles lacht.	everything rejoices, everything laughs.
Höret nur,	Yet listen,
des erblühnden Frühlings Pracht	the glory of spring's blossoming
ist die Sprache der Natur,	is nature's very language
die sie deutlich durchs Gesicht	that in visions plainly
allenthalben zu uns spricht.	it speaks to us everywhere.)

Hearing in seeing creates a knowledge that is first shown rather than searched out; then, through many experiences, it expands itself more and more into a cosmic consciousness of oneness. Jacob Böhme (1575–1624) tells of an experience he had when he was twenty-five years old. "Surrounded by the divine light, and replenished with the heavenly knowledge; insomuch as going abroad into the fields to a green, at Görlitz, he there sat down, and viewing the herbs and grass of the field, in his inward light he saw into their essences, use, and properties, which was discovered to him by their lineaments, figures, and signatures."[9] Knowledge and overwhelming joy are one! It is a joy ignited ever anew by the beauty of creation. Anglican Thomas Traherne heralded it as an experience of oneness in which the subject feels fused with the whole cosmos. Being freed from restriction *(Entgrenzung)* and finding home *(Beheimatung)* go together as basic aspects of nature mysticism. "Your enjoyment of the world is never right till every morning you awake in Heaven; see yourself in your Father's palace; and look upon the skies, the earth and the air as celestial joys. . . . You never enjoy the world aright till the sea itself floweth in your veins, till you are clothed with the heavens and crowned with the stars; and perceive yourself to be the sole heir of the whole world, and more than so, because men are in it who are every one sole heirs as well as you."[10] Enthusiasm does not brook esoterics. Liberation from restriction in which "the stars crown you" goes together with a kind of return home that distances one from the world of affairs and violence; in that way it prepares for resistance.

A Morning Hymn: Harriet Beecher Stowe

> Still, still with Thee, when purple morning breaketh,
> when the bird waketh, and the shadows flee;
> Fairer than morning, lovelier than daylight
> dawns the sweet consciousness, I am with Thee.
>
> HARRIET BEECHER STOWE

This morning hymn from the Presbyterian hymnal is a simple expression of nature mysticism. Its author, Harriet Beecher Stowe (1811–1896), was a teacher in New England. She married a theology professor and the stories she wrote for newspapers and journals were regarded by many as sentimental. Finally, in 1851, she wrote the world-famous *Uncle Tom's Cabin, or Life Among the Lowly.* She wrote it initially in installments for the widely read *National Era,* the mouthpiece of the opponents of slavery. At first, the reviews were devastating; she was accused of ignorance of the true conditions and that, as a woman, she held sacred conventions in disregard "with an unbridled lasciviousness!" There were rebuttals, counterportrayals, even mocking epics. She protested that God had guided her hand. Soon the book was received with enthusiasm far beyond the circle of abolitionists. It became the cult book of resistance, echoed in the comment alleged to have been made by Abraham Lincoln: "So, this is the little woman that started this big war!" It is astounding how highly her European contemporaries valued the literary and moral qualities of the book that today is most often regarded as much too shrill and much too sentimental. In the nineteenth century it was called "the most valuable contribution of America to literature." Tolstoy put it on the same level as Dickens's *A Tale of Two Cities,* and Heinrich Heine even compared it to the Bible.

The mystical morning hymn does not speak of the realities of trafficking in human beings or of their humiliation and torture. It lives wholly from a piety that is of white women who sing the praise of the "Thee" of God found in nature. God and the soul, that is the theme, and the soul is "alone" with God. Dawn mirrors their union, which nevertheless—ever so traditionally—is more beautiful and lovely than nature's manifestations.

> Alone with Thee, amidst the mystic shadows,
> The solemn hush of nature newly born,
> Alone with Thee, in breathless adoration,
> In the calm dew and freshness of the morn.
>
> Still, still with Thee! As to each newborn morning
> A fresh and solemn splendour still is given
> So does the blessed consciousness awaking
> Breathe each day nearness unto Thee and heaven.[11]

This hymn is really understood only when one hears it in the musical setting of Felix Mendelssohn (1809–1847). Shadows are called "mystic," adoration is "breathless," and the consciousness of being with God "sweet"—one of the favorite words of women's mysticism in the Middle Ages. The word "still" has a crucial place; it has to do with the ability of letting go on the mystical road. To be still means to be free of worries and desires. Still is much more than simple absence of noise. The New Testament tells of Jesus rising up during a storm and commanding the wind to be still; a great *galene* (the Greek word for the stillness of the sea) set in (Mark 8:26). In a verse by Friedrich Rückert, set to music by Franz Schubert, we read: *Du bist die Ruh, der Friede mild, die Sehnsucht Du und was sie stillt* (You are the calm, the gentle peace, you the yearning and what stills it). In mystical tradition this stillness can be experienced and it means both God's invitation to enter into it and to hand life over, to give oneself to God.

So shall it be at last in that bright morning
when the soul waketh and life's shadows flee.
O, in that hour fairer than daylight dawning
Shall rise the glorious thought I am with Thee.[12]

Early morning was traditionally the time for contemplating one's death and in so doing understanding it as an awakening to true life. Life on earth was seen to be night and shadow (life's shadows) that fade away before the eternal dawn *(Eichendorff)*. The mysticism of nature and its stillness converge with the mysticism of the hour of death.

Harriet Beecher Stowe is a woman who embodies the unity of what mysticism and resistance can mean. Upheld by the civil rights movement of the abolitionists of her day, she let herself be upheld also by the inner stillness that filled her pious hero Uncle Tom (severely critiqued today for sound political reasons) with a humility that was hard to endure. He was beaten to death because he refused to administer beatings. That critique does not diminish the historical achievement of Stowe's having participated in the resistance against the criminal system of slavery, particularly since in the novel she depicts an alternate option for blacks: before being sold into the South, Eliza, a domestic slave, and her son flee to freedom.

Within the context of the unforgettable debate of James Baldwin about black identity, the word "sentimental" has become more and more problematic for me. Sentimental may mean being incapable of feeling anything and, to make up for it, luxuriating in overblown, petty sentiment. If so, it can be well documented in the SS bosses who loved their Beethoven, but not in the white New England woman who, precisely because she was "with Thee," lived in indignation about the slave-holder state. Often seen traditionally to be a women's role, belonging to the inner world of religion, becoming "still" on the road of mysticism is the "ground"—not in the sense of causality—for the clear and even clamorous language of the No! uttered in resisting.

Monotheism, Pantheism, Panentheism

Within Jewish and Christian tradition, all mystic experience repeatedly came under suspicion of having eradicated the clear separation of creator and creature. Instead of orienting themselves by doctrine, book, and hierarchy, people, overcome precisely by experiences of nature mysticism, felt the ocean pulsate in their veins and felt the nearness of God in the morning light. It is in ecstasy, coming from creation experienced directly and as if for the first time, that an amazed oneness arises, a oneness in which reverence, sense of beauty, liberation from restriction *(Entgrenzung)*, nature piety, mystical fusion, and pantheism flow together and become hard to distinguish. According to an apocryphal saying, Jesus told his followers: "Lift up the stone and there you shall find me; split wood and I am there"— highly pantheistic words.[13]

This pantheism and its identification of the whole universe with God is in contrast to biblical monotheism and its affirmation of the superiority over the world of the God beside whom humans "are to have no other gods." According to Augustine, God is the creator of the world and we are to enjoy God; creatures are meant for our use rather than our joy. *Uti* (to use) and *frui* (to enjoy) must be rigorously distinguished and the perfection of humans is to enjoy God. Joy and delight are to be found in God alone and not in the created; this is the understanding shared by the mainstream of Christian tradition. Nature is to be met with love and sympathy, esteemed in amazement that keeps distance nonetheless, for nature is the means that can lead us to knowledge of "the source of all goods." Nature is no substitute for God: it reflects God but is not divine itself. For Bernard of Clairvaux, nature—loved and used as a teacher—is the book written by God, but certainly not something to be confused with God. The delimiting line between creator and creature is left untouched; pantheism is to be rejected as a heresy inasmuch as in its ecstasies it renders that line quite fuzzy.

Such rigid juxtaposition of monotheism and pantheism, intensified in modern times, has repeatedly been the cause of tension and repudiation. If infinite substance is one, possessing unnumbered attributes, if in other words, nature and God are merely two names for one and the same reality, as maintained by Baruch Spinoza (1632–1677), the most significant philosopher of pantheism, then orthodox theologians had to look upon this pantheistic nature mysticism as something heathen. According to Schopenhauer, pantheism is "polite atheism" because it necessarily thinks of the divine in impersonal terms.

In contrast, a rigid monotheism places God, the "wholly other," at the tip of a hierarchically conceived universe. It is the opposite of a pantheism in which God is the reality of the whole and a divine substance is said to be the ground of all there is. Under the influence of dialectical theology, many Protestant theologians of the twentieth century rejected *unio mystica* as a human work. Even a modern cosmological proposal like that of Jesuit Pierre Teilhard de Chardin (1881–1955) had to face suspicion of heresy and attempt to reconcile pantheism with Christian faith. But is that possible at all?

Several criticisms have been leveled against mystical crossings of the delimiting line and, in particular, against the experiences in nature mysticism of reality's one divine substance. One is that in pantheism the radical separation from God, namely sin, is not taken seriously. For example, Karl Barth criticizes Rudolf Otto's book *The Idea of the Holy* (1917, English translation 1926) for the "remarkable absence of any horrors at ourselves."[14] For his part, Otto seeks to distinguish rigorously between the lofty "spirit-mysticism" of Meister Eckhart and romantic nature mysticism, which he associates with William James's expansionist feelings.[15] Another criticism is that pantheism allows for no transcendence in the traditional, supernatural sense and that, at best, it concedes the experience of an immanent transcendence. Finally, pantheism dissolves God's personhood in favor of life-power, energy, oscillation, and radiation.

As I see it, the conflict between monotheism and pantheism is waged today on two distinct fields. The one consists in the difficulties that every Abrahamic religion has with mystical pantheism because it contains an element of anarchism, one that undoes domination. The distinction between creator and creature is, after all, not a purely religious matter. Various dualisms derive themselves from it, in particular those that like to think of themselves as in accordance with creation: man and woman, soul and body, human and nonhuman, spirit and matter, as well as such unbridgeable social dichotomies as parents and children, masters and slaves, and whites and people of color. Sexism, feudalism, racism, class-domination, and the desacralization of nature have again and again at least used this dualistic either/or in the dominant understanding of God for their purposes. The mystical counterexperience not of dominance but of oneness, those of a different piety that is centered in women, and the cosmos and nature mysticism were attacked as upsetting the powers and orders that be.

One of the most important contemporary critiques of religion is directed against the "merciless consequences of Christianity" (Carl Amery), Western culture heard the command "to subdue the earth" (Gen 1:28) only too well. It did not listen to the Bible's true creation piety, which in many places of the Wisdom literature and Psalms in the Bible bears definite features of pantheism (for example, Pss 104 and 46), nor the "groaning of creation" that Paul still heard (Rom 8:22).

The second field of the conflict appears to me to be the issue of God's otherness. Can it be thought of without getting caught in the patriarchal trap of power and imperial domination? There are, indeed, forms of mysticism that dissolve this otherness and that wind up in an egomania that blots out every dimension of strangeness. But most mystics experience the incomprehensibility of God precisely in the mystical experience of union as something growing larger rather than smaller. In biblical terminology, "otherness" is of the God who is not visible and tangible, who cannot be imaged or be put at one's disposition, but who has a voice and desires to be heard, even if only as a "silent cry." Otherness means permanent mystery, darkness and light in one, the mystery of the *loin près* (the far-near one), as Marguerite Porète calls God (see chapter 7).

Karl Rahner (1904–1984) wrestled with the problem of mysticism because he wondered whether the "natural phenomena" of mystical experience and immersion really were only natural or whether they were determined by supernatural grace, even when they were not named as such.[16] Rahner's interest is the grace of God that is at no one's disposal, but this passion is confirmed exactly by the mystical experience that "the basis of man's existence is the abyss: that God is essentially the inconceivable; . . . that he only becomes our 'happiness' when we pray to him and love him unconditionally."[17]

The concept of panentheism, representing a marriage of the two elements, offers a possibility of relating the mystical and orthodox positions more closely. Even though seen to be present (pantheistically) in everything, God is not diffused in the cosmos; the divine is (monotheistically) more than the world. The world is *in* God; this allows for a theology of "being in." Panentheism avoids the dangers of heterodox pantheism because its understanding of God transcends both the world and the soul.

Thus, God's otherness is maintained while the relationship of God and soul is sought to be depicted in a model other than the patriarchal one of domination and dependency. Pantheism, as it is presented particularly by the philosopher Alfred North Whitehead (1861–1947), modifies some of the classic male attributes of God, such as impassibility and omniscience, that rule out human spontaneity. When thought of mystically, God's being is not the kind of intangible, omnipotent, impassible, and independent power that sovereignly rules as it wills.

Panentheistic thinking posits the interdependence of God and humans between the sheer dependency of the clay pot on its "maker," on the one hand, and the independence of a tearless ruler called God that is equally void of relationality. Love cannot be thought of without dependency of one on the other. The lack of mysticism in the Protestant churches is perhaps above all a lack of lived mutuality in which—according to Teresa of Avila—fear *of* God is transformed into fear *for* God, the latter being without doubt a theme of twentieth-century spirituality. In place of an orthodox spirituality of creaturely obedience, Meister Eckhart, perhaps best known as a precursor of panentheism, insists on a different one: the mystical spirituality of creation. Angelus Silesius remarked in his *Cherubinischer Wandersmann* that without us God cannot be for one moment; if we cease to be, God must by necessity give up the spirit (see chapter 8). The difference may be clearly seen when we reflect once again on what "miracle" is on the basis of the first step: amazement. In monotheistic patriarchal perception, a miracle is an external intervention that suspends the laws of nature. God's rule over nature, the body, time, and earthly reality is made visible through the supernatural event. Mystical amazement, on the other hand, sees the original miracle in being itself, in creation, in a rose blooming. Of course, the mystic also sees when the lame walk, the deaf hear, and the hungry are fed. But the decisive aspect is not the sovereign intervention. It is in the interaction between "nature" yearning for healing, for a reversal of direction, and the inbreaking of "grace." I cite as an example the peace movement of the eighties when I experienced as a miracle the healing of the blindness of a people handicapped by militarism.

The natural sciences are not irrelevant for this kind of different religion. Rightly understood, they teach us instead a cosmic amazement. There is a kind of "panentheistic plunge"[18] into the source of all being that by necessity leads into critique of our social norms and values and to their transformation. Henry David Thoreau (1817–1862), sometimes called a father of today's deep ecology, says of himself, "The fact is, I am a mystic, a transcendentalist and a natural philosopher to boot."[19] Withdrawing from the world of professional work and false needs, he found a nondominating, mystical relation to the woods and animals, to light and water. In the face of a lake's calm, he speaks of the transforming power that comes from living in nature and from leaving an existence that is purpose-ridden and machine-like. He speaks of an unconscious obedience to the supremely just laws wherein we human beings become like a calm lake of pure crystal and what is deeply within us reveals itself readily. The whole world seems to pass before us and is reflected in our own depth. Marvelous clarity results from experience through pure media such as the simple life and an honest intent. And here we truly live and break forth with joy. But Thoreau's pantheistic romanticism is no mere flight from making a living, from the world of greed and self-destruction (the antecedent to the destruction of nature); it is the finding of self. In coming to know the woods, Thoreau comes to know that

> It is no dream of mine,
> To ornament a line;
> I cannot come nearer to god and Heaven
> Than I live to Walden even.
> I am its stony shore,
> And the breeze that passes o'er;
> In the hollow of my hand
> Are its water and its sand,
> And its deepest resort
> Lies high in my thought.[20]

Sharing and Healing: A Different Relation to the Earth

Karl Rahner's belief that the Christianity of the third millennium will be mystical or not at all has, in the meantime, become an insight of ecotheology as well. In our world, the two great theological themes of creation and redemption can no longer be treated as separable and independent. An individualistically understood "salvation of the soul" that does not liberate creation can no longer be taken seriously; the decline of such remnants of religious culture is only perfectly consistent.

For reasons that have to do with mysticism's approach, I have not set the concepts of "nature" and "creation" apart. To make amazement, wonderment, and reverence the point of departure is, initially, an aesthetic endeavor that is contingent on our ability to behold the other unconcerned with its utility, our ability not to be about things like the pigs Traherne speaks of (see also above, p. 99). That the other is not of our making, not our product and that we, rather, are a dependent part of the whole, renders the difference between an areligious and a religious perspective relatively unimportant. In the bliss of mystical experience, that difference melts away. However, I happen to think that the language of religion speaks more clearly because, even though it does not define what is not of our making, it at least names it tentatively through the reference to the origin. Attending to the language of my fellow human beings, I believe that many of them would never use the word "creator" but feel themselves very much included in the word "creation." That something lies before us, a cosmos outside ourselves, makes us strangers to the world that is produced and administered and at home in the other, the created world. The more we destroy nature, the more we long for it.

This mystical experience of nature points to the dependency of human beings. Into the place of an allegedly total autonomy there enters a knowledge that we human beings, latecomers to the planet, are dependent on plants and animals. What make life on earth possible in the first place are the sun, the photosynthetic power of green plants, and the existence of the primordial sea's simple bacteria, all of which are not only the source and power of life but also have created the ozone layer and the oxygen-filled atmosphere. To embrace this dependency, not only as a scientific insight, but existentially, is the first step into a different spirituality without which the preservation of creation will be impossible. The sciences can establish this knowledge of dependency but the transformation of our basic attitude, our liberation from the shopping mall, needs today a kind of mystagogical instruction. For we, caught in the web of the Cartesian era, need help in learning again that two-legged, four-legged, and winged creatures have much more in common than we have believed.

Water, air, and earth are common to all living earthdwellers. Experiencing relationship with all living things is a dimension of that relationship to nature found in the mysticism of a *tat tvam asi* (the other is like you). Simply stated, nature is no "it," no material to be utilized and slotted to be at the very bottom of a patriarchically conceived hierarchy. Nature is a living "thou."

In singing, "Every part of this earth is sacred to my people," the ecological movement borrows words from North America's First Nations and a nature religion that has become the model for many people. Cartesian philosophy and Newtonian physics have deprived nature of its sacredness, that is to say, its soul, by replacing the organic image of the creation as one great living whole with a mechanistic concept of nature. It is like a machine powered by mechanical forces. Within the contours of such thinking, creation is at best a big clock, initially wound up by God. In this system, the role of human beings or, to be more precise, of the white male human being, is to use and exploit the objects that were perceived as having no relation to him whatever. This male human being identified himself with the patriarchal God, situated outside the world and ordained to leadership.

At the final phase of this development, which is where we are now, two paradigms compete one against the other. First there is the Cartesian paradigm, which some ecologists simply identify with Christianity. The other paradigm, occasionally called "New Age," borrows from nature religions and often approximates Buddhist spirituality. I believe that mystical piety, taught, lived out, and experienced, will become a foundation for a changed time.

But the model of exploitation and its course toward catastrophe go on in their unbroken rule. Their hostility to creation becomes most apparent in our totally changed relation to time. In the Nations' creation myths, boundaries are depicted between day and night, summer and winter, seedtime and harvest, desert and fertile regions, youth and old age, living and dying: the patriarchy of industry has rendered all of them unimportant and has obscured or abolished them. What those myths dramatized as times of labor and of rest, seasons of fasting and of feasting, in sabbath days and years, is being systematically demolished. Space and time are seen to be the last fetters that the autonomous individual is now finally breaking in order to find domicile on the other side of creation, in the shopping mall of the global market's total disposability. This globalization includes human organs, sex objects, and experimental research animals. It does even more than that. It redefines the relation between nature and humankind: from dependency to disposition, from attachment to the rhythms of life to springtime forever available for sale, from relationship with every creature to absolute rule over them, from the very ability itself to enter into relation to having virtual reality making that ability superfluous.

Dependency is not seen as a mutuality of nature and humankind; it is overcome. The mania for omnipotence, once projected onto God, has in technopatriarchy attained most efficiently to world dominance. But omnipotence and mysticism are mutually exclusive. This applies not only in history of religion terms to the god who was called king, god of hosts, and ruler of the world, but very much also to the idols of today's world that listen to names like progress, growth, and abolition of space and time.

The experience of being one with nature, the mysticism of everyday life, is the foundation for many resistance groups that work against the destruction of nature or even its substitution by sham tourist paradises. Often without knowing it, such groups live out what bears them up: an attentiveness to God's presence in their experience of nature. Attentiveness is one of the most important virtues of mysticism (see chapter 10): it is about hearing, seeing, smelling, feeling, and knowing that we are not alone but that we may live in the midst of other life. According to Goethe, love always contains an element of voluntary dependency. Many places in the poetry of nature mysticism express this insight. Robert Frost wrote, "Our very life depends on everything's / Recurring till we answer from within."[21] Such mutual life-dependency respects creation, but not in a narrowly monotheistic sense in which only the Creator, Maker, and Father acts unilaterally, exercising power. A living energy that permeates all creation and in which we take part presupposes a different kind of thinking, one holding a good power that fills others with power. *Empowerment* is the new, feminist horizon wherein creation is seen as power that shares itself. We shall understand the divine power of creation correctly when we detach it from the images of patriarchal power to command and experience it—in the image of Hildegard von Bingen—as *viriditas* (green power), the life-energy that shares itself. This energy causes all creatures to shine in the beauty of their perfection. "The way we are, we are members of each other. All of us. Everything. The difference ain't in who is a member and who is not, but in who knows it and who don't."[22] These words tell of the mystical, nonhierarchical relationship of all living things, which is a cosmic bond that must lead onward to ecojustice.

Ecojustice is a new word that is used by certain political groups. It bespeaks an attentiveness to the presence of the other (and why not say the divine?) through the interdependence shown to us in nature's recycling system that we are now learning to imitate. Two elements of the biblical tradition are to be found in ecojustice. The first is the amazement in the face of God's presence in nature. This is a primary experience of the holy that is not ours but on loan or entrusted to us. We do not communicate with God by distancing ourselves from the body, by denigrating the body, or, denying it altogether. Rather, we communicate by celebrating creation as sacrament, as the presence of God experienced here and now. The liturgical tradition of Christianity, other than its dogmatic one, has not denied nature but hallowed it. Christ is present in bread and wine, in body and blood; many liturgies today, arising from a fear for God, understand creation as the cosmic body of God. A new, sacramentally shaped piety is in the making.

The other element is the prophetic call for the justice that grants all living beings their share of life. The biosphere is a community of living beings bound one to the other, and any damage done to one being necessarily avenges itself. Both nature and economic order strike back and hit the *maîtres et possesseurs de la nature* (the masters and owners of nature) that Descartes talked about. How do we wean ourselves from being masters and owners? I think that mystical spirituality of oneness with nature is the best preparation for the other life we are looking for. Dealing sacramentally with bread and water, one's own body and our nonhuman sisters and brothers, and with energy, the cosmos itself will grow from the abyss that is our domination-free ground.

7. EROTICISM

Paradise is love. Every lover was in paradise for fleeting moments. But whoever lives in God's love lives there for good. Human love, too, is a feeble glimmer of eternity. Ones sees eternity shine in that fleeting moment but not with clarity.

ERNESTO CARDENAL

Heavenly and Earthly Love and Their Inseparability

WHAT EROS IS TO SEXUALITY, mysticism is to religion. According to the Romantic writer Wilhelm Schlegel, mysticism is "what the eye of the lover alone sees in the beloved," the force that urges onward, the dynamic that presses toward the unification of everything that is separated. To be sure, there are atrophied forms of sexual and religious activity, without eros. There are oft-repeated habits, frequently technically expert, but they have no part in ecstasy. They are to be counted in what Buber called "the commotion" of an eros-free functionality that artificially and often cynically shields itself against mysticism. Those who at any moment know why and to what end they do this or that, have shut themselves off from the power of the rose that blooms without a why or wherefore. In the face and for the sake of this energy that repeals rules and roles, eroticism seems to me a better name than love or sexuality for this place of mystical experience. Love is an ambiguous word and sexuality too technical a term for this place of mystical experience.

One cannot think of mystical experience and certainly not speak of it without eroticism. All religions testify to intersections of eros and religion that arise from a sacred power. Hildegard von Bingen—to name an example that applies to much of women's mysticism—speaks of the human libido in metaphors of heat and fire, the very ones she uses when naming the divine energy. There are many texts where, based on the meaning of words, one cannot distinguish the mystical love for God from human eros. In Sufi tradition, for example, one cannot always sort out who is addressed in prayers and in vows of love. Certain texts from the late Middle Ages manifest a playful language that delights in confusing eroticism and religion. In the nuptial chamber, faith "takes off Christ's clothes so that the bride may see the groom without his covering"; a Benedictine nun prays that "Jesus might give himself wholly to her, enter fully into her soul and impregnate all her organs and feed them with all his love in order to beget a fruitful progeny."[1]

But these erotic wordplays have much older and deeper roots. Even if one reacts with mistrust or abhorrence to such mixing of eroticism and religion, one cannot deny the purely linguistic observation that repeated connections are made between mystical and sexual experience, and that it cannot be given expression without drawing on eroticism. The preferred place of mystical experience is eroticism. In the Talmudic tradition we read: "When the Israelites came to the temple in Jerusalem for the three feasts, the veil (of the Holiest of Holies) was opened before them and they were shown the Cherubim in intimate embrace. And then they were told, 'Behold, the mutual love between you and God is like the love of man and woman.'"[2] The Zohar (ca. 1280–1286) is the most important text of the Jewish mystical tradition known as Kabbalah. It interprets the creation of the human being in a two-gendered form as the basic characteristic of creation, indeed of createdness in general. "Adam" is not the name of the first male but of the first human who, according to Genesis 5:2, is understood to be an androgynous being. "'Male and female He created them.' From here we learn: any image that does not embrace male and female is not a high and true image. . . . Come and see: The blessed Holy One does not place His abode in any place where male and female are not found together. Blessings are found only in a place where male and female are found, as it is written: 'He blessed them and called their name Adam on the day they were created.' It is not written: 'He blessed him and called his name Adam.' A human being is only called Adam when male and female are as one."[3] Martin Buber summed up this understanding in a simple sentence that excludes a heterosexist understanding: "In the beginning was relationship." The otherness of the other is declared as well. Only on account of Adam's sin has the human being lost this original androgynous relatedness. In this tradition, every man and every woman living alone is understood to be only "half a body."[4]

The basic conviction that the two different beings or sexes are dependent on each other is reflected as well in the Kabbalist teaching about the emanations of the divine power known as the *Sephirot*. The sephirotic realm itself is structured androgynously: the masculine and feminine aspects of God are the *Tipheret* and the *Shekinah*, respectively. Tipheret, the wholeness, the male as the active power, is sometimes depicted as the tree of life while Shekinah, God's indwelling, is Israel's communion with God in the midst of sinful and suffering humanity.[5]

Is the love humans experience of divine origin, or do they owe it to the fact that they have physical urges? This critical question arises because of how the web of life is torn asunder by something deeply rooted in patriarchal thought. Swedish theologian Andres Nygren worked out the distinction between *eros* and *agape* in his systematic study *Eros and Agape* (1930–1936) and interpreted those two basic concepts within the framework of a hierarchical perspective. Agape is the relation of the perfect to the imperfect, the condescension of the higher to the lower. Eros, on the other hand, grows from the experience of imperfection, the yearning of a lover for the exalted. According to Nygren, in Christianity agape becomes the unique and fundamental motif because it points to God's condescension in Christ; God did not condescend to humankind out of desire or need but simply out of a spontaneous and gracious love for human beings. In Nygren's view, whenever eros, which in this context means the eros of mysticism, determines the Christian understanding of love, agape is threatened, even destroyed. Opposing their commixing, Nygren insisted on the separation of eros and agape.

I speak of this classical antimystical position because it is presupposed in many discussions between mysticism and orthodox theology, between mystics and clerical powerholders. Eros and more particularly sex have nothing to do whatsoever with holiness and God's love. The wholly other God "loves" humans but does not need them; God is sufficient unto Himself![6] The love humans have for one another and their interdependency are, in the orthodox position, something fundamentally different from their relation to God. To call sexual love "heavenly"—even to experience it as such—is an unacceptable confusion of levels. On principle, giving and receiving are separated; activity is the divine, guiding, and male principle; passivity is the human, reacting, and female one. The relations between God and human beings are understood here in accordance with the unexamined ideas of patriarchal order.

It is the aim of this chapter to bring divine and human love closer together again as the use of the term eroticism suggests. Teresa of Avila was not the only one to have declared, "There is only one love."

The Song of Songs

The basic biblical text about love is the Song of Solomon. It is a collection of love poems, a work of high literary quality, where the voices of a young woman and a man are heard. For a long time, up to the beginning of the second century C.E., the dispute raged as to whether it belonged at all to the Jewish canon of sacred writings. The church fathers and later exegetes repeatedly raised the question: why is the ancient love song in the Bible at all? Is it not the only book in the Bible that does not mention the Eternal One? The text speaks unabashedly of kisses, breasts, cheeks, and thighs—is not the love of which it speaks purely human, that is to say, an utterly profane matter? Conversely, readers critical of the church ask today whether it is not high time that bodily existence and desire be neither vilified nor extolled to the skies but, rather, be affirmed directly as it is. Must we not get away from the mythical-supernatural transfiguration and proceed to a logical-natural explanation?

The classical tradition of interpretation has steadfastly and in "mystical defiance" resisted this trend toward the secularization of both sexual experience and its mythical interpretation. It did not let itself be drawn into the either/or choice presupposed in the questions above, between heavenly and earthly, human and divine, and immanent and transcendent. In *The Star of Redemption* (1921), Jewish philosopher Franz Rosenzweig (1886–1929) addresses those traditional religious interpretations that know that there is only *one* love. He defends them against a secularizing and allegorizing flattening that has become dominant since Goethe and Herder. "The Song of Songs was recognized as a love lyric and precisely therewith simultaneously as a 'mystical' poem. One simply knew that the I and Thou of human discourse is without more ado also the I and Thou between God and humans. One knew that the distinction between immanence and transcendence disappears in language. The Song of Songs was an 'authentic,' that is, a 'worldly' love lyric; precisely for this reason, not in spite of it, it was a genuinely 'spiritual' song of love of God for humans. Humans love because God loves and as God loves. Their human soul is the soul awakened and loved by God."[7] In the history of interpretation there are different readings of the Song of Solomon that, taking immanent transcendence seriously, proceeded as Rosenzweig describes. The oldest of these is the Jewish reading that recognizes that the relationship between God and God's people is depicted in the Song of Songs as a love relationship. Israel is the bride, an impetuous, desiring young woman, and God is the lover who lets himself be found. The liturgy for the Sabbath day of Pesach assigns the recital of the Song of Songs: the feast of the liberation from slavery is brought together here with the happiness of the lovers. In mystical tradition, sex is not only a personal act but an opportunity for communion with God.

Christianity has inherited this interpretation and put the church in the place of the people of Israel. The *ecclesia* is seen to be the bride of Christ; however, at an early stage, the shift from the collectivity of the faithful shifts in the interpretation to the individual soul that yearns for and experiences union with God. One may find such a reading in Origen (185–253 C.E.). This so-called bridal mysticism, which Bernard of Clairvaux reclaimed with an elementary linguistic passion, had decisively influenced the history of Christian mysticism. "The Bride, if I dare say so, are we," Bernard notes. In his interpretation of the Song of Songs, the soul-bride exclaims: "I find no rest until he kisses me with the kiss of his mouth. I am grateful that I may kiss his feet, grateful also to kiss his hands. But if he likes me at all, he should kiss me with the kiss of his mouth. I am not ungrateful— but I do love. . . . I beg, I beseech, I implore: he should kiss me with the kiss of his mouth!"[8] The extent of erotic imagery in the mysticism of the high and late Middle Ages is quite overwhelming. On the soul's way from first approach to consummation, there is playing, fondling, taking off clothes, becoming naked, penetration, kissing in the most diverse forms—from smothering the small of the back or other individual parts with kisses to French kissing—all of them expressions of a mystical eroticism. Here is Bernard of Clairvaux once again. "*O amor praeceps, vehemens, flagrans, impetuose . . .* O stormy, violent, burning, surging love who do not permit that one should think something other than you. . . . You tear down orders, pay no heed to ancestry, know no measure. Propriety, reason, modesty, counsel, judgment—all these you make your prisoners."[9]

Mysticism got a bad name precisely on account of this excessiveness of mystical passion, particularly that of women. The great woman poet Mechthild von Magdeburg (see also chapter 8) spoke of the divine-human relationship in a forthright language that is daring when compared to the polite restraint of love poetry. "O Lord, love me mightily and love me often and long; the more often you love me the purer I become; the more mightily you love me the more beautiful I become; the longer you love me, the holier I become here on earth."[10] For her, God is always "sick with love," and it is this different, undifferentiated piety that celebrates the erotic force in creation; it does not charge it with being of the fall and locate it in an "evil drive." Instead, this piety understands the erotic as something that is in the Creator's very self. What destroys the human being is to be separated off rather than being united. Eros is one of God's names.

The *unio* with the origin expresses itself not only with the help of erotic language. It teaches, it "mirrors"—in the medieval sense of the word—what eros does with us in terms of transforming us. Richard of St. Victor (d. 1173), in his *Tract on the Four Grades of Passionate Love*, distinguishes between four stages of God's love; they image the classic triad of *via purgativa, via illuminativa,* and *via unitiva,* in its two stages (see also chapter 5). Richard's four stages are called:

- purifying, awakening love
- binding love, which accompanies up to the third heaven
- love that unifies with God's will
- love that leads to perfect love of God and human beings, a love that aligns the soul to Christ

In relation to erotic mysticism, it is important to recognize that two movements are intertwined here. God's descending movement corresponds to the thirsting soul's transcending movement. In the first stage, God enters the soul and it learns meditation. Here the soul attains to its own life, which it did not know, before the one encountering it *(das Gegenüber)* made the soul become acquainted with God. The soul did not know itself without the You, an experience that many people have in first love. The soul is made pure for when the soul enters into the love relation with God, it must depart from Egypt, which in this context is the material world and its commotion. The exodus, the exit from slavery as a root symbol of the Jewish experience of God, is claimed in the medieval tradition of mysticism and related to the way the soul takes. The soul is "awakened," meaning that it becomes free.

Marguerite Porète and the Enrapturing Far-Near One

Erotic life always occurs in the alternation of losing oneself and finding oneself again in others; roaming aimlessly and immersing oneself, existing incompletely, undiscovered, partially only, and being found.

The Song of Songs expresses this movement of alternation with its frequent change of place: gardens, roads, vineyards, and the concomitant hurrying, coming, fleeing, being held back, and searching. This movement is a basic feature of the erotic force.

One of the most beautiful names given to the beloved in the lyricism of the troubadours and the poetry of mysticism is that of *loinprès* (the far-near one). It represents the play of love *(ludus amoris)* and the go and come *(va et vient)* of erotic mysticism.[11] It is for him, the far-near one, that the soul waits in anticipation. He is simultaneously far and near, deep and high, bright and dark, in the words of the mystical trinitarian hymn of the mustard seed *(granum sinapius)*.[12] The beloved cannot be named in a single word. The words of nearness, happiness, fulfillment, and sweetness are in themselves limited. They cannot express the power of the erotic in such a way that it truly remains the power that cannot be possessed and for that reason is "other," far away, eluding, and ever giving itself anew.

The term *loinprès* (the enrapturing far-near one) is used for the one who encounters; it is found in a book of instruction for women mystics, passed on for centuries as a text of an anonymous writer. This late-thirteenth-century tract is called *Mirror of the simple, annihilated souls and of those that tarry solely in desiring and demanding love*. It is a mirror that images the soul's way into love in seven stages. It ascends from the valley of humility and over the plains of truth all the way to the mount of love, away from the loss of self into union with God. "Mirror" here means not only a depiction of the other life, but also instruction about how to be about becoming simple, free from dependency on possession, status, power, and prestige as well as from "know-how" about God and from being subjected to the rule of the virtues. The sole certainty of life is found in the love that destroys all else. In a unique way, the book combines eroticism and a kind of happy nihilism for the sake of God.

If there is one saint for the idea of mysticism and resistance, then it is the name of the long-hushed-up and forgotten Beguine from northeastern France's Hainant region, Marguerite Porète (ca. 1255–1310). She lived what she wrote. On July 1, 1310, she was burned "alive as a relapsed heretic" at the stake on the Place de Grève in Paris, today called Place de l'Hôtel de Ville. The spiritual and worldly authorities of the day were present as was a large crowd of simple folk, many of whom wept. Centuries later, Marguerite de Navarre, the sister of King Francis I of France, wrote about this nameless woman and her book: it "was filled with the flame of love, so ardently that love and love alone was her sole concern, the beginning and end of everything that she said. . . . How attentive and attuned this woman was to receive the love that immolates her own heart and of all those who listened to her!"[13]

We do not know very much about the life of Porète, but we know more about her trial. It is presumed that she was a Beguine in Valenciennes; soon after that religious association of women came into being, there is evidence of the presence of a community of Beguines in that town. It is not likely that Porète belonged to the itinerant and begging Beguines. She was acquainted with contemporary troubadour lyricism as well as Dionysius the Areopagite, and her education suggests that she may have been of noble lineage. Her *Mirror* is a most artfully structured conversation of different voices. There is the teaching voice of Love (*fine amour*, as perfect love is called here in courtly language), the questioning voice of Soul *(l'âme),* and its counterpart, the voice of Reason *(raison),* wrinkling up its nose in puzzlement, coming to be called in the course of the conversation "one-eyed" and even "a sheep."[14] A literary drama ensues in which poetic sections are artfully integrated. Perhaps Porète recited the text in the public square in the manner of a minstrel or in spiritual companies; the dramatic structure of her text is eminently suited for it.

Certain topics of women's mysticism are absent from this work; neither visions nor auditions are mentioned. Absent too are the formulae of modesty or references to feminine weakness. Perhaps Porète left out these necessary protective mechanisms deliberately. And there are none of the erotic details that are typical for the period, such as allusions to living his passion with Christ. Her style has little darkness. Was it then the simple clarity of the *Mirror* that caught the eye of the censor's office and the Inquisition? They certainly suspected this mysticism of being of a kind with the heresy of the Brothers of the Free Spirit.

The *Mirror* came into being quite likely before 1300. It was banned during the rule of the Bishop of Cambray between 1296 and 1306 and publicly burned at Valenciennes, in the presence of the author. Possession of a copy of the book or the dissemination of its teaching was subject to excommunication. Nonetheless, the work found extraordinarily rapid dissemination. Like no other early mystic text in the vernacular, in subsequent years it made a triumphal march through Europe's orders and Beguine houses. It appeared as an anonymous work, in different versions and four languages. What may well have contributed to this was that the first Latin translation of the French text was long held to be a work of the Flemish mystic Jan van Ruysbroeck, who himself was regarded to be an opponent of the Brothers and Sisters of the Free Spirit. And so it was that anonymity and the erroneous ascription to a male author allowed the work to survive. As late as 1439, thirty-six confiscated copies of the book were stored in the offices of the relevant papal commission. Only in the middle of the twentieth century did Romana Guarnieri establish who the person was that had authored the *Mirror*, a fact that had been obscured for centuries.

It was probably because she had allowed the book to go on circulating that Porète was charged again and brought to Paris. The General Inquisitor took charge of her case. She was told to swear the oaths required for the examination and to provide information about her teachings. She refused both. For eighteen months she was held in a Paris jail with the intent to make her change her mind and recant. She consistently refused in a kind of *résistance* that was later to mark the life of Quakers. The authorities then tore a number of statements from their context, cited them as heresy, and tried to have Porète recant. This effort failed in the face of her steadfastness; a Beghard close to her and one of her coworkers, threatened with death by fire, recanted on her behalf and had his death sentence commuted to life imprisonment. A commission of highly respected and learned theologians was set up and the list of incriminating statements was placed before them. All twenty-one men condemned the work of this "simple and free soul" *(l'âme simple et annihilée)*—in the positive sense of utterly unburdened.

As one reads the text, in a few places one is overcome by the feeling that Porète may not have anticipated the fate of execution, of fiery death, but that she consented to its possibility. An incomparable tone of inner freedom fills her language.

LOVE: This Soul, says Love, takes account of neither shame nor honor, of neither poverty nor wealth, of neither anxiety nor ease, of neither love nor hate, of neither hell nor of paradise.

REASON: Ah, for God's sake, Love, says Reason, what does this mean, what have you said?

LOVE: What does this mean? says Love. Certainly the one knows this, and no other, to whom God has given the intellect. . . . And this Soul, who has become nothing, thus possesses everything, and so possesses nothing; she wills everything and she wills nothing; she knows all and she knows nothing.

REASON: And how can it be, Lady Love, says Reason, that this Soul can will what this book says, when before it said that she had no more will?

LOVE: Reason, says Love, it is no longer her will which wills, but now the will of God wills in her; for this Soul dwells not in love which causes her to will this through desiring something. Instead, Love dwells in her who seized her will. . . .[15]

Why was Marguerite Porète burned to death? Purely political reasons may have been at play for the king to demonstrate his orthodox disposition to Rome by sacrificing a Beguine suspected of heterodoxy; a woman, that is, without the protection of marriage or the head of a religious order.[16] But a year after her death, at the Council of Vienne, religious differences were named in a bull on the errors of the Beguines and Beghards. These differences have their own distinct significance that also affects the subsequent history of the mystical movement of women. The mystics' understanding of perfection is decisive here; it creates two conflicts in relation to the understanding of the church and to the meaning and function of the virtues. The immediacy of the experience of God is in no need of mediation; the soul can do without the mediating function of the institutional church and its offices when it becomes absorbed in the *loinprès*. And so Marguerite Porète distinguished between *Sainte Église la Grande* (the Great Holy Church), which is the Church of the Spirit, and *Sainte Église la Petite* (the Little Holy Church), which is the empirical and scholastic church whose uncomprehending queries are more often placed on the lips of reason than are made to testify to love or the soul.

This opposition is intensified by how the virtues are dealt with in the *Mirror*. Their role and participation in the soul's approach to God diminishes as the soul ascends. As the soul has less and less desire for masses, sermons, fasts, or prayers, so it becomes more and more free from the rule of the virtues. In a dramatic scene, the soul admits that "for a long time and for many days" it was in the service of the virtues but now has been "placed outside their service" by love. This transition is accented by a change from speech to song.

Soul: I confess it to you, Lady Love, says this Soul, there was a time when I belonged to them, but now it is another time. Your courtliness

has placed me outside their service. And thus to them I can now say
and sing:
Virtues, I take my leave of you forever,
I will possess a heart most free and gay;
Your service is too constant, you know well.
Once I placed my heart in you, retaining nothing;
You know that I was to you totally abandoned;
I was once a slave to you, but now am delivered from it. . . .
I am parted from your domination, in peace I rest.[17]

"Just as the 'annihilated soul' has no more need of the virtues, so it
is no longer concerned with God's consolations nor with God's
gifts."[18] Distinguishing between the giver and the gift is an essential
first step that appears frequently in mystical tradition. God is not to
be loved for the sake of what God gives but for the sake of God's self.
And as erotic love always embodies more than what its reasons yield,
so much more does this *amour fou* (foolhardy love) that strains for
the far-near lover. Because the soul is wholly focused on God it
should not or cannot concern itself with what it expects from God.
The condition of the "emptied" soul, existing solely from *divine
amour* (love for God) is called *foy sans oeuvres* (a faith without
works). That formula points ahead, as do a few other ideas in the
Mirror of this heretical woman, to the Reformation's discovery of
"righteousness by faith alone without the works of the law."

This freedom from every form of religious utilitarianism relates
Marguerite perhaps most deeply to Meister Eckhart. He arrived in
Paris one year after her death and became involved as a result of his
pastoral commission with the Beguines. He took up many of Marguerite's basic ideas and gave them theological expression in a less
offensive manner. The soul's annihilation is one of them; it was conceived of as an unknowing and an undesiring. Unknowing is an
aspect of the tradition of Dionysian negative theology that can no
longer bear "presumptuously affirmative talk of God."[19] For reason
can finally come to know only what God is not, whereas the soul, the
more it experiences the goodness of God, knows so much more
clearly that it knows nothing. The wonderful name of the far-near
one expresses exactly this unknowing that is more than knowing.

Marguerite's notion of un-desiring reaped her the charge of qui-
etism; like Eckhart's perceptions of "letting go of" or "being distanced from" all dependency, including even one's dependency on
paradise, un-desiring is part of the union with God which transforms
the soul "into a being without being, which is being itself."[20]

In this liberating annihilation, God works within the soul, without it, and for it. Formulations like "in her, for her, without her" (*en elle, pour elle, sans elle*) express both at the same time: the soul that has no more will—and is free of virtue—and the closeness of the beloved who is in it and for it. "But this Soul, thus pure and clarified, sees neither God nor herself, but God sees Himself of Himself in her, for her, without her. God shows to her that there is nothing except Him. And thus this Soul understands nothing except Him, and so loves nothing except Him, praises nothing except Him, for there is nothing except Him. For whatever is, exists by His goodness. . . ."[21] Contemporary accounts of Marguerite's way to the stake convey an inkling of this "non-nihilistic negativity" in which there "is nothing except Him," describing it in such terms as dignity and composure. The depth of her resistance, apparent in her refusal to testify under oath, her silence before her accusers, and her desire for nothing on the way to the stake, grows from the conviction of being at one with the *ravissant loinprès* (the ravishing far-near one). The soul loses its name in God just like the river that flows into the sea.[22]

The Bitterness of Ecstasy:
D. H. Lawrence and Ingeborg Bachmann

There are different ways of engaging the mysticism of the erotic, one of them being the one traveled thus far. It begins with the testimonies of mystical experiences, which are examined for the erotic images they contain. This approach gives rise to two further problem areas. The first of these I call "mystical critique of patriarchy." It is directed by the simple question whether the erotic images for the union with God can be identified as being female or male. Is not the soul, including that of the man, always female? It takes on female traits at least when the soul is depicted in a bridal relation to God, thereby referring back to the original oneness of man and woman in Adam. There is another important question to be put to texts of erotic mysticism. What emphasis does a text place on missing the other, desiring and longing for her or him, and how does it seeks to depict fulfillment and union? How much darkness and light and how much distance and nearness can mystical language convey? Can one speak of transcending ecstasy without noticing ecstasy's bitterness?

This latter question leads to a very different way that begins with the erotic experiences themselves, which are found in people's everyday lives and depicted in stories, songs, letters, or works of art that are of nonreligious origin. The mystical questions to such testimonies are these: to what extent does human erotic experience lend itself to naming transcendence from a petrified presence and a different, perhaps mystical, wholeness? In what manner is mystical desire for union present in erotic desire? How does it begin and when does it die? Is there a mysticism of everydayness that is grounded in erotic experience?

I want to discuss two literary figures of our century who both saw and named the fearful and dark margins of radical love. I begin with D. H. Lawrence, the English writer, renowned for his work *Lady Chatterley's Lover* and his endeavor to renew the world on the basis of a panerotic power. In his novel *The Rainbow* (1915), he wrote a chapter on "The Bitterness of Ecstasy," which can contribute a good deal to the transcendence as well as the unfulfilled aspects of human sexuality.

It is a love story that ends with the words, "It is finished. It had been a failure."[23] But here there are no external circumstances, no evil world, that separate the lovers from each other; the failure lies entirely within themselves. Ursula does not want to marry because she is afraid that the social self will simply take over the real self that they had just discovered. In both lovers, there lives a powerful awareness that they have found "another country," another world in which the old, constricted one had dissolved and is now gone. In this new world, one moves freely, without fear of one's fellow human beings, without disquiet and defenses, but instead, calmly, indifferent, and as one desires. In the Middle Ages this condition would have been called *ledig* (unburdened, freed).

The ecstasy the two experience for weeks and months transcends diverse forms of their lives, that is to say, it has unmasked them, rendered them superfluous and superceded them in a condition that lies "trans" (beyond) the world as we know it. They become nameless. "She was no mere Ursula Brangwen. She was Woman, she was the whole of Woman in the human order. All-containing, universal, how should she be limited to individuality?"[24] The ecstasy transcends normal language, expected behaviors, and rational control and immerses the lovers in the symbol of a darkness that they share with creation. "So they stood in the utter, dark kiss, that triumphed over them both, subjected them. . . ."[25] One dimension of the mystical experience of ecstasy is the passivity of being overwhelmed. The symbol of darkness is played out against autonomy, consciousness, and rationality. Erotic ecstasy transcends the time that normally governs us; the lovers step out of it because they absolutely want their own time. It is said of Ursula, "But it was as if she had received another nature. She belonged to the eternal, changeless place into which they had leapt together."[26] The temporality, mortality, consciousness, and control of the I all disappear in the Dionysian symbol of darkness.

The social self, with its dependency on money, time, obligations, and conditions, is experienced by Jan as "an ashen-gray, cold world of rigidity, dead walls and mechanical traffic, and creeping, spectre-like people. The life was extinct, only ash moved and stirred. . . ."[27] The contrast of social and real self, the old and the new land, the died-out ashes and the vibrating darkness dominates this depiction of a love. Why does this love have to fail?

One symptom of clinging to the ecstasy of transcending is fear of the marriage in which by necessity the social self triumphs over the real self. But this real self is threatened not only from the outside. The ecstasy of love is dependent on another darkness. Lawrence describes it as the relation of what is known and what is unknown. One morning, the woman watches her lover as he washes and dries himself. "His body was beautiful, his movements intent and quick, she admired him and she appreciated him without reserve. He seemed completed now. He aroused no fruitful fecundity in her. . . . She knew him all round, not on any side did he lead into the unknown. Poignant, almost passionate appreciation she felt for him, but none of the dreadful wonder, none of the rich fear, the connection with the unknown, or the reverence of love."[28] What is this necessary element of the unknown, the undiscovered, of the dreadful wonder that cannot be held onto in this grandiose venture of love? It is suddenly understood as something missing by both of them, and this lack leaves everything behind destroyed. Do not all lovers need this relation to the unknown, this never totally nameable? Do they not always have to love more than what they know of each other and what is knowable? Is love, understood as the venture of a purely immanent-mystical experience, not necessarily condemned to fail?

Religious tradition answers this question by referring to the amalgam of mystery, both frightening and fascinating *(mysterium tremendum et fascinosum)*. Only the far-near one can stay near. Only the one never wholly known can be known. Deprivation, separation, and ecstasy's bitterness keep its "sweetness" alive. Perhaps that is one of the reasons why, in spite of its horrid history of abuse, religion is so irreplaceable, so indispensable: it depicts this otherness, this darkness in the midst of light. Mystical love for God holds together both what causes us to tremble in fright and what never ceases to fascinate us.

What Lawrence calls "ecstasy's bitterness," Ingeborg Bachmann has dramatized mythically in her play *Der gute Gott von Manhattan* (The Good God of Manhattan). Two people meet in New York, quite by chance; they drop the conventions of a fleeting travel acquaintance and try a "distance arrangement," finally arriving at the boundary line, which they cross, and hopelessly fall in love. The space and time, all the constraints that they had hitherto lived in, are left behind in intoxication and self-forgetting. The mystical night-side of love surrounds them. In rushing from the world—as al-Hallaj or Marguerite Porète had done—they disturb the order of that very world. The other member of the cast, an allegedly "good" god, believes in "an order for everybody and for every day by which one lives every day."[29] The madly-in-love couple have fallen away from that order. That is why the god, a kind of enlightened gang leader, tries to assassinate the two lovers. But he encounters the woman only, who had stayed in the mythical-ecstatic condition while the man had given in to the normal desire to be alone for a half-hour, thereby escaping assassination. In him, as Lawrence would say, the social self has overcome the real self that has flared up briefly.

Correspondingly, the god who represents that order regards love as "a dangerous disease that brings with it too much intoxication and self-forgetting." He recommends instead the rule of healthy human reason and accommodation to general custom. "I believe that love is on the night-side of the world, more corrupting than every crime, than all heresies. I believe that wherever it emerges, a turmoil like that before the first day of creation erupts. I believe that love is innocent and that it leads to the demise. . . . I believe that lovers justly go up in smoke and always have."[30] The assassin, the good god who stands for order and conventionality, is not acquitted; the judge, who secretly agrees with him, lets him go. The woman dies and the mysticism of love with her. In the world where the judge, the accuser, and Manhattan, as that world is called here, are in agreement, there is no room for her.

Here, as in Lawrence, the mysticism of love seemingly cannot be lived out. The ironic title of the "good" god who cares for order excludes the other god of mystical transcendence. And yet people perish from the impossibility of the love that belongs to the night-side of the world, against order and conventionality.

Bachmann's play was written in 1957, in other words, before the sexual revolution and the Pill. In the meantime, order and conventionality have accommodated themselves to the market that needs sexuality as merchandise and packaging. The bitterness of mystical love, presented in the play as an absurd undertaking, has only become sharper. The god of our world does not tolerate people "absenting" themselves. Transcending is prohibited. Even though it is not imposed dictatorially, in consumerism and entertainment, or "fun," this prohibition exercises no less a totalitarian rule.

Such impossibility is met today with cynical smiles. There is mourning behind Bachmann's cool tone: her play ends in impenetrable silence. Years later, she wrote a speech that she entitled "Die Wahrheit ist dem Menschen zumutbar" (the human being's capacity for the truth can indeed be expected). Bachmann was fully aware of how impossible such an expectation is, but neither was she prepared to relinquish it.

What does the failure of mystic love mean in this world of ours? Is mysticism an absurdity, a socially irrelevant momentary diversion, worth no more than the official religions that on occasion make use of it? Can we never be at all what we do? Have we fallen asleep for ever in the prison of our world?

Sacred Power

If there really is love, it has to meet two conditions. It has to bring about a kind of mutuality in which the unknowability of the known is preserved, the otherness of the other. Only in this way can love impart participation in sacred power, in the shared power of the holy. This power is called holy because its nature is not to rule over others or to exercise domination that is sustained by dominion. It is "holy" because it is in essence a sharing of power, an empowerment in which everyone has a share in the power of life. Both basic features of mysticism of eros, mutuality and sacred power, are what the two literary figures just mentioned, Lawrence and Bachmann, are looking for and fail to find.

A mystical understanding of the erotic relationship must reflect in a new way activity and passivity, giving and taking, singleness and duality. A wretched and false perception of human sexuality reigns in the Western world's thinking since Aristotle. All activity, all life-creating power, is seen to reside in the man's seed. In contrast, the role of the female is described as being merely the seedbed, the receptacle. In this way, activity and passivity are turned into gender-specific role models, and the assignment of dominion and control determines even sexual behavior.

Mysticism of the erotic, especially women's mysticism, but also that of men, in which the soul is understood as something female, has shaken these foundations of patriarchal order. An understanding of mutuality nurtures the thinking of such mysticism: giving and taking, desiring and claiming, being loved and loving continually flow one into the other without one being primary or foundational and the other secondary. Rumi declared that "it is not only the thirsting who seek water; it is water that also seeks the thirsty."[31]

"There is no clapping of hands with one hand alone." This expresses that in love the boundaries of time, space, and assigned role are crossed over; mysticism is an ever renewed deconstruction of socially constructed sexual roles. It forever subverts and transcends the relations of domination and submission. Hildegard von Bingen assumed that, before the fall, Eve looked up to God and not to Adam! And Teresa of Avila presupposed that the marital relation to a man deprives a woman of the dignity that she obtains alone in the immediate relation to God.

Since the individualism of the Enlightenment, the relation between self and others has been loosened from many body-alienated and ascetic institutions and won more freedom. But the relations between the sexes have not become new and not been conceived in terms of greater mutuality. Instead, they are seen more as a competition and a struggle for power. Freedom was defined in purely male terms: as the freedom from dependency. Goethe's question about "mutual dependency, this most beautiful condition—how could it be without love?" seems forgotten in the face of sheer self-limitation to individual autonomy. In the "free" societies autonomy related to the individual reigns, as heretofore, as the highest good, defined as self-possession and self-direction. This grants perpetuity to the struggle for power in human relationships and blocks the recognition of the indeed transcendent power, namely the sacred power that is lived in being shared.

But the love that crosses fixed boundaries is endangered also by a modern self-sufficiency that from the very outset denies mysticism of the erotic. Paul Mommaers writes, "Human love is not a well laid out little paradise in which the tendrils of the heart remain deeply intertwined. An expansive space is needed, the unfathomable 'ground' has to open up or, to put it in more personal terms, the gardener has to be allowed in."[32] The failure of mystical love in this world of ours often leads to a fear-induced scaling down of expectations, visions, and the like. Many expect from the very beginning that in their love relation there will be no mystical wholeness in which "I am what I do." Others attempt to privatize their love so that it has nothing to do any more with that "expansive space" alleged to be essential to it. But that is when the little paradise turns into a kind of hell for two. Worldlessness is not the space of mysticism of the erotic; sanctifying the world is. What corresponds to the unreserved opening one to the other, wherein habit and role are left behind, is not the totality that excludes all others but the involvement of the self in and with the others' otherness.

"Allowing the gardener in" means also to find another relation to the other. The other is like you, said Martin Buber, and the other is not like you. Both statements belong together and can be lived only when correlated. Love is not simply complete concord; there is also the other's strangeness and one's being frightened by him or her. Perhaps the innermost difficulty of the two people in Lawrence's novel is their denial of otherness and their tendency to lay total claim to each other. There is something like the sacredness of the other, untouchable and at no one's disposition, that must plunge us into a powerlessness; the common, sacred power can be derived only from there.

At times I ask myself whether this otherness can be lived without recourse to the language of religion, without "allowing the gardener in." It is not because she might conjure up something we really do not wish for. All mystics know that the incomprehensibility of God grows rather than diminishes when God's love comes close to us. But is that not precisely the same with the incomprehensibility of the other? We are not rid of the bitter, the dark, especially when we finally come to learn to celebrate the power of the erotic by sharing it.

Just as a world without poetry has squandered the mystery of the snowflake, so does a world without religion suffocate from its merciless functionalism. When there is no more mystery, the mystery of the other will also have died: everything is already known and predictable. Love knows all by itself how and when to scale down, without pressure. It may be true that mystic-erotic energy has subverted and transcended the patterns of patriarchy within the old monotheistically formed cultures. If so, then one may ask whether this same sacred power within us does not also know how to transcend the arrangements of sexual consumerism and of the little private paradise within the world of neoliberalism and its world of consumer goods.

In this world of ours, religion is as superfluous as it is indispensable. It is superfluous in a functionalist sense because it has given up its old roles. Science now explains the world; state and economy regulate the community; and a common ethic crumbles into ethnic mores. In a mystical sense, however, religion is indispensable particularly for people who love. For religion still names our poverty and reminds us still of the power in us that holds together and heals. Religion still speaks of the sanctity of life for all that we can locate in love.

8. SUFFERING

Have we ever tried to love God where no wave of emotional
enthusiasm bears us up and we can no longer confuse ourselves
and our life-urge with God, where we seem to be dying of a love
that looks like death and absolute negation and we appear to be
calling out into nothingness and the utterly unrequited?

KARL RAHNER

Job: The Satanic and the Mystical Wager

MY FIRST ENGAGEMENT OF SUFFERING as a place of mystical experience took place some twenty-five years ago when I wrote the book
Suffering (Leiden), in the series *Themen der Theologie* (Themes in
Theology). I distanced myself from all Christian masochism as well
as from apathy, which as the inability to suffer resides in the belief in
progress. I was taking hesitant steps toward establishing a position
which, in the broad democratized understanding proposed here, I
would call a mystical affirmation. The biblical book of Job played a
noticeable role.[1] My discussion was shaped by Ernst Bloch whom, as
I see it today, I followed all too uncritically. I refer less to his Marxism than to his perspective fixated on struggle that leads to a deficit
in mystical thinking.

Today I have a different view of the narrative of the innocent suffering of that pious man from the land of Uz. For me, the basic issue
on which it focuses is no longer the struggle with the ruler of the
heavens but the struggle of mystical love with God. Can that love
sustain itself even in suffering? The author of the book of Job wres-
tles with such questions. Can faith in God be free of ulterior motives
and interests? Can there be such a thing at all? Is there something like
pure religion that does not act from fear of punishment and that is
not intent on reward? Or is religion always a deal, a transaction
where people expect to reap well-being, fortunes here and beyond,
health, wealth, and affirmation and enter into certain commitments
as a result? Is *do ut des* (I give so that you will give in return), the
market principle, an all-governing basic law of human life? And what
about the mystical dreams of an amazement unalloyed with interests,

of the soul's unattachedness and freedom, of the *sunder warumbe* (the utter absence of any why or wherefore) and the rose's blooming for no reason at all, of singing and glowing free of purpose? Do all these wreck on the bitter reality of the injustice of human life?

The book of Job raises this question with astonishing radicality. It does so in the prose narrative of chapters 1, 2, and 43, which biblical research often labels pejoratively as folklorist enclosure, framing the great, poetically, and rhetorically well-crafted speeches of Job's friends and God. The prelude in heaven tells of Satan, roaming the earth, proposing a wager with God. By means of the pious and righteous "servant of God," he wants to prove that love for God lasts only as long as it yields a return, as long as one can count on reward and just retribution. God rejoices in Job's piety and praises him, "there is none like him on earth," to which Satan replies, "Does Job fear God for naught?" (1:8-9) The Hebrew term *chinnam* means "without payment, for nothing, without recompense"; it is used again a little later in the sense of "without cause, without purpose" (2:3).

As Gustavo Gutiérrez has shown convincingly, the intent of Satan is to unmask religion. Piety, faith, and trust in God are all utilitarian aspects that the enlightened Satan sees through. They stand and fall with the expectation of reward, of a corresponding favor returned. Job's friends are of the same opinion: suffering is to be understood only as just punishment. They want to free Job from his delusion of innocence. From a literary perspective, this is a highly interesting fusion of populist narrative prose and polished poetic rhetoric.

Satan can think of understanding religion only in terms of manipulating God in the interest of advantages humans seek to derive. In a religion that is intent on the self, there can be no real encounter between God and the human being. Instead, what happens in it is the construction of an idol. That there could be "the loving and completely free meeting of two freedoms, the divine and the human"[2] is something Satan cannot imagine; it is beyond him to think in other than mercantile categories.

But Job keeps his faith "gratis" and thus helps God win the wager. Even when he utters words of utter despair, it is the day of his birth that Job curses, and not God. What Satan hopes for does not happen, namely, that Job speaks ill of God. At no time does Job say that God is unjust; instead, he questions the theology of rewards and interests.

In the course of the Job's discussion with friends, a different process sets in. Job connects his fate with that of other innocent sufferers. Alerted by what is happening to him, he accuses God concerning what others are experiencing. Job discovers his sisters and brothers whose land has been stolen, their animals impounded, and their clothing and shelter taken away. "God pays no attention" to injustice (24:12) and remains deaf. In the course of complaint and accusation, Job changes as he relates the impoverishment of the poor and their innocent suffering to his own situation. Thus, in the debate about suffering he reaches in his own way the prophetic voice of the Hebrew Bible, in which the oppressors are called murderers (24:14) and the equality of all human beings is attested (31:15ff).

This siding with the poor does not solve his own problem; it does not end his ill fortunes. But in a certain sense, it represents a different wager with Satan, the substance of which is not the demeanor of the innocent but that of God. "Bet you that . . ." is the voice of a wager made in mystical love. I bet you that . . . God is the father of all victims of injustice, that their situation will not remain as it is today, and that the historical losers in the global economy are not forgotten, superfluous beings that can be ignored. In his book, which is an interpretation of Job from the context of the reality of the Third World's impoverishment, Gutiérrez cites several voices of people who, like Job, have fallen into misfortune innocently. Like him, they bring together the prophetic biblical tradition, which offers resistance and mystical love that is free of ulterior motives.

> We know there is no promised land
> nor any promised stars.
> We know it, Lord, we know it
> and we labor on, with you.
> We know that a thousand more times
> we have to hitch the wagon anew
> and a thousand times
> build our wooden shack
> on the dirt all over again.
> We know that in so doing
> we'll recover neither our costs nor gain profit.
> We know it, Lord, we know it
> and we labor on, with you.
> And we know
> that on this shabby stage,
> a thousand and more thousand times,
> we must play the old tragic-comic play
> without applause or recognition.
> We know it, Lord, we know it

and we labor on, with you.
And you know, Lord, that we know it,
that we all know it, all of us!
(Where is the Devil?)
That today you can make a wager
with whomever,
a wager more certain than with Job or with Faust.[3]

This poem by Leon Felipe came into being in the context of the repeated slum clearances endured by the poor, whose huts of corrugated iron or cardboard are bulldozed. At the same time, the poem is an unsentimental description of the labor of base-communities, who always begin anew after a wave of destruction. In place of the satanic wager represented here by the book of Job and by Faust, the poem's "we" makes a better bet with God. What these impoverished ones propose is a mystical wager that does not accept misery in apathy or resignation but, instead, clings to the prophetic appeal to what in the creation story is called a "good" life. The Bible's two voices, the mystical and the prophetic, belong together; indeed, whenever they assume that they can do without each other they lose themselves. The ethical-prophetic voice speaks in the place of God and, in that respect, it speaks "about" God; but that is not enough. It needs a language other than the one that knows God's will and articulates it. It is dependent on the language of mysticism, which is always a speaking "to" or "in" God.

With its being-in-God, religious-mystical language responds to the experience of suffering on the part of the innocent, with the mystical wager mentioned in the poem, a wager that is itself derived from the biblical experience. In the book of Job, Satan loses his wager: irrespective of the consequences, Job does not cease to love God. Job lives the *sunder warumbe*. People in this biblical tradition can pronounce the "we" of the poem and attain to an innermost assurance that will not let itself be put off. "Still, you remain my joy, Jesus, even in the midst of suffering" *(Dennoch bleibst du auch im Leide, Jesus, meine Freude)* is what the Protestant tradition sings in a hymn.

In a conversation about the mysticism of suffering, Karl Rahner said something like the following. There seem to be moments in every human life where common, day-to-day love, barely distinguishable from rational egoism, suddenly faces the alternative of loving without reward, to trust without assurance, to venture where it appears only that a senseless adventure lies before you that will not yield profit to anyone. But just such nonprofit love is the foundation of every mysticism of suffering.

There is a famous poem by Rumi in which the supplicant is ready to despair of God because "for many long nights" he has prayed in vain.[4]

> "How well you implore!" Satan said derisively.
> "But where is God's responding 'Here I am!'?
> No answer will come down from the throne!
> How long will you shout 'O God!'—Don't waste your time!"

The supplicant falls silent in his suffering and Chidr, a messenger from God, brings him a mystical answer. Protestant theologian Friedrich August Gottreu Tholuck, a significant figure in the nineteenth-century continental Awakening, took up this answer in his dissertation on Sufism (1821). He wrote, "What could be more abstruse and daring?" The abstruse mystical text in which Rumi voices God's answer is one of the great passages of mystical love in the midst of Godforsakenness.

> Your shout "O God!" is my shout "Here I am!"
> Your pain and your imploring is but a message from me.
> And all your striving to reach me—
> is a sign that I draw you to me!
> Your love's anguish is my goodwill towards you.
> In the cry "O God!" are a hundred "Here I am!"

Between Dolorousness and Suffering

Mystical piety arises from the fulfillment that Bernard of Clairvaux used to call "deification": *Sic affici, deificari est* (to be so touched or fulfilled is to be deified).[5] Such an experience can be exemplified in nature, eroticism, and other places. But can it also be had in pain, deprivation, and suffering? How can ecstasy happen here, this being "outside" oneself, or the wholeness in which "I am what I do?" Does not suffering always mean that I am exactly *not* what I do when other powers are doing something to or against me?

In our current spiritual context there is no aspect of mystical experience that is as foreign, disputed, and open to misinterpretation as the reality of suffering. Does suffering even have any place left in a society fixated on performance and experience? Can its meaning be sought, prayed for, meditated upon, and discerned? Is it really true that getting rid of or avoiding suffering is something for which no price is too high and no anaesthetic too precious? "An Indian teacher of wisdom said, 'if suffering and redemption from suffering are no problem to you, you will hardly muster the energy and the persistence needed to search for the self. Pleasure lets you go to sleep, pain wakes you up. Through blessedness alone you cannot come to know yourself, for it is your true nature. You have to look the opposite in the face, into what you are not, in order to find enlightenment.'"[6] What does it mean "to look the opposite in the face?" Every form of mysticism of suffering found in the different religions faces critical questions. Within the Christian tradition, those questions are particularly sharp because this tradition always fostered an extreme, often pathological obsession with suffering that is referred to as dolorousness *(dolorismus)*. The other forms of addressing suffering receded into the background here: the fight against suffering as embodied by Prometheus and Heracles in Greek mythology, but also the pious and patient submission to God's will within an imperfect world. In Islam, for example, Muhammad indeed teaches that "patience is one half of religion," but this does not mean that suffering is understood as something necessary for salvation or that it is especially virtuous to invite suffering into one's life.

This is where Christian tradition imports a different emphasis. If God, too, is one who suffers, then suffering is not simply something bad to which one can surrender or stand up in resistance. It becomes instead a reality that has something to do with the far-near God and that fits into God's incomprehensible love. The way of suffering that is not just tolerated but freely accepted, the way of the passion, becomes therefore part of the disciple's way of life.

Suffering does not necessarily separate us from God. It may actually put us in touch with the mystery of reality. To follow Christ means to take part in his life. According to Paul's Letter to the Colossians, it is the believers' task to "complete what is lacking in Christ's afflictions" (1:24). In Christianity suffering is not explained, for example, on the basis of Satan's power or the sin of humans; it is viewed positively for the sake of Christ. At times it is even transfigured, as the place of encounter with God where we make a gift (sacrifice) and God invites us to her/himself by bearing the suffering with us.

In the history of Christian mysticism, from the High Middle Ages until at least the Enlightenment, "the concentration on the physical pain and psychological agony of the Savior . . . [is] perhaps the most typical characteristic."[7] Erotic mysticism and mysticism that is focused on the passion often flow one into the other, as in the infectious *Laude* of the spiritualist poet Jacopone of Todi (ca. 1236–1306): *Cristo amoroso, et eo voglio en croce nudato salire* (Christ, most beloved, I too will go naked onto the cross and there, in your embrace, die with you).[8] For many pious mystics, it is more important to behold the man of sorrow and embrace the bloodied bridegroom than to meet the risen Savior. This longing finds its climax in stigmatization, the emergence of Christ's wounds on one's own body, as first attested to in Francis of Assisi. From this basically new evaluation of suffering developed a polarity of different, often overlapping ways of living one's life, and mystical trends that may be categorized as dolorousness *(dolorismus)* and compassion *(compassio)*.

What is dolorousness? In the Middle Ages, there were hermits who had themselves walled in for life, most often next to a church. It is said about a recluse from Magdeburg, who, on account of her crippled condition was called Margareta Contracta, that "suffering did not cause her concern; what troubled her was that no suffering could suffice her."[9] Such craving for suffering no longer distinguishes between fruitless, avoidable, and self-inflicted suffering and that which Paul accepted "for the body of Christ's sake," that is, for the sake of the community that suffered persecution in the Roman Empire. *Compassio* in this sense is not suffering that people bring upon themselves through unparalleled demands of asceticism. It arises in the immediacy of innocent suffering and from solidarity with those who have to bear it. Dolorousness draped in mystical yearnings has nothing to be glossed over. It patently bears the marks of masochistic substitutionary satisfaction.[10] In a horrendous example of such obsession and dependency, Mechthild von Hackeborn (1242–1299) scattered glass shards on her bed "for repentance's sake" and then tossed and turned "until her whole body dripped with blood so that she could neither sit nor lie down because of the pain."[11]

Heinrich Seuse, too, suffered for sixteen years from a similar addiction that took the form of fasting, sleep deprivation, cold, iron chains, self-flagellation, and wearing a nail-studded cloak. This man, who was regarded as a remarkably gentle and empathetic shepherd of souls, rubbed salt and vinegar into his wounds. This is quite astonishing, seeing that Seuse had studied with Meister Eckhart, whose work is quite void of images of hell, Satan, and punishment. Eckhart makes no reference to such doloristic disciplines and *purgatio* (purification as the first stage of mysticism) plays no part in his thinking. Eventually Seuse was healed from his obsession with suffering when, in an apparition, he was told that God no longer desired such behavior. In a gesture of liberation, he hurled his instruments of torture into the Rhine.[12]

Is it at all possible to understand the desire for suffering and the yearning for even more suffering? I think that it is possible only in conjunction with the other basic Christian concept, *compassio* (suffering with Christ and all who suffer). Mystical love for God makes us open to God's absence: the senseless, spiritless suffering that separates humans from all that makes for life. The privation and eclipse of God ought at least to be felt and suffered. The nausea caused by this world of injustice and violence ought at least to be perceptible; it ought to increase to the point of physical vomiting, as is told about so many highly gifted women from Catherine of Siena to Simone Weil. That kind of nausea is an experience of compassio.

John of the Cross says that "the suffering for the neighbor grows the more as the soul unites itself through love with God."[13] This kind of suffering is not imposed, as in the manner of illness, nor is it chosen, as in extreme ecstasy. It arises from a relationship to the world that is not immersed in the I alone. Instead, in its anguish about unliberated life, it is drawn into suffering, which is—in terms of the hardly exhaustible double meaning of the word—from the passion of the impassioned heart into the passion of the road of suffering and pain. It is not the self-imposed form of ascetic dolorous suffering that is the voluntary element here but the risk contained in every partiality for the victims of history and every commitment to the cause of the losers.

This is made evident in one of the most beautiful texts of the mysticism of suffering written by Mechthild von Magdeburg. This text may be interpreted in the sense of compassio as suffering with Christ what he suffered. Following Christ's call to be tormented with him, there is a recitation of suffering that is part of the sparse knowledge we have of Mechthild's life context. "Thou shalt be martyred with Me; betrayed through envy; tempted in the desert; imprisoned through hate; denounced through slander; thine eyes shall be bound that thou mayest not recognize the truth; thou shalt be beaten by the fury of the world; brought to judgment in confession; thy head struck with rods; sent before Herod in derision; stripped in dereliction; scourged with poverty; crowned with temptation; spat on with contempt."[14] Most likely, Mechthild was born into a noble family; at age twelve she experienced for the first time what we might call a disrobing of the ego. From that time she yearned for a life free of marriage and unconnected with the monastery but given to meditation and piety. She spent many years in a community of Beguines in Magdeburg. She reaped enmity as a result of the visions, prayers, and reflections that she wrote down beginning in 1250 C.E. on the instruction of her father-confessor, and which lacked nothing in the critique of and biting scorn for nobility and clergy. Under quite dramatic circumstances she fled from Magdeburg and found shelter in the cloister of Helfta, where Gertrude the Great and Mechthild von Hackeborn also lived (see chapter 15).

The passion of Christ is mirrored in the experience of Mechthild von Magdeburg's loving soul who, on account of her ecstasies, is scorned, mocked, and despised and, because she is a woman, is denied education and humiliated religiously using confession as an instrument of power. Elsewhere there is an allusion to Mechthild's critics who want to burn her book, which calls to mind the fate of the other great Beguine, Marguerite Porète. And just like her, Mechthild von Magdeburg refused to opt for a life free of suffering by submitting to established authority. In the two-fold sense of that word, she chooses the passion of solitude in place of a passion-free life. This voluntary nature is a mark of mystical life. Compassio means, in the first place, suffering with the crucified Christ. The cult of the cross is hotly disputed these days. Represented in churches and schools, at crossroads and on mountaintops, it once served to educate one in suffering with another. According to Christian understanding, until the end of the world, as Blaise Pascal put it, Christ still hangs on the cross; namely in the victims of injustice, every one of whom is to be regarded as a sister or brother of Christ (see also Matt 25:31-46). Without compassio in this encompassing sense there can be no transformation of suffering. Eventually the great majority of humankind hangs on the cross of empire and, in an extended mystical understanding of suffering, with her species and elements our mother earth, too, hangs on the cross of industrialism. Without compassio, there is no resurrection. Every mystical affirmation of love that pursues no ulterior motive includes the acceptance of suffering. As Mechthild says, it is "the hammer of love that nails us to the cross."[15]

"Even When It Is Night": John of the Cross

This togetherness of courtly love and cross, of love and suffering, of the near and the faraway beloved is found in the mystical theology of the Middle Ages. What is new in Counter-Reformation Spain is the inner knowledge of "the dark night of the soul," that found its way into a poetry that thinks of darkness and highest bliss as one. Darkness, night, and suffering cannot be excluded from the wholeness of God as some New Age piety promises. As affirmed by John of the Cross, one of the greatest mystics and poets of Christendom, faith is "a dark night for the soul . . . and the more it darkens the soul the more it also gives it its light."[16]

For John, whom the poets of Spain elevated to be their patron in 1952, night became the central symbol, the "most original creation," as Edith Stein put it. His most beautiful poems lovingly play with the symbolic word repeated in almost every verse: *noche oscura* (dark night). In his works composed later, *Ascent on Mount Carmel* and *The Dark Night,* he did nothing but exegete and systematize his poem *En una noche oscura* line by line.

That exegesis is mystagogy in the best sense of the word. It addresses the difficulties that face beginners, the more advanced and those who have arrived. John identifies these three groups with the distinction made in mystical tradition, *purgatio, illuminatio,* and *unificatio* (see chapter 5), but he does so in a new, what might almost be called psychological, spiritual depth of the inward look. He consoles those who believe that "the scruples of the soul and its reluctance" derive "from a diseased constitution,"[17] or those who feel that God has abandoned them because they "searched for God in a feeble and unsuitable manner."[18] He uses repetition to explain what, in my view, he had named more profoundly and with less dogmatic warrant both in his pastoral care and in the systematic justification of his genuinely poetic mysticism. Both mystic poetry and mystagogical prose are concerned with the soul's transformation into God (*transformación del alma en Dios*) as the ongoing dynamic movement of spiritual life. And so, as a spiritual director, he lifts the paradox of the *entender no entendiendo* (comprehension without comprehending) in order to deepen it as a mystic.

This transformation happens "even when it is night" as he repeats at the end of every verse of one of his most beautiful poems about the source that bubbles over and flows forth.

That eternal spring lies hidden,
How well I know its hiding place,
Even when it is night.

In the dark night of this life
How well I know in faith the sacred spring,
Even when it is night.

I do not know its source, for it has none,
But I know that every source comes from it.
Even when it is night.[19]

"Even when it is night" (*aunque es de noche*) runs like a red thread through John's sense of mystical presence, a thread of what in Johannes Tauler's work is called *gotliden* (suffering God).

Nothing is more alien to Spanish poetry than the portrayal of realities; its language lives in freedom for the paradoxical symbol. Reality is antecedent—and not worthy of language that is at one and the same time poetry and prayer. Comprehension comes subsequently, it clatters along afterwards. What is spoken in poetry is what cannot be spoken in any other way, namely, the "disrobing of the ego," the submersion and the forgetting of oneself in the other. The German poet Stefan George (1868–1933), a leader of the revolt against nationalism in German literature, renders this as follows:

Thus I remained and forgot myself
Inclining my face toward the beloved
The world waned. I sank
And my sorrows sank away
Buried in the midst of lilies.

John of the Cross weaves into language what dolorous mysticism deeply yearned for, namely, stigmatization, Christ's wounds breaking forth in one's own body. Originally, the stigma was a wound, an injurious stab wound inflicted on Greek and Roman slaves as a mark of identification, comparable to the numbers tattooed on the wrists and forearms of concentration camp inmates. In this sense the poetry of Saint John lives from an open wound.

Night had a special place and value in the life of Saint John of the Cross. He loved to spend much time under the starry sky in order to experience "the silent music, the euphonic solitude."[20] One of his community brothers reports the following: "In the peace of the night,

John spent several hours alone in prayer. When he arose from prayer, he fetched his companion and, reclining in view of a brook on a green meadow, spoke with him about the beauty of the sky, the moon and the stars. Sometimes he spoke of the gentle harmony of the heavenly spheres and their movements. He would ascend then into the very heaven of the blessed. His companion would warn him of the dangers of the evening dew, to which John was to have replied, 'let us go, I understand, Reverend Sir, that you wish to go to sleep.'"[21] Later he would gladly allow his own monks to leave for "prayer excursions" under the open sky or in the solitude of quietness in the cloister gardens.

John was three years old when he became acquainted with poverty. His father had died and his mother dragged herself and her three children from one relative to another begging for work or bread. Later he worked as a servant and, while a student, as an orderly. At age twenty-one he joined the Carmelite Order but only his meeting with Teresa of Avila (see chapter 4) took him into the reform wing of the order that was characterized by seclusion and contemplation, as well as a rigorous hermitic life. As Edith Stein, a twentieth-century Carmelite, writes, "participation in the cross of Christ is to be the life of the Discalced Carmelites."[22]

Teresa's reforms needed to incorporate the male part of the order. With the cry of Rachel on her lips, "Give me children, or I shall die!" (Gen 30:1), Teresa looked for "sons," capable brothers who could advance the reform of the order. John, the most important of these sons, worked next to Teresa between 1572 and 1577 at Avila, as a spiritual director and mystagogue among the "unshod" Carmelites, that is, those who reestablished ascetic rigor and the priority of contemplation over the apostolate.

The price he had to pay for this was high. In November 1577, Carmelites of the Old Order (the "shod" Carmelites) abducted him. They were moving against "renegade" brothers and sisters with the same destructive fervor they manifested toward Jews and Moors. He was condemned and banned from Old Castille; in December he was carried off to Toledo and thrown into a windowless dungeon. As a "barefoot" Carmelite, he was not allowed to cover his feet with the two blankets allotted to him, so that during the ice-cold nights his toes froze several times. In the summer months, his dungeon became unbearably hot. Fresh air or a change of clothes were denied him as was conversation or spiritual consolation. In the end, his clothing began to rot. Three times a week, the prisoners were allowed to leave their cells to take nourishment. The "remorseful" among them were seated at tables while John was singled out to pick up his food—water, bread and sometimes a sardine—with his mouth from the ground, while crawling on his knees. On Fridays, after the meal, the monks were "disciplined," as the torture was called, which ended with the monks, walking in a circle, beating one another on their backs. John had to strip his back bare, and every time his blood would flow during this torture, which lasted as long as it took the monks to recite the *Miserere*. In August 1578, taking a daring nighttime leap over the walls, he succeeded in escaping from his incarceration.

This information about the abduction, solitary confinement, abuse, and successful escape appears in his poetry in allusions, such as "on the secret ladder, disguised, hidden by darkness." The other story in which he makes use of biographical material is that of the Song of Songs; here the bridegroom (God) and the bride (soul) find each other. Once again in the rendition of Stefan George;

> O night you that leads me
> O night sweeter to me than dawn
> O night you that didst unite
> the friend with the beloved
> the friend having gone into the beloved.

John of the Cross did not rend asunder light and dark, fulfillment and denial, losing oneself and being found. Both sides belong inseparably together because God wants to be the dark side of God's glory. God is always also the other of God's self; the intuition of this is what sustains John's mystical poetry. He prayed to Christ for cross, suffering, and contempt, and he received all of them in all their bitterness to the end of his life when the general chapter of his order ruled him unworthy of any office and responsibility. They packed him off to a hermitage, and the plan to remove him to Mexico failed only on account of his poor health. A few months passed after this humiliation and then he died.

For John of the Cross, the night is always a symbol also of purification,[23] of the senses being stripped,[24] of the deprivation needed by the I that has fallen into dependency (see chapter 12). He differentiated between the stages of the active purification of desire that the I has to bring about, and the passive one that comes from God. The step from meditative reflection to contemplative observation is also the step from activity to passivity. In this passivity the I ceases to be at work, to analyze, and to look for an escape. It falls into emptiness. Contemplation renders us defenseless and delivers us into the dark night.

John set about to make sure that even the finest and most concealed form of spiritual pleasure be stamped out in the passive night of the spirit.[25] Every spiritual consolation is stripped away and "pure" faith without recompense is called for. In this he resembles Martin Luther. John's experience of love, perhaps one may say his love story with God, is marked by alternation of dryness, drought, and mystic betrothal, an alternation of self-deliverance to God that necessarily includes pain.

In the formulations of dogmatic theology it is quite proper to say that God has become revealed "with finality" in Christ as love. The mystical question that is put to this and similar statements concerns the darkness of God. God's irrevocable darkness cries out in the suffering of the innocent, the losers of history, in Job's lament. What happens to God's darkness in the revelation of love? Is it triumphalistically muted? Are those who dwell in darkness consoled with a hereafter? The mystical answer to such questions is that love does not render darkness harmless through religious prattle but, rather, deepens it and makes it more unbearable. For the sake of this unbearableness, some mystics have preferred hell to heaven. To *deus absconditus* (the hidden and mute God), for example, in the gas chambers, which corresponds to *homo abyssus* (the human being caught in the abyss). And to the dark night of the soul corresponds, if it be a serious contemporary appropriation of what John of the Cross experienced, to the dark night of the world which we live today.

"Better in Agony than in Numbness": Twentieth-Century Mysticism of Suffering

The mystical experience of God, which always includes the possibility of missing God, arises from the concrete situation and necessarily returns to it: transforming, acting, suffering. A spirituality that unfolds apart from real history and seeks to be left alone by it may match certain features of piety. But this is not "mystical" in the sense developed here when it shuns the cost of God's presence in the world's activity and its suffering. The "dark night of the soul" does not fall outside the historical world in an allegedly pure encounter of

God and the individual soul. At least in the tradition we call Judeo-Christian, that encounter is always marked by the irksome and irrevocable presence of the other whom the Hebrew Bible called "the neighbor." The "dark night" that can purify perception and spirit so that they may be guided from the onset of darkness, to midnight, and on to dawn, is always a night the place of which can be named. The "dark night of the soul" experienced today is based in a "dark night of the world." Its eclipse of God is given expression in a variety of accents or with different names of hopelessness, such as "cross" (Edith Stein), "misfortune" (Simone Weil), and "agony" (Reinhold Schneider).

I begin with the dark night of the Jewish people and, at the same time, of the world of those twelve years of German history about the horrors of which, according to Reinhold Schneider, "no insightful person can assert that it is impossible to repeat them."[26] A Roman Catholic woman and mystic of Jewish birth gave that night the traditional name, "cross." Edith Stein (1891–1942), a philosopher and Edmund Husserl's assistant, was first an atheist and subsequently a Carmelite sister. She wrote a study on John of the Cross in 1941 titled *Kreuzeswissenschaft* (Science of the Cross). "A *scientia crucis* can be had only when one comes to experience the cross most profoundly. I was persuaded of this from the very beginning and said with a full heart: *Ave Crux, spes unica!* (Hail, Cross, unique hope!)."[27] Born into an educated, Jewish, merchant family, from early on and without much ado she called herself an atheist. What oriented the way of an intellectually gifted phenomenologist to mysticism was, above all, her experience of suffering. One of her closest philosophical friends from the time of her studies in Göttingen was killed in 1917 at the front in Flanders. His partner, Ann Reinach, who during the First World War converted from Judaism to Christianity, responded to that senseless death quite differently than Edith Stein had expected. In the midst of pain she accepted her suffering in light of the cross, without regarding it as a pointless blow of fate, or sinking into deadening dullness or self-destructiveness. She saw it as her personal participation in the cross.

Edith Stein said that this encounter was "the moment when my disbelief broke down and Christ shone forth, Christ in the mystery of the cross." Years later, when she was received into the Carmelite community, she confessed that "it is not human action that can help us but Christ's suffering. To take part in it is what I desire."[28] In 1933, at age 42, Edith Stein entered the Carmelite community at

Cologne, a step that deeply pained her religious Jewish mother. All attempts of her sisters and brothers to stop her failed, including their offer to support her financially when, in April 1933, she lost her job for reasons of her Jewishness. A twelve-year-old niece asked her at the time why she was doing this now? Her niece later wrote, "By becoming Roman Catholic, our aunt forsook her people. Her entry into the monastery gave witness to the world outside that she wanted to separate herself from the Jewish people."[29] That is how it appeared to her family, but it was never true for Edith Stein herself. She did not cut herself off but went with her people on their way, albeit in the perspective of theology of the cross that to the majority of Jewish persons could only be incomprehensible, if not unbearable.

Reflecting on the mysticism of suffering and its biggest symbol, the Roman Empire's instrument of torture, must by necessity confront traditional Christian anti-Judaism. Edith Stein was not immune to it even though she rejected the absurd notion of the collective guilt of Jews for the death of Jesus. She deeply desired that all Jews would convert, and she suffered much from the rejection on the part of the Jews of the Messiah promised to and longed for precisely by them. In her last will and testament, composed on June 9, 1939, she wrote: "I pray to the Lord that he may accept my living and my dying . . . as an atonement for the Jewish people's unbelief and so that the Lord may be accepted by his own and that his reign may come in glory, that Germany may be saved and that there be peace in the world."[30] Burdened with the false judgment concerning this alleged unbelief, which has become more apparent even for Christians since Auschwitz, Edith Stein lived in solidarity with the Jewish people as a conscientious Christian. In 1942, when the SS took her away to the transports headed for Auschwitz, she said to her cloister sisters, "Pray for me!" She took her biological sister Rosa, who was mentally disabled, and went with her into the gas chamber. She took Rosa by the hand with these words, "Come, we go for our people."[31]

Edith Stein understood the fate of the Jewish people as "participation in the cross of Christ." It is not a dolorousness that seeks suffering and then chooses which one to shoulder; rather, it is a mystical approach to the reality that comes from the passive experience of being overwhelmed to accept voluntarily the suffering of the downcast and insulted. In Roman Catholicism, such acceptance is often called "sacrifice," which is in my judgment an insufficient term. In what others call "fate," acceptance finds the suffering God and calls her/him "Love," and thus the accepting person becomes a participating subject instead of remaining a mere object of the power of fate. Acceptance deprives icy meaninglessness of its power because it clings to God's warmth also in suffering. In this context, sacrifice does not mean that a God hostile to life and humans has to be placated with blood, or that a saving quality accrues to suffering as such. Rather, that concept expresses the participation of humans who do not acquiesce but who, in mystical defiance, insist through their suffering that nothing become lost. It is in this sense that in 1930, twelve years before her death in Auschwitz, Edith Stein spoke of the *holocaustum*, what the Bible calls the complete sacrifice, when she thought about her attempts to reach half-hearted or unbelieving people with her words. "After every meeting in which the impossibility of influencing someone is palpably present to me, the urgency of my own *holocaustum* becomes even more intense."[32] And, at the end of 1938, when several of her siblings had already emigrated from Germany—all others were subsequently murdered by the Nazis—she reflected on the name she took as a nun, Theresa Benedicta of the Holy Cross: "To me the cross means the fate of God's people that was beginning to make itself felt even then. I thought that they who understood that it was the cross of Christ would take it upon themselves in the name of all."[33]

To think of Auschwitz as a continuation of Golgotha is horrendous for a Jewish mind. I became personally aware of this during a conversation with Wanda Kampmann, a historian, whose book *Deutsche und Juden* (Germans and Jews) appeared in 1963. I said at the time that Christ had been gassed in Auschwitz; she could not stand that way of speaking. I was startled and felt ashamed, for I really believed—and still do—that Christ cannot be understood and loved without seeing the ongoing crucifixion done to his sisters and brothers. On the other hand, I had the feeling that in uttering it I was betraying this truth. Today I understand better the dread of a Christian co-optation of an event that needs its own language, the Jewish language, and that has found it in many forms. I will not cease to question critically the silence of dominant Christian theology that does not wish to see Christ's ongoing suffering in the Shoah. In that sense, Edith Stein remains a mystical-theological teacher of "what it means to be betrothed to the Lord in the sign of the cross. Admittedly, one will never comprehend it because it is a mystery."[34]

The craziness of Edith Stein may well be compared to that of the French woman Simone Weil and perhaps be expressed in Reinhold Schneider's pointed formulation that identifies agony *(Agonie)* and numbness *(Narkose)* as the options open to us in the face of suffering. This expresses a basic conflict that applies to every mysticism of suffering of the past and present century. The conflict consists of the contradiction between the avoidance of suffering, not-having-seen and not-wanting-to-see anything, and seeking to protect oneself with the diverse and increasingly improving means of numbing, on the one hand; and the preferential option for victims wherein people voluntarily enter into the pain of others and, in the extreme case, choose the pain of death, on the other. "Numbness" is a metaphor for apathy, "agony" one for compassio.[35]

Simone Weil, too, chose agony before numbness. Rarely did a modern intellectual human being so passionately, absurdly, pathologically resist every alleviation of pain, every social privilege, and every right to numbing as she did. It is said that when she was a child and was helping her parents move to another place, she found out that her burden was lighter than her brother's. She refused to walk any further until she was given a heavier load. In a certain sense, she did the same throughout her whole short life.

Like Edith Stein, she occupied herself intensively with the study of John of the Cross. Like him, she desired to overcome her natural dependency, especially on nourishment and healthcare but also the dependency on the reason that has to be subjected to faith, in favor of an inner emptiness that renders one open to God. Her concept for the dark night of the world is *malheur* (meaning not only unhappiness or sorrow, but affliction, a condition compounded of pain and distress). It emerged for her in the context of the factory job that she held for one year while studying at the training college for secondary school teachers in Paris, interrupted by her medically unexplained excruciating migraine headaches. That self-chosen experiment, rooted in her trade union and socialist engagement, gave her a sense of what it means to live without dignity and rights.

On June 26, 1935, while on a bus, she recorded in her factory diary certain feelings that were to become everyday reality for Jews in Germany. "How can a slave like me get on this bus and use it just like everyone else for a payment of twelve centimes? What uncommon advantage! Were I told to get off because such convenient means of transportation were not there for me to use and to go on foot instead, I believe that I would find that quite natural. Slavery has utterly deprived me of the feeling that I have any rights. It seems like sheer grace to experience moments when I do not have to experience human brutality."[36] *Malheur* (a totalization of suffering) causes people to become deadened and to give up on themselves as well as to be unable to resist or accept suffering. During her time at the factory, "the affliction *(malheur)* of others penetrated [my very] flesh and soul. . . . The mark of slavery was stamped on me forever, like that mark of shame that the Romans branded with a hot iron on the foreheads of their most despised slaves. Ever since, I have regarded myself as a slave."[37]

The manifold attempts of self-sacrifice in Simone Weil's life have to be understood from this radical perspective from below, from that of the victims of history. She worked like a Trojan in factory and farm. She took part in the Spanish Civil War on the side of the anti-Fascists. She advanced the idea of frontline nurses who would give aid at the very places of death, only to be ridiculed by Charles de Gaulle. She joined a parachute action in France so that she might fight in the underground. In the end, she died as a consequence of eating only as much as was apportioned to Jews who had been left in France—a hunger ration she had imposed on herself as a token of her solidarity with them. "When you, steadfastly clinging to love, sink to the point where you can no longer suppress the cry, 'My God, why have you forsaken me?' but then hold out there without ceasing to suffer, you will finally touch something that is no longer affliction *(malheur)* and not joy either, but the pure, supra-sensual, most inward essential being common to both joy and suffering."[38] Simone Weil did indeed despise numbness; in agony she cried out to God rather than do without such cries. She did not regard Christianity as a "supernatural remedy for suffering"; miracles or punishments or interventions of supernatural power have no place whatsoever in her thinking. She insisted that Christianity's greatness lies in that it seeks what she called a supernatural use for suffering. In her work, as in the book of Job, *malheur* (this "inconsolable bitterness") and the love of God are juxtaposed, but that is something that she is not conscious of, given her inherited Christian anti-Judaism.

This mystically experienced oneness of joy and suffering shines forth from the agony present in many experiences of suffering free of numbness. It is an inconsolability that stays steadfastly in the love for God. "To love God, beyond the destruction of Troy and Carthage and without consolation. Love is not consolation. It is light."[39] Those sentences were written prior to Auschwitz. Are they still valid after Auschwitz?

"Inconsolability" is a concept that Heinrich Böll endeavored to introduce into the discussion of aesthetics.[40] Dietrich Bonhoeffer

(1906–1945) expressed the basic idea in his well-known poem "Christians and Pagans" and did so with great Protestant simplicity. It is not hopelessness or despair or consolation in the sense of a present or future abolition of suffering but, in the first instance, a holding firmly onto agony against every possibility of escaping into numbness. "Christians stand with God in God's suffering." From the initial situation of seeking help from God ("pleading for help, praying for fortune and bread") that is common to pagans and Christians and which Bonhoeffer would have called "the religion of those not come of age," the way of discipleship leads to "being dragged into the messianic suffering of God in Jesus Christ" in which human beings share in God's impotence. "This is the very reversal of everything the religious person expects from God. Humans are called to share in God's suffering, to suffer with God the godlessness of the world."[41] Such an understanding of suffering—both "of age" and mystical—is close to that of the Roman Catholic writer Reinhold Schneider (1903–1958), whom one may call a "charismatic in the description of misfortune." In a "time without consolation" Schneider defended himself against his own faith-doubts. "It is much better to die with a burning question on one's heart than with a faith that is not quite honest anymore; better in agony than in numbness."[42] In the Nazi era, he secretly distributed carbon copies of his sonnets. His diary entries, *Winter in Wien* (Winter in Vienna) completed just a few days before his death, connect with this tradition of looking down into the abyss. These entries are, in his words, "soliloquies of outer and inner misery."[43] They testify to the struggle of a Christian with the insuperable night that Schneider interprets as "the cosmic and historical absence of Christ." He tries to fashion a picture of the times in relation to what has come to be known since as "the military-industrial complex."

I became aware of the historical background of his struggle only upon rereading his book in the spring of 1996, as the transports of atomic waste materials rolled through Germany. It was the nuclear pacifism of the fifties that opposed Germany's armed forces being equipped with nuclear weapons. In his Viennese winter, Schneider held discussions with atomic physicist Otto Hahn and futurist Robert Jungk and knew that "today's most significant research is made 'on the orders' of His majesty the atom."[44] The protest of the academics and researchers known as the Göttingen Eighteen of 1957 gave rise to the movement "War on nuclear death." The plan to arm West Germany with nuclear weapons was stopped at the time but the hope to separate science from militarism failed. "Who is there who does not know that the No! of the Eighteen will be countered tomorrow by a Yes! uttered from a thousand throats and that the powers of history have utterly co-opted the labors of the protestors to date?"[45] What Schneider suffered from and thought about goes beyond his life's chief topic, the conflict between conscience and power, that continued to be pondered in Vienna in a certain nostalgia for the Hapsburgs. Science had let go of the alleged neutrality of research and tied itself into the complex that is the dominant twentieth-century power of history. "Research, the apex of the mind, has discovered the goal, namely power, and now runs after it in the same way as power runs after research; we run in a circle of death not knowing what is apex and what is goal."[46]

The convening of a major atomic conference in Vienna and the plan to establish there the "international uranium stock exchange of the world" gives the title of that diary *Winter in Vienna* its double meaning: it is a winter of the mind and the soul. One is astonished by his predictions of subsequent and by now actualized developments. "We have just begun to conquer 'the cosmos as our battleground,' as an American major-general declared in the euphoria of an explorer. For that is our true relation to the cosmos."[47] Of course, the projects for the military exploitation of space continue as before, except that since 1989, the year of the big change, they have been given different names. "We are given assurances that we are making headway in ridding the world of cancer, of the afflictions of time and of our fear of time—and hence of time itself."[48] Here is a prophecy that the globalization of the world's economy during the eighties has fulfilled. "Science will give birth to a tyranny that surpasses the heresy trials."[49] I see this coming true more and more in how human beings and human material is made available to gene technological research even without consent.

A reader of international journals, Schneider assembled with great meticulousness the scientific data of catastrophes, such as strontium 90 in the bones of children,[50] or the tiny, eyeless thieving ants that bleed their victims white to the point of their own death, and of "the self-inflicted death of the urge for life" that he substantiates in numerous examples.[51] By now that kind of hopeless outlook has become commonplace, but Schneider's response is not that of intellectuals who demonstrate their superiority over every protest by showing how much they know about death. Hopelessness is no ritual in Schneider because he opposes it ever and again from his faith stance. "Faith has now only this road left: through the grave; faith's life is the mysterious, subterranean agony and its place the chapel of Christ's fear of death."[52]

However well acquainted he was with the "frightful melancholy of nature" and however clearly he distinguished between the old battlegrounds of history and the "zone of destruction before which we cringe,"[53] he renounced the numbing relief offered by the total privatization of consciousness and held fast in the irresolvable contradiction between what he subsumed in the language of facticity and what, seeking refuge in a church, he prayed for every morning. "Praying beyond faith, against faith, against unfaith, against oneself, everyday the furtive walk of the bad conscience to church—in opposition to oneself and one's knowledge—as long as this imperative is known, grace is present; there is an unfaith that is part of the order of grace."[54] Reinhold Schneider lived in this conscious inconsolability. "It is the entrance to the cosmic and historical absence of Christ, if not even a dimension of it: the place before what is insuperable in the night that is insuperable. Is that experience, coming out of the despair of the cosmos and history, the despair before the cross, the Christianity of today?"[55] This mysticism of suffering reverses the old assertion of consolation: God is always greater than the evil that takes place *(Deus semper maior)* and turns it into the opposite *(Deus semper minor)*. An unresolvable contradiction remains between cognition and prayer for Schneider: Christ "the one who suffers with us on earth . . . is more helpful than the risen one."[56] This is a view that could have come from medieval mysticism of suffering except that it was derived from the contemporary night of the world.

Remaining in inconsolability is a way of listening to "the silent cry." I want to illustrate this by means of an encounter I had during a demonstration against the atomic waste removal transports in 1996. An elderly man stood up after my speech: with passion-filled bitterness he spoke about the twenty years that has been wasted in the resistance against the nuclear enterprise, how illusion followed illusion and false promises only gave way to broken promises, how friendships and trust were destroyed. One defeat after another. Finally he said, "If only there was at least a hint that the development of nuclear energy was to be stopped! We could negotiate about the temporary or final storage of the toxic waste; there could be discussion between superpower and resistance, between the commerce of death and life. The most difficult thing for me is to carry on carrying on in the face of a power that is unbroken and that couldn't care less." I heard "the silent cry" more clearly in those words than elsewhere and saw more sharply the steadfastness in agony without which there can be no resistance. As Reinhold Schneider put it, "Our task would be to set the faith of powerlessness against the unfaith in power."[57] The old man at our demonstration did not put this mysticism into words, but his remaining in inconsolability was a genuine *mystique vécue* (a lived-out mysticism of suffering).

9. COMMUNITY

To live like a tree, single and free and
in brotherliness among the trees of the forest
that is our dream.

NAZIM HIKMET

The Hidden Sacred Sparks: Hasidism

THE SIMPLE DESIRE OF HUMAN BEINGS to live "like a tree, single and free" took the Turkish poet Nazim Hikmet (1902–1963) into the resistance, into exile, and finally into a twelve-year prison sentence in Turkey, which broke his health. He wrote the poem "Das ist unser Land" (This Is Our Country) in prison. Before and after his imprisonment, he lived for long periods in Moscow; perhaps the emphasis on the words "single" and "free" is in relation to conditions there. The relation of tree to forest, of individuality to sociality, of *liberté* to *fraternité,* is proposed ever afresh while, at the same time, it is a perennially new mystical dream.

The concepts of mysticism and community exist in a complex tension one to the other. Irrevocably, the principle of individuation seems to be a precondition for the way inward. "God and the soul, the soul and God" that is what the great liberal theologian, Adolf von Harnack, in line with Augustine, referred to as the heart of religion. Why should it not serve to depict the experience of something that, when it happens, focuses individuals on themselves? As a mass phenomenon, mysticism of personal experience often strikes us as ludicrous and sometimes repulsive. Reports from fourteenth-century monasteries, telling of "the whole company of sisters going into rapture during the liturgy and the entire convent lying dead-like on the chancel floor or convulsed with laughter or weeping,"[1] rather reinforce the necessity for solitude.

Collective mysticism evokes fear: from the medieval processions of flagellants after the outbreak of the plague to the torchlight march-pasts of the Nazis and the collective frenzy in our football stadiums or rock concerts. Yet, at least in premodern forms of every mysticism, there is found a desire to live a common life that is different. A

157

simplistic distinction between the enlightened individual and the blind masses does not resolve what is at the heart of that desire. The group, the congregation, the federation, and the community of a movement each represent a different order of togetherness. That is what has often protected individual members, at times even assuring their survival. In addition however, every community has an inward-directed significance, envisaged as the "more" that makes the whole greater than the sum of its parts.

What does an individual need the community for? In what spiritual sense? In premodern times the question hardly posed itself in this way. In modernity it has frequently been answered negatively: "If only I have him, if he is mine alone. . . ." This manifests pietistic individual religiosity that needs no togetherness. But isolating the individual is intolerable to mystical thinking where God is always joined to the individual being. In such thinking this God needs the community even when the I imagines that it can become whole without the community. If, according to Eckhart, God is "of all the most communicable," then being-in-God, including our suffering of God, cannot be privately appropriated and enshrined into the purely personal happening. The communication Eckhart alludes to is related less to, but is not exclusive of, collective experience. It is focused more on the exchange following the experience, that is, the unending endeavor to bring mystical experience into language. Self-enclosed inwardness of the soul, boasting that "nobody really understands me" (and drawing the ire of as early a writer as that of *The Cloud of Unknowing*) is insufficient. When it comes to fulfilling what is really signified by "I am what I do," it is as inadequate as an all too self-sufficient self-realization. Community, like the attempt by the "Sisters and Brothers of the Common Life" to begin something new, is a conscious renunciation of solitude with God. The experience of inner strength and the assurance of fulfillment seek to communicate themselves. Good power is that which distributes itself and makes others strong; "power is empowerment" is true also of mystical power.

This was understood particularly by mystics who legitimated themselves not merely by the mysticism of their personal experience but by developing a reflective or narrative understanding of the experienced cognition of God. When my consciousness expands, my knowledge deepens and my being changes. A process is just beginning at the conclusion of which there is much more than the salvation and illumination of individual souls. Genuine mysticism, in this context understood as revolutionary mysticism, goes beyond the spiritual egoism that shapes so many esoteric scenes. Genuine mysticism goes out into the ongoing creation of the world in which we participate. As Jewish mysticism teaches: the world can be redeemed, and it is not merely that individual souls are saved out of it. Mystical participation in redemption unites the individuals who work on it, but who do so without being able to effect it.

Nowhere is this element of community seen so clearly and so unmistakably as in the Eastern Jewish movement of Hasidism. It can be perceived as a uniquely nonelitist Jewish "mysticism for the masses." According to Hasidic teaching, nothing in the world is unworthy to God for revealing Godself to the human being who is truly searching for God. The Hasidic understanding of salvation is defined in terms of what the Lurian Kabbalah calls "the sacred sparks" that need to be discovered and then liberated by means of ordinary, everyday deeds. The Hasidic person proves God's love in all creatures, yes, in all things. According to Martin Buber, salvation consists in the world being hallowed.

It is in this sense that the founder of Hasidism, the Ba'al Shem Tov (1699–1760), fetched the Kabbalah down from the angels and placed it securely into the hands of simple folk, who live in *devekut* (in constant communion with God) and, in their everyday life, make this affiliation with God's will visible. Every *tzaddik* (leader of the religious community) has a spark of Moses within, or as Rabbi Dov Baer put it around the year 1770, "the *tzaddikim* have made God to be their unconscious part, if one may say so."[2]

The Hasidic renewal movement took place during one of the worst periods of Jewish history in Eastern Europe. Weakened by Cossack uprisings and wars, Poland blocked Jews from the more profitable trades: mining and leasing ore and salt mines, custom and taxation lease holding, and the purchase of property in the countryside. Jewish freedom and their rights to choose their livelihood were restricted to manual labor; at times their right to residence was curtailed. This is the background to the rise of the Hasidic movement in which impoverished and intimidated people came together and formed communities.

Friendship is a key concept in Hasidism and, at the same time, a defense against the isolation and loneliness forced on them by government, aristocracy, and anti-Semitic clergy. The exhausted and unlearned villagers discovered anew how to articulate that they belonged to God's people, Israel. Whatever we know of the Ba'al Shem Tov, surrounded as he is with fables and rumors, he did change the atmosphere and quality of Jewish life in hundreds of villages and small towns. In the midst of their own miserable circumstances of life, Jews began to remember their origins and, in effect, their dignity and learned to see hope in their own tradition. The sacred sparks, hidden within animals and tools, in speech and in silence, as well as in work, seek to be "raised up to their source"[3] through the action of the pious. The hallowing that results is also pure; in Eckhart's sense of *sunder warumbe*, it is action with no ulterior motive. "Pay heed that whatever you do for the sake of God be itself in service of God" reads one of the instructions given by the Ba'al Shem Tov concerning our dealings with God. All action must be "purpose-less" *(weiselos)*, direct to God. "Concerning food: do not say it is the purpose of eating that you may gain strength for the service of God. That is itself not a bad purpose but true fulfillment comes only when the deed is done itself for heaven, for that is where the sacred sparks are fashioned."[4]

Merchants, shopkeepers, dry-goods makers, rabbis, coachmen, and clowns are figures around whom this mysticism of everyday life dramatized itself and turned into narrative. It did so with a fascinatingly consistent disdain for the modern division of life into sacred and profane spheres. This piety is interested neither in the practice of asceticism nor in forsaking the world; everything happens within the everyday realities of eating and sleeping, working and dancing, teaching and learning. Mutual sharing of consolation, community, and prayer are basic elements that, indeed, do not ignore the other radical modern separation of individuality and sociality, given the fact that the narratives always deal with highly individualistic men, but they overcome it. The fact that women are nearly unseen and unheard in that Hasidic world is an absurd contradiction to this communal nearness to everyday life.

A favorite Hasidic image for the community is the ladder. Occasionally, the *tzaddik* is perceived as the ladder. More often, however, every person of higher or lower estate is pictured as one of the rungs. This should not be interpreted in terms of a hierarchical power arrangement. Instead, it is a repudiation of spiritual arrogance of every sort and it signifies the humility of equals. Communion with God means that every person gives and takes, teaches and learns. No one is dispensable on this ladder and lifelong learning is as normal as breathing.

It is told of the Ba'al Shem Tov that once he stood deeply immersed in silent prayer while all his friends had already finished their prayers. They waited a long time for him but finally, in order to conduct their business, they left the house of prayer. Returning after several hours they found him still in prayer. Because of that "painful separation," he told them the parable of a glorious many-colored bird of most rare beauty. The bird alighted on the top of the tallest tree. According to the *Zohar*, the bird is an image of the Messiah. The king of the land—an image of God—ordered the bird to be fetched down; several thousand persons gathered under the tree and made a ladder. One climbed up onto the shoulders of another until the last one, at the top, could reach the nest. "It took a long time to build this living ladder. Those who stood nearest the ground lost patience, shook themselves free, and everything collapsed."[5] In this image of the ladder, everyone is a participant who can work for the Messiah's coming only together with everyone else. The king's will is not yet fulfilled.

Community, the Sinai of the Future: An Examination of Buber's Relation to Mysticism

Community is a place where in togetherness a ladder is built and divine sparks are fashioned and become visible. But is community really a dimension of mysticism? Is mysticism itself not altogether profoundly formed by personal experience, by a religiosity that perceives itself as something quite individual, often in decided contrast to religious institutions and establishments? Are mystical love for God and formation of community not mutually exclusive?

My awareness of the problems raised in connection with this question grew as I discovered contradictions in the thought of Martin Buber, the one from whom I have learned ever so much concerning both mysticism and community. The more Jewish he became, the more he distanced himself from mysticism, once a subject of great enthusiasm for him. I try now to portray his way of thinking in three phases that I identify with his own concepts of "ecstasy," "I and Thou," and "community."

Before World War I, Buber published *Ecstatic Confessions* (German edition, 1909), an anthology of mystical writings. In his introduction to it, he described ecstasy as mystical experience, as lifting the individual above the divided and individualized world of "commotion" (see chapter 2). This personal primordial experience of "rapture, illumination, ecstasy" may be seen as something "timeless, without consequences" and also basically asocial, as Buber noted later in his life.[6] This critical approach to mysticism and his incipient abandonment of it became evident in remarks Buber made during the First German Conference of Sociologists, in October 1910, in response to Ernst Troeltsch.

As a theologian and sociologist, Troeltsch (1865–1923) had a strong interest in the historical elucidation of the idea of community in Christianity. Social ethics seemed to him to be at least as relevant as individual religion. Where these two intersect is where he researched social movements inspired by mysticism. Buber asked Troeltsch whether mysticism was a sociological category at all, or whether it should be viewed instead as "religious solipsism." "It also seems to me that mysticism negates community—mysticism does not struggle with any organized community, nor does it set itself up as a counter-community, as a sect would. Instead, mysticism negates community, precisely because for mysticism there is only one relation, the relation to God. . . . The [mystic] remains thoroughly isolated in his belief *[Gläubigkeit]*, for nothing else matters to him than to be alone with his God."[7] Troeltsch's attempt to perceive of mysticism and community conjoined is what Buber rejects, signaling already his subsequent antimystical turn. A personal experience in 1914 marks his separation from a purely religious, individual mysticism free of the world. "It was nothing unusual that happened. One morning, after a period of 'religious' enthusiasm, I received the visit of a young person unknown to me. My soul was not in it. I showed no less friendly openness than I normally do . . . but I failed to guess the question that he did not articulate."[8] Only later, after the young man's death, would Buber learn of the crisis his visitor had been experiencing. Years later he reflected on that visit in an essay entitled "A Conversion" *(Eine Bekehrung)* from the mysticism of religious experience to the turn towards the Thou: "Since then, I have left behind that kind of 'religiousness' which is nothing more than an exception, a matter of being taken away, of stepping outside, or ecstasy, or else it has left me behind. I possess no more than the everydayness from which I am never taken away. Mystery no longer opens itself, it has withdrawn or it has taken up residence here where everything happens as it happens."[9] The mildly ironic sentences beginning with "or else" indicate that the renunciation of mysticism or religiousness is not final and complete.

In place of the juxtaposition of ecstasy and commotion there is the "I and Thou" (published as a book with that title in 1923), which represents the dialogical thinking that for Buber had long prepared itself in the Jewish-Hasidic context. What matters is not the individual, elevated, qualitatively unique religious experience, but the life of religion in the world's everydayness. After completing his two-volume work *Tales of the Hasidim* (1927, English edition 1947–48) he discusses the question of Hasidic piety with the reticence—well known to me—characteristic of all who cannot embrace the customary separations and questions concerning what is worldly or godly, profane or sacred, ethical or religious, theological or political.

> Is *Hasidut* to be called piety?
> Earthliness I came to learn from it.
> Is it to be called goodness and mildness?
> You have woven it too firmly into time.
> Close to heaven, it is close to commotion,
> thus I render it "love for all that is."[10]

This Hasidic closeness "to commotion" perhaps best expressed Buber's separation from his early phase. His rootedness in reality is expressed in that aspect. Dialogical thinking does not consist of an ahistorical togetherness of I and Thou unrelated to community, as has sometimes been erroneously believed, but of the concreteness of commonality, as Buber found it in Hasidic tradition. Philosophically he formulated it as a sociality that is rooted in language itself, in being addressed and giving response. Only in sociality does the subject become subject. "What help is it to my soul that it can be transported again from this world into that unity *[Einheit]*, when this world has, of necessity no share whatever in that unity—what does all 'enjoyment of God' profit a life rent in two?"[11] The ecstatic union the soul experiences is not denied in I and Thou but is examined in relation to its consequences. Is that union "concentration of all forces" attentive to actual reality or mere immersion that "wants to preserve only what is 'pure', essential, and enduring, while stripping away everything else. . . ."?[12] Does it mean preparation for the engagement with the world or "sufficient satisfaction" with the I that immerses itself?[13]

If mysticism means fleeing from this world, leaving history, society and community behind, then Buber is no longer a mystic since his move towards dialogical thinking. When life's fulfillment is sought in experiences that exclude every form of community, as Buber elucidates it in connection with Aldous Huxley and his mescaline-induced states of euphoria, then the individual renounces the "commonality" that is given to us in language, dialogue, word, response, and responsibility. In such forms of mysticism, language and creation are negated. "The 'chemical holidays' of which Huxley speaks are holidays not only from the small I enmeshed in the commotion of its purposes, but also from the person participating in the commonality of logos and cosmos."[14] In this sense, a living community like the Hasidic one "explodes the customary understanding of mysticism."[15] But in those harsh dissociations, Buber perhaps hung on to more mysticism than he was prepared to admit. He critiqued otherworldliness and flight from the world, spiritual egoism, and a kind of gnostic intellectualization of religion. But it is precisely in the this-worldliness wherein God encounters us in unpredictable ways that the purpose-free God of mysticism lives. In the emphasis of the very now, wherein God desires nothing but pure attention to the now, lies the mystical understanding of time as present. Buber never believed in the orthodox ideas of God's revelation in Scripture and tradition alone. He knew that no symbol is adequate for God and that the life between one human being and another can itself become a symbol for God. He was critical of any mysticism that finds God wherever people leave behind the world with its temptation to hoard possessions. He saw a bigger mystical task in remaining in the world and resisting within the world the urge to possess both things and power.

In every religion, Buber sees a confrontation between *gnosis*, which he critically labels as "know-it-all," and *devotio*, a dedication and piety that manifests itself as "service of the divine, understood as an opposite *(Gegenüber)* and presented as such ever and again."[16] "The gnostic cannot serve and does not want to serve."[17] Devotio, on the contrary, can extend as far as self-sacrifice in martyrdom. Hasidism helped Buber to oppose false mysticism and opened him to a true, democratic mysticism of everyday life. It took from the Kabbalah only "what it needs for the theological foundation of an enthusiastic and unexalted life in responsibility, the responsibility all individuals bear for the part of the world entrusted to them. . . . The holy manifests itself now not in the seclusion of ascetics and their schools but in the joy the masters and their congregations find in one another."[18] In philosophical terms, Buber developed the I-Thou relation in the direction of "commonality" through an interpretation of a statement by Heraclitus about *koinón* (the community organized on a legal basis). The understanding of community grew from the personal over-against-ness *(Gegenüber)* of the I-Thou relation. In what is linguistically awkward, perhaps as a result of the damage sustained by the word "community" at the hands of the Nazis, Buber searches for the "essential We," the "true We" that he sets apart from the collectivism contained in the pronoun "one." "Only humans who are capable of truly saying 'you' to one another can truly say 'we' together."[19] And in this "we", he perceives "the directness . . . that is the decisive precondition of the I-Thou relation."[20] Community cannot seal itself off in self-transfiguration for it is always oriented toward actualization, the building up of God's community, the new beginning. In this sense, speaking with the Buber of 1919, "true community [is] the Sinai of the future."[21]

I want to elucidate what is meant here by mysticism in terms of an experience I had during a large peace demonstration. After repeated sneering questions by journalists as to what we handful of people thought we could accomplish, I became angry and said something like this in my speech in Bonn. "We are not only we. We are many more. The dead of both World Wars are here with us. They are still waiting for the life that the apparatus against that we are marching here took away from them. They belong to us and not to the venerators of war memorials. They help us to hold our places here."

Without Rules and Poor, Persecuted, and Free: The Beguines

Coming into being at the end of the twelfth century and flourishing for nearly two centuries, the Beguine movement is one of the rarest examples of a mystically inspired new form of life created by women for women. Together with the mendicant orders of the Franciscans and Dominicans, it forms part of the emergence of poverty movements. It embodies the search for a lifestyle different from a piety that makes itself known as enthusiasm, as "ardor" and charismatic experience, but it also distances itself deliberately from the church's hierarchy. Marguerite Porète spoke aptly of this movement as Sainte Église la Petite (the Little Holy Church) (see chapter 7). The Beguines put into place new forms of common life and self-administered commonality that connected with the traditions of monastic life through the commitment to celibacy and poverty. However, their new forms maintained a different relation to the world and a different independence in their lifestyle as female laypersons. One might almost call this independence "autonomy"; but, given the unbroken, deep piety of this women's movement, the better word for it is "theonomy." That mystical directness to God does, indeed, foster a greater need for autonomy for both individuals and groups is made evident by this medieval women's movement: in an ocean of patriarchal, hierarchically directed injustice, the Beguines created islands of freedom for women. The revolution that occurred there was spiritual. It refused to bow down to the world's secularity in relation to sexuality and property, as well as creating a new way of life that also found new forms of expressing the inner life in language and ritual.

There were an estimated one million Beguines, or 3 to 4 percent of the female population. The movement spread rapidly in Holland, the Rhine region, France, and Switzerland, carried chiefly by women from the lower nobility and the urban patriciate. When joining a Beguine community, it was not necessary to make the gift of a dowry: the very opposite to entering a monastery or, even more so, a marriage. In the twelfth and thirteenth centuries, there was a surplus of unmarried women. Many men chose male communities of the religious orders or the priesthood; others, as apprentices and journeymen, were forbidden to marry and remained single well into their thirties. Hence many women could not marry. It is more important, however, to understand how many women, especially those with mystical sensibilities, did not wish to marry at any price. To them marriage appeared to doom them to horror: the incessant sequence of births, the dependency on the husband who had the right to administer corporal punishment, and the absence of economic self-determination that was changed only occasionally for widows. But above all it meant the exclusion of women from education and spiritual development, a fate that many young women tried to elude only to face dramatic conflicts with their parents. To cite just one example: at age nine, in order to escape marriage, Ida von Nijvel (1198–1231) ran away from her home, holding only her Psalter in hand, and sought refuge with the Beguines.[22]

In small groups numbering three to twelve sisters, these women could live a happier, more pious, contemplative, and also self-determined life. The community offered them the protection that a single woman living alone could not expect to find elsewhere and a different lifestyle that made room for common worship and for prayer and some education. Beguines who had enjoyed a certain amount of education—it often excluded Latin—advanced the reading of Scripture in the vernacular; they preached and taught, they gave counsel and pastoral care to other women.[23] So it was that the community that offered shelter was, as with the Hasidim, also a community of learning.

Several stages may be distinguished in the two centuries of Beguine history.[24] The first spontaneous development is rooted in the religious awakening and the search for a deeper spirituality that had arisen in the new urban centers of Western Europe and Italy. Women wanted to live lives dedicated to God and to religion but outside the traditional existence of vows or rules. Not all of them ruled out marriage, nor did they want to withdraw from the world. They wanted to find their preferred way of life within the culture of the city, as an alternative to marriage and monastery.

Beguines lived in their own homes or in those of friends or relatives. The door of the house displayed a white cross as a mark of identification. The women wore simple dress and a wide-brimmed hat. In many places they earned their livelihood by manual labor such as baking bread, brewing beer, making candles, spinning, weaving, and sewing in the emerging clothing industry. Other tasks included caring for the sick and dying and burying the dead. Many Beguines also joined together under the unofficial direction of monks or clerics sympathetic to their aims. There were no community rules and no perpetual or long-term vows.

The unmarried, the married, and widowed lived together in chastity and poverty. Every household developed its own form of spiritual life, prayer, spiritual exercises, and silence. But as the movement became greater and more familiar, the absence of ecclesial supervision and official approval by the hierarchy proved threatening. If the Beguines healed the sick, they could very well also be witches. If they read mystical tracts or even copied them, they could well be suspected of heresy. If they were nonresidents, going up and down the countryside begging, there could well be danger that they might join the many currents of the radical heretics especially since the Waldensians, Cathari, and Bogomils practiced a relative equality of women. Or it was assumed, not always without foundation, that nonresident Beguines supported themselves by working the streets.

Beguines in settled forms of existence found the support of the Cistercian order, in particular in one of their passionate advocates and protectors, the Dutch priest Jacob von Vitry (ca. 1165–1240), who later was made a cardinal. In 1233, a papal bull, "Gloriam virginalem," indirectly recognized the houses and communities of the Beguines. This initiated a development that brought the Beguines more and more under clerical control and organization. Many houses were forced to adopt a modified rule and to submit to ecclesial supervision of their spiritual life. Their erstwhile freedom to choose the priest who cared for them was curtailed. Nevertheless, the Beguines' lifestyle and their new forms of manual labor still differed markedly from those of monastic tradition. Officially Beguines continued to be treated as female lay people in the local parish.

The municipal authorities regarded their houses as purely female communes and granted certain privileges, such as protection and dispensation from taxes, as long as they put themselves under clerical authority, often of the Dominicans. And yet in the early decades of the fourteenth century, a wave of persecution befell the Beguines and the numerically much smaller male groups of the Beghards. It attacked especially the itinerant Beguines but also suspected many of the resident women of heresy. Suspicion was cast on the entire movement of poverty and freedom of the spirit that had its mystical foundation in the belief of the sinlessness of the soul that is immersed in God and thus needs no acts of virtue nor the church's mediation of grace. This suspicion and its concomitant hounding and smear campaign among the population had its effect on the Beguines, who may be regarded as the "comparably freest" of the orthodox groups of women.[25] But even a relatively orthodox mysticism is never void of consequences and their independent conduct of life proved risky for the Beguines.

Governed by no ordering rule, poor, persecuted and free: that is how one may describe these communities in which many of the greatest women mystics, such as Mechthild von Magdeburg (see chapter 4), Marie d' Oignies, Hadewijch of Brabant, lived and found homes. At the heart of their community is an anarchistic leaning. Individual freedom is respected in every dimension, even in their architecture. Beguine settlements were surrounded by protective walls, fenced off by moats and gates, and incorporated many small and quite diverse apartments. Beguines also had a certain anarchist tendency, sometimes described among scholars as feminine, to regard institutional structures as secondary and for having little enthusiasm for handling the organizational formalities of a group. Women moved from one community to the next and changed in and out from family life to a Beguine community or a nunnery. Many of them could not be tied down by a permanent affiliation. In his poem "Beguinage Sainte Elizabeth, Bruges," Rilke discerned this aspect clearly: "The high gate seems to hold none back, / the bridge leads gladly in and out."[26] One notices even in the chroniclers of that time how hard they try to present a founding narrative of the Beguines, to identify their principals, and to clarify what their order of life was. It hardly occurred to those writers that there may indeed be informal arrangements that give ordinary life religious meaning. What is fascinating is precisely this informality: it is a surplus of freedom, of "being without" (*ledig*) in the mystical sense of the word. Communal life in this sense may make one a participant in what Eckhart calls "purposelessness" (*Weiselosigkeit*). "I am confirmed in naked divinity, in which never an image nor form existed. . . . as long as the good person lives in time, his soul has a constant progression in eternity. That is why good people cherish life."[27] These sentences by Sister Katrei of Strasbourg, from the dialogue with her confessor, are erroneously attributed to Meister Eckhart. Katrei was an itinerant and mendicant Beguine who in 1317 was prohibited from participating in the sacraments. It is not known why and what happened to her thereafter. That "good people cherish life" in common is true for the many women whose names have not been handed on. According to Rilke, Beguines "go to church in order to understand better / why there is so much love in them."[28]

The Society of Friends and the Inner Light

If there exists a modern, living embodiment of communal mysticism, it is the Society of Friends, known more popularly by the originally derisive name of Quakers, given them soon after their foundation. This name came into usage because, during their silent devotions or their spontaneous, unprepared speeches, Friends, moved by the Spirit, would sometimes begin to quake. In 1668, some 60,000 followers of the "Inner Light" in England formed a loose association—a Christian religion without dogma, without church buildings, and without paid clergy. For three reasons I find this religious society modern, reasons that differentiate Quakers substantively from many other splinter groups and esoteric sects. Firstly, Quakers are mystics who orient their mysticism to the here and now in a this-worldly way. Secondly, they are not organized hierarchically but democratically, and thirdly, they live their faith in an everyday political praxis of freedom from violence in any form whatsoever.

A student spoke of her first visit to a Quaker house for worship; a friend had asked her to come. The people sat in silence on rows of wooden benches facing one another. After ten minutes, having become nervous, she asked when the service would begin. The answer came in a whisper, "it has already begun." The visitor waited for the minister to enter, but everyone else was sitting there so calmly and peacefully that she no longer dared to ask again. This lasted about forty minutes. Then one of the participants stood up and spoke. The student was surprised that the minister had been present all along. When he sat down, a woman got up and spoke. By now the visitor was utterly confused; there were a few more minutes of silence and then everyone began to greet all the others. The meeting was over. "Where was the minister?" the visitor asked her friend, who burst out laughing.

Gradually the student understood that every woman and man present at worship are what elsewhere are called the clergy and that the gathered silence was the worship of God. She learned that this is less a new teaching but much more a new way of living that has its foundation in what Quakers have called for three hundred years "waiting for the Lord." It is practiced in silence. This silent waiting is their worship of God, a mystical preparation. In this preparation, often the many cares and worries or life's fears are uttered first; at times the false longing for the idol that will finally turn stones into bread are also named. But silence also creates a calm leading into an emptiness into which the strength that is not one's own can enter. The biblical expression of waiting enunciates this silence, which initially means no more than openness. "But they who wait for the Lord shall renew their strength, they shall mount up with wings like eagles, they shall run and not be weary, they shall walk and not faint" (Isa 40:31). Quakers have made a connection between this waiting and the mystical presence of God (*praesentia Dei*). They have not hoped for a miracle worker or another world beyond but for their personal participation in the redemption of all, for their own liberation from fears and conventions, constraints and lack of courage, in a word, for their "wings."

At the beginning of this mysticism there is communal silence. The friends gather together in silence, uniting themselves and one another with silence. It is not a matter of individual meditation that coincidentally takes place in the context of a group. By turning inward, all attune themselves to one another. The silence of Quaker devotion replaces Protestantism's customary sermon, the well-phrased words of which would only disturb the silence in which I learn to listen. The sacraments are not needed because the conduct of life itself is a sacrament.

Some months later, the young woman whose bewilderment I described experienced the togetherness in communal silence and wrote about it: "After about half an hour, I came to be present to myself and, at the same time, entered into relation with the other members of the meeting. I felt myself to be in communion with them; in a deep sense, I felt a kind of love for them and being loved by them. What was peculiar about this experience was that I had never met some of the people present at the meeting. And yet, I had the feeling that I knew them profoundly and that they were profoundly aware of me. In fact, a woman offered up a spoken contribution and referred directly to a problem that weighed heavily on my heart. This moment of my life was an experience I would call God, an especially sacred moment in my life. Then I tried to integrate it into the other aspects of my life, as a sort of example, by expanding the possibility of such right relations to everyone else around me." What for many is an extraordinary esoteric experience, available only to the few, is for Quakers a normative reality of mystical life. It is the "inner light" that Quakers seek to involve in every devotion, in every business meeting, and in every new day. "The true light that enlightens everyone was coming into the world" says the Gospel of John, which is particularly valued (John 1:9). The light represents the ongoing activity of the Spirit in every human being. In terms of another, often used expression, it is "that of God" in every human being.

Quakers do not use the traditional image of the little spark in the soul *(scintilla animae)*, which plays an important role particularly in Eckhart, even though this "spark" is exactly what George Fox and others expressed rather clumsily in the phrase "that of God in you." It is God's analog in the human being, eternal and uncreated, an ontological relation of the soul to God. Perhaps they were concerned that the notion of the spark, or the little spark, might mean that the light is divided, one part in one person, another part in another. But there is only one light and the closer we come to it, the closer we are to one another, using Plotinus's image of the center and the rays.[29]

George Fox (1624–1691), a man whom Walter Nigg called a "Don Quixote of religion," was an inflammatory enthusiast in puritanical times. When he was twenty-three years old, he saw the inner light in a vision. For him it symbolized the spirit against the letter, silence against chatter, experience against dogma, and equality against all who build inequality on authority and power, be it of the state or religion. His mistrust of the official Anglican Church was immense. He spoke with disdain of the "towered houses" and was tormented by the ringing of church bells. He frequently interrupted preachers, standing in the church's doorway, a hat covering his head, and uttering threatening words toward the pulpit, causing great excitement in the gathered congregation. It often resulted in Fox being beaten up, banished, and, later on, jailed for years. What aroused his ire, above all, were the priests who, without ever having experienced or even looked for illumination, presented themselves as servants of God but, in truth, comprised a "society of cannibals." It is "not enough to have been educated in Oxford or Cambridge in order to become capable for and efficient in the service of Christ."[30] To this day it is difficult for many Friends to speak of "Quaker theology." The Friends believe in Scripture—George Fox knew it by heart—but they also believe that the Spirit transcends Scripture and that the inner light is experienced by all human beings without human mediation. "The inner light," "the inward teacher" are names that the early Quakers gave to their experiences of the Spirit. They believe that everyone can meet the "Christ within," even though he has different names in different ages and places and is not tied to any form of religion. This light is open to everyone and, yet, it is not simply the natural light of reason. In a conversation that Fox had with Lord Protector Oliver Cromwell, he vigorously resisted this rational interpretation.[31]

In every human being is "that of God," hidden, eclipsed, often forgotten. Linguistically a clumsy expression at best, "that of God in everyone" is the foundation of human dignity. In addition, it is the admonition to believe in it, to discover it in each and everyone and to respond to it. Fox said, "Walk joyfully on the earth and respond to that of God in every human being."[32]

The belief of Quakers that God is present in everyone finds a clear expression in the practice of treating all people alike. Long before the French Revolution the Friends practiced *egalité* in everyday life. Fox traveled the country, lifted his hat to no one, high or lowly, and addressed everyone on a first-name basis, without title. He saluted no one. American soldiers who had become Quakers were not initially rejected because of their pacifism, but because of their allegedly disrespectful demeanor toward their officers. In the seventies in the United States, I met an old Quaker lady who did not rise to her feet in court and, as a result, was given an additional sentence.

The clearest expression of this egalitarianism, founded in mystical religiosity, is to be found in something that the Reformation had promised but did not keep: the "priesthood of all believers," namely in the question of the role of women. Here one thinks of Margaret Fell (1614–1702), the brilliant woman who toiled with George Fox and later became his marriage partner. In 1667, she published a book titled *Women's Speaking Justified*, in which she provided the basis for the right of women to preach. The basic conviction of Quakers was—and is—that God reveals Godself "without respect of persons." Divine revelation is not reserved for particular groups of people only; social location, biological age, physical strength, property, color of skin, or gender do not have a specific role in God's plan. The clarity with which Margaret Fell attacked the literalistic constraints of biblicism also earned for her years in prison.[33]

The way of Friends may be described as one leading from silence to "that of God in us" and on to "concern." Worship of God becomes truly what it is meant to be when everything that insults the sense of equality and justice is addressed. In the world of feudalism and slavery, of wars and their scientific-technological preparation, in the world where the majority goes hungry and is deprived of rights, Quakers have for three hundred years of their history clung to their mysticism (see also chapters 11 and 13). Their concern is the task that arises from clarity about the will of God and cannot for that reason be refused. It is the task of the meeting to respond to it communally.

Acting as a consequence corresponds to beginning in silence. In the history of Friends, this has again and again led to resistance against state, law, economy, and the military. It is a voluntary resistance, not directed by one's personal interests. Quakers do not resist only because they are black, impoverished, disadvantaged, or afflicted by disability. For those who are not impeded or affected, it is also a dimension of their dignity to regard themselves as "damaged" through the damage and destruction inflicted on others. A mystical understanding of community in this sense presupposes a different sort of globalization in which it is not only war that is repudiated. The causes of war in us ourselves are also opposed.

10. JOY

Such a soul bathes in the sea of love,
that is, in the sea of delight
that streams forth from the Godhead.
It feels no joy for it is joy itself
and bathes and flows in joy
without feeling it.
For it inhabits joy and joy inhabits it.

MARGUERITE PORÈTE

The Mystical Relation to Time: Thich Nhat Hanh

THE INNERMOST PLACE of mystical certainty may be designated in the everyday word "joy." Without feeling, expecting, or, for that matter, missing joy, we cannot talk of God's mystical presence. Happiness, too, spawns presumption and hunger. Those who know no music miss nothing when there is no music; those who know it suffer when there is none. The joy, jubilation, and ecstasy that inhabit the soul for no reason, cause, or purpose change the soul in different ways. Society's distinctions and the roles it prescribes are all muddled up, and the relation to bodiliness and the body's self-expression becomes more intensive. Joy is the ground on which mysticism and aesthetics made connection, for both are in reference to beauty.

But more than this, mystical joy changes our experience of time and, concomitantly, our language. I have already indicated that the different language of mysticism is not a means to take possession of the world but to gather us together in the now (see also chapter 4). The time of mysticism is the time of the pure now, the now that is not distracted. In many worship services of black churches in the United States, I again and again experienced the power of the beseeching "right now," invoked in prayer, hymn, or just silence. Such invocation of the Spirit who is among us "right now," "this very morning," was foreign to someone coming, as I do, from a mystically underdeveloped, chilly Protestantism. The "right now" opened new doors for me. It allowed me to participate with others in a joy that I was bathing in. As Marguerite Porète puts it with great precision, it was a joy that was not simply what one feels "about" something. I hesitate to call it a "service," but the closeness of God in such a gathering is not only hope for a different life where all tears will be wiped away. It is certainly not mere nostalgic recollection of a lost paradise. Recalling the good beginning of life and hoping for its reestablishment are siblings of the pure now, but they cannot take its place.

On the contrary, in the pure now the various dimensions of time wherein we move with fear, scheming, worries, and expectations may become void of their hypnotizing power. There are experiences in which we stop asking "and then?"—a question that functions to trivialize the now, no matter how normal it may sound. On the other hand, a pure, fulfilled present roots us in what is now. This kind of immanent transcendence causes our constructions of time to collapse. Instead of being "anxious" about what we are to eat and to drink, how we are to clothe ourselves (Matt 6:25) or to pass the examination, or where we are to go after a farewell, we stay in the now. Every purpose becomes purposeless and every mediation unmediated. The now of joy is what it is, without reduction to anything else: the now of joy.

There is a different name for this new relationship to time in which we give ourselves unreservedly to the present and thereby are made ready for the joy that is not tied to any object. It is what Buddhists call "attentiveness." A Zen story tells about a man of the people, who one day asked Master Ikkyou whether he would write down a few sentences of the highest wisdom for him. Whereupon Ikkyou took a brush and wrote the word "attentiveness." The man asked whether that was all; would he not write some more? Then Ikkyou wrote the same word again. The man was disappointed and said that he still could perceive neither excellence nor depth in what the Master had written. Now Ikkyou wrote the word a third time. Close to anger the man wondered what that word "attentiveness" was supposed to mean. Ikkyou's answered, "attentiveness means attentiveness."

The quality of attentiveness cannot be produced, even though its preconditions may be practiced and learned. Leaving the tradition of the Western world, I want to refer here to one of the most important current Buddhist teachers living in the West, the Vietnamese Thich Nhat Hanh (b. 1926). I first became aware of him during the Vietnam War, when he was one of the leading representatives of the peace movement. At that time Martin Luther King proposed Nhat Hanh's name for the Nobel Peace Prize. After being exiled, Nhat Hanh went to Paris. As a Zen master and teacher of meditation, he founded the Buddhist monastic community of Plum Village in southern France in 1982.

Many of Nhat Hanh's works involve the concept of "mindfulness," which puts a different relationship to time at the core of meditative exercises. "There are two ways to wash dishes: the first is to wash dishes in order to have clean dishes; the second is to wash dishes in order to wash dishes." What the *sunder warumbe* is in the language of Meister Eckhart is made clear here by means of a simple, everyday process. The first way to wash dishes consists of getting the task over and done with so that one may finally get to drink the eagerly awaited cup of tea. Washing up is a tedious burden that one gets done with expending as little time and energy as possible. The critical question to be put to this everydayness is: what happens to time in such performances, what becomes of our life's time in those unimportant moments? "We are not alive in the time when we wash dishes, in fact, we are utterly incapable of perceiving the miracle of life while we are standing at the sink. When we can't wash the dishes it looks as if we also can't drink our tea." We always think of something else and are unable to truly live even one minute of our life. Attentiveness is a way of putting down roots in the here and now; it is an ability to exist that is practiced by a conscious and particular way of breathing and by meditation.

The mystical relationship to time is fundamental not only for the I that is becoming attentive, but also the purposes and goals that orient our activities. Being present to a beloved person who has fallen ill, or for a poisoned river, must be borne by such attentiveness lest it wither away in activism. "When you are being carried off by your sorrow, your fear, or your anger, you cannot really be present to the people and things you love."[1] Attentiveness is what C. S. Lewis expressed in the phrase "I am what I do" (see also chapter 1). Even though I have worked with that magnificent phrase for many years, it never occurred to me to associate it with washing dishes. Would it be because I do not live in a Buddhist monastery but in a large family? A false overevaluation of the spiritual over the commonplace reigned over me, an inattentiveness—as I now see it—to life in the now. Meditative attentiveness to every process, however trivial, is precisely what the Eastern praxis of meditation can teach us. It allows us to be alive in every moment and not just in a few of them. "The miracle is not to walk on water but on the earth."[2] The time is now, the place is here, the time of life is today.

Through Buddhist meditation, the way to that state is learned and practiced quite differently than in the mysticism formed by Christianity. When speaking of the difference between Eastern and Western mysticism, the study of mysticism has always upheld the difference between mysticism of experience and mysticism of illumination. Thus far, it is only boundary persons who have sought to overcome this contrast; they attempt not to dramatize the experience as totally now-related and not to interpret it only in a psychologizing manner. Learning from Buddhism in this context means two things: to bring the experience closer to the exercise that seeks to bring about illumination and, secondly, to understand the illumination as that which in theistic language we may call God's nearness to us. My intent is not to achieve religious egalitarianism but to further a nonpolarizing capacity for learning. We do not have to be "disrobed of the Ego" in order to gain a different relationship to time and learn to live in attentiveness.

Attentiveness to the now also contains a critical outlook on Christianity's linear understanding of time; the ancient orientation toward eschatology and the "last things" has probably something to do with the deeply disturbed relationship of Western occidental people to time. If "having no time" is a sign of quality and success, then it signals a lack of attentiveness. The great historian of religion Friedrich Heiler used to say, "Europe needs quiet, in other words: it needs Buddhism." If it is really true that the almond tree actually blossoms in your front yard, then experience is less dramatized and freighted with exclusive subjective uniqueness and actually seeks to be part of your everyday life. That a different sense of one's use of time can indeed arise in a society of people hounded by work and consumption in equal measure may perhaps explain why Buddhist meditation has such a strong attraction today.

To live with Zen means to breathe when breathing, to walk when walking, to drink tea when drinking tea. The half smile on the Zen master's lips, present even when work is tedious and unpleasant or the wait is long, is close to what Eckhart called *Gelassenheit* (the state of having let go). Attentiveness is the precondition of joy. Just as the gong in a center for meditation reminds us from time to time to return to ourselves in the here and now, we all may become "bells of attentiveness."

Publicans, Jesters, and Other Fools:
The Abolition of Divisions

In the mystical sense, joy is something not tied to objects or certain experiences of delight. Joy is more a matter of "rejoicing *in*" rather than of being "glad *about*." Those who lose themselves in God lose their total dependence on the body's well-being and exchange it for an interdependence of what happens "in the heart," on the one hand, and what happens "in the time of sorrow," on the other. It is not patience with or acquiescence in suffering that is taught but an active, self-determined acceptance of reality that cannot destroy one's being-lost-in-God.

The connection between radical attentiveness, prayer, and joy pervades Jewish mystical thinking in its diverse phases but never so brightly, so every-day-related, and so clearly as in Hasidism. Melancholy is the dust in the soul that Satan spreads out. Worry and dejection are seen to be the roots of every evil force. Melancholy is a wicked quality and displeasing to God, says Martin Buber. Joy, on the other hand, is such a great good that the Hasidim tells the strangest stories about it. The following tale is told of "the Seer" of Lublin.

> In Lublin lived a great sinner. Whenever he wanted to talk to the rabbi, the rabbi readily consented and conversed with him as if with a man of integrity and one who was a close friend. Many of the Hasidim were annoyed at this, and one said to the other: "Is it possible that our rabbi, who has only to look once into a man's face to know his life from first to last, to know the very origin of his soul, does not see that this fellow is a sinner? And if he does see it, that he considers him worthy to speak to and associate with?" Finally they summoned up the courage to go to the rabbi himself with their question. He answered them: "I know all about him as well as you. But you know how I love gaiety and hate dejection. And this man is so great a sinner! Others repent the moment they have sinned, are sorry for a moment, and then return to their folly. But he knows no regrets and no doldrums, and lives in his happiness as in a tower. And it is the radiance of this happiness that overwhelms my heart."[3]

Obviously, this happiness, this joy is "that of God" in this otherwise unrepentant sinner, separated from God and congregation. "One day, another rabbi went to the marketplace, as was his custom, and met Elijah. He asked the prophet whether there were any children of the world to come in the square right now. The prophet pointed to two brothers who were just passing by. When the rabbi asked what they were doing, they told him, 'We are jesters. When someone is sad, we try to cheer him up and when we see people quarrelling, we try to make peace between them.' "[4] Gershom Scholem calls these pranksters "righteous men after the heart of the Ba'al Shem. They do not sit at home, thinking about their own salvation. They labor in the busy and dirty marketplace just as he liked to do."[5]

For Hasidim, joy is not a gift of blessing from beyond; it is present much more in the thoroughly earthly humor that is reminiscent of the mad wisdom sayings of Buddhism. *Kavanah* is an intentional concentration or attentiveness to God. According to Abraham Heschel, "Kavanah . . . is more than paying attention to the text of the liturgy or to the performance of the mitsvah. Kavanah is attentiveness to God. Its purpose is to direct the heart rather than the tongue or the arms. . . . Kavanah in this sense is . . . not a yoke we carry but of the Will we remember."[6] This concept initially was reserved for the prayer offered in the synagogue or an individual's meditation but was reinterpreted in Hasidic tradition to include the wider dimensions of great immediacy and applied to the praise of God in actions as diverse as those of the marketplace. Rabbi Bunam said: "Once when I was on the road near Warsaw, I felt that I had to tell a certain story. But this story was of a worldly nature and I knew that it would only rouse laughter among the many people who had gathered about me. The Evil Urge tried very hard to dissuade me, saying that I would lose all those people because once they heard this story they would no longer consider me a rabbi. But I said to my heart: 'Why should you be concerned about the secret ways of God?' And I remembered the words of Rabbi Pinhas of Koretz: 'All joys hail from paradise, and jests too, provided they are uttered in true joy.' "[7] How are jests hailing from paradise? Do they belong to the secular sphere that is divided from the sacred one? The Hasidic answer is because they create space for joy. "And so in my heart of hearts I renounced my rabbi's office and told the story. The gathering burst out laughing. And those who up to this point had been distant from me attached themselves to me."[8]

Joy, laughter, and delight are so powerful because, like all mysticism, they abolish conventional divisions, in this case the division between secular and sacred. The often boisterous laughter, especially of women, is part and parcel of the everyday life of mystical movements. Julian of Norwich (ca. 1342–1416) insisted, contrary to monastic tradition, that laughter become a component of the Benedictine rule that had hitherto categorized laughing as a peculiarity of the *stultus* (fool). Even though Christ never laughed, according to the testimony of Scripture, Julian unhesitatingly declared that "it pleases him nevertheless when we laugh, to our consolation and filled with joy in God, that the foe has been overcome."[9] "A story is told of a pupil who asked his rabbi for permission to go to a *tzaddik* in another town and to study Talmud with him. He tries to find him until he finally is sent to the keeper of a tavern. The *tzaddik*—and here the story becomes quite Zen Buddhist—is behind the bar washing glasses. He asks the young man to help him every day until the latter returns to his village on Friday evening. He tells his rabbi back home that he learned nothing at all and that he only rinsed out glasses in a tavern. But his rabbi says to him, 'Don't you know that when *He* washes glasses, he cleanses the world and so sets the sparks free that are encrusted in soiled matter and leads them back into the soul of the world?'"[10] That is how publicans, storytellers, and unrepentant sinners become bearers of joy.

The Ba'al Shem Tov knew that sad people are subject to sin because Satan draws the soul down whereas joy lifts it up to God. So, why not give joy a hand with a little brandy? And why not sing the sacred words of the Psalms in melodies of the Cossacks?

The difficulties the Hasidim had with the traditionally orthodox are reflected in the question whether to separate or to integrate. In many Hasidic songs there are Russian tunes. Asked whether that was permitted, one rabbi said: "Of course, for that is how the melodies are reclaimed." People, too, become reconciled in dance and music, as a story of the Ba'al Shem Tov shows:

[A seven-year-old] boy was stood on the table and in his silvery voice sang a Hasidic dance song without words that went straight to the feet of the villagers. In a reel of wild happiness they danced around the table. Then one of them, a young fellow, stepped forward from among them and asked the boy: "What is your name?" "Shaul," he said. "Go on singing," the peasant cried. . . . in the midst of his wild leaps and bounds, he repeated over and over in charmed tones: "You Shaul and I Ivan, you Shaul and I Ivan!" . . . About thirty years later, Rabbi Shaul, who had become both a wealthy merchant and a Talmud scholar of sorts, was travelling through the country on business. Suddenly robbers attacked him, took his money and wanted to kill him. When he begged them to have pity on him, they took him to their chieftain. He gave Rabbi Shaul a long penetrating look. Finally he asked: "What is your name?" "Shaul," said the other. "You Shaul and

I Ivan," said the robber chief. He told his men to return Shaul's money and take him back to his carriage.[11]

Dancing and Leaping: The Body Language of Joy

There is a French Marian legend about a storyteller who gives up his fickle life and enters a monastery. But the life of the monks remains strange to him; he knows neither how to recite nor chant a prayer. He pours out his lament to the Virgin Mary and she tells him to serve God with what he can do, namely to dance and leap. From that moment on, he skips the divine offices and dances during those times. He is called to the abbot and believes that he is about to be expelled. But the abbot only says, "With your dancing you have glorified God with body and soul. But may God forgive us all those lofty words that pass our lips without coming from the heart."

This story takes up an important theme of mysticism, that of bodiliness. It expresses both the dimension of union, of becoming one with each other, and the conflicts that religion, based in word and scripture, have had with such boundary-crossing experience. Laughing, singing, and dancing play a role in the mysticism of otherwise highly diverse religions. "Someone who is in God is drunk without wine and full even without meat. Someone who is in God is delighted and full of amazement, needing neither food nor sleep," writes the poet Rumi.

It is said that he welcomed the birth of his son by dancing for seven whole days.[12] This son, named Alim, later established the manner in which the order of the "dancing dervishes" danced their rituals. When Rumi was buried, the ecstatic dance of the huge crowd of mourners lasted for hours and on his coffin were written these words:

> Come to my grave not without drums
> For at God's feast grief is unseemly
> I am stupor, the wine of love my source.[13]

As many testimonies show, dancing is an expression of an inwardly experienced, overwhelming joy that not only wants to give itself bodily expression but "must" do so. "If I am to do much springing, you yourself must do the singing" is what Mechthild von Magdeburg says to Christ, the leader of the dance.[14] "Praise-dancing" is her word for what the soul does in anticipation of the bridegroom's arrival. Meister Eckhart says that "God will rejoice, yea, He will rejoice through and through: for then there is nothing in His depth which is not stirred by joy."[15]

Among the many different reasons advanced by orthodox hierarchies against mystical experience and ways of living, dancing is especially suspect. For outside observers, such as the (male) biographers of mystically gifted women, the spiritual freedom of the nuns or Beguines that were beyond control was forever a source of fright and at times revulsion. The physically visible expressions of joy—loud, hearty laughing, clapping of hands, leaping and dancing that can only be called daring—were foreign to them. They became afraid of those enthusiastic states in which women "laughed and grew merry from divine love and acted as if they had lost their senses, leaping and singing. One would laugh, another weep, a third shout in a loud voice, and many remain silent. Seeing them one would have thought that they were drunk."[16] They could do no other but show their inward joy in a bodily dance; after all, David's psalm before the ark of the covenant was their biblical model: "My heart and flesh sing for joy to the living God" (Ps 84:2).

Here, too, boundaries are crossed, namely those of orderly, dignified, proper behavior and of assigned roles. And in mystical ecstasy another boundary is abolished, the one tradition has erected between understanding and enjoying. Mechthild von Magdeburg describes this dancing or leaping as follows: "There I leap into love, from love into understanding, from understanding into enjoyment and from enjoyment beyond all the human senses. There I shall remain and yet circle still higher."[17]

At that time, the Catholic Church had imposed a ban on dancing in sanctuaries. Dance and liturgy were vigorously separated and only in 1994 is dancing mentioned affirmingly as a possible form of liturgical celebration. But mystics like Mechthild or poets like Jacopone di Todi could not care less about such fear-driven prohibitions.

> It never entered my mind, Jesus,
> that in the dance I am the dancer,
> but the force of your love, Jesus,
> has most certainly led me to dance. . . .
> I had already forgotten
> that I had begun the dance,
> joy fills every heart, Jesus,
> so that words are lacking.[18]

It is no accident that the rediscovery of the mystics Hildegard and Mechthild by the women's movement during the last two decades is coupled with a conscious relation to bodiliness. The spoken word alone cannot express the jubilation and the power of joy that are there without explanation. The dream of paradise makes itself known in the now of the body's language. In many aspects of the women's movement, a new pleasure in ritual or just spontaneous dancing is apparent. The now of accomplishment seeks celebration and dancing, for verbal articulation no longer suffices especially for women who have found new self-awareness. What this may look like in Christian day-to-day life was communicated to me in a letter from a quite ordinary village congregation where people had decided "to let Christ's passion and Easter pass through their bodies in dance" during the night before Easter Day. Another boundary that is clearly crossed over here is that which divides professional and laity. The mysticism of joy cannot tolerate this apportioning of roles and calls for everyone's self-expression. After a worship service where I had been asked to deliver the sermon I received the following letter from a young woman.

> When at the close of the service at St. Christopher's the band struck up for a "hallelujah," I was moved to "dance it out" before the altar. I asked a woman who stood next to me, herself radiating with joy, to leap and turn with me. She was about fifty and it clearly caused her great delight to conclude the service with dancing. While we were swinging and turning, she asked me, "do you also study theology?" whereupon I laughed out, "No!" But later I began to think about her question. I became aware of two things: there are some who feel that there is a need of institutional competence for the praise of God. Why do I need to study theology when I end the worship of God with dancing? The other, more significant to me, is that in this question, asked in that situation, there is an instruction, a desire and a longing of the congregation addressed to its "superiors." It is this: teach the people whom you send to "study God" to dance; teach them to invite us over the fences to join in the great, divine feast of joy, for we are ready for it; teach them things other than—or not only—educated words!

In many of the medieval movements of mysticism, particularly among women, there was, as a result of the social constraints upon them, a deep longing to be "disrobed" of day-to-day life, to have more power, and become "free" and "unrestrained." They yearned for time to meditate, to become educated, and they made use of the language of their bodies that speaks more than words to communicate this longing. But this wish to be whole would be misinterpreted were we to reduce it to the "love parades" and "ecstasy parties" current nowadays among "experience junkies." What they had in mind was more than what was granted them at the time and also more than what today is commercially appealing. Joy wants to inhabit us and not merely drop in for a visit.

The Relation of Mysticism and Aesthetics

Whenever love succeeds and life turns out well, the longing for wholeness is not really stilled; rather, it grows with fulfillment. We learn to cry not only through pain but also through life's riches and its beauty. There is a deep relation between mysticism and aesthetics, between the joy of God and beauty: relatively little thought has been given to this thus far. The audible mark of that relation is what tradition names in the old word "praise." Praising is an aesthetic activity in which something is perceived, seen and made visible, extolled, celebrated, and sung about. It is loved out of darkness into light.

Many psalms contain a self-exhortation that strikes us as peculiar. "Praise the Lord, O my soul!" "Praise, my soul, the Eternal One!" "Praise Him, O my soul!" The hymns of the church take up this language and urge the soul: "arise, my soul, and sing!" or "Rise up, my heart, rise up with joy!" It sounds as if humans had two souls, one that is capable of mystical joy and another that broods or just gloomily ponders on. The awakened one urges the other not to remain fixed on itself in heaviness and weary of life. In one of his hymns, Paul Gerhard takes up the old mystical phrase, "go out of yourself," and rewords it as, "Go out, my heart, and seek out joy!" As if the one soul said to the other: You, my melancholic soul, unacquainted with praise, don't hang around in yourself, look outside yourself, let go of yourself! Become able once again of not hearing the wind as a noise and, instead, of listening to its voice.

The oft-lamented spiritual impoverishment of today has to be recognized above all in this inability to praise life. People may see the clouds chasing along, feel the wind, and notice the fish playing in the water. Yet they may not see, feel, and notice because they are not amazed by it. Instead, they are caught up in themselves. Giving praise does not easily come on its own; to name what has been inflicted on life is something that suggests itself much more readily. Praise has no easy task because it has to be read into things, thereby getting close to the productive aesthetic state. A midrash on Psalm 104, in which the soul is called upon to give praise, declares that the world becomes visible only where it is lifted up in song. Perception (*aisthesis*) succeeds only when people experience beauty and sing of it. In this sense, we are all guardians of joy and responsible for making life's beauty visible and audible. It is when a hymn, such as "peacefully round us the shadows are falling," is sung that evening can arrive.

In the Middle Ages, spiritual advisors always warned against a state that had a variety of names but was difficult to describe: inertia, ill pleasure (*acedia*), nausea, laziness (*pigrita*), dullness (*tarditas*). All these terms pointed to a joyless, antimystical condition: an idleness that can be highly busy, a nauseousness with life that has learned the morbid art of seeing only decay and destruction in everything, a laziness of life that makes us too sluggish to look for God's radiance in creation or to make it shine again. Not to be able to cry and to rejoice, to curse and to pray, were regarded at that time as an ill-fortune and disturbance. In many cultures those two ways of expressing ourselves belong together, for example, in the culture of America's First Nations (see also chapter 1).

In our postindustrial world today there is weariness of life, a mournfulness without an object. This is reminiscent of the dullness that the Middle Ages worried over and fought against. What is different is that the voices of self-exhortation are too faint among us. Whining is easier than praising; it requires no great skills. One can often notice sighing gratification and hear gratified sighs. There are times in life when we are so badly beaten down that no tongues are left to sing praise; however, it is imperative that we take responsibility at all other times for joy of life, which at the same time means responsibility for beauty.

Mystical jubilation lies hidden in everything and that is why it is contagious. John of the Cross breaks out in praise:

Mios son los cielos	Mine are the heavens
y mios es la tierra	and mine is the earth
Mios son las gentes	Mine are the people
los justos son mios	The just are mine
y mios los peccatores	and mine are the sinners
Los angeles son mios	The angels are mine[19]

Do the heavens, angels, and sinners not become more lovely when they are sung to in such bliss? Mystical joy needs and produces beauty. It is a pure act *(actus purus)* in which they whom joy has overtaken become participants in creation. With all the seraphim and cherubim they exclaim, "behold!"

Next to love, Francis of Assisi (1181/82–1226) probably lived and embodied no other state of the soul as much as joy. He told his community brothers, "It is the devil's greatest triumph when he can deprive us of the joy of the Spirit. He carries fine dust with him in little boxes and scatters it through the cracks in our conscience in order to dim the soul's pure impulses and its luster. But the joy that fills the heart of the spiritual person destroys the deadly poison of the serpent. But if any are gloomy and think that they are abandoned in their sorrow, gloominess will continuously tear at them or else they will waste away in empty diversions. When gloominess takes root, evil grows. If it is not dissolved by tears, permanent damage is done."[20] At the heart of Franciscan spirituality is to be found resistance against melancholy. This is not to be confused with deep, genuine mourning. Francis did not fear it, but he flees from the joylessness and negativity of life that is coated with the devil's fine dust, the dullness of the senses that lets us see, taste, and hear nothing. That bland, all-embracing sadness neither weeps nor prays because it has taken away our ability to feel. It is said that whenever Francis felt even the littlest touch of it in his heart he took refuge in prayer. Praying, singing, praising, dancing were his antidotes to this sadness. When an illness overcame him he began to sing a hymn of praise to God in all God's creatures. Francis ran away from the dull inaccessibility that brings with it a joyless emptiness and ran to prayer and, mysteriously, into tears.

He was only forty-four years old when, nearly blind, he lay on his deathbed; he asked the people around him to sing because that would lift the burden of his pain. He composed one song after another, and his companions became annoyed, thinking that someone dying should be serious. Tears in their eyes, they sang his hymns to sister sun, brother wind, sister water, brother fire, and mother earth. And he inserted the line before the final stanza, "Praise to you, my Lord, through our brother death."

III. MYSTICISM IS RESISTANCE

11. AS IF WE LIVED IN A LIBERATED WORLD

———⊰◆⊱———

> As far as possible, we ought to live as we believe we should live
> in a liberated world, in the form of our own existence, with all the
> unavoidable contradictions and conflicts that result from this. . . .
> Such endeavor is by necessity condemned to fail and to meet
> opposition, yet there is no option but to work through this oppo-
> sition to the bitter end. The most important form that this will
> take today is resistance.
>
> THEODOR W. ADORNO

The Prison We Have Fallen Asleep in:
Globalization and Individualization

ONCE AGAIN I TAKE up Rumi's idea of the "prison" in which we
humans who have no thought of God have fallen asleep (see chapter 2). I try to describe our First World prison at the end of the millennium. As I see it, this prison is determined by two trends that
match perfectly: globalization and individualization.

Since 1989, we live in a standardized, globalized economic order
of technocracy that demands and achieves total disposition over
space, time, and creation. Its engine runs on, driven by the coercion
to produce more and confirmed by technological success of unimag-
inable proportions. And this engine is programmed for ever more
speed, productivity, consumption, and profit, for about twenty percent of humankind. In all of history, this program is more efficient
and more brutal than comparable empires and their towers of Babel.
Within this super-engine, human beings are not only "alienated"
from what they might become, as Karl Marx observed, but they are
also addicted and dependent as never before.

One of the spiritual difficulties in our situation is the inner connection between globalization and individualization. The more
globally the market economy structures itself, the less interest it
demonstrates in the social and ecological webs in which humans
live, and the more it requires the individual who is without any relation whatsoever. The partner that our global market economy needs
is *Homo oeconomicus*. This is an individual fit for business and
pleasure, showing no interest in the antipersonnel mines that his car

manufacturer produces, no interest in the water that his grandchildren will use—not to mention interest in God.

As the agent of justice and protector of the weaker, the old nation state is downsized, dismantled, and disempowered. At the same time, the individual is built up as the being with unlimited capacity for utilization and consumption. By now, choice, purchase, presentation, and enjoyment have long found their own forms of religious staging and production: it is called "cult marketing." The religion of consumerism no longer needs the old and milder forms of the opiate of the people. Much more efficient opiates are for sale everywhere.

Living within the super-engine, I do not find the New Testament and many other items of the religious tradition of humanity mythologically encoded. Instead, I find them enlightening and clarifying. The New Testament describes the normal condition of human beings under Roman imperial rule as being-in-death. "We know that we have passed from death into life" (1 John 3:14). Here, normative submission to the all-governing power is called death. Alienation, sin, and addiction are different names for the spiritual death that masquerades as life, the death that surrounds us. In the same manner, Paul speaks of us having been "enemies" of God (Rom 5:10). This expression also contains nothing that we have to dismiss as mythological projection.

Instead, the tradition of religion helps us to identify correctly our role at the apex of world society: we are enemies of the earth, enemies of more than two-thirds of all human beings, enemies of the sky above us, and enemies of ourselves. Hildegard von Bingen speaks of the "stench" of death that hangs over our earth. Whoever believes that we can evade it subjectively has already made an arrangement with the super-engine. Such a person uses the engine unknowingly, profits from "its positive side," and in so doing experiences the slow death that the engine has planned for the soul.

Within globalization, corporate world dominance collaborates with a novel form of unrelenting individualization that has no attachment to our fellow creatures. This collaboration appears to be beyond hope. Many regard it as a headlong rush toward the apocalyptic end; thoughtful people among them accept it as our unstoppable fate. Can we still live "as we believe we should live in a liberated world?" This would mean insisting on another vision of our life together, a vision that nourishes resistance.

But are such visions not long gone or turned into harmless private eccentricity? Are there any forms of resistance at all; is there any point to protesting or studying civil disobedience in new ways and practicing it? And has not the spirituality of mysticism itself, from which resistance could emerge, already become an aspect of the market against which it promised to offer protection? I struggle with my own fear of the world and the feeling that religion is dying in a spiritless materialism. It is no coincidence that I seek help exactly among those who know the "dark night" of history and of the eclipse of God.

When we only stare at the lords of this world and the mass of individuals rendered harmless, we do not yet have new eyes for seeing. Fear of the world then encircles us and locks us up in the most exquisitely furnished jail that has ever existed. The New Testament offers a new perspective. Its sociological world is neither the masses nor the individual but the groups that set out on a new way. In the course of Christian mysticism, every rebellion appealed to the early churches and their situation in the ancient imperium. They looked back to a time in which it was not a patriarchically ordered hierarchy that decided what belongs to God and what belongs to Caesar. Instead, it was the groups themselves who appealed to the justice of God against that of the emperor. Their understanding of religion was not the performance of rituals that are judged harmless in Rome as in Washington. Religion as a private matter is a contemporary liberal idea. It knows nothing at all of the mystical ardor that another embodiment and reality of life has always needed and which it has always sought.

The early church refused to involve itself in several of the social benefits and obligations of the empire. Christians did not go to the theaters, the public baths, or the circus. They also shunned what Roman culture called *circenses*, games to entertain the masses and divert their attention from real problems. The public executions staged by Rome for deterrence effect were command performances, but Christians still tried to stay away. Every event connected with the military, the swearing of oaths or the offering of incense to the emperor, was seen to be of the devil. In a minority Christian culture, abstinence, separation, dissent, opposition, and resistance flowed one into the other. It was to precisely these forms of negation of the dominant culture that later dissidents looked back upon. Ernst Troeltsch contrasted these dissidents to what in his work are known as "church" and "sect." His understanding of groups working for social reform illumines the sociological location of mysticism. In a third type called "group," he combined the Protestantism of the Radical Reformation and mystical movements.[1]

This thinking presupposes that mysticism enables community even where its manifestation is extremely individualistic. Of necessity, mysticism desires to get away from the privatization of joy, happiness, and oneness with God. The dance of the love of God cannot be danced alone; it brings people together. God's conviviality, of which Ruysbroeck writes, brings people out of the "purely religious" activity that is said to be harmless. The understanding of human dignity, freedom, and the openness for God or the divine spark cannot be reduced to a special religious space where God can be served and enjoyed but not shared with the 80 percent of our superfluous people.

In the present scenario there are global players on one side, and satiated, isolated individuals on the other. But the groups who are committed to voluntary effort, critical openness, and taking their own initiative are the bearers of hope. Politically speaking, these nongovernmental organizations, among which I count those sections of the Christian church that are alive, are the carriers of resistance. From a spiritual perspective, they embody a different subject than the one that has fallen asleep in the prison of consumerism. What sustains those groups? What keeps them awake? Why do they not give up? I believe that it is elements of mysticism that cannot be extinguished.

God is the nothing that seeks to be everything, says Jacob Böhme. My fear tells me that in the world of globalization this "nothing" is less and less noticeable, that more and more the silent cry is drowned out. But the nothing that wants to be everything generates its own imperturbability, yes, its own mystical defiance. Böhme conceives of God as a movement, as something flowing, growing, driving, as a process. When we engage ourselves in the process we become part of the God-movement and are connected with all others.

When we are part of the movement of nothing, it means that we too live with our nothing, confront our nothing or, as mystics have always put it, that we become annihilated. Without such "disrobing" of faith wherein it becomes stark naked, we cannot take part in the process. Here in the third part of this book I address the ego, possessions, and violence, which are the focus of the disrobing of resistance. To be ego-less, possessionless, and nonviolent is to be identified with the nothing that wants to be everything even among us.

Often tiny, sometimes at a loss as to what to do next, and frequently unorganized, groups of resistance come into being before our very eyes. In order to spot these new hope-bearers, to understand

and strengthen them, and protect oneself against one's own fear of the world, it is good to look for the element of mystical resistance in them. The subject that weaves itself into the web of networks and grows into resistance cannot be destroyed. That subject is and remains a "member" (see chapter 6), even if it does not always know it. The nothing that wants to become everything is also at work in and among us.

Out of the Home into Homelessness

"Mysticism *is* resistance." Years ago, a friend said this to me and I wanted to know how to picture the relationship between mysticism and resistance. The experiences of unity in the midst of commotion—hearing the "silent cry"—necessarily puts us in radical opposition to what is regarded as a normal way of life.

At the theological seminary in New York where I used to teach, we were once asked about our religious experiences. There was an embarrassed silence; it was as if we had asked our grandmothers about their sex life. A young woman eventually spoke up and offered to present, in a week's time, an extensive report on her experiences. Accordingly, she told us that as a very young girl in the American Midwest, she had spent many hours reading in bed at night, without permission. One winter's night, she woke up at four in the morning, went outside, and looked at the stars in the clear, frosty sky. She had a once-in-a-lifetime feeling of happiness, of being connected with all of life, with God; a feeling of overwhelming clarity, of being sheltered and carried. She saw the stars as if she had never seen them before. She described the experience in these words, "Nothing can happen, I am indestructible, I am one with everything." This did not happen again until about ten years later when, in a different context, something similar took place. The new context was a huge demonstration against the Vietnam War. There, too, she knew that she was sheltered, a part of the whole, "indestructible," together with the others. Struggling for words and with her own timidity, she brought both experiences together under the rubric of religious experience.

Suppose that this young woman had lived in fourteenth-century Flanders; she would have had at her disposal other traditions of language allowing her to say, "I heard a voice" or "I saw a light brighter than everything else." Our culture confines her to sobriety, self-restriction, and scholarly manners of expression. How she fought these constraints and the very fact that she did so makes her unforgettable.

Mystical experience is bliss and simultaneously it makes one homeless. It takes people out of the home they have furnished for themselves into homelessness, as it did to young Gautama, known later as the Buddha. I sensed a bit of this ascetic homelessness in the student's report and in her feeling of being drawn more and more into a nonviolent life. The least that can be said is that being touched by religion produces a condition that evokes alienation; in terminology that conveys a degree of loathing, the New Testament specifies it as alienation from "this world." Distance from everyday reality does not necessarily legitimate the big word "resistance," but it does point to a different life. Bliss and homelessness, fulfillment and quest, God's presence and the bitterness of God's absence in the everyday, violence-riddled reality belong together.

Is mysticism necessarily connected with this resistance? The thesis can be questioned from two different positions. Observers far removed from mysticism will look upon mysticism more as a flight from the world, an introversion and concentration on the well-being of one's soul. To them the privatization of religion will seem to be the essential aspect within mysticism. They will find the many examples of conflicts included in the first two parts of this book to be beside the point, even though such conflicts arose from mystical sensitivity. Such interpretation strangely flattens out the dimension of the love of God that is essential to every form of religion—as if ritual and being consoled were all there is! Most of the great men and women of mystical movements have also spoken clearly in their theory against a complete withdrawal from the world. For a time being, they indeed practiced the contemplative "way inwards," but their aim was consistently the unity of the contemplative and the active life, of *ora et labora* (work and prayer). The notion of mysticism as a flight from the world is much more a result of the bourgeois idea that religion is a private affair.

But there is also a very different objection to the idea that mysticism is resistance. It comes from a context that is quite far removed from religion and much closer to what political ethics calls resistance. It is represented by postreligious thinkers who concede that in the course of history, mysticism may have on occasion played a part in resisting the numerous forms of barbarism. However, for such thinkers, rational arguments can now provide sufficient support for the refusal to go along obediently with any further barbarization of society. The apparent persuasiveness of this view seems to arise from a certain overestimation of rationality, usually associated with the left. To me it expresses a kind of naive faith in the goddess Reason.

I am personally acquainted with many groups that practice pacifist and ecological resistance and, above all in the world's poorest countries, economic resistance. I learn from them ever anew that experience, analysis, and insight alone are too weak to bring us out of the prison in which we are asleep. We need a different language that keeps awake and shares the memory of liberation and the promise of freedom for all. We need a different hope than that of political strategies and scientific prediction.

For Martin Buber, the difference between secular and religious movements striving for a renewal of society lies in how they relate themselves to what he called the foundational substance of tradition. Is that substance rejected in principle? Is the "axe to be laid at the root" of the existing order, or is there a relation to tradition that does not eliminate tradition as such? In his view, revolutionary movements work with the knowledge of "how it was meant to be; they begin with the hidden spark in every human being and want to wipe clean the mirror of its distortions, bring back again what was lost and repair again what was destroyed."[2] The category of "again" promises liberation from the compulsion to win.

The failure of state socialism perhaps has an in-depth relationship to the totality of its repudiation of received culture, tradition, and religion. It did not invoke the time "when Adam delved and Eve span," nor any memory of the good story of the beginning of life in creation. The new elites were always the authors of their own being; there was no good beginning. They wanted something completely different and not the *renovation* and the renewal of the face of the earth that is promised in Psalm 104:30. What mysticism can contribute today to the substance of resistance movements is this relation to the origin of life that is often expressed in a phrase like "surely, this is not all there is to it, it wasn't meant to be like this." Whoever desires the new needs the memory and the feast that, even now, celebrate the renewing.

The concept of resistance that meets us in many places of mystical tradition is broad and diverse. It begins with our not being at home in this world of business and violence. Abstention, disagreement, and dissent lead on to simple forms of nonconformist behavior. The American Quakers who helped black slaves escape to the North often got into trouble for their love of truth and their deeply rooted preference for plain speech. When asked whether they had seen a slave pass by on the road, they did not say "No," for that would have transgressed the commandment of truthfulness. Instead, they said, "I saw no slave," staying with the truth that the black person they had seen was a child of God and nothing else. They did not share the implicit belief that such a person could be named a slave. Children of Quakers were sometimes entrusted with hiding refugees so that their parents could truthfully say that they knew nothing about illegal guests.

It is not always easy to keep up this relation between love of truth and protecting the persecuted. In many forms of resistance, there was and is a necessity for secrecy. Whenever possible, the early Quakers preferred to confuse their persecutors "with truth rather than with lies." During the years of the Cold War, Quakers traveled to Poland with aid supplies and were asked by American secret agents what ships they had seen in the harbor. They would reply, "If we had seen any, we would not tell you. It would be deceiving the Polish government to say that we came to help and then spied for the U.S.A." This principle of open and honest talk and disclosure of intentions plays an important role in nonviolent actions. Several Quakers informed the authorities of their acts of civil disobedience, but only after the asylum-seeking refugees had safely crossed the borders.

The broadest notion of resistance assumed here arises from the distance established from what is regarded as the normal world, a world founded on power, possession, and violence. Consequently, in different situations the notion varies between evasion, dissent, abstinence, refusal, boycott or strike, reform or counterproposal, dialogue, or mediation. Yet, however radically mystical consciousness practices and strives for changes in conditions based on possessions and violence, the connection to those who think otherwise is steadfastly maintained. No one is excluded or eliminated. Such consciousness is deeply marked by "revolutionary patience" that sets out from the experience of what has always been good.

I remember an act of civil disobedience when we occupied a nuclear weapons facility in the Hunsrück Mountains in Germany. We spoke the Lord's Prayer together. About forty people faced the huge military vehicles that drove in and out and we said, "Your kingdom come." Never had I heard that petition as I heard it then. Never had I known as clearly how different the kingdom would look without the instruments of death. Never had I felt as I did then what it means to pray. The mysticism of the good beginning and of its reestablishment and resistance against the terror of violence were present to all of us at that moment as genuine forms of life. We knew something that we could not clearly name at the time. Thanks to Jewish mysticism, I see more plainly now. "Every individual in Israel who calls on God in prayer places a crown on God's head, for prayer is an act of crowning God, of acknowledging God as king."[3] The image of the coronation of one who, according to orthodox Christian opinion, needs no coronation and certainly not at the hands of ordinary, sinful people shows how far mystics can proceed especially in a situation of resistance.

I have long thought about what verbs go with mysticism and resistance. Which verbs can we can utilize in order to express mysticism and resistance as a unity? Is there such a thing at all as mystical activities? Is praying also a kind of fighting, like weeping, smiling, keeping silent? Years ago, young people in Zürich wrote an ironic mystical slogan on the walls of their city: "We have enough reason to cry even without your tear gas." In this sentence, crying is a mystical activity, a response to the "silent cry."

Acting and Dreaming: Becoming Martha and Mary

"To know God means to know what has to be done."[4] Emmanuel Levinas (1902–1995), the Jewish philosopher of religion, was utterly skeptical toward every form of enthusiasm, ecstasy, or mysticism. Distancing himself to a certain degree from Christian tradition, he insisted on an adult religion, which had "come-of-age," and on the indivisibility of knowing and acting. "Ethics is not the corollary of the vision of God, it is that very vision."[5] Resistance is not the outcome of mysticism, resistance is mysticism itself; that is how I understand Levinas's statement. The concept of God that goes with mysticism understood this way may, according to Rudolf Otto, be called "voluntaristic," that is to say, God does not live rigidly, self-sufficiently, and immobile in "his" being. God's being, that which we can know of God, is the divine will to build up the reign, the kingdom of God.

This Jewish root of thinking God has often been obscured and buried in Christian tradition. And the perception of mysticism as pure inwardness, mere withdrawal from the world, has caused difficult debates. How are we to think about the relationship between the work we do in the world around us and what we do within ourselves? Bernard of Clairvaux called the former "good" but called the latter mystical disrobing, "something much more beautiful."[6] The aesthetic dimension of mystical bliss is understood here as rarely before. Without the dream of a different relationship of the world around us in the widest sense of the word, without songs, rituals, or dancing, resistance cannot succeed. "If I can't dance," said New York anarchist Emma Goldman (1869–1940), "I don't want to be in your revolution."

Following its dualistic principles, medieval theology often established an order that, corresponding to that of spiritual and worldly life or theory and practice, ranked the contemplative life higher than the *vita activa* (the life of action) (see chapter 6). But it was precisely this superordination of contemplating over acting that great mystics like Eckhart or Teresa of Avila criticized and overcame.

The test case for this view in the realm of Christian thought is the interpretation of the New Testament narrative of the two sisters, Martha and Mary, who had Jesus as a guest in their home (Luke 10:38-42). One acted as his host, the other listened to him speaking.[7] Ever since Augustine, Mary's quiet attention to Jesus' words and Martha's restless caring about the body's everyday needs have been interpreted as images of the *vita contemplativa* and the *vita activa*. The former was held to be of greater value, to be more spiritual and essential, while the latter, however necessary, was of a lower order. In this tradition, Martha is seen to be useful but somewhat limited, while her sister is seen as spiritual, refined, and more saintly. "Pure" theory is elevated above mere praxis; in the course of Western intellectual history, this relationship gets passed on, according to the patriarchal gender roles, as work of the head and manual labor.

Martin Luther later took this valorization and made it even more acute when he contrasted faith and mere "works." But long before him, Meister Eckhart raised a bold objection that reflects the spirit and discussion of the blossoming movement of women. He places the still uncompleted Mary at the beginning of spiritual life while the active Martha is much further ahead. "Martha feared that her sister would remain stuck in her feelings of well-being and in sweetness."[8] Then this spiritual counselor completely reverses the sense of the biblical text that assigns "the better part" to Mary and, identifying himself with the activist Martha, says: "Therefore Christ spoke to her and said, 'Set your mind at ease, Martha, she too has chosen the better part. This [viz. Mary's inaction] will come to an end in her . . . and she will be blessed like you!'"[9] This reversal is not only about rehabilitating Martha and active behavior but also about abolishing the division of human beings into makers and dreamers, activists and introverts, and the differentiation between the productivity of action and the receptivity of piety. By not separating Martha's acting from Mary's contemplative devotion but, rather, conceiving of Mary in Martha, Eckhart does away with the false superordination as well as the compulsive choice between two forms of life, the spiritual and the worldly. In the perspective of mysticism, this hierarchy is untenable. Real contemplation gives rise to just actions; theory and praxis are in an indissoluble connection. Even if one were in a state of rapture like Paul, it would be better still to prepare a pot of soup for a needy neighbor![10] In the words of Teresa of Avila, "Believe me, Martha and Mary need to be together to host the Lord and keep him with them for ever, or else he will be badly hosted and be left without food."[11] What "food" Christ is to be served is explained by Teresa from her own praxis, "gather up souls in any manner whatsoever so that they may be saved and praise him for ever and ever."[12]

The point is neither to practice an introverted mysticism nor to engage in an extroverted critique of the age alone, but to find one's *vita mixta* in this sense between contemplation and activity. This was made manifest in the Middle Ages, above all in the many attempts of mystical women to involve themselves in the church politics of their day without neglecting in any way voluntary poverty and asceticism. The combination of contemplating and acting is rooted in the mystical understanding of the relationship to God as a mutuality of receiving and giving. "What we have gathered in contemplation we give out in love," says Eckhart.[13]

Ruysbroeck describes the mystical human who lives in communion with God and with everything else there is. "This person possesses a rich and gentle foundation that is secured in the riches of God. Hence the need incessantly to flow into everyone who needs these riches."[14] The words "foundation" and "to flow into" depict the connection of mysticism and resistance not as cause and effect but as a unity.

But oneness with God, beginning in action, can also discover the mystical unity that undergirds resistance. Albert Schweitzer (1875–1965), a great physician and religious thinker of the twentieth century, thought in terms of such a tradition of ethical mysticism. Far removed from esoteric rituals but very close to current forms of resistance against nuclear industry and commerce, militarism, juridically legitimated xenophobia, and ecological blindness, he describes in idealistic language what is experienced in the activity of resistance. "Whenever my life devotes itself in any way to life, my finite will-to-live experiences union with the infinite will in which all life is one."[15]

Let me take an example of this oneness from the current North American farmworkers movement. Cesar Chavez (1927–1993), whom Robert Kennedy called "one of the heroic figures of our time," fought all his life so that Mexican immigrants, the Chicanos, would not be subject to the powerful landowners and without any rights whatsoever. It was a struggle against racial and economic discrimination, for contracts and voter registration, and, above all, for minimum income for itinerant workers, many of whom were children. At the beginning of the movement, it was simply a matter of those workers not being summarily shot to death by the white landowners when the workers dared to organize themselves. Chavez knew poverty intimately. He began to work in the fields and vineyards as a ten-year-old, together with his bitterly poor family, roaming the Southwest near and far. In his arduous travels, he built up a syndicated organization of isolated, lost, and often illiterate farmworkers and got them to go out on strike. Another very important means he used in these struggles was the organized boycott of produce, especially table grapes and wines; in the mid-seventies, seventeen million adult American citizens heeded the appeal to boycott the giant corporations who refused to grant even minimal rights to the farmworkers.

Unlike the European workers' movement, this organized resistance by farmworkers is based in a deep piety. Cesar Chavez was a practicing Roman Catholic who prepared himself carefully for every action through fasting and prayer. He once fasted twenty-four days before a large and very dangerous strike. Every time he prepared himself his enemies would say, "Watch out! Cesar Chavez is up to something. He's praying."

For him, resistance did not begin by putting the burden of responsibility on God, as a thoughtless understanding of prayer would want us to believe. It began by making God the ally of the exploited. Fasting can become nourishment, and prayer a mystical fortification that was regarded as a necessity for the nonviolent farmworkers. It was accepted as such. Chavez and the others responsible for the United Farm Workers lived on a subsistence income that amounted to no more than $5,000 per year.

During the summer of 1988, Chavez maintained a "fast for life" that lasted thirty-six days in protest against the pesticide poisoning of vineyard workers and their children. "If you are outraged about existing conditions, you cannot be free or happy until you give all your time to change them and do nothing else but that." All who knew Chavez described him as free and happy.

The Fruits of Apartheid

In mysticism there is a negation of everyday reality that is related to the amazement present at the beginning of the journey. All of a sudden there is a sense of distance from the common thoughtless intoxication with or captivity to the world. I became personally aware of this when, in the seventies, I bought a big bag of oranges to take with me for a visit to East Berlin. I was to meet with a group of Christians on the other side of the Wall and wanted to do something nice for them. Elisabeth Adler (1926–1997), a woman of the ecumenical movement and one-time director of the Protestant lay academy in East Berlin, took the bag and looked to see where the oranges had come from. "South Africa," she said, "I don't eat those." I have rarely been as ashamed as I was at that moment. I knew that opposition to apartheid was an important matter, especially for women who organized this resistance. I had simply forgotten this in my "common thoughtless captivity to the world."

The resistance movement of Protestant women's work against the racist system is an example of how resistance can generate publicity, with such simple means as letter campaigns, picketing, information sessions, and prayer vigils. What was new above all was the consumer boycott that was conducted under the slogan "Don't buy the fruits of apartheid!" It had soon expanded to affect banks and travel agencies that supported the policies of apartheid through their business with South Africa.

The report of a woman from the Rhineland, who had helped organize the boycott, has made a number of things about resistance clear to me in the most simple and everyday sense. In her Rhenish accent, she told us how she had gone to a branch of a large German bank in a small town in order to inform the employees there about apartheid. Unexpectedly the manager of the bank walked in. "If I had known that, I would never have gone in there." She felt she could not speak to a bank manager. But she soon realized that the almighty manager knew nothing of the reality of South Africa. He had no idea about infant mortality, separation of families, and the burden of debt on the people. And at the same time she discovered her newly won strength in the knowledge she had gained in a year and a half. Her own courage to speak that had grown in the process. The manager grew silent while the woman and her companions talked and the employees listened.

I interpret this example in two ways. This is a story that leads to action. It says that people who have decided to resist know more than the experts on death. The cumulative knowledge of the resisters develops its own strength as soon as they apply it confrontationally and persuasively. The misery of the solitary analyst who always knows better—trumping every discussion with "It is much worse than that!"—is precisely the misery of privatization of knowledge. Such a person hoards knowledge, refines the analytical vocabulary, and nuances the arguments but is hardly in a position to share the knowledge with the deceived and cheated. Every bit of knowledge turns into knowledge of death; the discoloration of the forests and the coughing of children confirms that we are impotent. Paul calls this "worldly grief" (2 Cor 7:10) in contrast to the grief that is of God and that leads to resistance. About this grief as God desires it, he writes, "See what earnestness this godly grief has produced in you: what eagerness to clear yourselves, what indignation, what alarm, what longing for change, what zeal in bringing the guilty to account" (2 Cor 7:11). How do we get from worldly grief to the grief that is of God? That is the theological question about the resistance of people in the rich world. We are at once overeducated and under-powered. We have knowledge that has no consequences for action and makes us helpless. Knowledge is not power, as the classical workers movement believed, but impotence. We do not use our education sensibly in the sense of turning back from the way we have found out to be wrong, namely the way of industrial society. We use it toward even greater hopelessness. In the rich world we still have to learn resistance.

In the light of the theological initiatives in the Third World, I have often felt that the key term for us cannot really be "liberation," related to specific historical events like the exodus from Egypt, the banishment of a tyrant, or the occupation of a landowner's estates. Instead, our key term is "resistance," as the long-term praxis that is learned in Babylonian exile: refraining from eating the fruits of apartheid, publicizing the profits of arms manufacturers and traders, providing deserting American soldiers with a telephone number.

To grow into resistance means also to claim the power that has been given to all created beings. The woman in the example above reappropriated the power misappropriated from her, namely to live as one endowed with a mind and a heart. The American peace movement speaks of "own one's power," pointing out that we, living without resistance, are not in possession of the powers given to us. The woman in the bank's foyer claimed her own power. In many places women and men who are falsely treated, irradiated, and paralyzed by powerlessness rise up again and claim their share of the power of life. They "arise," as the Bible puts it. They rediscover their own ability to resist. The reaction of these minorities to the media's manipulation of the Gulf War, whose victims were made invisible even more effectively than during the Vietnam War, is an illustration of the reappropriation of objective truth and subjective dignity.

The woman from the Rhineland taught me something else as well. Her story is, after all, a biblical story: like Jeremiah she did not want to speak, and like Jonah she did not want to go to Nineveh where prophets are ridiculed and sent packing. She experienced the miracle of what the Bible calls "the strength of the weak." The basic experience of resistance is receiving the gift of power. An exodus from imposed and self-generated impotence takes place. Life gains a new direction that can be detected from small signs whenever people feel confident to speak to the almighty bank manager, school principal, and base commander. "Speak, that I may see you!" said Johann Georg Hamann, a contemporary of Immanuel Kant. Often, all too often, the minorities in the rich world are still invisible.

For me, the step from impotence to the power of the weak is more important than another transition that many of us attempt again and again, namely, moving from an unconscious, unsuspecting, tolerated impotence into a paralysis of analysis that leads to despair and to the resigned exclamation, "there's nothing you can do about it." What I am commending here is a practical-existential step that includes confronting the life-threatening power. It is costly, and it disunites and unites anew. It is an irreversible step that we can forget or undo only at the price of self-betrayal. This step is a break with the bourgeois half-measure that ponders endlessly whether the other side might not be right as well; it is a break with the violence that so lives in me that I submit myself to it without a fight.

At a South Africa conference in Frankfurt in 1982 I asked a number of activist women to say something about mysticism and resistance. Some of them were quite critical about the word "mysticism." They staunchly defended themselves against what the word implied, namely, the withdrawal into a kind of piety or the withdrawal from reality into prayer. One woman spoke of sister activists for whom the "problems of the world" were too hot and who then relativized everything in their discussions that had to do with action and resistance. Often she heard the remark, "God doesn't really mean for things to be that specific and concrete. Everyone has to find her own answer to it." In 1978, after several years without church, Bible, and prayer, this woman had taken her first trip to South Africa. There she came upon a community of people who were actively opposed to the system of injustice ruling there. They also lived intensively with the Bible, offering prayer and intercession, and celebrating spontaneous services of Holy Communion. She told how she became quite naturally part of that life: "For me it was like coming home. I became aware of two things. First, the congregation gives us as much as I am prepared to put into it and that there is need for a place of community where action (= resistance) is shared. Second was the recognition that I was part of a large company of fighting, believing, loving, and suffering human beings. I suddenly realized that praying was important for me, that I needed it. Not as a retreat from (dreadful) reality but much more as a time of holding still to face that reality in its horror and beauty, face it as a part of it, but also to experience at the same time that it is not the last word." At that time in 1982, the end of apartheid could not be foreseen and the critics of the resistance and boycott movement declared again and again how pointless those actions were. Still, the women kept on working, counseled and encouraged by their South African partners. Asked what she had to say about mysticism and resistance, another coworker from Frankfurt said,

> I knew right away that this concerns me and that this is what I am about. The word "mysticism" is not really part of my vocabulary. I rarely speak of piety, but most often of faith. That is like an abbreviation, a figure of speech for my life before God, with God, in God, and from God. I think of being one and being whole with God and with me, of being well.
>
> Mysticism *and* resistance: the "and" adds nothing contrary but connects what belongs together. Mysticism, immersion and entering *is* resistance and makes for resistance against the failure of imagination and hopelessness, against the "constraints of circumstance" and violence, against unfaith and sin.
>
> Picketing: it is to stand in for people you don't know, to bear their names. But how close and familiar they become! Jabulae Ngwenya, Alexander and Khosie Mbatha, Emma Mashinini . . . they enter into

my everyday life, are part of my thinking and doing, are closer than my neighbors, influence my decisions and are present in my prayers.

Intercession: even reflective Christians wonder what good it does. They misunderstand praying as something special, from particular causes and with particular purposes. But prayer is really the natural expression of my life before God. For I am never "alone" before God with my most individual and personal cares, doubts and hopes. The others, the whole "body of Christ" is there. Only in South Africa did I really come to know what this mystical term means.

"Don't buy fruit from South Africa!": I protest against my power-lessness, my entanglement in economic structures where I am exploited and exploit others. This protest makes both manifest: what is and should be, sin and its conquest.

South Africa is one of the few examples where the nonviolent resist-ance of economic boycott, sustained by millions of people, especially in the United States, contributed to a liberation, with relatively little violence and without civil war. I do not know whether this would have been possible without what is spoken of here as the "mysticism of liberation" of South Africans and of their friends all over the world. And I ask myself, in fear and doubt, whether such forms of resistance can still be effective in the global economy of "global part-ners." Nevertheless we need precisely such stories of resistance and its indestructible hope.

12. EGO AND EGO-LESSNESS

—≫◆≪—

Why should I be anxious? It is not up to me to
think of myself. It is up to me to think of God.
And it is up to God to think of me.

SIMONE WEIL

The Ego: The Best Prison Guard

THERE IS A STORY about an Egyptian monk who was tormented by
temptation. One day he decided to leave his cell and move to another
place. As he put on his sandals he saw another monk not far away
who also put on his sandals. "Who are you?" he asked the stranger.
"I am your own ego," came the reply. "If you are leaving here on my
account, you should know that wherever you go from here I shall
always go with you."

This story may not be quite as old as it sounds. The hope of escaping from the old ego by changing one's place, clothes, roles, or partners is not restricted to hermits. There is something coercive about
that hope. It is a manifestation of the ego, the best guarantor of the
prison wherein we have fallen asleep. Our ego is the agent that does
not allow the bundle of desires, drives, and needs in us to come to
resolution. That is precisely how it shores up in us such a profound
dependency on this world.

Ego-lessness, propertylessness, and nonviolence belong together.
They are the cornerstones of the change of life that comes from the
spirituality of mysticism. Buddhist monk Thich Nhat Hanh (see
chapter 10) speaks only when he has something to say; a presentation of the ego in the manner of talk shows is not intended. He lives
a simple life with his monks, without alcohol and as a vegetarian.
Nonviolence is the foundation of his peace work that includes
encouraging American veterans of the Vietnam War to help Vietnamese children today. There is an attempt to turn the tide away
from the ego, property, and violence and into a different freedom.
This search for a different life can be seen also in many unknown,
"lowly" folk. I want to let them speak here, on different levels, in
different forms, and with different consequences. To speak of

democratizing mysticism means also to discern it in the everyday forms of nonconformist life.

Ego, property, and violence are real and cry out to be relativized or to become redundant. But ego and ego-lessness are connected. They are paired in the same way as property and propertylessness, violence and nonviolence. In discussing each pair, I cannot isolate the naturally affirming term from the negating term that points to liberation. I need to keep both terms together, for who wants to dissipate in ego-lessness or be completely without property? It is not a matter of an either/or choice. Instead, it is a growth process that always develops new forms. The most difficult and convoluted component of this critical life process is the relationship of ego and ego-lessness. Frequently there is a desperate search "to find oneself" and finally, to find time, space, and freedom for oneself. Yet that search thoroughly negates any sense of leaving oneself and the mystical desire of getting rid of one's ego. It is precisely for that reason that it also fails to satisfy the realistic practical desire "to gain one's life" and finally come to enjoy it. But mystical desires can be as little denied as "that of God" in us.

I return once again to the tradition of Sufism that made the remembrance of God, *dhikr* (calling on the name of God), one of its most important rituals (see chapter 2). To remember God dissolves dependency on the ego because the ego is said to be a concretization of "God-forgetfulness" and the human brain the organ of that forgetfulness. Sometimes the brain is compared to a sponge that has soaked up images of this world to overflowing: an amazingly apt simile for today! Our body is "like Noah's ark inundated by the Flood" that washes us into the hands of the principalities and powers of this world. How can we survive that flood? What does it mean to remember God? How do we become free from ego fixation?

Sufis practice a basic principle of spiritual psychological counseling, namely the *ka'anna* (to act as if). The teaching sheikh always assigns the learning pupil something more and higher than what matches the pupil's degree of maturity and development. Symbolically speaking, the sheikh dresses the murid in a garment that is always too big, so the pupil has to grow through action by imitating the teacher. The ego is not engaged here at the level of what it can do now and so it does not even have to try to flee from itself like the monk putting on his sandals. Instead, an exercise in attentiveness, a stammering ritualistic repetition, is given to the pupil with the expectation that the being is discovered in the self that can learn to go beyond its boundaries.

In the first step of the audible or external *dhikr,* God is called upon as "He." It is the step of God's absence. Bodily movements, rhythmic swaying, and sudden leaping on one's feet accompanied by loud exclamations are all part of the next step. In this step, God is now called "You." In the third and secret step, the unity of God and the self is expressed. In relation to the ego that performs this step-by-step process of remembering, the transition from the absence of God or God-forgetfulness to the presence or remembrance of God can be interpreted as the ego being placed in the accusative, as Levinas puts it. *Me voici* is an accusative that is not derived from any nominative. The ego loses its place as the acting and determining subject in priority over every relationship. If Martin Buber's sentence is correct that "in the beginning was relationship," then the ego exists because it was beheld and addressed, accused and made use of.

Buber reflected on this problem in one of his childhood recollections. As an eleven-year-old, visiting his grandparents' farm, he developed a friendship with a dapple-gray horse. He would spend his time gently stroking the horse's neck. What he experienced from contact with the animal, he said, was the other, the enormous otherness of the other, but it did not remain something alien. The horse would snort softly; it was as if a conspirator gave an accomplice a signal that only the latter should be able to perceive. Suddenly, one day, the boy accidentally broke the relationship. While stroking the horse, the boy became aware of how much this action delighted him, and he suddenly felt his hand. This playfulness went on as before but something had changed, it was no longer "It." And when the next day, he went back to stroke his friend's neck, the horse would not lift his head. Buber describes in these terms what was destructive in the event: he had let the other exist only as his own experience, merely as a "my-ness."[1] In other words, he had not gotten rid of the ego. Instead, he had inserted himself as "my-ness," destroying the relationship. In Levinas's terminology, Buber had placed the ego that was already in the accusative into the nominative.

It is necessary to forget the ego, and that is exactly what mystical tradition has in mind when it connects remembering God and forgetting the ego. The process wherein the ego ceases to forget God is the same as the one wherein it begins to forget itself. Remembering and forgetting are two sides of one act. Forgetfulness of the ego, replacing the normal forgetfulness of God, is mystically speaking part of immersing and losing oneself, of falling in love, that is to say, one of the activities in which we depart from ourselves. A human being does not obtain a face by looking in a mirror, like the monk in the story told earlier. Having a face includes looking at something different and being captured by something outside ourselves. Losing ourselves in something that is not us is the most wonderful way of disempowering the ego and in this sense becoming free.

The mysterious "way inward" is not one on which one finally comes to know and find oneself. Instead, it is a way on which being possessed by the ego loses its power. The ego liberates itself because it knows itself as having always existed in the accusative.

A different relation to the ego and its needs would be one of the spiritual preconditions of a different style of life that does not build on plunder and rape. How did people come to perceive ego-lessness as liberation and understand freedom as freedom from the ego? Mystics of every tradition have fought against flooding the ego with objects that foster covetousness. In the worlds of poverty, this had subversive meaning; there was a noncoveting freedom from money and goods and a defiant independence from "the good life" and luxury. "Riches I heed not" sang the people conscious that next to the idol there are other values worth striving for.

In current globalized production, the remnants of that independence have to be eradicated. The consuming ego of the consumer must not show such disinterest in looks, accessories, outfits, and an environment shaped according to style. Instead, it is bombarded with ego-propaganda. Needs are altered in the sense of "more often," "faster," "more," "right away." The education in ego fixation is conducted worldwide by the media, adroitly using the real needs of human beings that traditionally are all affirmative: I would like to "be" more attractive, musical, quick-witted, appreciated. Those "being-needs," present in different degrees in all human beings, are titillated in advertising and, before they are recognized as such needs, are changed into "having-needs." I see the empty white beach, feel how wild and inviting it is, and am skillfully diverted to the product that I am to "enjoy" instead, which means buying it.

The ego is not only to be made greedy for new things. It is also to become thoroughly dependent on the possibilities of choice and the abundance of options. Buying is itself staged as a religious act in the temples of consumerism. The motto of the postmodern world and life therein may well be, "I consume, therefore I am." The artificial creation of needs is an essential component of economic life; the countermodel of "live simply so that others may simply live" is denigrated as sheer romanticism. We are further removed than ever before from an economy that sustains subsistence and is not hounded by progress. To be "over-choiced" with thirty different kinds of bread does indeed develop the shopper's awareness of differentiation and sense of taste. However, from the ego that is becoming dependent on such a surplus of choice, it also takes away the time and energy for other life pursuits. The ego is diverted and, with the help of the world of consumer goods, "turned in on itself" (*homo incurvatus in se ipsum*), as the tradition used to depict the sinner.

The least to be learned from the tradition of mysticism is that becoming empty in a world of surplus, learning to switch off, and limiting oneself are small steps in the liberation from consumerism, and that perhaps freedom cannot be imagined without letting go (see also chapter 5). To enter into the way from the ego to ego-liberation is a beginning in resistance. In the consumer culture of plundering, the ego turned into an addicted identity functions as the best guard in our jail; it controls and effectively suppresses our attempts to escape. We need a different relation to the ego that includes egolessness as the liberation from impositions and constraints destructive of life and that perceives the ego in terms of communal participation. Even Plotinus (205–270 C.E.), who strongly influenced Western mystical thought, remarked "Man as he now is has ceased to be the All. But when he ceases to be an individual he raises himself again and penetrates the whole world. Then, becoming one with the All, he creates the All."[2]

Going even further back in time, trying by this circuitous route to get closer to the point, I refer to the Chinese mystic and philosopher who is believed to have lived during the fourth century B.C.E. and became known by the name of Lao-tzu, "the ancient master." He understood the ego to be "a gift on loan to us by the universe." What is on loan is not taken as a possession but as a temporary and care-filled and loving acceptance of something that connects us with others around, before, and after us. An ego on loan is at home in the cosmos rather differently than the one possessed as one's own; it can leave itself behind and weave itself into larger webs. "Go out of yourself and let yourself go" (see chapter 4) is the medieval version of this kind of freedom. To be able to walk away from the ego fortified in possessiveness means to recognize what has been given as something on loan. By no longer having to be purely individual, the ego participates communally in the universe. The utterly unfathomable Tao, present before heaven and earth came to be, can be seen as the mother of the world (saying no. 25) or as the mother of ten thousand beings (saying no. 1). In this sense, Tao, the impersonal deity, has also a personal side. Lao-tzu, who came from a region of matriarchal culture, uses the image of mother but also speaks of the primordial father of all things (saying no. 4). What is decisive is the relation to the primordial ground of the universe, for it is this relation that creates a kind of ego-lessness in the temporarily loaned ego.

There is a story about the great impressionist painter Claude Monet (1840–1926) that throws light on this different relation to the ego. On Monet's eightieth birthday, a photographer from Paris visited him, wanting to take pictures of him. But Monet said coolly, "Come back next spring and take pictures of my flowers in the garden, they look more like me than I do." A mystical answer! Becoming ego-less does not begin with the superego's demands or rituals of purification but in the amazing sharing of the one life that is in everything.

"Go Where You Are Nothing!"

Ego-lessness is not a task to be performed; initially, it is happiness— the flowers in the garden really do resemble Monet more than his photo. A greater freedom is possible as fear and inconsolability fall away and, yes, consciousness, this needy individual being, recedes. "My soul was so captivated and delighted that I had no thought about my own salvation, and scarce reflected that there was a creature such as myself," writes an eighteenth-century man about a moment of mystic rapture.[3] Egocentricity melts away before the sun of mystical union.

According to Meister Eckhart, the goal of human life is to become free from oneself and all things. This freedom from the ego is not only a supra-temporal religious-ethical idea; the ego to be relinquished plays its particular role as the agent of "this world" where its binding function can be abolished in the process of letting oneself go. Today it oversees us in the prison of the false economic order by aligning our needs with that order. It makes sure that we venerate, research, and pay for the violence named "security." It makes us dependent on what Eckhart called the spirit of "mercantilism," or what John of the Cross identified as "cravings."

In his sermon on Jesus driving merchants and money changers from the temple in Jerusalem (Matt 21:12), Eckhart contrasts becoming rid of the ego with the mentality of mercantilism (see chapter 4). He begins by identifying God's temple with the human soul that God "wants to have emptied." Then Eckhart asks, "Why did Jesus drive out those who bought and sold?" What is to be said against those merchants and money changers, honest business people that they were, cheating no one, keeping their religious duties like fasting, keeping awake, and praying? What is wrong with mercantilism and its spirit?

Eckhart preached this sermon in Cologne, an emerging trading site that at the time had become the most important center of trade between Western and Eastern Europe. Eckhart was neither reclusive nor naive. His undisguised allusions to the world of economics prove him to be a critic of the mercantile spirit because it makes self-centering and ego fixation, what Eckhart also calls "selfness" *(Eigenschaft),* the basis of life. In the thinking that characterizes a mercantile mind-set, the world in divided into subject and object, seller and buyer; service is reciprocity. Everything is bounded by the gradually pervading circle of goods / money / goods to which the ego has to submit. Ego-centering is part of the mercantilists' foundation for what in later capitalism was openly referred to as the "enlightened self-interest of the individual" and embraced as the driving force of the economy. Eckhart recognized the profound significance of this thinking inasmuch as it relates not only to the economic domain, but also to the relationship of human beings one to another and to God. Indeed, this basic conviction includes God: "He" owes something in return to those who have rendered pious service to "Him." There is to be nothing that is not "quantifiable," to use a current term. Merchants have a claim on reward commensurate to service rendered. But God is not for sale and "truth does not desire any kind of mercantile exchange. God does not look out 'for number one,'"[4] contrary to the merchants and money changers that Jesus expels from the temple.

The issue about the ego's attachment to itself and the question of the possibility of freedom from the ego have to be raised against this background. The consciousness of the market collides with the hope of eventual liberation from the ego. Wherever the ego's understanding reigns as the subject of the economy, the ideal of freedom from the ego that the monks, Beguines, and mystics promoted comes into conflict. Ego-lessness may indeed be tolerated on occasion as a private alleviation of the worst personal aberrations, but as a goal of life, ego-lessness is irrelevant and foolish. As the late Middle Ages knew, ego, property, and violence have an inner connection. Being rid of self-interest and the annihilation of the ego must be understood as radically contradictory to the basic reality of the market.

The opposite notion to mercantilism is what Eckhart calls "being rid" *(ledig)*. This word has a number of meanings: unburdened, without imposed conditions, not being a serf, unencumbered, unoccupied, idle, or, as in current usage, unmarried. The soul that has stepped out of the self is said to be *ledig*. It has not made itself dependent on real or imagined needs, on the market of surplus choice and the self-interest of buyers and sellers. "If you wish to be completely rid of mercantilism, . . . you must be completely unbound, as nothingness is unbound and is neither here nor there."[5] Eckhart accuses the merchants in the temple of being "bound to their own ego, to time and number, to the before and after."[6] That bondage is the merchant's "handicap." To become free from what is one's own is to be a virgin, Eckhart once said, "unimpeded by any image of what I was when I was not yet."[7]

In their different way of living, what the Beguines were striving for was independence. In their perception, freedom was not defined as freedom to buy and sell. The true freedom of ego-lessness consists in the congruence of one's own renounced will with the will of God. It is the absence of what Rudolf Otto names in the beautiful trio of "created, individual and sundered will"[8]; they have been given up or annihilated. A line from Eckhart's poem about the mustard seed goes like this, "Your own ego must become naught" *(Dein Eigenes Ich muss werden zunicht)*. According to Kurt Ruh, this is "the religious core-assertion"[9] of all Eckhart's writings. Today, if we too can learn anything from Eckhart, it is this ego-lessness as the spiritual foundation for a different vision of common life than the one dictated by the total market.

John of the Cross is another teacher of freedom in ego-lessness (see also chapter 8). He maintained that freedom cannot dwell in a heart that is ruled by desires, that is, in the heart of a slave. Rather, it lives in a heart set free, the heart of a son. In one of his frequently cited great meditations he says,

> If you desire to season everything,
> seek your delight in nothing;
> if you desire to know everything,
> seek to know something in nothing;
> if you desire to possess everything,

seek to possess something in nothing;
if you desire to be everything,
seek to be something in nothing.[10]

The words *todo* (everything) and *nada* (nothing) are repeated again and again. The text describes how they belong together. Without using the word "God," he speaks of the longing "to be everything." He reflects on this yearning after having spoken to the *todo* wherein is embodied the search, the great desires of the learner. But the aim of the reflection is not to find the object of the search. It is to change desiring itself. Whoever wants everything must first be disrobed and annihilated, and must first attain to a humble detachment of the spirit. The way to everything leads into nothing and beyond.

If you desire to gain what you do not enjoy,
you must go where you enjoy nothing;
if you desire to reach what you do not know,
you must go where you know nothing;
if you desire to reach what you do not possess,
you must go where you possess nothing;
if you desire to become what you are not,
you must go where you are nothing.[11]

The word "desire" in the first section is elucidated in a paradoxical pattern and then expanded in the second section in the words "go where." "To go where" is more than an end in itself; it is taking to the road and moving on. The places of poverty where we are propertyless, powerless, and without importance are places where we learn to relinquish knowledge and power, possession and status. What does this "go where you are nothing" mean? Am I to look for joylessness? Am I to seek confirmation of my ignorance, acknowledge that I am poor, and declare my own impotence?

I understand this "go where" as more than an inner process of consciousness-raising. It is also the real experience of real people who resist the principalities and powers that rule over them. The citizens of the democratically organized rich world have access to places where they are *not* simply nothing. They can elect parliamentary deputies; they can appeal through courts of law and attempt to make their voices heard, however increasingly restricted that is turning out to be. And yet, repeatedly, in essential issues concerning creation, our fellow creatures, the disenfranchised and human laborers, experience failure. And then nothing seems more normal than to give up and let what cannot be changed stay as it is. "Go where you can accomplish something!" seems to be the imperative that has more rationality. What is to be learned from mystical ego-lessness goes beyond this.

John of the Cross speaks of the dark night that we enter into unprotected, without all the security mechanisms that we use for consolation and diversion. "Go where you are nothing" means trying to make manifest what has no lobby for its work, what exposes you in your nothingness, your inconsequentiality, and the negation of the self. And you are not to be ashamed of your nothingness. You are to let go of your fear of being nothing and be free for "the nothing that wants to be everything."

Those who have freely chosen this way of becoming ego-less, in the sense of having no power and authority, include many highly gifted twentieth-century people with affinities to mysticism. The great philosopher Ludwig Wittgenstein (1889–1951) chose to give away his millions and become a grade school teacher. Simone Weil worked on a factory assembly line. Albert Schweitzer went into the jungle at Lambarene. They all chose a place where they were nothing. "Go where you are nothing" also holds true for those who, in trying to block transports of nuclear waste, face the superior strength of a heavily armed police. At the atomic waste site of Gorleben in Germany, resisters—and life itself—are nothing.

Asceticism: For and Against

There exists a somewhat anti-Christian commonplace phrase that says, "forget your ego, but never deny your self." On the contrary, in connection with following after Jesus, the New Testament speaks without inhibition of the denial of self (Matt 16:24) and even of hating one's own life (John 12:25). The distinction between "ego" and "self" seeks to keep both the liberation from the ego, ego-lessness, and the new being of the self that is eventually discovered. Christ-in-me or the Buddha-nature of every human being are names for this self that has come free of the ego.

One of the great difficulties within mystical tradition and praxis is the overlap of the learning that leads to the ego and that which leads to the self. This overlap makes for a lack of clarity. It is often in the very experience of losing or forgetting oneself that there grows a kind of ego-inflation, a narcissistic super-elevation that believes it can satiate itself by losing the ego.

What Eckhart called "being caught in sweetness" (see also chapter 11) appears in some accounts from the late Middle Ages as a kind of craving for experience. It yearns for inundation by the unconscious and then, when a dry spell sets in, it suffers from deprivation, that is, from the very ego that it should have already "forgotten" or relinquished long ago. One has the impression from this mysticism tinged with neurosis that the yearning for ego-lessness was the best warrant for the inflationary ego.

Most older cultures as well as the so-called nature religions (see chapter 1) use the term "asceticism" to speak of the exercise of repressing the ego, to reduce its claim, and to check its obtrusiveness. A variety of ascetic practices that prepare for and lead to ego-lessness have played a role in the history of mysticism. Among them are sustained or periodic fasting, abstinence from certain food or drink, observance of place-specific taboos, chastity, isolation—to such degrees as having walls erected around oneself—sleep deprivation, flagellation or self-martyrdom called "discipline," homelessness, unceasing itinerancy, and self-humiliation. Asceticism is a way of interrupting oneself, weaning oneself of habits; it changes our way of life and how we accommodate ourselves to the times and spaces we inhabit.

According to John of the Cross, the soul must clarify its relation to things even before its ascent to Mount Carmel. For only then can the two-faceted purification of appetites, desires, and demands begin: the active one carried by the spiritually guided soul itself and the passive one initiated on the higher steps by God. The four natural sensations of joy, hope, fear, and pain are to be mortified and set at rest. Thus the recommendation to "seek always what is difficult and never what is easier, . . . not what consoles but what exhausts, not the advantageous but the disadvantageous, not to demand but to desire nothing." By means of this kind of self-teaching, natural sensuality and delight in one's own success are to be purified so as to free the meditating person to receive the supernatural. This recommended route even reaches the stages of self-despising: "Occupy yourself with abasement and desire that everyone did so."[12]

I relate to those radical demands of ascetic tradition in a divided, that is, a modern way. I will endeavor to name my No and my Yes. I have critical questions about human needs and people that engage in asceticism. Ascetics engage in limiting, taming, and denying human needs that are often spoken of without differentiation in the word "appetites." Are the appetites false that compel us to quench our thirst, sleep when tired, and seek warmth in the cold? If a form of ego-lessness is derived by an asceticism that thwarts those appetites, what does that mean? Is the presupposition of such asceticism not the dualism of spirit and nature? Does it not in its extreme form lead to the destruction of the physical body rather than to the healing and hallowing of the whole body?

The second question to the ascetic tradition is connected with the false dualism that calls for the dominance of spirit and the subjugation of nature. To whom is it to be directed? Is that ascetic tradition appropriate only for celibate men, or could it be lived also by women who are pregnant, nursing, and responsible for other people? Is this praxis of freely chosen renunciation perhaps meaningful only where the basic needs of life have already been met? The disempowerment of the ego that mysticism needs presupposes an independent ego capable of making decisions. Where one is striving for ego-lessness there has to be an ego. Is this ego not almost always thought of as a male, self-determining, autonomous ego?

Every patriarchal culture assigns sacrificial roles to women and burdens them with self-denial. Ego-lessness is commended as a virtue to those who are not permitted to develop an ego on account of societal constraints, which we buttress by role-fixing ideologies. For a long time, asceticism masked sexism, but today other methods are used to the same end. Today it is consumerism, as the preferred means for excluding women from autonomy and power, that masks sexism. It is not ego-lessness that is the noble aim but fixation on the infinite need to possess. With the aid of such needs people are kept from becoming human beings. In a kind of post-ascetic formation program in pure self-realization, the power that resides in beautiful ego-lessness is denied.

In the last few years, many Third World women have repeatedly expressed the desire that their children be spared the burden of ignorance or the lack of education, of unwanted subordination, and of the ego-lessness that is forced perennially on precisely the poorest women. If asceticism is to be something different today than this premodern denial of autonomy and self-determination, it must be conceived of differently and in nonsexist terms. It must start from the existing dependency of the ego on the world of consumer goods, a dependency hailed as autonomy and free choice. The issue today is a different relationship to things, not the mortification of the body. In the context of globalization, asceticism means simplicity in the sense of simplification of lifestyle and needs. This means less, smaller, less often, and more consciously.

We have known for a long time that poverty can destroy the body and render the soul deaf and insensitive. What has yet to be learned is that overabundance of things and enjoyments also devours the soul. An appropriate relation to things, one that does not overwhelm the senses, cannot grow when things are everpresent for our consumption. For example, a child who has thirty dolls to play with will give none of them a name, cannot love or hate anyone of them, will not develop a fantasy life with them, and will soon be bored playing with them. What that means is in complete accordance with and in the interest of the market as the great dictator. The child will want to have more and more new things without thereby being able to drive away boredom. A child growing up this way has learned quickly to look for life's intensity in quantity, but that search is futile. An appropriate relation to things, one that allows the erotic dimension of our being to come into its own, cannot develop as long as we consume things indiscriminately simply because they are always overabundantly available. Overabundance destroys the intensity of people and their capacity to enjoy and to be related.

In cultures where asceticism developed and was practiced, people knew that one can suffocate when every option is a readily available one. Without self-limitation, without fixed boundaries—like those given in creation between day and night, summer and winter, being young and growing old—life loses its humanness. Asceticism means to renounce at least for periods of time the options that present themselves. In bygone cultures of poverty there were times for fasting, waking, withdrawing, and keeping silence. Perhaps people believed that life itself could be saved by giving up parts of it.

In rich societies, the fundamental idea of sacrifice is highly suspect; it contradicts the basic constitution of the world of affluence. Sacrifice, as well as those who are to do the sacrificing have indeed been much abused. Even so, voluntary sacrifice, freely renouncing status, and limiting career or other options available to oneself can consolidate one's capacity for happiness. This seems very apparent to me in ecological resistance movements. No one can feel at home in a world that has to be bought and used up. We ourselves as well as the environment are damaged by consumerism; it dulls the senses so that people no longer know how to smell, taste, feel, and see. A world without sensuality—replaceable anytime by the "virtual reality" of video and computer—is also a world without sense; the relationship between sense and sensuality is more than etymological. All of the senses live through sensuality and no sensuality has a life apart from culture.

Asceticism is most often associated with relinquishing and ego-lessness. But a limitation that is sought after, freely chosen, and affirmed has also to do with enjoying life, with mystical joy. The self that forgets its ego dives deep into the universe; it is enabled to make itself of no account and that also means that it can open itself. To step out of oneself means to know amazement. When I see a child overwhelmed with joy at seeing a dog, I no longer question life. I am immersed in amazement when I hear a child singing or watch the migration of cranes flying north in the clear spring sky. All of this is part of asceticism in the sense of becoming ego-less. Things them-selves have a song and a language of their own, pointing beyond themselves and praising God in hidden, divine names. The ego that has become ego-less sees in amazement that a piece of goodness lies in life. Beauty heals and beauty makes devout, but in order to notice beauty I need to dismiss the ego. I must learn to see with the eyes of Claude Monet.

Tolstoy's Conversion from the Ego to God

In the modern world many examples can be found that reveal detachment from preestablished worlds of life and their dictates to the ego. I want to cite the life story of the great Russian writer, Leo Nikolaevich Tolstoy (1828–1910). His religious conversion also rep-resents a mystical coming to life wherein arises a different relation to the ego and to society.

At the age of fifty, Tolstoy's life was in crisis, as described in his *Confession* (1879), a work composed of memories and religio-philo-sophical reflections. There are no external causes for the crisis; Tol-stoy felt healthier and stronger than friends his own age, his family life was happy, and his two novels had won for him great success as a writer. Suddenly, in ever more frequent moments of confusion or "faltering," he was asking himself how to live, what to do. Looking back over his life he was becoming aware of the emptiness into which he had fallen.

"One can live only so long as one is intoxicated, drunk with life; but when one grows sober one cannot fail to see that it is all a stupid cheat. What is truest about it is that there is nothing even funny or silly in it; it is cruel and stupid, purely and simply."[13] The ego experiences itself as part of that cruel and stupid world. Gone is the interest, excitement, and joy of life that had marked the life of the writer and popular educator, who came from an aristocratic family, who had served as an officer in the Crimean War, and who jeopardized his estate through his compulsive gambling. "It was an aspiration of my whole being to get out of life. Behold me then, a happy man and in good health, hiding the rope in order not to hang myself to the rafters of my room. . . . I . . . increasingly kept asking myself how to end the business, whether by the rope or the bullet."[14] In his reflective searching, he turns to Buddha, Socrates, Solomon, and Schopenhauer, on account of their pessimism, the wisest of all humans, and it is only in hesitant steps that Tolstoy separates himself from a disgust with the world to which the romantic aesthetic ego of his spiritual environment had accommodated itself so well. He recognizes *Weltschmerz* (world-weariness) to be a characteristic of the upper class to which he belongs and from then on regards it as conventional, aestheticistic, intoxicated with art, and motivated solely by personal ambition.

After this break with his former existence, Tolstoy's zeal for truth brought reproach. He was called a fanatic for whom art was no longer all-sufficient. Shortly before his death, fellow novelist Ivan Turgenev (1883) implored Tolstoy to return to literature. But Tolstoy's renunciation of the art that served only the ego's self-enrichment was irrevocable. From that time onward, he wrote "folk-tales" whose heroes are uneducated serfs and peasants. He wanted art to be for everyone and to speak to the soul of the people.

As a young man and after reading Voltaire and Rousseau, Tolstoy fell away from the Orthodox faith. What it had to offer seemed to be unrelated to reality and unable to withstand rational knowledge. His personal crisis was at the same time a crisis in the belief in progress as it was represented by the educated Western world and its devotees in Russia. The crisis led him to approach the old world of faith, a world taken for granted by the majority of the peasants who owned nothing and among whom this lord of the manor lived. Foremost in his new way of life was serving one's neighbor. "I gave up the life of the conventional world, recognizing it to be no life, but a parody on life, which its superfluities keep us from comprehending."[15] In the classic sense of the term, a purification of the ego began and he became free from and rid of the bonds to his own class. Their clinging to what is superfluous and insincere, their lack of interest in the ordinary life of the great majority of people, and their mania for luxury, aesthetics, and refinement stood in an unbridgeable contrast to what Tolstoy now wanted to know and talk about. He was interested in what "people really live by."

The only option he saw was conversion, in the manner of the Sermon on the Mount, to a conscious faith in God. As before, what separated him from the Orthodox Church was his rejection of fundamental teachings like transubstantiation and the Trinity. However, an even more decisive impediment was his uncompromising stance on war and the death penalty and his sharp condemnation of intolerance toward people of other faiths. The Russian Orthodox Church excommunicated him in 1901.

His passion and unconventionality, his moral pathos, and his lack of ambiguity in matters of luxury and violence arose from this turn to premodernity in a seamless manner. What changed was his relation to the ego that was often advanced by modernity as the highest court of appeal, becoming the only god that was left. "The less God / the more ego" is how the process of modernity may be summed up. Here the ego takes shape in ambiguity: in pleasure and in constraints. With less God around, the ego can enjoy itself undisturbed while it is also subjected very differently to the constraints of self-examination and constant observation. It can no longer lose itself to anything and so becomes its own, albeit merciless god.

The step into ego-lessness that Tolstoy took in embracing his conversion is a step towards disempowering the ego. Power is given back to the good, shared power of God. In one of his late masterful tales he describes a snowstorm on the steppes that overtakes two people, "master and servant," threatening their lives. The servant Nikita is an industrious, good-natured *mushik* (peasant), who talks to all the animals and is exploited by his master. Poorly clothed, he patiently and without complaint awaits his death from exposure. The master is a *nouveau riche* merchant whose business pursuits have brought them to this hopeless state of being lost in the snow. He tries at first to escape from the blizzard on horseback, leaving the useless servant to his fate on the ice-covered sled. The horse comes back and when the master sees the old man half-frozen, his profiteering, greed-nurtured egomania suddenly vanishes. The master lies on top of the servant, warms him with his fur coat and body heat, and saves the servant's life while freezing to death himself in the storm. Told in simple language, this is a mystical conversion of a merchant and "master," who suddenly believes that he is Nikita and Nikita is he, and that life is not in himself but in Nikita. He dies with the words, "Nikita lives and, therefore, so do I."

Freedom from the "Ring of Cold": Dag Hammarskjöld

The ego and becoming ego-less were also factors in the life of Dag Hammarskjöld (1905–1961), a Swedish mystic who was also a high-ranking political figure. From 1953 until his murder in the Congo, he was Secretary General of the United Nations. Hammarskjöld worked tirelessly and uncompromisingly to resolve conflicts without recourse to weapons and to establish the UN as an instrument of peace in the midst of the turmoil of decolonization. Only after his death and the subsequent discovery of his diary entries in his New York apartment did it become known that this highly respected politician was a Christian mystic. His thinking was shaped by the traditions of Eckhart, John of the Cross, Pascal, Henri Bergson, Saint John-Perse, and Albert Schweitzer.

An aristocrat of the spirit from the high nobility of Sweden, Hammarskjöld was unusually talented and light years removed from all mediocrity, informal chatter, and trivialization. He was cool and unapproachable—a solitary figure who maintained an irrevocable distance between himself and others as well as to the constantly and radically suspect ego, not to speak of every form of mystical "sweetness." He writes about his own isolation: "He had no need for the divided responsibility in which others seek to be safe from ridicule, because he had been granted a faith which required no confirmation,"[16] that is to say, in Eckhart's sense, "without a why," free of purpose. For him, that mysticism and action belong together was unquestionable. Mystical experience in "[f]reedom which is at one with distance" was for him "a freedom in the midst of action," and "[i]n our era, the road to holiness necessarily passes through the world of action."[17]

Hammarskjöld is a human being of modernity. He is painfully aware that with the disappearance of God the ego moves forward to become the sole divinity. More than half of his short diary entries reflect on the ego. "Its efforts to shelter its love create a ring of cold around the Ego which slowly eats its way inward to the core."[18]

This highest-ranking civil servant in the world suffered from growing isolation, which was dictated as much by that top position as by his education and character; but, most profoundly, it was grounded in the ego-centeredness that follows upon the absence of God. Ego-fixation is not in the first instance a moral problem but *the* religious problem of the ego that believes in reason. "The less God / the more ego" applies here, at least that is how Hammarskjöld himself saw it. "God does not die on the day when we cease to believe in a personal deity, but we die on the day when our lives cease to be illumined by the steady radiance, renewed daily, of a wonder, the source of which is beyond all reason."[19] The mysticism of the good beginning in creation, the vital power of amazement that is there before asceticism, and the halting search for a God who is thirsty and wants to be needed—these are the goals "beyond reason." Hammarskjöld knew early on that one can approach these goals only as one leaves behind dependency on the ego. It is from this dependency, this "icy ring" that he suffered his whole life. "You are your own god—and are you surprised when you find that the wolf-pack is hunting you across the desolate ice-fields of winter?"[20] Not without reason does he call his entries, often written in a crystal-clear opacity, a sort of white paper on his negotiations with himself and with God. The negotiation will succeed only as the ego is rid of itself, hands itself over, and sacrifices itself, which is one of Hammarskjöld's key concepts that perhaps prefigures his own end. To this day, whether he died at the hand of an assassin or in a traffic accident remains unclear.

But how can the ego become mystically free when it has been so schooled as to see right through itself in whatever disguise, when it knows so incorruptibly and desperately who it is? In 1941 Hammarskjöld took stock of his own ego—often spoken of as "he"—that always revolves only around itself. It is a devastating summation. With unparalleled ironic acuity, he juxtaposes positive praise of the ego—he was upright, modest, protective of life and others—and bitter clarity about this ego. "He stood erect—as a peg-top does as long as the whip keeps lashing it. He was modest—thanks to a robust conviction of his own superiority. He was unambitious—all he wanted was a life free from cares and he took more pleasure in the failures of others than in his own successes. He saved his life by never risking it—and complained that he was misunderstood."[21] In this account of the ego there is no whimpering, no prevarication, no secret hope for pity. Hammarskjöld did not pray for the supernatural intervention of a divine power; the faith he struggled for was no nostalgic kindergarten religion. It was a grown-up, this-worldly mysticism.

He has been called one of the loneliest people of the twentieth century. It took long years of despairing of the ego before, coinciding with the appointment to high office, he could embrace the mystical voices that had grown ever clearer. He was not someone who became a mystic overnight. But ever since the turn of the year 1952/1953, the new presence of God is unmistakable in the greater directness of Hammarskjöld's style, the biblical references, and the meditative, sometimes lyrical language. "Not I, but God in me" he can say in 1953.[22]

Before this knowledge of being called, there was a search for life's being, a search where radical self-criticism and equally radical doubt were joined. He remarks sarcastically, "On the bookshelf of life, God is a useful work of reference, always at hand but seldom consulted."[23] Hammarskjöld accuses himself of solipsism, greed for power, and a death-wish.[24] He lives in an incessant self-critical observation, such as "joyless and a killer of joy,"[25] and he feels "disgust at . . . [his] own emptiness"[26] and loathes the nothingness of the ego. "What I ask for is unreasonable: that life shall have a meaning. What I strive for is impossible: that my life shall acquire a meaning. I dare not believe, I do not see how I shall ever be able to believe: I am not alone."[27] Thus, the brilliant political rise of Hammarskjöld was accompanied by a merciless critique of the ego and a helpless, desperate search for someone or something that can soften its overwhelming importance. As for many mystical thinkers, the question remained also for him whether this is about a personal God or life's energy and power. "I don't know Who—or what—put the question, I don't know when it was put. I don't even remember answering. But at some moment I did answer Yes to Someone—or something."[28] In the midst of these reflections on the self the mystical concept of becoming naked emerges. One of the oldest longings of all people of mystical sensibility is to be rid of disguises to the point of becoming naked. "Clad in this 'self', the creation of irresponsible and ignorant persons, meaningless honours and catalogued acts—strapped into the straight-jacket of the immediate. To step out of all this, and stand naked on the precipice of dawn—acceptable, vulnerable, free: in the Light, with the Light, of the Light. Whole, real in the Whole. Out of myself as a stumbling block, into myself as fulfillment."[29] To become naked is one of the great metaphors for the ego finally set free. It expresses in one term two experiences that Hammarskjöld names "stumbling block" and "fulfillment": to take off the clothes that make us different, to put away the glasses, wigs, and masks, and to throw away titles, diplomas, prizes, and trophies. The other ego, having become ego-less, called "fulfillment," is free to give itself and to disregard itself.

Nearly all mystics live in an odd combination of humility and pride. Bayezid is said to have spoken these words to God, "when I am with you I am worth more than anyone, and when I am with myself I am worth less than anyone."[30] Hammarskjöld says much the same in the following entry. "Except in faith, nobody is humble. The mask of weakness or of phariseeism is not the naked face of humility. And, except in faith, nobody is proud. The vanity displayed in all its varieties by the spiritually immature is not pride. To be, in faith, both humble and proud: that is, to *live*, to now [sic] that in God I am nothing but that God is in me."[31] The relation to one's own ego changes in the state of "God in me." The finally discovered "Yes to God" means "Yes to Fate: yes to yourself."[32] Again and again the idea of sacrifice emerges both as sacrificing oneself and as accepting suffering in the sense of following after Christ. The way of triumph is the one that leads to downfall; the price for engaging oneself for life is to be reviled and the deepest humiliation means "the only elevation possible to man."[33] Even the sacrifice that does not yield healing and certitude, and even the despised sacrifice wherein the ego gets rid of itself means freedom in submission. The foundation on which the ego exists that has become ego-less is that God needs human beings and does not have to be looked on as an idol of fate that rules with a free hand just as it pleases. This cooperating of God and the human being who has become free of the ego is one of the basic certainties of mystical life. "I am the vessel. The draught is God's. And God is the thirsty one."[34]

Success and Failure

How do we become free of the ego? In the twentieth century, Simone Weil provided a new instruction in preparing oneself for this work. In her endeavors she took up the notion of "attention," perhaps from Buddhism. In one of her most beautiful essays that deals with "a Christian conception of studies," she combines school and university studies, generally associated with scholarly, scientific thinking, with the mystical sense of dedication that integrates and focuses us. "If we concentrate our attention on trying to solve a problem of geometry, and if at the end of an hour we are no nearer to doing so than at the beginning, we have nevertheless been making progress each minute of that hour in another more mysterious dimension. Without our knowing or feeling it, this apparently barren effort has brought more light into the soul. The result will one day be discovered in prayer."[35] Simone Weil explicitly brings attention and prayer together. "The quality of the attention counts for much in the quality of the prayer."[36] Every exercise directed to our ability to be attentive changes us inasmuch as it diverts us from focusing on the self. "Even if our efforts of attention seem for years to be producing no result, one day a light that is in exact proportion to them will flood the soul."[37] From this sort of understanding that hovers between concentration and attention a new freedom from the ego can emerge. It is perhaps the greatest step in the "un-forming" that Heinrich Seuse speaks of in his mystical journey toward the "acquiescing" human being. It is preconditional for being "conformed to the image of Christ," which Simone Weil regards as the preparation for prayer. "Students must . . . work without any wish to gain good marks, to pass examinations, to win school successes; without any reference to their natural abilities and tastes, applying themselves equally to all their tasks with the idea that each one will help to form them in the habit of that attention which is the substance of prayer."[38] The purpose-free nature of Eckhart's *sunder warumbe* can hardly be put more clearly. "Attention consists in suspending our thought, leaving it detached, empty, and ready to be penetrated by the object."[39] In this emptiness something evil in oneself is unintentionally destroyed and a kind of inattentiveness disappears. Simone Weil makes use of the beautiful examples of writers' work in which one enters upon "a way of waiting . . . for the right word to come of itself at the end of our pen, while we merely reject all inadequate words."[40]

To reject the inadequate, not to be satisfied with it, is mystical activity. Emptiness is a better condition for the soul than being flooded with orientations that turn the ego into a helpmate of destructive reality. In rejecting inadequate words, we also reject inadequate feelings, images, conceptions, and desires so that in true prayer false desires vanish and others, greater and perhaps more mute ones, arise. Here the classical philosophical distinctions between activity and passivity is abolished. The ego becoming free acts and, at the same time, lets itself be acted upon.

What do ego-lessness and becoming unattached mean in connection with today's mystical way in the form of resistance? Concepts like asceticism, renunciation of consumerism, and using less and simpler ways of living make it apparent that the way of conscious resistance has to lead from ego-fixation (that globalized production requires as a partner) to ego-lessness. What is missing is a reflection that shows more clearly how complicit we are ourselves in the consumerist ego that the economy desires. I want to elucidate this in terms of a question that every nonconformist group, every critical minority wishing to contribute to the establishment of a different life has to face, namely, the question of success.

Decisions about possible actions are weighed in a world governed by market considerations by one and only one criterion: success. Is it necessary now to boycott certain aspects of consumerism, to blockade nuclear waste transports, to hide refugees threatened with repatriation, or offer pacifist resistance against further militarization? Whenever such topics are raised, questions like the following are regularly heard: "What's the use of protesting, everything has been decided long ago?" "Can anything be changed anyway?" "What do you think you will accomplish?" "Whom do you want to influence?" "Who is paying attention?" "Will the media report it?" "How much publicity will it have?" "Do you really believe that this can succeed?" Sadly and helplessly, many people say, "I am with you, but this symbolic or real action is of no use against the concentrated power of the others." Questions and responses like these nourish doubt in democracy, but worse, they jeopardize partiality for life. Behind questions like these lurks a cynicism that shows how powerfully the ego is tied into conditions and relations of power.

Martin Buber said that "success is not a name of God." It could not be said more mystically nor more helplessly. The nothing that wants to become everything and needs us cannot be named in the categories of power. (That is why the "omnipotent" God is a male, helpless, and antimystical metaphor that is void of any responsibility.) To let go of the ego means, among other things, to step away from the coercion to succeed. It means to "go where you are nothing." Without this form of mysticism, resistance loses it focus and dies before our very eyes. It is not that creating public awareness, winning fellow participants, and changing how we accept things is beside the point. But the ultimate criterion for taking part in actions of resistance and solidarity cannot be success because that would mean to go on dancing to the tunes of the bosses of this world.

To become ego-less, unattached, and free also involves dismissing the agent of power *within* us who wants to persuade us that given the huge power of institutions, resisting has no chance of succeeding. To become unattached means, in addition, to correct the relation of success and truth.

I use my own experiences from the years of the German peace movement to elucidate the point. I assumed, with a certain naiveté, that the questions journalists put to me were motivated by an interest in truth. I thought it important to find out whether particular nuclear bombs could be used for defense apart from exclusive use in first-strike offensives. I wanted to have figures showing what armaments cost and then to relate this to what those moneys could do for the education and healthcare of children. I believed that the connection between arming ourselves and letting people starve was what had to be made known. And I assumed that those who asked me questions were also interested in such often concealed truths.

It took years before I understood that the majority of media representatives had quite different interests. They did not want to know and write about who the victims of arming ourselves are; they "covered" demonstrations and protesters only from the perspective of securing viewers for that evening's news telecast. The interest in success, asking questions such as "who are you anyway and whom or what do you represent?" had increasingly superceded interest in truth. Attempts to revive an interest in truth, to make the victims visible instead of mindlessly orienting oneself to the winners, had little chance. Long years of mass movements for a peace no longer constructed on arms, for economic justice and solidarity, and for the integrity of creation have not succeeded. Discouragement over this is a bitter and undeniable reality.

Is what Bonhoeffer called "shoving a spoke in the wheel" something that we can do at all today? Mysticism of ego-lessness helps me deal with God's defeats in this world. To get rid of the ego means not to sacrifice truth to the mentality of success, to become unattached and not to uphold success as the ultimate criterion. An Italian mystic of the fourteenth century, at one time a wealthy cloth merchant, let himself and his companions be bound and driven with blows and insults through the streets where once he made his money. Just as Christ had been regarded as a madman, so these friends of God wanted to be regarded as fools and idiots (*pazzi e stolti*).[41]

Something of this foolishness is found in many forms of organized resistance. Women are met with rudeness and invective when they hold vigils for tortured prison inmates. To become free from the coercion of compulsory success is a mystical seed that is not always at the fore of consciousness but that does sprout precisely in the defiance of "keeping on keeping on." A slogan was coined in the antinuclear energy movement that reflects some of this defiance of ego-lessness,

Wer sich nicht wehrt, lebt verkehrt (the person who does not put up a fight, lives a wrong life). A Hassidic rabbi puts it in more pious language, maintaining steadfast in prayer, he said: "and if you don't want to redeem Israel yet then redeem the goyim alone."[42]

There are many mystical teachers who can help in satisfactorily reaching the point of no return with what they teach us concerning the unattached ego, about going out of ourselves, and about freedom from constraint. Thomas Merton, a Trappist monk and a leading opponent of the Vietnam War, wrote about the mystical foundation of this freedom in a letter to James Forest in 1966: "Do not depend on the hope of results. When you are doing the sort of work you have taken on, essentially an apostolic work, you may have to face the fact that your work will be apparently worthless and even achieve no result at all, if not perhaps results opposite to what you expect. As you get used to this idea, you start more and more to concentrate not on the results but on the value, the rightness, the truths of the work itself."[43] He advises the younger pacifist to become free from the need to find his own affirmation. For then "you can be more open to the power that will work through you without your knowing it."[44] Living in mystical freedom one can say then with Eckhart, "I act so that I may act." Being at one with creation represents a conversion to the ground of being. And this conversion does not nourish itself from demonstrable success but from God.

Years ago, American friends persuaded me that the best way to remember the infanticide of Bethlehem, when King Herod ordered all children under the age of two to be killed (Matt 2:16-18), was for peace activists to go to the Pentagon on the second day of Christmas, which is dedicated to the remembrance of those innocent children, and pour blood on the white pillars there in order to give witness to what is planned and commanded there. I went along, but with many doubts. Was it only a gesture, a kind of theatrical production? What success would it achieve? The clearer that question became to me, the more astounded I was that my friends in this mystical peace movement, shaped by the Catholic Worker movement (see chapter 13), had left this question behind them. They had become free of it and their freedom seemed greater to me than my own.

13. POSSESSION AND POSSESSIONLESSNESS

When the bishop of Assisi once spoke to Saint Francis about his life so rich in deprivation and his lack of possession, he was told, "My lord, if we wanted to have possessions we would also need to have arms for our defense. But that is where the quarrels and fights come from that so often impede love for God and neighbor. That is why we do not want to possess temporal things in this world.

FRANCIS OF ASSISI

Having or Being

A MYSTIC SUFI SAID of Jesus that he had become so detached from worldly things on his pilgrimage "that he only had a cup and a comb in his possession. But he threw away the cup when he saw a man drinking from his hands and the comb when he watched a man using his fingers instead of a comb."[1] In its own crazy way, the story points to the unending process from having possessions and to being without them; the gesture of throwing away the cup and comb speaks of liberation and beauty. It reminds me of a middle-income worker in the Black Forest region who wrote to me that he had "thrown away" his car after having studied about dying forests. It takes him almost three times as long now to get to work but he feels freer than ever before. The letter of this unknown man has a kind of clumsy beauty.

Many religious traditions regard possessions as something damaging to the soul; poverty is held up as an ideal. Possessionlessness *(faqr,* as Rumi calls it), is "a strong physician," a wet-nurse that nourishes and educates the human being; it is also the "home of all beauty."[2] What does this disconcerting hymn of praise to possessionlessness signify? In the Sermon on the Mount, why are the poor said to be blessed here and now, not in some beyond? For what reasons should owning a utilitarian object like a comb or car be harmful?

Possessions are often regarded as a kind of life-threatening drug, impeding the power of judgment. "Sloth and cowardice creep in with every dollar or guinea we have to guard."[3] Having contributes to rendering the ego dependent. In having dead things the ego approaches being dead itself. Possession occupies those who possess and contradicts the ideal of having life. Even things that make daily life and work easier are seen to be a kind of seduction into the mentality of possessors and the existence shaped by having. Buddhism calls this craving, and the traditions of Judaism and Christianity call it avarice.

The desire to possess is marked by an unceasingly growing, voracious element that manifests itself in the simple desire to have more, but also in the growing dependency on consumerist habits that people do not want to give up. The ego loses its benign distance from things to be used and is ruled by the urge to possess them. This rapidly infects other aspects of life. Like objects that one wants to have available, partners, relatives, and friends come to be seen as having to be possessed. The ownership relation that develops and prevails assumes a natural right to dispose a person like an object. Enjoyment and pleasure obscure clear judgment because, as John of the Cross put it, there is no conscious enjoying of a creature without wanting simultaneously to own it. Desiring or craving, knowing or disposing, and having or possessing are conjoined in something that is called domination.

In his famous sermon on the first beatitude concerning poverty, Meister Eckhart names the three conditions of "inward poverty": to desire nothing, to know nothing, and to have nothing.[4] All three forms of mystical poverty are focused on the nothing whose concrete form and most important metaphor is, in Christian mysticism, construed as becoming naked. This nothing is what can neither bind nor rule over me. Having nothing means having it at one's disposal and being ruler over it. The philosophically more naive author of *The Cloud of Unknowing* says in connection with this un-formation, "Do not leave off, but press on earnestly in that nothing with an alert desire in your will to have God, whom no man can know. For I tell you truly that I would rather be in this way nowhere bodily, wrestling with this blind nothing, than to have such power that I could be everywhere bodily whenever I would, happily engaged with all this 'something' like a lord with his possessions."[5] In his *Having or Being*, psychotherapist and social scientist Erich Fromm develops the question of "having" on the basis of Eckhart's sermon. It is "being" that Fromm juxtaposes with the craze to possess that he sees at work in both capitalism and the former state socialism. The little word "or" between having and being is the new element of his thesis. It is not a matter of a friendly coexistence of having and being, of "having" as the prerequisite for eventually achieving "being." "Our judgments are extremely biased because we live in a society that rests on private property, profit, and power as the pillars of existence. To acquire, to own, and to make a profit are the sacred and inalienable rights of the individual in the industrial society. What the sources of property are does not matter; nor does possession impose any obligations on the property owner."[6] This being oriented by having is said to be rooted in human nature and, for that reason, unchangeable. But it is what destroys the relation to the neighbor, to nature, and to the ego.

Fromm makes a very helpful distinction between possession for functional purposes and acquisitiveness that is without use-value, serving only to consolidate the ego's social status and to secure the future or to satisfy an ever more autonomous, unmitigated avarice. Of course, Fromm knows that humans cannot live without having things. However, he believes that for some forty thousand years since Homo sapiens first emerged, humans thought of and lived in terms of utility-possession and did not submit to the coercive commandment to "go and have!" According to Fromm, it was only advanced capitalism that brought about an altered mind-set in which "being" human is redefined as "being" *if* or *what* you have. Even in the thirties, advertisements of savings banks in Germany made presumptuous proclamations that "you are somebody when you have something." Such a mind-set reflects the rapid turnabout from use-value to the cult of private ownership and concretizes what mystical tradition warns against: that intrinsically enjoyable possession becomes a burden that must be secured, and that the master and owner becomes the slave and servant of his property. The promised "castle" turns into a prison.

In a twofold way, mystical tradition helps resist the tendency to define being in terms of having. The radical demeanor of the Jesus of the Sufis, who throws away cup and comb so that he might be free, and the craziness of Saint Francis who tolerates money only on the manure pile, give evidence of resistance and beauty that are made visible in the greater freedom from having to have and having to own. They are mystical gestures that invite us to resist. But they also have a reformist side, related to everyday life inasmuch as throwing away possessions instructs us how to make functional, limited, simplified use of our possessions.

What can be learned here is that often making do with less means having more energy and time for other things. Our relation to things becomes more relaxed in that we can look upon them as things that have been given for the short term, on loan so to speak. No longer claiming autonomy, they lose their power over their owners. The Sufis and many other traditions that are radically critical of possessions point to the jubilant leap into freedom.

But the tradition that praised poverty and becoming unattached always distinguished clearly between voluntarily chosen poverty and that into which people are thrown without being asked. The two may overlap inasmuch as even inherited or imposed poverty may be embraced voluntarily, welcomed as a gift of God, and turned, after the fact, into something freely chosen. Nevertheless, the difference between an imposed fate and the freely chosen "different life" is in no way abolished.

Let me give an example from the United States. In the early sixties in Georgia, in the Christian community called "Koinonia," an interesting attempt was made to join together black and white agricultural workers in a kibbutz-like way of life. The white participants were primarily middle-class college students. They had consciously chosen a lower social status, without career and property. The regional blacks, children of the impoverished farm population, could not go along; they had just begun to find knowledge, education, and to learn the use of the necessities of life. Despite high idealism and goodwill on both sides, the upward mobility consciousness of the one group collided head-on with the downward mobility aspirations of the other. The attempt failed even though, today, the community continues to wrestle with the question of how voluntary poverty is to be lived out.

Naked and Following the Naked Savior: Francis of Assisi

Just as there needs to be an ego in order to achieve a form of ego-lessness, there has to be some property before one can learn to throw it away. No one teaches this as much as Giovannio Bernardone, the son of a rich cloth merchant of Assisi, who for his love of lady poverty has become a figure of world history (see also chapter 10). Francis married lady poverty. When one of his novices absolutely had to have a prayer book of his own and asked for one again and again, Francis finally told him, "Once you have your Psalter you will become covetous and want to have your own breviary. And once you have your breviary, you will seat yourself at the lectern like a learned man and it will not be long before you will say to one of your companions: brother, come here and bring me my breviary."[7] Property creates dependency while it destroys a group's brotherhood and sisterhood. Affluence makes for superordination and subordination, domination and barriers; and precisely because these barriers have to be defended, it makes for war. Unity, participation, and solidarity always include a rejection of everything that separates us, all that divides and breaks up life. This is true for the group as much as in relation to nature.

Once Francis was sitting close to a fire and his linen trousers began to burn. A brother wanted to douse the flames, but Francis prevented him because he did not want to hurt brother fire. Another variation of this story has it that Francis's hut was burning down and someone saved his trousers. Francis no longer wanted to wear them because they had been taken from brother fire. Fire was his brother and water his sister. It is as if he knew already the implications for the natural world of an ownership mentality, namely, the mind-set that Descartes later came to define as humankind's task to be *maîtres et possesseurs de la nature* (masters and owners of nature).

Poverty was apparent in everyday lifestyle: the brothers provided for their food by begging and gathering leftovers and scraps that were often nauseating. When Francis was invited to dinner by a cardinal in Rome he put his beggar's bowl that he had brought along on the sumptuously decked-out table and ate what had been given him: bread crusts and half-rotten fruit. The brothers built their shelters, small huts of wood—not stone—in humble, ordinary style. There was to be nothing worldly about tables and vessels; everything was to depict poverty and remind the brothers that they were pilgrims and strangers. Once, in his unique instinct for symbolic action, Francis began all by himself to demolish a house that the people of Assisi had erected for the brothers. And when an eminent personality came to join the order, Francis pronounced that he had to leave behind even his scholarship so that, free also of this possession, he "could throw himself naked into the arms of the naked Christ."

The early thirteenth century saw the rise of a new economic era in the city republics of upper Italy. A growing population and the economic upturn had restructured the medieval makeup of cities. The age-old significance of rural economy was waning and, next to the aristocracy and clergy, there arose with a new self-awareness the bourgeoisie to which affluent cloth merchants like Francis's father belonged. New forms of trade developed in the flourishing towns of

Lombardy. The upper classes imported and consumed luxury articles like silk and spices from the East. At the same time, modernization of the technologies of the skilled trades created new industries, especially that of cloth-making. People who once worked the land were uprooted and even the existing minimal social-patriarchal protection through dependency on the estate owners disappeared. More and more wage-dependent workers, women and men, roamed the streets. One of the representatives of the new poverty movements that simultaneously came into existence, Peter Waldo of Lyon (d. 1206 C.E.), called them "God's poor."

The new era was no longer based on the exchange of natural goods but on the traffic of money. The language of the banking business that emerged at this time bears to this day an Italian stamp. Profiteering, speculation, and market swings determined the economic destiny of even the newly poor. At the same time, this early capitalism sustained a bourgeois citizenry profoundly fascinated by money, property, success, and upward mobility. The mysticism of poverty that Francis developed has to be seen against this background. His break with his father is a break with the values of the bourgeois world. He does not take over the father's cloth business and is cursed by him. In this change of lifestyle from affluence to poverty, Francis exchanges dominant values and even emotions. The revulsion felt by bourgeois humanity for leprosy, running sores, and uncleanness is transferred by him to what stinks and is unclean in his eyes: money. He kisses a leper's hand that the illness has already eaten away, but even to touch money is a taboo for him. Marriage to the noble lady poverty leads him to despise money even as a mere means of exchange. "No brother is to pick up money or coins, to accept or to have received them in any way whatsoever, neither for clothing or books nor for payment for work, for we are to have or to expect benefit from money or coins no more than from stones." So states the unofficial rule of 1221. A brother had picked up a piece of money left behind by someone in the church; Francis ordered him to carry it in his mouth to the nearest dungheap covered with donkey manure. However free the brothers were in giving poor women church decorations and Bibles so that they could buy bread, they themselves treated money with contempt. The order accepted no gifts of money. It was to be despised as much as the devil himself. Money and excrement were to be valued equally.

But for them poverty was not only an ascetic notion helpful for avoiding the dangers of affluence but also a total renunciation of the self and subsequent giving it to God. The mystical demands to "let go" of the self and the world were met in the marriage to lady poverty for "she brings to nought every covetousness and avarice and worries of this world."[8] Francis heard the gospel and its instructions to the disciples as if it were a message addressed to him. Jesus' rules of life for the women and men who follow him had given him one last cause to convert from a courtly, chivalrous culture that had an aesthetic fascination for him and from the life and world of early capitalism. "Heal the sick, raise the dead, cleanse lepers, cast out demons. You received without pay, give without pay. Take no gold, nor silver, nor copper in your belts, no bag for your journey, not two tunics, nor sandals nor a staff, for the laborer deserves his food" (Matt 10:8-10). What Francis heard on February 24, 1208, was this: go and preach, even without formation or ordination! No gold, no silver, no money not even for alms! No bag for provisions! One habit only! No shoes, no staff! It was an amputation of every superfluous item, of every precaution for life, and, at the same time, of every protection that an institution like the church could provide at the time. It was also a refusal to be recognized as a regular order, a refusal of the legal privileges associated with such status, and a refusal of priestly ordination. Poverty in the institutional sense means to be excluded from privileges.

A group of like-minded people soon gathered around Francis and were recognized as minor brothers. They came from various classes; aristocrats, rich burghers, as well as utterly uneducated, coarse "country bumpkins." Irrespective of whether they were clerics or lay folk, they all lived in the order without any distinction. "No brother is to hold a position of power or a ruling office, especially not among the brothers themselves. No one in this way of living is to be called prior; instead all are to be known simply as minor brothers. And all are to wash one another's feet" (rule of 1221). For the Franciscans such a rule meant that the Middle Ages' structure of estates that also enjoyed religious legitimation was left behind. The traditional monastery where the personal poverty of the monks and nuns was sustained by the common property of the monastic community was replaced by urban living quarters and by the actions of preachers of repentance who were not tied down to one particular location. The minor brothers understood their homelessness as a delineation from the older understanding of poverty held by the orders established earlier. At the same time, this nonsedentary life in cities and towns corresponded to the life of the broader masses that had been torn out of the old bonds to the land and feudal conditions and driven into the cities.

Thus, the early Christian ideal of poverty had gained a new meaning—and it was hotly disputed. Nearly a hundred years after Francis's death, on November 12, 1323, Pope John XXII declared as heretical the thesis advocated by the poverty movements that Christ and the Apostles had neither private nor common possessions. In the course of this feud over poverty, numerous opposition groups and individual spiritual and other radical individuals were persecuted by the Inquisition and publicly burned at the stake. Through this action, the principle *nudum Christum nudus sequi* (naked and following the naked Christ), which is mentioned as early as in St. Jerome's correspondence and depicts the ideal of "Christ's poor" in the eleventh and twelfth centuries, was negated in the interest of the power politics of Rome.

In the course of history, the churches developed two different ways of dealing with their radicals. They expelled them or attempted to domesticate them. The Cathari, Waldensians, the radical wing of Francis's followers, and the Fratricelli were expelled, which according to the existing imperial law meant that they could be persecuted, killed, and deprived of their property. Francis himself was robbed of his sting, smoothed out ecclesially, and decimated in terms of his dreams. Radical stories told about him, such as those gathered by Thomas of Celano, were prohibited and his biography suppressed. An expurgated version of Francis's life, written by Bonaventure, was declared the official biography. What was left was a gentle friend of nature, with a few oddities, who loved poverty more than anything else. What it no longer explained is against whom he told his stories or in whose favor. Posterity was shown a man who loved all birds, all human beings, and suffering. Francis did not preach to all beautifully chirping birds but, at least according to Umberto Eco, told the vultures and other birds of prey in the cemeteries the things the rich city councillors did not want to hear. Authorities and the gentry were subject to his radical critique. He embraced and kissed lepers not only in the sense of humble charity but because he wanted to liberate them from exclusion, from being told that they did not belong. One of them had a part in Francis's conversion from being a happy gourmet and troubadour-musician to a man of poverty. If, as Eco maintains, leprosy is a sign of those who are disenfranchised, oppressed, uprooted, and pushed around, then it is precisely this exclusion of people we fear that Francis was intent on eradicating.

His goal was not an aimless and self-delighted asceticism; rather, he sought to live the vulnerable openness of love that gives itself without condition, protection, and reassurance.

Many stories about this man show how the boundary between sacredness and profanity is removed. The anarchy of love restores order; it ridicules social division built up on the basis of possessions. It knows no limits. Mockery is one of its tools. Breaking conventionality is a sign of affection for all. Francis is a fool *(pazzo)* and not a good-natured simpleton. He acts out ever anew what really ought to be valid everywhere: the eradication of the boundaries that are drawn from the obsession with possessions.

The renunciation of possessions, clothing, medals or other insignia of honor, and consciousness of status and one's ego is the mystical sense of this freedom from having. But it is also a renunciation of the privileges that the earlier monastic communities claimed as their own. The Friars Minor need neither legal protection nor civic prerogatives, which church or state could have afforded them. And at the same time they consciously repudiated weapons, which is that other important covering sought by the naked, vulnerable human being. Freedom from possessions, freedom from the possibility of exploiting others, and economic justice, these alone can be the foundation of a nonimperialistic peace as the Bible envisaged it in its insistence on justice as the cornerstone. If we had possessions, Francis would say, we would also need weapons. He held on to the inescapable link of poverty and peace. For human beings, possessions destroy the nakedness in which we are born. After having been deprived of his possessions and children Job exclaims, "Naked I came from my mother's womb" (Job 1:21 RSV). Possessions are the abolition of this original condition because they are at once protection and armor, distancing people one from another by concealing them behind affluence.

The theme of becoming naked, of disrobing and defenselessness, is a basic theme of mystical freedom that runs like a red thread through the entire life of the Poverello. During the big showdown with his rich father, Francis publicly takes off his clothes that had marked him as a child of the merchant-bourgeoisie and, in the presence of everyone witnessing the court case, throws them at his father's feet. Later he sends one of his brothers, clad only in underwear, to preach in a church. Then, equally undressed, he follows and preaches about a naked Jesus on the cross, devoid of any insignia of power and glory. Francis spent his short life after his conversion by disposing of everything that could protect him against the wounds of love. Nothing was to stand as a buffer between himself and the naked Christ: no solid house, no money, no legal security, no power, and no protection. When he lay dying, he was undressed and laid naked on the ground.

In the Abrahamic religions, God is again and again praised as the "eternally rich One" who holds the fullness of life in both hands. Paradoxically, the way to this richness leads through poverty. Possessions, privileges, and power, all basic institutions of common life, are ever abolished anew in this attempt to come naked before God, without covering and defenses in the vulnerability that every love creates. Love, every love, renders one naked.

John Woolman and the Society of Slave Owners

A more modern, more unprepossessing name for this process of the soul that renounces possessions by becoming naked is "simplicity." In the spirituality of Quakers, simplicity means a reduction of material needs, abhorrence of luxury, simplification of lifestyle, and, correspondingly, a different relation to gainful employment. The testimony of Quakers to simplicity demands that one live out of one's divine center, unencumbered by any hindrance, trusting that our loving already looks after our needs. This somewhat awkward description of freedom comes from a Quaker handbill and declares that freedom consists in responding in holy obedience to the guidance of the Holy Spirit who arises from the depth of silence and prayer.

The diaries of eighteenth-century American John Woolman (see chapter 1) are, in their very closeness to day-to-day life, a testimony to the "and" in the subtitle, "mysticism and resistance." In the spirit of mystical experience, he describes this relation to possessions and to letting oneself be given over to the Spirit. On account of his life of divestment and modesty, Woolman was called the Quaker saint. He was an unassuming, relatively little-educated tailor from New Jersey who at times appeared somewhat odd. He was a third-generation American from a family who had fled from England when Quakers were persecuted there. Following his father's wishes, Woolman began to work for a shopkeeper who had bought two Scottish "servants": at that time, Scottish prisoners of war in England were sold as slaves. One of them fell deathly ill and "being delirious, used to curse and swear most sorrowfully, and after he was buried I was left to sleep alone the next night in the same chamber where he died. I perceived in me a timorousness. I knew, however, I had not injured the man but assisted in taking care of him according to my capacity, and was not free to ask anyone on that occasion to sleep with me."[9] The fear of the twenty-one-year-old of this "test" is clearly apparent in the entry composed fifteen years later. This was Woolman's first encounter with slavery, with the kind of ownership that is ready to walk over dead bodies. Shortly afterward, he had to write a bill for his employer that concerned the sale of a young black person. Woolman, a rather inward-oriented and shy young man, told the man making the purchase, himself a Quaker, that slaveholding was a practice inconsistent with the Christian religion.[10] When another of the Friends asked him to prepare the ownership certificate for a black female slave, he refused. These questions to be put to slave-owners about their sense of justice and their way of life would occupy Woolman for his entire life.

In the year 1800 there were still almost 1,300 slaves in the state of New Jersey; in Woolman's youth around 1740, there were far more than that. Slavery was as normal, even among many Quakers, as driving a car is now. Slavery was questioned as little then as are our habits of consumption today, such as the wearing of textiles that are produced in the *maquiladoras* by disenfranchised, literally enslaved women who work in the textile factories that serve the global market. Woolman sought to break through the normality of this way of living. He began where he lived, among the citizens who had become rich but who did not actually defend slavery or profit directly from the trade of human beings. These people, however, sustained this injustice as its accomplices and profiteers. It was the realistic view of the "middle way" that determined John Woolman's life work, and he came to focus more and more on the connections between legally recognized possession and exploitation. "The love of ease and gain are the motives in general of keeping slaves, and men are wont to take hold of weak arguments to support a cause which is unreasonable."[11] The methods of his resistance were the simplest imaginable: conversation with all who owned slaves, on the one hand, and his own lifestyle, on the other. Forever unprepared to compromise, he entreated slave owners in a spirit of loving concern. He truly believed in his opponents' ability to change and this Quaker belief in "that of God," to be found also in those who kept slaves, nourished their own, often secret wish to live a different life. At every meeting of Friends, Woolman endeavored to explain that hunger for possessions causes deadly harm to both rich and poor alike and that oppression destroys both oppressor and oppressed. He posed a simple question to the oppressors: how much longer would it be before they will have become deaf to every kind of moral question? Into the toil of liberation he incorporated his other plan of action, the repudiation of luxury and consumerism.

Woolman gained credibility through another form of everyday resistance, namely, his personal rejection of whatever advantage and benefit that derives from injustice. He earned his living as a merchant, then as a tailor and, occasionally, as a teacher. He grew fruit, prepared contracts, and wrote legal documents. This work put him in touch repeatedly with slave owners who desired to bequeath their slaves legally to descendants. Woolman could not in good conscience compose such a last will and testament. Instead, he began to speak to those who called on his services, most of whom were devout, affluent Quakers, and tried to dissuade them from their intent. In so doing, he gradually developed a very clear position on slavery. In his frequent and distant travels that eventually took him to England in connection with slavery, he was dependent on Quakers for hospitality. But when he saw how the field slaves of a farmer were dressed—many of whom, particularly children, wore nothing at all—and their state of health, he preferred to sleep in the open fields. The next day he would go to the owner in question and talk with him about slavery and the treatment of slaves.

He did not want to profit from kindnesses that were "the gain of oppression. Receiving a gift, considered as a gift, brings the receiver under obligations to the benefactor and has a natural tendency to draw the obliged into a party with the giver."[12] This kind of unmasking and refusing complicity is part of the simplicity of lifestyle. Simplicity, the rejection of consumerism and opting for possessionlessness, is a modern, social form of what medieval mysticism called "becoming unattached." In the course of almost a century, Woolman became one of the most important grassroots workers in the process that liberated at least the Quakers from participation in crime.

In 1696, a group of Mennonites and Quakers composed a letter against slavery, but only after long-drawn-out negotiations did the yearly meeting, held at Philadelphia in 1776 (nearly a century before the Civil War), officially condemn the practice of slavery. Members had to set their slaves free, and slave owners were visited and examined. Quakers found to be involved in the trade of slaves were excluded from the community of Friends.

Woolman refused to drink from silver vessels customarily used in the homes of his hosts. This often caused embarrassment because people had no other ones on the table. He also refused to wear clothing that had been dyed because of the brutal exploitation of slaves in the West Indies, who were exposed to the poisonous vapors of the dyes. He stopped eating sugar because slaves had to produce it. He refused to pay taxes for the war against the First Nations people and accepted no payment when soldiers were billeted in his house. When traveling to England, he did not take his passage in the passenger section but in the 'tween deck of the sailing ship, under the conditions of the ordinary sailors who were continuously soaked through and through. Arriving in England, he walked on foot from London to York because he knew how cruelly the stagecoach crew and the horses were treated. When looking at the "furniture of our houses and the garments in which we array ourselves" he wondered whether "the seeds of war have any nourishment in these our possessions or not."[13] Behind such questions was his conviction that when we surround ourselves with superfluities or desire wealth in a manner contrary to true wisdom, we cannot help but become guilty in a certain form of oppression.

In critiquing the desire for luxuries, Woolman also developed a different understanding of labor. Until 1756 he himself had worked as a tailor but gave up that trade saying that it had been his general practice to buy and sell things really useful. He did not wish to trade in things that served chiefly to please people's vanity since he felt that it weakened him as a Christian. He himself stayed poor because he spent no time accumulating wealth. Woolman believed that every human being should work in order to live—and not live in order to work! Everyone ought to do some kind of useful work but neither too much—like the slaves—nor too little—like the masters. (Later Gandhi came to call such work "bread-work.") Woolman considered too much work to be detrimental to a person's spiritual well-being and to the needs of the community. He distinguished between "a people used to labour moderately for their living, training up their children in frugality and business, and those who live on the labour of slaves."[14]

All these forms of refusal, boycott, renunciation, and alternate life that is lived out already here and now have a mystical ground. It becomes manifest in a dream that John Woolman had when he was seriously ill and could not even remember his own name.

Being then desirous to know who I was, I saw a mass of matter of a dull gloomy colour, between the south and the east, and was informed that this mass was human beings in as great a misery as they could be and live, and that I was mixed in with them and henceforth might not consider myself as a distinct, or separate being. In this state I remained several hours. I then heard a soft, melodious voice, more pure and harmonious than any voice I had heard with my ears before, and I believed it was of an angel who spoke to other angels. The words were *John Woolman is dead.* . . . I was then carried in spirit to mines, where poor and oppressed people were digging rich treasures for those called Christians, and I heard them blaspheme the name of Christ, at which I was grieved, for his name to me was precious. Then I was informed that these heathens were told that those who oppressed them were the followers of Christ, and they said amongst themselves: "If Christ directed them to use us in this sort, then Christ is a cruel tyrant.[15]

At times, the mysticism of simple needs sounds somewhat homespun or even doctrinaire. But behind this moralism there is something that is set alight by the decisive question raised by possessions and the obsession with them. Slavery is the radical, most gruesome consequence of the craving for possessions. In slavery, disenfranchised human beings, robbed systematically of all autonomy and dignity, are turned into commodities, into things to be used and objects to be sold. This absurd division of people who are born as slaves and destined to be such and those who are masters and owners who have no sense of wrongdoing is based on a philosophy of life that regards having, ownership, and the individual's self-interest as the sole foundation of the economy. The mystical view of the unity of all life contradicts that technological-rationalistic view.

Something of this different thinking that arises from the perspective of God can be seen in John Woolman's dream. Mystical thinking is rooted in a sense of not being different from the "others," those who have no possessions and no rights, those of different color and the other sex. The indistinguishable mass of fellow creatures that the dreaming John Woolman saw in the mines is integrally part of the inextinguishable longing for oneness. Possession separates just as Ego does. God, of whom Eckhart says that she is the only reality that we ought to have as a possession and which renders all else unnecessary, binds together all who set themselves apart by means of possessions and the lusting after them. This is what Woolman saw in his dream: in the state of "as great a misery as . . . could be," he saw those who had nothing and himself "mixed in with them." In the sense of contemporary mysticism, this can mean nothing other than that they who make up the 20 percent of the owners of the world belong together with the remaining 80 percent "in the state of as great a misery as . . . could be."

Voluntary Poverty: Dorothy Day

In the spring of 1972 a conversation took place at the University of Notre Dame in Indiana between two extraordinary women of the twentieth century. Both beautiful in the wisdom of advanced age and engaged for the right of all human beings, they met for a lively and at the same time personal exchange. They were the Jewish philosopher Hannah Arendt (1906–1975) and the Catholic radical Dorothy Day (1897–1980). Listening to them, a priest whispered into a friend's ear, "They are incarnations of intelligent goodness and generous intelligence, Mary and Martha, the sisters of Bethany" (see also chapter 11).

In my search for a tradition of resistance in the twentieth century, I have repeatedly encountered this "intelligent goodness" of a woman who thought and lived mystically. Many in the United States regard her as *the* American saint of the twentieth century because she combined piety, pacifism, and voluntary poverty with an utter normalness. As a social reformer, agitator, and activist, Dorothy Day took Martha's active and organized life into strikes and boycotts. At the same time—after her conversion—she lived the life of Mary in daily participation in the mass, fasting and contemplating regularly, and spending many hours in prayer.

In Roman Catholicism, there is a deeper aversion to the belief in possession and, in particular, to the notion that possessions are the visible signs of God's blessings as in Calvinistic Protestantism. This aversion goes back to premodernity, for which reason it may perhaps hold out some hope for the world of postmodernity. The people who gathered around Dorothy Day and the Catholic Worker movement lived in possessionlessness and voluntary poverty. They did so in a world that regards possession as a legitimate right and takes lifelong striving for possession for granted. Dorothy Day and her leftist friends dreamed the old utopian-socialist dream of building the new society in the husks of the old, as the Industrial Workers of the World used to put it. They wanted to make real a new life now and not only after a revolutionary assumption of power. Neither the dangers of the slums of North American cities nor the frequent jail sentences for civil disobedience—they called it "divine obedience"—could prevent them from pursuing this goal.

In the spring of 1917, Dorothy Day—nineteen years old—was jailed for participating in a protest demonstration at the White House against the treatment of suffragettes who were demanding women's right to vote. In jail she took part in a hunger strike against the way women were treated and fell into a deep depression. "That I would be free again after thirty days meant nothing to me. I would never be free again, never free when I knew that behind bars all over the world there are women and men, young girls and boys, suffering constraint, punishment, isolation and hardship for crimes of which all of us are guilty. . . . People sold themselves for jobs, for the pay check, and if they received a high enough price, they were honored. If their cheating, their theft, their lie, were of colossal proportion, if it were successful, they met with praise, not blame."[16] A rather remarkable feature of Dorothy Day's life was the ability, reminiscent of the Franciscan tradition, to identify herself with others, particularly those who evoke repulsion in us. "I was the mother whose child had been raped and slain. I was the mother who had borne the monster who had done it. I was even that monster, feeling in my own breast every abomination."[17] During the twenties she was part of the radical Bohemian scene in Greenwich Village in New York City. She interviewed Trotsky for *The Call,* a small anarchist-socialist paper that paid her five dollars a week for her journalistic activity, an amount that was paid to many women at that time in factory jobs. She was a drinking-partner of Eugene O'Neill, had several, mostly unhappy amorous relationships, and had an abortion that she described in a novel. The author who had fathered the child left her and advised her to soon find herself a rich man to marry. She took the advice and spent a year in Europe when the marriage fell apart.

In a subsequent relationship she experienced pregnancy and the birth of her daughter as a deep and overwhelming happiness. For a Communist monthly she wrote "Having a Baby," an article that was so successful that it was reprinted in workers' journals all over the world, including in many Soviet papers. Shortly thereafter, at age thirty, she received baptism in the Roman Catholic Church, which meant breaking with her deeply respected anarchist-atheistic partner. It was no coincidence that she embraced the faith after the birth of her daughter, Tamar. In her biography she wrote later that no human being could receive or persevere such a huge flood of joy as she experienced after the birth of her child. And with it came the need to worship and adore.

It was the encounter with a homeless vagrant, who was also a Catholic philosopher and an anarchistic socialist, that led to the establishment of the *Catholic Worker,* a monthly paper published since 1933 and to this day available for one penny. Peter Maurin, the radical personalist from France, envisioned a social order in which it would be easier for people to be good. The *Worker* was to be radical and Catholic at the same time, reflect Catholic social teaching, and advocate a peaceful "green revolution." What developed was help for the poorest of the poor, hospitality for the homeless, and later on, soup kitchens and consciousness training, called "clarification of thought."

The volunteers who worked in the rapidly expanding soup kitchens of the *Catholic Worker* asked bakers and grocers for leftover, stale-dated, and unsaleable produce from which they prepared soup for their numerous guests. Among them were urban vagrants, homeless, physically or mentally challenged people, runaways from institutions, others whom society had given up on, or, who in many cases, had given up on themselves. Many were alcoholics who spent their welfare money on alcohol or drugs. Their only warm meal of the day was what they received in the soup kitchen.

At the end of the seventies, when I was on a visit to the Lower East Side of Manhattan and, together with many young volunteer helpers, dished out soup, it cheered me that the poor did not have to queue up but were invited to sit at a table where we served them. I had a long conversation with Dorothy Day that was constantly interrupted by homeless women and a few men. The aging Day mentioned in passing that again and again people came into her room, would stay for a time, taking away things, or leaving things behind. The renunciation of personal possession that she practiced included private space. In this sense, voluntary poverty is the renunciation of personal possession of material as well as nonmaterial goods. One dimension of this poverty is to be in the service of the poor. To share material, intellectual, and spiritual possessions with others and, above all, to share the most valuable of what we have, our time, with them is an aspect of the mystical understanding of poverty; having become praxis, it is an utterly clear mysticism.

What is "voluntary poverty?" In an article for the *Worker,* Dorothy Day speaks of the two towels she uses. Do we need more than that? As Thoreau says, too many things make life superfluous and suffocate us. "We must be what we expect of others" is one of the personal principles of the people of the *Catholic Worker*. Dorothy Day often cited Dostoevsky's words that it is a hard and dreadful thing to demand love from us. When I met her, I accidentally overheard an exchange concerning someone whom I did not know. The other person said, with great dismay in her voice, "she is supposed to have a savings account," and Dorothy Day shook her head sadly.

Dorothy Day was a brilliant writer. She would set out from a carefully observed aspect of reality and slowly render it transparent to the wider webs of greed, oppression of the poor, and class-struggle from above, all the way to prison and war, which she regarded as the offspring of the two basic powers, money and violence. She regularly contributed small articles to the *Worker;* most of them begin with a meeting, a situation, or a piece of meticulously observed reality, which she would describe sometimes humorously or at other times cuttingly. In the small, everyday, and often seemingly banal fact, what is essential becomes clearly visible. It is a classical journalism that reflects the general in the particular and names it. Some of her columns read like stories from the gospel; they do not sentimentalize or romanticize the poor and yet are full of wonder. They contain a spirit that expects the miracle around the next street corner—or at least finds it missing.

Dorothy Day's conversion was prepared in her political engagement for the poorest of the poor and in her radical critique of a system that is founded on wage labor, prison, and war. After her conversion she retracted none of her social critiques; instead, she discerned everything that sought to stabilize lust after property and craving for possession. The other great topic of her life, the engagement for peace, has an inner connection to the critique of possessions that make weapons and antiaircraft and missile defense exercises a necessity. She remained an anarchist and became more pious and more radical.

And so two themes became crystallized in her life: poverty and pacifism. As a caregiver in hospitals, an inmate in prisons, and a resident in slums, Dorothy Day experienced in many ways the unequal distribution of the means of life, the privileges and impoverishment of ever growing masses of people, as well as the results of misery in prostitution, alcoholism, and brutalization. But only her conversion to Catholicism led her to realize an old socialist—and Christian— goal, which is to be "in this world but not of it" or to give reality to the new life in the husks of the old.

How far this voluntary poverty can go is made apparent in an interesting document, a letter from the *Catholic Worker* to the Treasurer of the City of New York. In preparing for the construction of the subway system, the city had expropriated the property on which the building of the community stood. Two-thirds of the compensation was paid in advance, the remaining sum a year and a half later. It amounted to $68,700 to which the city had added interest at the customary rate, a sum of $3,579.39. As the publisher of the *Catholic Worker*, Dorothy Day wrote to the treasurer's office in July 1960:

> We hereby return the interest on the money we recently received from you. We do not believe in loans with interest. As Catholics we are familiar with the church's early teaching. All early councils forbade the trade of money-lending and declared it reprehensible to gain money by means of interest-yielding loans. Medieval canon law prohibited the trade and, in a variety of decrees, ordered that profit gained in this manner was to be returned. Christian insistence on doing good obliges us to loan without interest, to give freely and even in cases of expropriation like ours, not to resist but to accept with a glad heart.
>
> We do not believe in the profit system and that is why we cannot accept profit and interest on our money. People who view human welfare from a materialist perspective are intent on making profit. But we seek to fulfill our obligation by offering our service without demanding payment from our brothers and sisters, just as Jesus commanded us in his gospel (Matt 25). In the judgment of a Franciscan brother, giving interest-yielding loans is the principal scourge of culture. The English artist and author Eric Gill called profiteering and war the two biggest problems of our age.
>
> Since we have addressed these problems in every issue of the *Catholic Worker* since 1933—the freedom of human beings, war and peace, the human being and the state, the human being and work— and since Holy Scripture teaches that the love of money is the root of all evil, we use this opportunity to practice our faith. As a sign of overcoming this love of money, we return the interest money to you.

For decades, Dorothy Day was observed by the FBI as a communist, particularly after a visit to Cuba and her positive reports on housing, healthcare, and education there. She was no communist because her anarchism and religion forbade her to bring about the other, better life through the power of the state. Her philosophy may be described as personalism in the sense of Emanuelle Mourniers, Jacques Maritain, and Martin Buber; it is at the same time Christian-communitarian. Common life in mutual responsibility is meant to replace the ordering and protective elements that capitalism subjugates to the market.

But her relation to possession and possessionlessness has still another root that I would like to call mystical in the wide sense of *mystique vécue* (mysticism translated into concrete life). It is not only a kind of pious selflessness that manifests itself in a lived-out voluntary poverty. Coming free from every form of greed roots itself in becoming one with Christ. For it is he who appears in the face of the poor, the prostitute, and the criminal. The presence of Christ in the poor is accepted and transforms the relation to time. The priority of the now over all planned and predictable history is a result of orienting oneself in terms of being rather than in having.

What moved me most deeply about Dorothy Day is something I found out only after her death. Like every human being who hungers and thirsts for justice and peace, she too experienced phases of utter exhaustion, sadness, and grief. The word despair seems inappropriate, but it cannot be that far removed from what she went through. In such times, I was told, she would withdraw and cry. For long hours, days at a time, she would not eat but just sit and weep. She never withdrew from the active, struggling life for the poorest of the poor and never ceased to look upon war and preparation for war as a crime against the poor. But she wept. When I heard this, I understood a bit better what prayer can mean in the midst of defeat, how the Spirit consoles humans and leads them into truth, how one thing is not at the expense of another, and where consolation is purchased with the renunciation of truth. That Dorothy Day cried for days means both consolation and inconsolability at one and the same time. She knew why she liked to repeat Teresa of Avila's words, "The whole way to heaven is heaven itself."

Middle Roads and Crazy Freedoms

"As far as the spirit of poverty" is concerned, Simone Weil writes in a letter to Father Perrin, "I do not remember any moment when it was not in me, although only to that unhappily small extent compatible with my imperfection. I fell in love with Saint Francis of Assisi as soon as I came to know about him. I always believed and hoped that one day Fate would force upon me the condition of a vagabond and a beggar which he embraced freely. Actually, I felt the same way about prison."[18]

This yearning for poverty and its results, forced upon or freely chosen, sounds crazy. All the mystics of poverty described in this chapter share in this craziness: Jesus who threw away cup and comb, Francis who had money dumped to the manure pile, John Woolman who went on foot rather than to participate in the exploitation of servants, Dorothy Day and her two towels. They all knew the difference between lady poverty, to whom Francis married himself, and the misery that destroys spirit and soul as it destroys the body. In consistently freely choosing possessionlessness, they enlarged their freedom from consumer dependency and the craving to have things. Mysticism of poverty can only be understood when one thinks of it in connection with freedom. A German folk song says, "My concern I have rested on nothing" (*Ich hab mein Sach auf Nichts gestellt*): this unconditional nothing is a source of joy and not of renunciation or even self-torture. The basis of spiritual renewal is not the guilt feelings that frequently arise in sensitized individuals in rich industrial societies. Instead, it is a crazy mysticism of becoming empty that reduces the real misery of the poor and diminishes one's own slavery. Becoming empty or "letting go" of the ego, possession, and violence is the precondition of the creativity of transforming action.

There are now a number of countermodels developed by groups that have taken some forward steps on the way from having to being, from possessing to *convivialidad* (a life where all is held in common, learning is mutual, and celebration is a thing of togetherness). I begin with a European minority church that draws on the twelfth-century mystic of poverty Peter Waldo, the heretic from Lyon. He, too, was one of the crazies who gave all their possessions to the poor of the city and thereafter lived from alms. "I am not crazy, as you think, but I have taken revenge on the enemies that have so long suppressed me and pushed me so far that I loved money more than God."[19] To this day, the Italian minority church of the Waldensians, building on this tradition, regards poverty as a condition for outward credibility and inner freedom. Conspicuous consumption is seen as a destruction of the self and the resources of these congregations are put into projects benefiting the poor. Ministers earn less than teachers in Italian elementary schools, and some of them leave home to work in other countries. As Christ had all riches and made himself poor, so this church tries to enter into God's riches and become a church of sharing. Every mediation of religion through a pope or the Madonna, through the saints or money, is rejected. In Sicily, the Waldensians maintain a kind of Protestant kibbutz (*servicio cristiano*) by working a farm and teaching school. This service played a significant role in the decision of many poor people to leave the Mafia, drug trafficking, and prostitution.

One may ask to what extent such forms of "live simply so that others may simply live" are mystically motivated and whether it is not more a matter of a Bible-adhering piety on the part of those down-to-earth Waldensians than mysticism. Be that as it may, theirs is a religion that in an old Protestant defiance affirms poverty and denies the striving for possession that rules the globe. It is more than a so-called "civil" religion and its accommodation to the destruction that is embedded in craving to possess.

The resistance that grows from the revulsion against reducing life to "earning a decent income and consuming without limit" develops new forms in which, even when they are thoroughly secular, I find a mysticism of the middle way. Lifestyle and patterns of consumption change among us above all in the face of the earth's destruction. Every eradication of species or forms of life on this planet is also our destruction of forms of God's presence among us. The togetherness of the earth's living beings is so threatened that resistance against lusting after profit and consumption grows even in a world that understands itself to be postreligious. This resistance does not necessarily have to assume the shape of radical possessionlessness, but the recollection of the craziness of the mystical tradition helps in finding ways that at least keep open an understanding for the truth that some things cannot be possessed, bought, and sold. Some of these resistance-shaped signs of hope have to do with possessionlessness in the sense of divestment as the shedding of one's vestments or depriving oneself of them. Other such signs seek to find alternative ways of investment.

I have in mind the many contemporary attempts to submit our ecologically and socially unrestrained economy to ethical norms. In the so-called free market, companies that destroy the rain forests and manufacture landmines or technologies of torture are generally not controllable either nationally or transnationally. Money, too, functions to reduce the diversity of reality and the needs of humans to naked numbers. People who invest their money are not confronted with the consequences of investment. A more global economy means it is less visible what happens with the allegedly innocently growing capital or what human-rights violations are behind our cheap consumer goods like orchids or textiles. Ethical investment acts against this.

Action plans for this kind of resistance have been in place ever since the Vietnam War and apartheid. In the United States today, annual investment of more than 450 billion dollars is undertaken in line with ethical criteria and not according to the criterion of maximum return. More and more, there are those who boycott companies that profit from war, racism, arms production, and the destruction of nature. Instead, they invest in companies that demonstrate ecological and social responsibility; they gather information that liberates the money trade from being an invisible abstraction unencumbered by ethics. Motivated primarily by religion, these people try to influence companies through the interventions and votes of critical shareholders.

In the eighties, I was present at a shareholders' meeting of one of West Germany's leading banks. There I witnessed how it was possible to elicit reflection and critique in relation to trade relations with the Apartheid state. The first task of critical human rights groups is to have questions about profits delivered to the owners of money superceded by questions about the working conditions their money creates, for example, among female workers in textile factories. The negative criteria governing investment become clearer and more acute year by year: no manufacture of arms, no reliance on nuclear energy, no animal experimentation, no environmental pollution, and no marketing of radiated foodstuffs. The growth of such nongovernmental organizations is a sign of hope in the ability of humans to distinguish between sensible and life-destroying power to possess and not simply to venerate the golden calf.

The mystical vision of freedom, of "letting go" of the world, interprets possessing as being possessed. That vision appears to be something infinitely bigger and more unreal than such little endeavors as dealing responsibly with the power of money. But then it may well be that "that of God in us" is present in both the big crazies and the small practical ways of dealing with the principalities and powers under which we exist. The retreat of a Thomas Merton to the solitude of a Trappist monastery is not that far removed from an annual intervention in the shareholders' meeting. The craziness of giving things away is a symbol that transmits an idea of genuine freedom. The practical reason that fights against the ruling ideology of the innocence of money has part in that freedom. Craziness and reason are not nearly as far apart as technocratic education makes us believe. According to Gotthold Ephraim Lessing, they who do not lose their mind over certain things have no mind to lose.

I want to refer to two fairy tales that give us an idea of these crazy freedoms. The first, told by the Brothers Grimm, is a mystical, humorous tale of Happy Hans, who becomes poorer and poorer and thereby freer and happier. According to this story, superfluous things, such as a lump of gold, make life itself superfluous. Hans becomes poorer, lighter, and more cheerful. In this tale happiness cannot be "had," earned, or bought; it is something of "being." Meister Eckhart says that we are to have everything in such a way "as if things were loaned rather than given to us, that is without any claim to possessing it." This is exactly what is told in the story of clumsy Hans who is always cheated and becomes less and less burdened.

The film *Le huitième jour* (The Eighth Day) (1997) by the Belgian Jaco Van Dormael tells a contemporary fairy tale about the collision of two worlds in the encounter of two men. Harry is a leading business man, always meticulously dressed and surrounded by an aura of an icy blue-gray light. His job is to teach managers the art of sales talk: "Look them straight in the eye! You must exude success! Enthusiasm is infectious!" Harry races through the world, armed with a cell phone. In the morning, an automatic wake-up call awakens him, and a few minutes later two slices of toast leap from his toaster. Soon after we see him in a line of endless bumper-to-bumper traffic on his way to the bank; he makes telephone calls while driving. He forgets to pick up his children and his neglected wife leaves him. On the road, this advertising strategist is stopped by a mentally disabled man, Georges; somewhat disgruntled, Harry gives him a ride. Georges no longer knows his address and wants to go to his mother who, as becomes clear eventually, has died years ago. He lives in a special home. On an excursion to the seashore, the residents of the home occupy a circus. At night he and his companions, in exuberant delight, turn on the merry-go-round and, in turn, dance, howl and cause destruction. Georges is an impulsive and, at times, frightening man, filled with a happy spontaneity. He likes Harry and without intending it, he heals the workaholic through befriending him. Trust, laughter, and a new relationship with his children and nature become real again.

In watching this film, even the naive observer wonders who is really crazy, the handicapped or the normal ones, those who are good for nothing or the successful managers. What relation do these two have to flowers or the sea, to children or one another? Apart from the somewhat contrived ending, the film is a cheery fairy tale that deals with a successful man's healing by a mentally challenged man, of someone possessed by someone free. The framework of the film is provided by reference to the creation narrative; it is an unbelievable mixture of biblical verses and how they are perceived by the challenged man. Georges says that on the fourth day God created the motorcycle. And, he says, on the eighth day, God created Georges and all those with Down's Syndrome.

Mysticism disenchants and enchants all at the same time. The power of possessions—symbolized here not by a lump of gold but by cars, the latest technology, bankers, and perfected lifestyles—is disenchanted. Knowing nothing, doing nothing, weeping, and being able to laugh without reason are enchanted. What results is friendship and new freedom that approximates the craziness of mystics.

14. VIOLENCE AND NONVIOLENCE

It is beyond dispute that a child, even before it begins to write the alphabet and gathers worldly knowledge, should know what the soul is, what truth is, what love is and what forces are hidden in the soul. It should be the essence of true education that every child learns this and in the struggle of life be able more readily to overcome hatred by love, falsehood by truth and violence by taking suffering on itself.

GANDHI

The Unity of All Living Beings

Mysticism creates a new relation to the three powers that, each in its own totalitarian way, hold us in prison: the ego, possession, and violence. Mysticism relativizes them, frees us from their spell, and prepares us for freedom. Those powers project themselves in very diverse ways. The ego that keeps on getting bigger presents itself most often as well-mannered and civilized, even when it seeks to get rid of every form of ego-lessness. Possession, which according to Francis of Assisi makes for a condition that forces us to arm ourselves, appears in a neutralized, unobtrusive form. The fact that the very entities with which we destroy creation—namely possession, consumption, and violence—have fashioned themselves into a unity in our world makes no impact, whether by design or through ignorance.

When women, like Dorothy Day, are not fixated on their own egos, or when fools without possessions, like some of Saint Francis's sons and daughters, live different, liberated lives, they are met with smiles of derision. But when they dare to take real steps out of the violence-shaped actuality of our condition, they come into conflict with the judiciary or wind up in jail. More than anything else, violence must hide itself and always put on new garments, disguising itself in the form of imperatives, such as security, protection, technological necessity, public order, or defensive measures.

Here is an inconspicuous example. In June 1997, a member of the White Fathers, a religious community that is part of the "Order for Peace," was fined for having demonstrated outside the Chancellor's Office in Bonn with a picket-sign saying "Cancel Third World

Debts." The office had refused to accept a petition, signed by 12,000 people, sponsored by the campaign "Development Needs Forgiveness of Debts." The harmless name of the violence behind which the Chancellor's Office was hiding is the law of inviolable precincts; under present circumstances it is one of the many, actually quite sensible garments of state power. But the law is abused when the office of state protects itself against democratic interventions and expects submission to or passivity in face of economic violence rather than a decisive No! of noncooperation.

This rather insignificant example of civil disobedience illustrates how people make use of violence. For many it is no longer good enough to behave nonviolently in their personal lives and to submit to administrative regulations. For in such nonviolence and submission, as the powerful of this world define them, the real violence that renders the countries of the Third World destitute is left untouched. To exist free of violence means much more than that: it means to think and act with other living beings in a common life. These forms of the freedom of opposition and resistance have multiplied in the last centuries also in Europe in the face of the militaristic and technocratic coercion. An essential and new role is played here by the basic insights of mysticism, such as those of the tradition of Gandhi as well as the Quakers.

In the eighties I was occasionally asked, especially within the contexts of civil disobedience against nuclear arms, whether I did not sense something in myself of the power and spirit of the other, the enemy: "Where is the Ronald Reagan in you?" I was in no mood to respond with a speculation about my shadow side. I do not think that a pacifist has to be complemented by a bellicist. Perhaps I did not understand correctly the seriousness of the question that seeks to grasp the unity of all human beings; to me the question seemed intent on neutralizing or mollifying what we were about. When I ask myself seriously what the principalities and powers that rule over me as structural powers claim from me, the answer is that it is my own cowardice that they seek to make use of. Those who submit to those powers also are part of the violence under whose velvet terror we live and destroy others.

Before he found his way to nonviolent resistance, Gandhi used to describe that time by saying that it was as a coward that he accommodated himself to violence. I understand this in a twofold sense. First, I submitted to external violence, which is to say I knuckled under, paid my taxes with which more weapons were produced, I followed the advice of my bank, and I consumed as the advertisers commanded. Worse still, I hankered after violence, wanted to be like "them" in the advertisements, as successful, attractive, aesthetic, and intelligent as they were. The existential step that the word nonviolence signals leads out of the forced marriage between violence and cowardice. And that means in practice that one becomes unafraid of the police and the power of the state.

The forms of resistance that revoke the common consensus about how we destroy creation have deep roots in a mysticism that we often do not recognize as such. It is the mysticism of being at one with all that lives. One of the basic mystical insights in the diverse religions envisions the unity of all human beings, indeed, of all living beings. It is part of the oldest wisdom of religion that life is no individual and autonomous achievement. Life cannot be made, produced, or purchased, and is not the property of private owners. Instead, life is a mystery of being bound up with and belonging one to another. Gandhi believed that he could live a spiritual life only when he began to identify himself with the whole of humankind, and he could do that only by entering into politics. For him the entire range of all human activities is an indivisible whole. Social, economic, political, and religious concerns cannot be cultivated in sterile plots that are hermetically sealed off from one another. To bring those sterile, sealed-off plots together in a related whole is one of the aims of the mysticism whose name is resistance.

In a long poem, Thich Nhat Hanh (see chapter 10) names the identification with all that lives in all its contradictoriness:

> I am the mayfly that flits on the river's watery surface.
> And I am also the bird that dashes down to catch it.
>
> I am the frog that happily swims in the pond's clear water.
> And I am the grass snake that devours the frog in the stillness.
>
> I am the child from Uganda, just skin and bones with
> legs thin as bamboo sticks;
> And I am the arms-trader selling the weapons that rain
> death on Uganda.
>
> I am the twelve-year old girl,
> refugee in a small boat,
> that was raped by pirates
> and now only seeks death in the Ocean;

and I am also the pirate—
my heart is not yet able to understand and to love.[1]

The poem is entitled "Name Me by My True Name" and the writer gives himself the most diverse names. He is the "caterpillar in the heart of a flower," a "jewel hidden in stone," but also a "member of the Politbureau" and, at the same time, its victim who, slowly dying, pays "its bloodguilt in a forced labor camp." Animals and plants become the "name" of the immersing and expanding I. In his poems, the Zen teacher and poet who developed the concept of the "engaged Buddhist" sends his learners on their own search for names, a search which, without them knowing it, can never end. Friends and foes are distinguished and named but not separated into classes, races, genders, or ideologies. Victims and perpetrators are distinguished; perpetrators such as the rapist are judged to be blind but not excluded—on them too does God's sun shine, as Jesus put it. That life has horrible, violent enemies is not denied. But this realism of naming is overcome into the mystical sense of being one. Difference is acknowledged but not absolutized in the destruction of community and the postmodern denial of every kind of universality.

Call me by my true name, please,
so that I may hear all at once
all my crying and laughing,
so that I may see that my joy
and my pain are one,
so that from now on the door of
my heart may stand open—
the door of sympathy.[2]

According to Buddhist teaching, dissociating the self is one of the four causes of suffering next to greed, hate, and infatuation. The division of I and non-I, in other words, the delimitation of the self from others, is the onset of violence. If I "am" not the fly—in the changed mystical sense that the word "to be" gains here—then I can also kill it. If I "am" not the trader of arms to Uganda, then I cannot enter into a dialogue about economic alternatives or a blockade. The trader remains for me an accomplice in murder and I remain a spectator. The everyday question, "What business is that of yours?" lives by the dissociation of the self and allows violence to spread. What does not concern the I does not exist, and in our culture the non-identity of the I and the non-I is virtually built-up and transfigured.

The dissociation of the I is a self-expression of actualized, legitimated, or suffered violence.

This violence is overcome when the belief in the I is expanded and transposed until, as the poem declares, one finally lives "recognizing oneself in everything." Buddhist wisdom teaches, "what I am, they are also; what they are, I am also; when one makes oneself thus equal with the other, one does not wish to kill or permit killing."[3]

The mystical foundation of the life that, according to Albert Schweitzer, "desires life in the midst of other life" is the foundation of the ever-to-be-searched-for freedom from the practice of violence and of the at least equally dangerous habituation to violence that rules among us. When one renounces one's attachment to the self, the consequences are truly great: no killing or acquiescence in it.

It is high time to stop playing the part of the "willing executioners" or of the allegedly uninvolved onlookers. The toil for possible alternatives to violence, which takes place, for example, in prison-work, in youth groups, and in the resistance against the violence of the nuclear industry, always recalls the spiritual basis of community. Devotions and meditative elements of very different kinds are today part of blockades or protest actions. The inner peace, as freedom from greed and the limitation of the self, translates itself into the practice of peace. The mystical peaceableness of the many "true names" leads to new forms of creating peace.

The Duty of Civil Disobedience: Henry David Thoreau

But is life without violence possible at all? When will the nations "learn war no more" (Isa 2:4) and when will it ever be more profitable to beat swords into plowshares? Tradition teaches that it is possible to break the spiral of violence and that therein lies our only hope.[4] The awareness of the oneness of all human beings and the knowledge that our true name really is not that of an individual personality heightens the responsibility for all who are threatened and enslaved by violence. How deep is our entanglement in violence in what we do and in what we allow to happen? How far have we already settled into the greater freedom from violence?

I want to return once again to Henry David Thoreau (see also chapter 6). He not only wrote an important work "On the Duty of Civil Disobedience" but also showed in his personal life traits of the deep, inextinguishable renunciation of violence in every form. A high school teacher in his hometown of Concord after his studies at Harvard University, he made no use of corporal punishment. This disconcerted the school administration as they regarded beating as an indispensable element in the interest of discipline. Thoreau was reprimanded. His response was most typical: he called out half a dozen of his pupils, smacked each one with the ruler, and quit his job.

Another remarkable story is about Thoreau's reaction to the death of Captain John Brown, an active fighter against slavery. Brown had created an organization, called by the code name "Railroad," to help slaves escape. Brown occupied an arms arsenal but was captured, tried, and hanged. Like no other event in his life, Brown's execution touched Thoreau, who clearly had taken Brown's side and called others to join him. Even mentioning Brown's name would cause his hands to clench up. After this shock he became bedridden, overcome by tuberculosis, from which he died in 1862. He writes this concerning Brown's death, "It took several days before I heard for the first time that he was dead—and I do not believe it after who knows how many days. Of all people that supposedly are my contemporaries, John Brown seemed to be the only one who had not died. . . . I met him at every street corner. He is more alive now than he ever was. . . . He no longer works in secret. He works out in the open and in the broad daylight that shines on this land."[5]

Thoreau's reason for writing this piece on resistance to the state was his experience of prison. During his two stays at Walden, he would occasionally walk into the town of Concord. One day, on his way to the shoemaker, he was arrested because he had not paid the poll tax for six years as a protest against the war with Mexico and the toleration of slavery. He was particularly irked by the latter, since Massachusetts had enacted legislation about the apprehension of escaped slaves. Thoreau spent only one night in prison—much to his chagrin—because an aunt put up bail. But the experience clarified his thinking and inspired him to write this resistance pamphlet that later on Gandhi distributed like a textbook among his pupils. French fighters in the *résistance* and English Labour Party theorists also passionately discussed the pamphlet. "Under a government which imprisons any unjustly, the true place for a just man is also a prison. . . . It is there that the fugitive slave, and the Mexican prisoner on parole, and the Indian come to plead the wrongs of his race should find them; on that separate, but more free and honorable ground, where the State places those who are not *with* her, but *against* her—the only house in a slave State in which a free man can abide with honor."[6]

Even today, this idea of the prison as a place of freedom in an oppressive system pervades the whole movement of nonviolence and of the "other America." This movement has its prison mysticism: prison can be where the human being is to be found in an inhuman world. The *Catholic Worker,* brothers Daniel and Philip Berrigan, and unnamed women and men believe in this "only house" that a free human being can inhabit in a time of furious arms production and the impoverishment of the majority of all the earth's inhabitants. How can one move beyond verbal protest to resistance in a violent militaristic state? One answer to that question is to coerce the state to put more and more people into prison through disobedience, tax boycotts, breach of laws, and resistance. This answer goes back to Thoreau; in 1848 he asked, "How does it become a man to behave towards this American government today? I answer that he cannot without disgrace be associated with it. I cannot for an instant recognize that political organization as *my* government which is the *slave's* government also."[7] The political issues Thoreau addressed were the war that the United States was waging against Mexico from 1846 to 1848 and slavery, the end of which the abolitionists were seeking. The provocation contained in Thoreau's thought has not been minimized on account of its historical distance from us today.

There is a similarity between the old slavery that was based on racial ideology and the new slavery forged by the triad of military-technology-economy. In the mid-eighties a grouping of "new abolitionists" came into being in the Sojourner Circle in Washington; they regarded the arms race as the crime that corresponds to slavery. To them, escalation of terror, preparedness for nuclear holocaust, replacement of politics by militarism, and crimes against the poor in one's own land as well as in the Third World were the new form of slavery under which we live.

Thoreau was a "screwball" who refused to administer corporal punishment to children. In our schools today children are no longer beaten with rods but only with the grades they are given. Thoreau was also not prepared to pay taxes for a war of conquest. He had another kind of life in mind. His word for the desire to become free from possessing too many things was simplicity. "The opportunities of living are diminished in proportion as what are called the means are increased. The best thing a man can do for his culture when he is rich is to endeavor to carry out those schemes which he entertained when he was poor."[8] To discover Thoreau means to let oneself be drawn into a discussion about true and false needs. And that is just what a culture of peace needs that is not built on the exploitation of others and the plunder of the earth. What initially sounds merely individualistic and harmlessly moralistic, namely to reduce one's own needs, actually has a lot to do with the peace that is not built on violence. Thoreau's influence is not based in his writing; his power lies in the existential experiment, namely to experience in one's own body what we really need to live, what is superfluous, and what is morally unbearable: war and slavery. It is the same love of life that Gandhi later called *ahimsa* that enabled Thoreau to live his life in the woods as well as to offer political resistance against slavery.

How can this encompassing love of life express itself in a democracy that is built on a kind of moral reduction and on the mediocrity that does not want to do what is unjust but tolerates it? How is love of justice to be combined with the concept of majority rule? "There are thousands who are *in opinion* opposed to slavery and to war, who yet in effect do nothing to put an end to them."[9] Thoreau criticizes those who are content to have an "opinion," and he calls for "a deliberate and practical denial of [the state's] authority."[10] He envisages conscious and active minorities to whom the government has to pay attention. His political hopes are founded on this active and conscious "wise" minority.[11]

His problem then—and ours today—is that the minorities are themselves paralyzed by a quantitative understanding of democracy. "Men generally, under such a government as this, think that they ought to wait until they have persuaded the majority to alter them."[12] But this waiting, this mere being of a different opinion, this nice democratic belief in the power of argument and persuasion is not enough. In a democratically legitimated system of injustice that justifies war and slavery, Thoreau seeks to give a new definition of what minority means. It is not enough to wait and to persuade. "A minority is powerless while it conforms to the majority; it is not even a minority then; but it is irresistible when it clogs by its whole weight. If the alternative is to keep all just men in prison, or give up war or slavery, the State will not hesitate which to choose."[13] Was Thoreau too optimistic? He believed that the state would renounce the system of injustice and declare it to be politically unfeasible, because every community is dependent on the cooperation of the deliberate and active minorities.

The decisive step is taken only when the minority no longer waits for the next election but, in face of democratically legitimated injustice, refuses obedience now. Conscience is not something that can be postponed to a later day. "It is not desirable to cultivate a respect for the law, so much as for the right."[14] That is why Thoreau calls on "those who call themselves Abolitionists—at once effectually [to] withdraw their support, both in person and property, from the government of Massachusetts."[15]

Thoreau was a moralist. For him it was simply not possible that people put up with a formally democratic justification of war and slavery. Instead, he called for anarchy: the refusal of any cooperation with the state even if its authority is democratically established and legitimated. He was for the now of action that cannot be postponed and for the minority consciousness that forms itself not merely in holding divergent views but in different acting and living. The same fool who left civilization behind and moved into a different freedom of nature also criticized democracy's stupefaction of the masses because it was submission to violence.

Mahatma Gandhi and *Ahimsa*

Every thinking, feeling human being may surely be expected to adopt at least one Indian word into their own vocabulary because it has become part of world culture and embodies the hope for liberation from violence. That word is *ahimsa*. We owe it to Mohandas Karamchand Gandhi (1869–1948), an Indian jurist, diplomat, and politician who, after his studies in London, spent more than twenty years in South Africa advocating for the human rights of the minority Indian population there. From 1915 onward he lived again in India and became the leading thinker and pioneer of the independence movement against British colonial rule. In 1948 he was killed by a Hindu fanatic who could not forgive Gandhi's advocacy for the untouchables and his efforts to reach an understanding with Muslims.

The mysticism of nonviolence owes its most important inducements to Gandhi. His mother, a pious Hindu, brought him up to exercise strict self-discipline in making vows, asceticism, and fasting. Later, in London, he came to know Tolstoy, with whom he had corresponded, and through him Gandhi also came to know the Bible. These encounters caused him to engage his own religious tradition with intensity.

In South Africa Gandhi developed the idea of *satyagraha,* the "soul power pure and simple" that is available to every woman and man, except that they often do not know how to set this irresistible force free. *Satya* literally means "that which is" or truth, while *agraha* means something like "to persist" or "a strong or stubborn inclination toward something" or even stubbornness. The unshakeable will, clinging to the truth, gives strength. *Satyagraha* is not only a theory or technique, it is a lifestyle. Gandhi did not invent the word; it is "as old as the hills" and to be lived out ever anew in the practical application of the individual. This inner power is set free as selfishness and egoism are eliminated. "Whenever you are in doubt or when the self becomes too much with you, try the following expedient: Recall the face of the poorest and most helpless man you have ever seen and ask yourself if the step you contemplate is going to be of any use to him. Will he be able to gain anything by it? Will it restore to him control over his own life and destiny? In other words, will it lead . . . to self-rule for the hungry and spiritually starving millions of our countrymen? There you will find your doubts and your self melting away."[16] *Satyagraha* is resistance as soul power; it is a weapon the strong pit against the sword of violence. Its foundation is *ahimsa,* the nonviolence that does not injure and causes no damage. Not only for seers, poets, or saints, *ahimsa* is also something for the people. Gandhi said of himself that he was no visionary; he considered himself to be a practical idealist. He also called *ahimsa* "the law of our species as violence is the law of the brute."[17] The root of the word *hims* means "to kill eagerly" while *a* is a term of negation. Thus, *ahimsa,* the "absence of every desire to kill," is the central theme on which Hindu and Buddhist morality is built.

People have already accommodated themselves to violence when they merely entertain the desire to kill, to remove, or to eliminate. In such desires the deep relatedness of humans one to another is destroyed. Nonviolence succeeds only when our faith in God is genuine and alive, according to one of Gandhi's convictions. In this context faith means as much as reverence for the basic law of the universe, which is precisely the unity of all living beings. It is injured even when we simply wish to win, looking on life as a kind of boxing match in which defeat always includes a humiliation of the other. Violence merely feigns the resolution of conflicts, whereas in truth it sows the seed of bitterness and enmity. Buddha teaches that victory brings forth hatred and that to be conquered creates suffering. The wise desire neither victory nor defeat. *Ahimsa* was for Gandhi the foundation on which he developed decisive action plans for the conversion of a whole society and its government. These plans have become the basis for most current forms of organized nonviolent resistance. First, there is dialogue or open negotiation; for example, the public announcement of forthcoming nonviolent, disruptive actions or blockades. Then there is noncooperation with or boycott of governmental regulations, like a tax strike or the boycott of particular means of transportation or other public institutions. Only the third action plan, civil disobedience, constitutes resistance against the authority of the state. During a blockade, when the nonviolent blockaders are commanded to leave (usually three times), their refusal to do so becomes a punishable action, risking fines or incarceration.

Ahimsa is present in all these forms of civil disobedience. It encounters the opponent with friendliness and sympathy but also with the firm determination to accomplish one's own goal irrespective of what goes against it. Unlike violence, *ahimsa* acts quietly and pervasively; the nonviolent are not conscious of their action. According to Gandhi, the subdued character of *ahimsa* does not impede effectiveness; on the contrary, it makes parrying it more difficult.

Gandhi's most important action in India was the march in 1930 to protest the salt tax imposed by the British government. This tax caused great hardship for the poorest of the poor, who each subsisted on one bowl of rice a day. After several unsuccessful attempts to enter into dialogue and negotiation, Gandhi announced that he and his coworkers planned to break the salt levy. Together with seventy-eight men he set out to the sea. The march resembled a triumphal procession; in every small community a thousand more people joined the nonviolent protest. Arriving at the coast, Gandhi took a handful of salt from the sea and everyone else followed his example. The young people sold salt in the towns, tax-free. Gandhi was arrested but the action went on without him. Police actions accomplished nothing.

In this *satyagraha,* the English colonial power completely lost face; it became apparent that it was not invincible. Indeed, it had to hand over power to those who submitted to police truncheons without offering physical resistance. Those beaten did not become winners, they became free.

"Our Weapon Is to Have None": Martin Luther King Jr.

At Union Theological Seminary, during one of my seminars on mysticism and resistance, a student came to me wanting to talk about Martin Luther King Jr. (1929–1968). Somewhat confused I asked, "King, terrific but—a mystic?" He asked me whether I knew about the kitchen table experience. I had no idea, but this is how I came to know something about the "dark night of the soul" in King's life.

It all began on a bus in December 1955 as a forty-two-year-old black seamstress was traveling home from work. Even though 40 percent of the inhabitants of Montgomery were black, seats on the buses were reserved primarily for whites. Rosa Parks was seated in the section segregated for blacks; as more people got on the bus the driver told her to give her seat to a white passenger. She was tired and remained seated. The driver called the police; she was arrested, and, as was the custom, put in jail. "I was not tired physically, or no more tired than I usually was at the end of a working day," she writes in her memoirs. "No, the only tired I was, was tired of giving in."[18] At the time, she was the honorary secretary of an antiracist organization that had been founded in 1909, in honor of Abraham Lincoln, to provide legal assistance and voter registration.

The evening following the arrest of this highly respected woman, young Reverend King invited well-known and influential black citizens to come to his church. The atmosphere was explosive. A boycott of the bus line was decided upon, and most black citizens honored the call not to ride the buses. For a year the buses drove their routes empty; taxi drivers took the strikers to their destinations for the price of bus fare. In the course of time, Baptist preacher King became the spokesperson for the local civil rights movement. At the same time he had to cope with threats and fears that the well-educated son of a Baptist minister had never encountered before. His father had taught him that "no one can make a slave of you as long as you do not think like a slave."

In January 1956, Martin Luther King Jr. was jailed for the first time under the pretext that he had exceeded the legal speed limit of 25 miles per hour by 5 miles. On the way to prison he became scared: the car he was being taken in was being driven out of town. Was he going to be lynched? A few months before, a black fourteen-year-old had been abducted and sadistically murdered; the three white perpetrators were never punished. With good reason to be scared, King also had reason enough for relief when he was taken "only" to the run-down jail, a place reeking of urine and overflowing with homeless people, vagrants, drunks, and thieves. "Don't forget us," they shouted as he was released on bail.

It was not much better at home: the family received between thirty and forty telephone calls and hate letters per day. "Get out of town or else. KKK." "You niggers are getting yourself in a bad place. We need and will have a Hitler to get our country straightened out." King and Coretta, his wife, could not disconnect the telephone because they depended on calls from their friends. They jumped every time it rang and had to listen to threats, unspeakable obscenities, and hatred.

A white friend informed King of a serious plot to kill him. King did not know which way to turn. He came home from a meeting exhausted, wrung out from a long day, and he went to sleep. Again the phone rang, he picked up the receiver and heard an ugly voice telling him: "listen, nigger, we've taken from you all we want. Before next week you'll be sorry you ever came to Montgomery." King could bear it no longer; he got up and walked the floor. For the first time he feared for his life. He went to the kitchen and put on a pot of coffee. Then he sat down at the table and wondered how he could leave Montgomery without appearing to be a coward. There was no alternative; he had to get away. He thought about his father. At this point, King Jr. was just twenty-seven years old. Something inside him said, "You can't call Daddy now. He's up in Atlanta, a hundred and seventy-five miles away. You have to call on that something, that being, that your Daddy told you about, this power that finds a way where there is none." Later King said that he discovered then that religion was for real, and that "I had to get to know God for myself." Sitting at the kitchen table and bowed over it, he began to pray aloud: "O, Lord. I'm down here trying to do what is right. . . . The people are looking to me for leadership, and if I stand before them without strength or courage, they too will falter. I am at the end of my powers. I have nothing left. I can't face it alone."[19] Subsequently, King himself told what happened to him then at the kitchen table in Montgomery. "It seemed that an inner voice was speaking to him with quiet assurance: 'Martin Luther, stand up for righteousness. Stand up for justice. Stand up for truth. And lo, I will be with you even unto the end of the world.'"[20] King heard the voice of Jesus telling him to keep up the struggle. He then heard or sang a hymn rooted in black piety: "He promised never to leave me, never to leave me alone." In that moment, King was to say later, he felt God's presence like never before. His fears left him all of a sudden, his uncertainty vanished, and he was ready to face anything. He made his decision, he did not quit, and he did not take the easier route of going along. He realized that suffering taken up voluntarily has a transforming power.

Years later King explained what this meant. He assumed that society was diseased with racism and hatred, and bent on keeping its privileges and advantages. These diseases are not healed if all that we do is to try to make misery known, for example, by taking photos of starving children in Africa. Such diseases become treatable when minorities actually stand up for justice in economic relations, and when they do not let themselves be defeated by failures and ridicule, by being told that they are inferior, or by being rendered invisible.

When white racists threw a bomb on the porch of the King house, enraged blacks gathered in a crowd, armed with pistols, knives, sticks, and stones. Arriving at the house, King implored the crowd not to answer violence with violence. Those who answer violence with violence, bombs with bombs, and killing with killing solve no problems but descend to the level of the enemy. He told the outraged people to take their guns home or to throw them into the sea. "Our weapon is to have none," he said. "When I decided that, as a teacher of the philosophy of non-violence, I couldn't keep a gun, I came face to face with the question of death and I dealt with it. And from that point on, I no longer needed a gun nor have I been afraid. Ultimately, one's sense of manhood must come from within him."[21] King had read Gandhi in his student days and for him also pacifism was not a "method for cowards."[22] He called hooligans reactionaries because they resemble too much their enemies; he himself was a moderate radical, proud of being "badly adjusted." He favored methods of direct action but only after precise analysis of the situation. Action is to be taken only after negotiating with the other side has been tried as long as possible. Nonviolence means to forego the desire to win and to avoid the defeat of enemies, which always includes their humiliation. The issues of peace, justice, and—as must be added today—creation are always the enemies' issues as well; they, too, need air to breathe. Their issue is also ours. Every form of the spirit of hostility has to be rejected. King called white racists "our sick white brothers," which angered some of his comrades in the struggle.

An important component of nonviolence for King was the unearned suffering that resulted from the conflicts. He said that there would be rivers of blood, but we are determined to make sure that it is not the blood of the enemy. And so the method or the different style of living out nonviolence gives precisely to the disenfranchised and powerless a different sense of their own dignity. This was rooted deeply in the piety of blacks, more deeply than King had initially assumed. Simplicity, clarity, depth—learned during centuries of suffering—is how King understood the Sermon on the Mount.

He had learned much from the black theologian and philosopher Howard Thurman (1899–1981), who, as a teacher of the way of mysticism, spoke on behalf of the disenfranchised and underprivileged. In his lectures on "Mysticism and Social Change," Thurman wrote in reference to the well-known words of the socialist Eugene Debs: "It is not only the socialist but also the confirmed mystic or the man seeking the fullness of the vision of God who must say truly, 'while there is a lower class, I am in it. While there is a criminal element, I am of it. While there is a man in jail, I am not free.' The distinction between personal selfishness and social selfishness, between personal religion and social religion which we are wont to make, must forever remain artificial and unrealistic."[23] The inheritance of this humane mystical tradition of unity is what King took up and, in his admirable rhetorical talent, declared it to be valid for his own people as well as for this century. "We shall match your capacity to inflict suffering by our capacity to endure suffering. We will meet your physical force with soul force. Do to us what you will and we will still love you. We cannot in all conscience obey your unjust laws and abide by the unjust system, because non-cooperation with evil is as much a moral obligation as is cooperation with good, and so throw us in jail and we will still love you. Bomb our homes and threaten our children, and, as difficult as it is, we will still love you. Send your hooded perpetrators of violence into our communities at the midnight hour and drag us out on some wayside road and leave us half-dead as you beat us up, and we will still love you."[24]

Between Hopes and Defeats

An old friend from the peace movement, a religion teacher by profession, was jailed for twenty days in 1992 for civil disobedience. She wrote about the experience in a privately circulated letter that begins with these sentences: "Our laws punish mass murderers. There is no law and no punishment for producers of weapons of mass murder and mass destruction." She told of life in prison but also about the protest that led to her sentence and particularly "the disarming demonstration by children with balloons that swirled all around the jail. Finally, standing on a chair in my cell, we managed to get a look through the barred window and saw all my beloved friends down on the street, five of us clinging to the window above them." At the end of her cheerful letter she reflects again on the prospects of nonviolent peace work. "When I consider what changes have come about in the last years and to which the peace movement gave significant momentum, the hope for the future of our earth that pervades me is quite apparent: the Wall came down, the Pershing II missiles were removed, the poison gas shipped away, the planned nuclear installations for Wackersdorf in Bavaria cancelled. I believe that we are and shall always be in God's hand." To become aware and then to transmit such signs of hope is important, especially when one's own perception is of a more pessimistic nature. I experienced bitterly the defeat of the peace movement in the Gulf War. We could not prevent the allocation of 18 billion German Marks as blood money. What is to be learned from this when one has to assume that this war is only the first in a series of new wars that have again become legitimizable? What new forms of noncooperation can be developed? What munitions trains need to be blocked? What deserters to be hidden? What hopes do we have for the wars to come?

To resist does not mean to imagine that the murder machine can be shut down. Actions of sabotage, disturbance, protests, and traffic blockades in our context pursue the political goal of winning majorities for peace and justice so that the expansion of the machinery of murder no longer finds acceptance. As Daniel Berrigan once put it ironically, the language of nonviolent action is a language for mentally challenged people who cannot communicate with the normal means. For illiterates, among whom Berrigan counts the officials of the Pentagon, front-page articles are quite irrelevant; therefore, blood on the white pillars and orderly desks of that institution! This human blood makes something visible just as the nearly 10,000 court cases in Germany against "reprehensible violators" made something quite apparent.

This fluctuation between defeats and hopes must be something a religious culture of resistance cannot avoid. Religiosity borne by "positive thinking" always strikes me as being embarrassingly void of spirit and opiate-like. This "dark night of the soul" cannot be voted out of existence, nor will buttons calling us to "Take Jesus!" help us to get over it, much less over the dark night of creation. That we are and shall always be in God's hand, according to the woman cited earlier, becomes credible when with Teresa of Avila we also know, mystically, that God has no other hands but ours. To be aware of the "silent cry" in our world means to become one with it.

I shall try to spell out once again this hope "against hope" (Rom 4:18) in terms of one of the most important tasks of any resisting love of creation, namely the issue of nuclear energy. The majority of the German population, according to the polls taken, is against the use of nuclear energy and is not assured by the promise of "greatest possible safety." What is to become of the radioactive waste in the coming centuries is completely unresolved. Nicaraguan writer Gioconda Belli depicts in her futuristic novel *Waslala,* set in the twenty-first century, how the Third World is turned into a garbage dump, including atomic waste that kills the children who rummage in the garbage. This radiation-contaminated future cries out for a different answer.

The resistance against the nuclear recycling installation at Gorleben in Northern Germany prevented it from becoming reality and postponed for over a decade the creation of the intermediary station for radioactive waste. It is not a solution but it is at least an indication of what is possible for nonviolent action. It was quite a different story at Wackersdorf where, as a result of the local population's and other opponents' protests, industry concluded that nothing could be gained but trouble. The very politicians, who to the very end had sent in troops against the demonstrators, pulled back and abandoned the project.

What is to be learned from this is that next to the direct action of "getting-in-the-way," resistance needs the other nonviolent action, that of influencing the influential. The decision whether technological mega-projects are to be built and put into use is made less and less by the politicians and jurists of the country in question than by those who profit from them. It is not possible for normal citizens to boycott nuclear energy. However, they can stop buying other products made by those firms as long as they refuse to give in to the demands of the nonviolent and simply stop processing uranium and plutonium. Boycott is a language these corporations understand. The violence against creation that so brutally dominated the second half of the twentieth century can be interrupted and replaced by democratic forms of doing business.

To this day, the violence of what Robert Jungk called the "atom state" (1977) is still on the increase in confrontations of this kind. Police forces still react on the basis of a graduated concept of escalation: they tell people to leave the area; when this does not happen they proceed to carry people away; should that be impossible, water cannons are brought in; and, finally, if all else fails, people are clubbed. The basic right of freedom from bodily harm is by no means suspended by friendly sit-ins; hence, violence in fact originates with the police, one of the consequences of which is loss of trust in the state under the rule of law. What seems even more important to me is a different, recent development that was observed by many people during the biggest nonviolent action of civil disobedience in Germany in early March 1997. It was the third "Castor blockade," named after the containers for nuclear waste. That some of the ten thousand bleary-eyed and tense blockaders would snap and revert to violence could not be ruled out. A new system of cell groups, organized by "mediators," integrated all newcomers, linked them into the network, and opened up a process of exchange and participatory decision-making in that every group delegated one person to the council of spokespersons. This model is interesting inasmuch as it builds, like Martin Luther King and the Civil Rights Movement, a piece of base democracy, thereby reestablishing through this work the dignity and responsibility of the powerless: they are needed!

Nonviolence has finally taken hold more firmly also in Germany. In the last few years the peace movement there has given itself over anew, and very productively, to the question of deserters. This critical incorporation is not only an aspect of addressing Germany's past; it also contributes to the enlargement of our understanding of resistance. We still have much to learn in order to desert the false flag that waves over us today. In face of this liberation for resistance, discussion about what ranks higher or lower in what we today consider to be resistance is of secondary importance, in my view even misleading. When a woman on social security openly boycotts the fruits of apartheid, she needs just as much courage as a young man who blockades a nuclear power station does. I see no difference in principle between giving one's signature, demonstrating, holding a vigil, boycotting, noncooperation, or blockading. Small actions, simple education, and mere symbolic acts are in this wider sense resistance against the violence of the economic system that governs us and systematically renders the majority of the human family destitute. These are also acts of resistance against the security system that safeguards this economic injustice with military force and against the system that in spite of repeated warnings continues its deadly attack on creation itself.

However small we judge our own power to be, it is certainly greater than we surmise or are prepared to concede. Learning to believe in that something that we envisage, in the divine—however vaguely!—as the power of life, also means not to give the last word to one's own assessment regarding success or uselessness. Submission to the idol of violence begins with the seemingly reasonable insight that we accomplish little with our own power; that we are zeros incapable even of indignation and outrage. But in truth "that of God," as Quakers call it, sleeps also in us and waits to become free and visible.

During a blockade I had a conversation with an older woman in the peace movement about our opponents. She said, "for some funny reason I can never be what I am supposed to be as long as the others are not what they are supposed to be. You, too, can't be what you're supposed to be before I become what I am meant to be. You understand? That's just how the world is, that's how it is structured." That is an everyday formulation of what Gandhi, King, Schweitzer, and many others meant by the mysticism of oneness. It is the foundation of nonviolence. We must be attentive not only to the most recent and most modern weapons systems but also to the "funny" inner voice that teaches us oneness, mutual dependency, and a nontechnocratic knowledge of the good creation.

15. A MYSTICISM OF LIBERATION

———◆———

When I see them,
the children of my people,
the world without voice:
emaciated,
bloated belly,
oversized head
and, very often,
empty, left behind,
as if it were missing—
it is Christ whom I meet.

DOM HELDER CAMARA

The Death and Life of Severino: João Cabral

THE FRAGMENTATION OF THE WORLD into center and periphery is generally known. There is life that is said to be productive and worth living, and there is life that is economically useless. Twenty percent of humankind have the right to use, to exploit, and to throw away, while eighty percent are superfluous, the losers. In the center of the world everything needed to live is available: banks and factories, administration and research, consumption and traffic. There all the treasures of the world are gathered up and within reach at any time. Whatever people plant and process in various regions of the world can be eaten in the center. Whatever people weave, film, or shape can be laid hold of in the center. Whatever has been thought of, planned, and invented can be had and be made in the center.

Living in the center of the fragmented world means there is nothing you cannot think of that cannot be produced and bought, accessed and possessed. Even if you are only a minor female clerk, in the center you feel that you are part of the power. At any given time you could buy, travel, and utilize. What is not up for discussion are the decisive words that, according to Helder Camara, are not our property: "to be" and "to love."

Far, far away from us, in some Third or Fourth World, there is a marginal sphere, the periphery. It would be an exaggeration to claim that everything that is available overabundantly in the center is what is missing at the periphery. There are banks at the periphery, except that they do not work with the people's money for the people; the money flows back to the center. At the periphery there are also factories, except that they do not manufacture what many need but what the center dictates. They work for export while the most needed things have to be imported. At the periphery there is also traffic: roads, airlines, railroads, but they do not create a grid. They only establish connection with what is most important, the center far away, elsewhere. There are raw materials, which are mined but not processed. There is abundance and luxury among a very thin layer of the population, but the masses have nothing to consume. There is technological progress but it reduces the number of jobs. Most of the people have nothing to eat, nothing to learn, nothing to do.

"Center and periphery" is a model for explaining this situation on our one earth. It makes apparent how the minority in the rich countries has rendered the majority in the poor countries dependent in every sense of the word: economically, politically, technologically, ecologically, and culturally. This model shows how the few rob the many and plunder, disenfranchise, and kill them. That this is accomplished not only with a knife or by a military dictatorship but far more thoroughly through structural, systemic violence is well known.

An understanding of the mysticism of liberation requires awareness of the anonymous violence that has been perpetrated on colonized peoples for centuries. However, the violence of the postcolonial period is of a different order. A poem, written in 1954–55, deals with this violence. Even though it was not written for the stage, it was produced by the student theatre of the Catholic University of São Paulo in 1966 and won the Golden Palm Award at the World Festival in Nancy. "The Death and Life of Severino" was written by the renowned poet from northeast Brazil, João Cabral de Melo Neto (b. 1920).

The poem begins with someone being introduced. A man tells his name, indicating his identity. But Severino has no "identification papers" and the simple act of telling his name fails to achieve its purpose. Identity is established by means of a name, the mother, the presumed father, the place of birth or residence, and visible marks. Yet, the attempt to zero in on Severino so that the audience may know who this person actually is, put a name to him and get hold of him, leads to the very opposite. As the angle of the lens widens, the focus becomes increasingly less definable so that namelessness is the final result. The words of the poet are simple, but his language contains an artful double movement of both naming and of not being able to name. In search of establishing identity, what becomes visible are the masses: "many Severinos in the same life situation." The man who fled the rural regions represents nothing unusual.

Life is described only after a description of death; the word "death" precedes the word "life" in the title. Stations of death are also the stations of one's life journey. One may speak of a longing for death, perhaps even of a mysticism of death, so much are all the encounters of this journey related to death. The journey follows the course of the river. It is the journey that a million Severinos begin, always with new hopes. It takes them away from the unproductive areas that they had been pushed back into, or from the regions destroyed and exhausted by monocultural agribusiness, through the forest regions to the plain and on to the city. From the lost cause of making a living from a plot of unproductive ground—the large estate owners control the productive land as well as the meager water resources and the superior technology—the road leads to the lost cause of the suburban slums.

On this journey, Severino meets himself again and again in the figures of the other Severinos. He meets himself as someone dead, murdered during one of the hunts that are carried out in the interior of Brazil against the still surviving aboriginal peoples. He meets himself emaciated and eventually laid out on a bier, people singing around him, done to death by the work in the landowner's sugar cane fields, out of work. He meets himself untutored, physically damaged by malnutrition. Severino meets himself in the dead that he comes across and in those who are still alive, maintaining themselves by doing death's business—burying the dead.

Cabral speaks on several levels simultaneously. He addresses the economically based fate of the masses that have been forced to flee from the land. He traces the route of the river through the various stages of the misery and history of the poor "everyman" called Severino. The geography of the country and the geography of hunger, the history of exploitation and the future are all seen together. The poem was written over four decades ago. Since then, Brazil has had its own widely heralded economic "miracle." Yet this miracle has left unchanged the conditions of the Northeast and the Severinic way of living and dying. Today's Severino also wants to take his life. Will he do so? The answer remains open.

The poem's conclusion once again reinforces the mystical aspects against the realistic ones. The journey of misery turns into a Christmas play. In the face of death and against all its forms, the carpenter's new-born child is praised; a neighbor woman and other friends bring gifts. Much like those of the earlier angels and shepherds, the gifts are not very practical for the struggle for survival. But in actuality, however difficult it is to transmit, the arrival of a new life means a defense of life.

> He is as beautiful as a Yes
> in a room full of No's.
> He is as beautiful as the second harvest
> that increases the sugar-cane field's yield.
> Beautiful, because he is a door
> that turns into many exits.
> Beautiful like the final wave
> that no seashore devours.
> He is as beautiful as the waves
> in their sum of infinity.[1]

The angels' hallelujah so long ago in the stable could not have sounded very different. The great hallelujah is never an explanation of reality and is in no way a substitute of the analysis that would lead to plans of action. I want to defend the language of mysticism in this chapter and defend it against the suspicion of counterrevolution. Mysticism wants nothing else but to love life, even where analysis has run its course and all that is left is to count the victims. To love life also where it has long been condemned to death, even from its very beginning, is an old human ability to go beyond what is. That ability is called transcendence or faith or hope—or listening to the silent cry. It is the most important movement that human beings can learn in their lives. The actors of the Pernambucan Christmas play make it happen in that they praise the child.

The most important human capacity for a mysticism of wide-open eyes is almost completely unknown within the rich world. With the most refined methods known to history so far, this capacity is being destroyed. Dying remains just as inexperienced as living, causing no one to change. Most citizens of my country cannot think of anything more in relation to the death and life of Severino than the Pill that, unfortunately, is not yet universally available. Birth-control technology would no doubt have prevented the accident that came into being in Bethlehem.

When I read poetry from Latin America, I often doubt who is really more hopeless, Severino or we here, and accordingly to whom hope is given.

Kneeling Down and Learning to Walk Upright:
The Theology of Liberation

Wherever theology undergoes changes, mysticism plays a part in it. In the second half of the twentieth century a movement of Christian base communities came into being in Latin America that bears the features of a mysticism of the poor. When a visitor asked such an ecclesial base congregation in São Paulo what had led them in coming together, the people told her, "we needed a pipe for clean water because our wells were contaminated." The European visitor wondered what that had to do with faith and was told, "Don't you think that God wants us to have clean water?"

From such base movements and their faith, called the "first act," *Teología de la Liberación* (Liberation Theology) nurtures itself, calling itself a "second act" of reflection. This theology was taken up in many parts of the Third World, in South Africa as in Southeast Asia, and by blacks in the United States and by Christian women all over the world. It is a Christian theology that is not centered on Europe; it renders the New Testament word *soteria*, hitherto translated mostly as "redemption" and related often exclusively to the salvation of the individual soul, as "liberation." For this liberation theology, *soteria* is what sets us free from economic, political, cultural, and spiritual oppression.

Does this kind of new and liberating understanding of Scripture and tradition have something to do with mysticism? One of the foundational biblical texts of this theology is derived from the narrative of Moses' calling. "I have seen the misery of my people in Egypt and have heard their cry" (Exod 3:7). God sees the misery of the enslaved people; indeed, the perspective of the poor is the perspective of the biblical God. God has a special preference, an option for them. God desires their liberation and Moses is to contribute to it. God hears their cry, and in and through God, Moses too hears the cry. All who walk the Exodus road with him also hear that cry.

In the sense of theology that liberates, the soul that is united with God sees the world with God's eyes. That soul, like God, sees what otherwise is rendered invisible and irrelevant. It hears the whimpering of starving children and does not let itself be diverted from real misery, becoming one with God in perceiving and understanding as well as in acting. For people in the slums, redemption does not consist of some great and far removed actor ending the misery of the oppressed. Rather, in coming so very close, that far-near one acts in and through those who have become one with that actor. In liberating movements, the mystical eye sees God at work: seeing, hearing, acting, even in forms that are utterly secular. In the contingency of literacy programs, or collaboration in building a school, God's action is manifest. It is a mysticism of wide-open eyes. This *mistica revolucionaria* expresses itself in numerous changes in practice and in the teaching of religion. I would like to speak about a few of them:

1. Replacing the hierarchical order that places the spiritual life (of Mary) above the merely practical-active life (of Martha), a new concept of *orthopraxis* relativizes the old concept of orthodoxy. In a situation where the majority is disenfranchised, truth cannot communicate itself only as a matter of correct belief and confession but is dependent on the struggle for liberation.

2. With the teaching office of the poor of the base community, liberation theology has created a new space for women, for people of color, for those who are untutored in the academic sense of the word, and for nonconsecrated lay people. In the base communities of faith, the new tasks needing to be done give rise to new, often little-defined offices and roles. The basic declaration that "the poor are the teachers" means at first that the poor pose the questions, such as that of clean water. They relate that question to Christ's passion and hear his cry "I thirst" in a new way.[2] Marching for water and Good Friday processions merge into each other.

3. Several elements are connected in a new way in this developing popular mysticism of liberation. A rediscovery of the original *religions of the indigenous peoples* with their music and rituals contributes to the reconciliation of the victims of the history of conquest with the religion of the conquistadors. In this process, the prophetic element of accusation and uncovering the causes is always conjoined to the pastoral element, namely the reconstitution of the dignity of the destitute. Judgment and consolation are experienced together.

4. A historical consequence of liberation theology has been one of the greatest persecution of Christians of this century. Numerous catechists, priests, female and male members of religious orders, and bishops have been murdered because they stood up for justice. Furthermore, in connection with the problems of land distribution and of aboriginal peoples' human rights, even more anonymous, undocumented people became—and continue to

this day to become—victims of repression, such as the parents and siblings of the Guatemalan Nobel Laureate for Peace, Rigoberta Menchu (b. 1959). Her father, a small farmer and catechist, tried to call attention to the massacres that were taking place in remote regions. He was burned to death in 1980, together with thirty-seven other members of the group that had occupied the Embassy of Spain. Her mother, a teacher, was arrested a little later, abducted, sexually assaulted, and murdered. The group to which both parents belonged was called "Revolutionary Christians." The Roman Catholic Church does not recognize them as martyrs, but the people of liberation theology celebrate them as martyrs of the reign of God who, on account of their engagement, were driven out or exiled, jailed or "disappeared," or tortured and murdered. Whole villages or base groups were wiped out by the death squads or the hired killers of the large estate owners.

In the face of this actual condition of repression, faith and hope do not function within a depoliticized, privatized piety but in a historically novel combination of kneeling down and learning to walk upright. These two movements, kneeling down and standing up, belong together and succeed only in tandem.

Introversion and extroversion are not mutually exclusive. If it is a fundamental mistake of clericalism to pay heed only to kneeling down, the modern practical illusion of walking upright—as free of religion as possible—is no better. The absence of real life cries out for wholeness and reconciliation. Every dream of the truly good life and every form of utopian longing in the most diverse cultures is religious and strives for a continuing liberation. It is achieved as little with the abolition of private ownership of the means of production as with the achievement of free elections. The danger of misusing religion as the opiate of the people seems much smaller to me today than the other danger that weans human beings from the language of their longings and their mysticism. This alternate danger shrinks people and their language to the acquisition of material needs. Meister Eckhart says about the just that they take justice so seriously that if God were not just, they would not give a fig for God.[3]

It is on account of this mystical dimension that today we cannot relinquish liberation theology, even though many of its high-soaring hopes of the seventies and eighties have come to grief in the meantime. The death sentence that neoliberalism is ready to pronounce on the Third World has also changed the spiritual situation of the poor. For example, in one of the poorest countries, Nicaragua, in the days of the Sandinista Revolution, there were street children without homes and parents. However, every morning those children went to school for free and without coercion. Now, this is utterly beyond their means. The economic impoverishment of "God's darling children" has become more desperate. The attempts to implement land reforms stagnate in most Latin American countries, education of and health care for the poorest of the poor have been cut back, and the globalization of the markets has destroyed every form of subsistence economy. It is important for survival itself in this phase of defeats to make known that liberation is God's promise to today's slaves. A theology is required that holds on to the dignity and the human rights of the destitute, even when this group of human beings is said to be superfluous, of no economic relevance, regarded as expendable, and treated as such in the most cynical statements of the experts. Defeats and new fears can diminish and weaken but not destroy the hope that arises at the margins as the power that drives history onward. "They can't expel God."

"When You Dance with Death, You Must Dance Well": Pedro Casaldáliga

A mystic of liberation theology, who was persecuted for years and threatened with expulsion, crafted the lovely sentence of the God whom even the bloodiest military dictatorship could not expel or get rid of. Pedro Casaldáliga, a bishop of Spanish origin and a poet of Northeast Brazil, developed a kind of "mysticism of death" in light of the threatened, disappeared, and murdered small farmers and Indios. In the face of threats, he lives out this mysticism and reflects it in his theology. "The presence of death helped me so much to feel myself in God's presence as if I had to give account in the very next moment."[4] That is still traditional theology, but when he addresses death as "a member of the family" or "bridegroom,"[5] something sounds new. In a song to death, he puts it as follows: "You encircle me, I encircle you, you to kill, I to live." This desire to protect, on the one hand, and the persecution that results from it, on the other, creates a whirl reminiscent of medieval imagery. It approaches a stance that has its origin in the mystical poetry of Spain.

One form of death is the daily pauperization of the small tenant farmers, driven from their land and now trying to work barren land, where children "absorb death already with their mother's milk."[6] The open repression and its violence is another form of death. Bishop Casaldáliga and a Jesuit friend once tried to come to the aid of two women who were tortured in the prison of the small town. A shot that was most likely meant for the bishop felled the visitor. Casaldáliga reported, "On that day I felt death to be really close, indeed physically, for João fell on my feet."[7]

Asked what the death of the people meant, and his own death that he sometimes longed for in the sense of martyrdom, he said, "First of all, death bowls me over. Death is always death despite all mysticism. . . . Sometimes I nearly despair and I ask God the reason for all those senseless deaths, those deaths that hunger causes, or the long, long ways people have to walk, the unavailable medical care or the injustice. . . . 'Killed dead ones,' as we say here, absurd, insane deaths. But, on the other hand, I believe in God and I believe in hope. For me hope has become a very sharp knife that becomes even sharper the more deeply it cuts into the flesh of the ever present death."[8] Two things are noteworthy about this mysticism of death that meets us here and there in the history of mysticism. The first is that in the situation of impoverishment, death is not only an individual problem that concerns individuals and perhaps their closest partners. For Casaldáliga, speaking of his own death always means speaking of the death of the people, of children, and of all who defend themselves. The death of the forests also belongs to that struggle.

One of the first martyrs of the ecological movement in Brazil is said to be Chico Mendes. Since 1977 he has saved thousands of hectares of rain forest from the illegal clear-cutting of the forest and resisted the expulsion of the population carried out by the large estate owners in the interest of McDonaldizing agriculture. Mendes became the organizer and spokesperson of 165,000 families in the Amazon region, who lived off an ecologically sound way of tapping rubber plants in the hitherto untouched rain forests. As a result of his engagement for a different way of relating to creation, members of one of the landowning families murdered him in 1988, like many other nonviolent blockading forest workers before him. In this event, many ecologically conscious people in Brazil and in the whole Green Movement came to feel the presence of death for the first time—not only death of the forests and the climate but also of the people directly affected. In mystical irony, Bishop Casaldáliga says that, "when you dance with death, you must dance well. There is no other way. You try to keep in step and not to lose the rhythm, to be correct, don't you?"[9] The medieval image of the Dance of Death is embedded into the theology of liberation. "But all those deaths that I have experienced here have made me feel lawlessness in the most dramatic way. Hence my passionate defense of justice and freedom."[10] The other element that may be learned from this mysticism of death is a peculiar freedom that transforms everything and changes even the necessity we call death. As indestructible as the structure of death seems to be and as hopeless as the crusades of Brazil's landless (who every time yet another child has died affix a diaper to the cross they carry with them) seem to be, in liberation theology death becomes an element of freedom. Death is not excluded from love, and death excludes no one from love.

Death is part of the domain of what Pedro Casaldáliga calls "becoming naked." That faith disrobes itself more and more is a traditional image in mysticism; the "garments" of faith are what Meister Eckhart often calls the "ways" of faith, its rituals and ideologies. Just as poetry in the literature of Spanish modernity "disrobes" itself more and more, so it is with faith. "In the measure in which faith becomes more and more naked, it becomes dearer and dearer to me, more and more my own, more and more of God and of all of us."[11]

Mysticism of liberation makes no distinction between movements associated with churches and secular movements. In the process of disrobing, the church becomes less and less definable "because it becomes less and less visible to me, more and more worldly and, at the same time, more and more otherworldly."[12] This church becomes more itself the more it loses power, economic power but also protective power for those who live out the liberating faith. "I hope that the last sacrament of my life will be death. . . . Looking at religious life today I would say that it becomes 'poorer' with each new day, losing respect and becoming less and less a matter of 'status.'"[13] It is not because of some subsequent resurrection but as a pure act that has nothing beyond itself that death is a sacrament. It is indeed the love for God, this inexplicable, uncoerceable, mystical love that even draws death into what is alive, lived wholly in the very now. If the phrase "I am what I do" depicts the mystical life, it also hold true for our dying.

> I shall die erect, like the trees.
> (They will kill me standing upright.)

The sun, as the sole witness, shall put its seal
on my doubly anointed body,
and the rivers and the sea
will become the paths of all my wishes
while the primordial forest joyfully shakes its treetops over me.
I shall say about my words:
I did not lie when I cried out.
And God shall say to my friends:
"I attest that he lived among you waiting for this day."
In the twinkling of an eye in death
my life will become truth.
Finally, I shall have loved![14]

The Voice of the Mute: Dom Helder Camara

One can learn about the mysticism of liberation theology best from those who live close to simple people, listen to their language, and know their fears. Dom Helder Camara (1909–1999), from northeast Brazil, was a political bishop and mystic. He wished nothing from the church as much as to see her rise up "courageously in search of its lost poverty."

That is why he, the co-adjutor to the archbishop of Rio de Janeiro, did not live in the bishop's palace but in a small room in his sister's place. As archbishop of Olinda and Recife (1964–1984) he scheduled his office hours for the poor in what he, with abashed irony, spoke of as the "so-called" arch-episcopal palace. But he lived in the sacristy. "Let's not make our moral power and our authority contingent on the make of our automobile" said the church leader who hitchhiked around his diocese. In 1965, at the conclusion of the Second Vatican Council, at which he made no public appearances while being a mover and shaker behind the scenes, he angrily exclaimed during a press conference: "Enough of a church that wants to be served, that always wants to be first, that does not have the humility and the realism to affirm the existence of religious pluralism."[15]

Since his seminary years, Helder Camara retained the habit of rising at two o'clock in the morning to listen to the silence and to meditate. "I set my alarm clock although I am very tired then. But it is just that time that I get things together again. During the day I have spent myself in every possible way: one arm is pulled this way, the other reaches out that way, one foot has gone to one side while the other went in the opposite direction. It is unity that has to be recovered."[16] In those hours, he would pray the breviary or write his little close-to-ordinary-life meditations. Here are some examples of these meditations. "If you had not given me the grace during my nightly vigils to drink the stillness and to submerge myself in it, letting it pervade me through and through, how could I guard that inner stillness without which one can hear neither human beings nor you, O Lord?"[17] Voicing God's presence again and again in beaten down and defeated life is at the heart of Camara's mysticism of liberation. In its language nothing remains fixed in mute self-immersion: the milkman's cart, the poor beggar, the pregnant woman, the newspaper vendor, and the street cleaner, all speak of God, as does a piece of wood, a sugar cane, or an old car. "Everything, really everything speaks to me of you, thanks to you."[18] It may be the little, forgotten provincial train station where the big trains "stop only as an exception. Doesn't it say anything to you? Or remind you of someone?"[19] It can be a simple puddle that reflects the sky, which is why the author is glad to see it, or else the floors of a highrise, passed through in an elevator that lifts up the praying Camara, tearing him away from the transitory. Here is a kind of the poetry, accessible to everyone in its linguistic simplicity, free of literary artistry, but precise, terse, and accurate. Taking up an old mystical image, Camara reflects on his writing: "When I write I want to be white paper in your hands, God, on which you can write what you like."[20]

And so the transition from the natural to the supernatural and from the real to the dream is "almost imperceptible," according to his own testimony. And yet, Camara is highly sensitive to language and attentively notes the destruction of language perpetrated on the poor. For example, when they are deprived of reading and writing, they are robbed not only of a technical tool for dealing with the world. The economic structure that prohibits the poorest, among them especially women, from learning, also keeps them from reading and praising the world, causing them to drown in silence. Like almost no one else, Helder Camara repeatedly pointed out that people who have no place to live, go to sleep hungry, and have been refused work, also grow mute and have no voice left to plead for their rights. Apathy is the sociological term for this condition of the helpless poverty of those who have no voice and, thanks to the barbarism of the economy, cannot gain one.

Helder Camara was among the first to describe with precision "the spiral of violence." He speaks of "violence number one," the institutional violence that injures the dignity and the most basic rights of human beings. He calls "war" not only the immediate violence done by weapons, but also the hunger and unemployment of the majority of humans, the destruction of subsistence economies in the interest of international business, and, concomitantly, the destruction of one's own dignity. This first violence is the cause of reactive "violence number two" that may take the forms of criminality or revolution. But only then does the spiral of violence turn and lead to "violence number three," to repression in all the forms of censorship, imprisonment, abduction, exile, torture, and murder.

Against this spiral, Camara opposes the passive resistance "without hatred and without violence," taken up by the majority of South and Central American Christian liberation theologians. This resistance will absorb more time than the poor have, but Camara is unwavering in his basic conviction that love is stronger than hate and that the right to speak the truth can be won by love and friendship. His speeches all attest to this basic idea, for example, the one entitled "Transnational Corporations and Today's Revaluation of Values" delivered in 1974 at the Symposium of European Managers at Davos, Switzerland. Nonviolence always also represents an appeal to the dignity of perpetrators. The game of liberation is played out before those receiving and those inflicting the beating. Camara's texts, therefore, are a pure gospel, excluding no one and, just like the vision of Mexico's Chiapas Indios in the nineties, is meant for "a world with room for all."

What is the ground where a hope grows that in an ever aggravating global economy sounds even more utopian? For Camara the world that has been pushed into muteness is the place where God is found.

> You could have forbidden—it was your right—
> that your decisive words: to be and to love
> would be subject to conjugation.
>
> I am not surprised at your timeless goodness
> with which you let the infinitives of your being
> be fragmented into times, persons, and modes
> like any old word.[21]

The God Camara believes in is not confined in himself. This God cannot be fragmented into "times, persons, and modes." Instead, it is a God who is born into the midnight of hunger and beaten-down life. One of the basic problems of every orthodox religion is avoided in this language, namely the separation of God and humans. God has become something like the shadow figures of the mute world. The God who "preferred the deepest night in order to be born in it" is not a winner. But the presence of God in beaten-down life is the foundation and ground of hope. However realistic, unerring, and clear-sighted Camara is in his texts, he is utterly incapable of not hoping; this could be what defines his mysticism. The ground of hope is at the same time its abyss, its void.

Even the night of children stunted by malnutrition is always God's night also. If there is a mysticism of mediated immediacy, a mysticism of agony instead of narcosis, of a Yes! in the midst of the No! of the world of misery, it is present here. In spite of their harsh clarity, Helder Camara's texts are inviting, beautiful. He makes use of aesthetic categories. His pictures for the unity of life, where no one is someone else's prey anymore, often are derived from the domain of music. Life's goodness is no longer inculcated with the rod of morality but with the appeals of an affectionate tenderness that cannot leave out anyone, a tenderness that is and remains subversive.

> When I stand before customs-officers and police-commissioners,
> I smile mischievously, for no one detects
> the divine contraband, the stowaway,
> whose highly discreet presence is visible
> only to angels' glances.[22]

Learning to Pray and a Different Mysticism

What does it mean to travel with the "divine contraband"? When liberation theology speaks of mysticism of "wide-open eyes," it repudiates the withdrawal from the world that is traditionally symbolized in the closing of the eyes. This does not imply that the divinity can now be seen bodily, or that God's only true name has been made known. Mystics cannot photograph God, just as theologians cannot prove that God is. Body and reason are equally helpless. The darkness or the silence of God cannot be taken up into an alleged immediacy. One may sooner speak perhaps of a "mediated immediacy" or in terms of paradoxes such as those of Pedro Casaldáliga when he calls out to Christ:

My strength and my failing are you.
My inheritance and my poverty,
my war and my peace,
the judge of my poor tears,
the cause of my hope.[23]

Thus, what mystics call "becoming at one" is never a possession that cannot be lost. What really happens in mystical union is not a new vision of God but a different relationship to the world—one that has borrowed the eyes of God. God is no private affair for a few who are naive enough or who are blessed with a fortunate disposition.

I want to go back again to the testimony of a medieval woman mystic who helped me understand being at one in a new and different way, in the sense of a contemporary liberation theology. Mechthild von Hackeborn from the monastery of Helfta once interpreted the mystical oneness of the soul with God not as an ecstatic-erotic fusion; instead, it is that the soul thus graced learns to make use of "God's senses." "She once begged the Lord to give her something that would always cause her to remember him. Thereupon, she received from the Lord this answer: 'See, I give you my eyes, that you may see all things with them, and my ears, that you may hear all things with them; my mouth I also give you, so that all you have to say, whether in speech, prayer, or song, you may say through it. I give you my heart, that through it you may think everything and may love me and all things for my sake.' In these words God drew this soul entirely into him and united it in such a way that it seemed to her that she saw with God's eyes, and heard with his ears, and spoke with his mouth, and felt that she had no heart than the heart of God. This she was also given to feel on many later occasions."[24] What happens really in the soul's union with God in terms of liberation and of healing? It is an exercise in seeing how God sees, the perception of what is little and unimportant; it is listening to the cry of God's children who are in slavery in Egypt. God calls upon the soul to give away its own ears and eyes and to let itself be given those of God. Only they who hear with other ears can speak with the mouth of God. God sees what elsewhere is rendered invisible and is of no relevance. Who other than God sees the poor and hears their cry? To use "God's senses" does not mean simply turning inward but becoming free for a different way of living life: See what God sees! Hear what God hears! Laugh where God laughs! Cry where God cries!

Part of that also is "to speak with God's mouth." But that implies a different, new, mystical prayer. The exercise in seeing how God sees happens in speaking with God as one speaks with one's friend (Exod 33:11). If there is a verb for the life of mysticism, it is praying. This superfluous activity, this unproductive waste of time happens *sunder warumbe*, (without any why or wherefore). It is as free of ulterior motives as it is indispensable. Prayer is its own end and not a means to obtain a particular goal. The question "what did it achieve?" must fall silent in face of the reality of prayer.

Leonardo Boff (b. 1938), one of the leading Brazilian liberation theologians, tells of meeting a woman who revivified his faith in God and his hope in God's reign. Her fifteen-year-old son, her only child, was on the city's garbage dump, rummaging for their livelihood, when he was killed by the police. His mother, hunched over with inconsolable pain, is like stone; she is no longer able to cry. Boff asked her: "Can you still believe at all in God?" He goes on to tell what he sees and hears. "I will never forget her eyes because I felt God's own gentleness in them; she looked at me and said, 'Me? Why would I not believe in God? For is God not my father? To whom else would I cling if not to God—and if I could not feel myself in his hand?'" Boff comments on this encounter: "Marx is mistaken. On this final stage, faith is no opiate but radiating liberation, a light that drives away darkness; it is life beyond death."[25] The prayer of the despairing woman is not a means of reversing what has happened. Nor is it an inner psychic discourse that delivers healing as its product. It is a mystical act because it does not regard the ground of the world as an ice-cold silence. The woman's prayer is what it is. It has moved beyond the pervasive assumption about prayers of intercession and supplication, namely that there is a purpose to be achieved. Unlike the pattern of prayer of some fundamentalists, there is no boasting of how many prayers have been answered. Instead, it creates a presupposition of mysticism for it takes for granted that they who pray have always been heard already. Violence has taken away the dearest the woman had, but death cannot take away the love in which she lives. The Father is with her. Who can separate them?

In such mysticism of prayer, the relationship of domination between God and humans has been transformed into one of love. That is precisely the mystical transformation that happens to prayer of supplication. The feudalistic patriarchal understanding of supplication often starts from the assumption that human beings have to go and knock on God's door and awaken "him" in order to present their petitions. The feudal lord then answers or refuses. If "he" has refused often enough even the most necessary things, the supplicant will go away and perhaps look elsewhere for salvation.

But in the true prayer of different religions, this utilitarian understanding is not the only dimension, not the beginning and the end. Religious language and its culture has always created other forms that embed supplication in lament and thanksgiving, in crying and praising. Even though in supplicatory prayer the human being—in the nominative—is still at the center, in performing mystical prayer the transformed human being replaces the former. It is the human being now who no longer only calls out but has always been called already—the human being in the accusative. The orphaned woman Boff talks about is a being in relationship, as is her God.

Mystics have rarely cultivated the prayer of supplication; they have worked at a relationship based on mutuality. They have known that there is such a thing as delivering the self to a grace that sets us free. This deliverance happens when we speak to God, make our accusations against God, and weep in God, which is, at the same time, to praise God—in spite of everything.

In this act of speaking, the mystery of the world is upheld as speaking and hearing. What Hölderlin expressed in his phrase, "since we are a conversation and can hear one of the other" is true in genuine prayer. The conversation that we "are" rather than "conduct" perceives us as respondents who are always already addressed. We are not isolated entities who in solitude cry out at the walls of nothingness. We do not produce ourselves; self-production is replaced by gratitude or grace.

The relationship to God also puts an end to the differentiation between active and passive behavior. All mystics have known that these categories are insufficient because all real experiences between human beings, and between God and them, are always both: radical gift, assault, being overwhelmed, and, at the same time, active accepting, opening one's hands, saying yes, drinking in. No more is anyone only acting or being acted upon. An activity that does not know the virtues of passivity, such as being able to wait, patience, letting go of oneself, and placing oneself into another's hands, becomes thoughtless and merciless. Only when I can experience myself also as a passive being can I know that I have not made myself and that from its inception life was goodness. Being called is always also letting oneself be called.

What changes in such a relationship of love is the modern, still dominant concept of autonomy, which prohibits self-deliverance because it implies the acknowledgment of dependence. Mutual dependence is the fundamental model that mysticism has put in place of domination. "I have it from God and God from me" is one of Angelus Silesius's many formulations of this basic understanding of love that cannot be thought of other than as being mutual. "That God is so blessed and lives without desire he has received from me as I have received it from him."[26] The mutuality signaled here is both dependency and self-deliverance. But can they be without domination and inferiority? To this question love responds with a resounding Yes! The dependency of someone who says to another, "I cannot live without you!" describes not coercion or inferiority, or dependency as sickness but something that elevates my freedom. I grow in the need for one who is different and removes my boundaries. I become more beautiful when I owe my beauty not to myself or my mirrors but to the one who calls me beautiful and whom I need.

Prayer also works in precisely this sense where love reduces domination by knowing itself to be dependent. Prayer is a language of love; whenever it is not, prayer is dispensable. Prayer is petition and teaches us to shape our desires more in accordance with life and together with others; at the same time, it is also delivery of the self into God's grace, but not in obsequiousness. Indeed, we are not self-sufficient. We ought not to exchange the premodern domination of a feudal-lord God for the modern domination of the *Herrenmensch* (the master-human being). It is possible, after all, to think of a different, domination-free model of relationship and to live in it, a model that may have a new chance in the postmodern world.

The basic understanding of the mutual dependency of God and human beings found in mystical religiosity has yet a very different dimension today than in the past. For now the notion of the self-sufficiency and domination of the two-legged creature over all other living beings and the elements, which are treated as mere resources, has grown beyond all imaginable measures. Appropriation, domination, subjugation, and use determine the relation to the world of nature and threaten the whole of life on the little blue planet. More and more people sense today that a different spiritual foundation for the earth's survival and all its inhabitants is necessary.

It is precisely among critical thinkers in the natural sciences that a new attentiveness is emerging to a domination-free, mystical religiosity. It has become clearer and clearer that everything that exists coexists and is bound into a network of relationships that we call interdependence. This approach to creation renders ever more questionable the notion of the absolute domination by our species. The anthropocentrism that today endangers the survival of creation and the multiplicity of its species is hostile to nature. In addition, it is without relation to God in depicting human beings as, according to Descartes, *maîtres et possesseur de la nature* (masters and owners of nature).

Creation itself is dependent on cooperation and on mutual assistance. Ever since his great "Canto Cosmico" of 1989, Ernesto Cardenal emphasizes in his synthesis of natural science, poetry, and music that this cooperation "has always been present at every biological level and is as old as life itself."[27] To inquire about the origin of cooperation means to inquire about the origin of life itself. In this endeavor, natural scientists discover in ever new ways that it is not the struggle for existence and the survival of the fittest that is the foundation. Instead, commonality and mutual dependency are the basis of evolution.

To entertain desires other than those prescribed is a preparation, a kind of school of prayer that we badly need. A mystical-ecological consciousness knows itself to be woven together with all that exists. All that is can live and survive only in the coexistence of relationships. This coexistence binds us together with the millions of years of evolution and, at the same time, with our grandchildren's drinking water. It cannot be ignored and no one has the right to foreclose on it. Coexistence needs a different world piety.

Mysticism as the future form of religion also relates to this unity of life. As its language, prayer brings the unity that is given with creation into awareness. Into the place of the cancer-like expansion of a few living beings and life-forms there enters the well-being of all. Give and take replaces the winner mentality. Is it possible for love to overcome the illusions of autonomy, self-sufficiency, and the praxis of exclusion? It is amply evident that we will have no chance at all without this mystical dream. To live in it already, now, is the hope of self-aware minorities.

I conclude with a description of such a life that is told by Quakers. In words of beautiful exaggeration yet, at the same time, utter realism, this picture of life speaks of three qualities that are open to everyone:

- boundless happiness
- absolute fearlessness
- constant difficulty

There are human beings who not only hear the "silent cry," which is God, but also make it heard as the music of the world that even to this day fulfills the cosmos and the soul.

AFTERWORD: A CONVERSATION

—⇒◆⇐—

"What is more splendid than gold?" asked the king.
"The light," replied the serpent.
"What is more refreshing than light?" the former asked.
"Conversation," the latter said.

GOETHE, "THE FAIRY TALE"

When I began writing this book, my husband, Fulbert Steffensky, read the first pages of the manuscript and spontaneously made some critical comments. I responded and the following conversation ensued.

FULBERT: What bothers me about mysticism is that it's really not something for simple folk. I can't imagine that my mother or my father could get anything from what you're trying to do here.

DOROTHEE: *(humming)*

Into his love	[*In seine Lieb versenken*
I will wholly plunge myself,	*will ich mich ganz hinab,*
my heart is to be his	*mein Herz will ich*
	ihm schenken
and all that I have.	*und alles was ich hab.*]

FULBERT: Piety, yes, but mysticism?

DOROTHEE: I suppose that mysticism is always piety, even when it takes on utterly degenerate forms such as Satanic Masses. If I understand the meaning at all of this Christmas carol by Friedrich von Spee (1591–1635), then I can also talk about *syntheresis voluntatis*. Your mother wouldn't have known what to do with that, but perhaps it could be useful to her clever grandchildren, who live without Christmas carols but not without philosophy.

FULBERT: Back again to my mother. I believe that she can appropriate every sentence of the New Testament tradition as nourishing bread on which one can live a normal and burdened life. But what is she to do with the curious religious ingenuities of a Jacob Böhme, or John of the Cross? Surely, the Gospel itself deals more with the simple and sensible desires of people: to be healthy and not having to despair of life, to be able to see and hear, to live for once without tears and to have a name. It's not about spiritual artistry but about the possibility of simply living.

DOROTHEE: But aren't mystics concerned precisely with the bread of life? As I see it, the problem is that people, including your mother, but certainly her children and grandchildren, encounter not just the gospel but something that has been distorted, corrupted, destroyed, and long been turned into stone.

Mysticism has helped those who were gripped by it to face powerful but petrified institutions that conformed to society; it still helps them today, albeit in a manner that is often very odd. What you call spiritual artistry may figure in it, but the essence of mysticism is something very different. One evening, without knocking first, I entered your mother's room. And there she was, the old lady, sitting on her chair with her hands folded—no needlework! I don't know whether to call what she was doing "praying" or "reflecting." But great peace was with her. That is what I want to spread abroad.

FULBERT: Perhaps my skepticism about mystics is not meant so much for them as for a certain craving for mysticism prevalent in the present religious climate. The high regard for categories of religious experience is growing at an inflationary rate. The religious subject wants to experience the self without mediation, instantly, totally, and authentically, in the manner she or he shapes personal piety. Experience justifies substance and becomes the actual content of religiousness. And then direct experience stands against institution, against the slowness of a journey, against the crusty, dark bread of the patient dealing with oneself. In this craving for experience, everything that occurs suddenly and is direct rather than institution-mediated—everything that's oriented to experience and promises religious sensation—becomes ever so interesting. I know, genuine mysticism is completely different from this. But that's how it's perceived.

DOROTHEE: I'm also concerned when immediacy becomes the chief category. I think that the great figures of the tradition of mysticism have chewed on some of your crusty, dark bread. As Huxley once said, there is no "instant Zen Buddhism." The "now" of the mystics is an experience of time that is no common experience. This has nothing to do with a teenage sense of life, the "right this moment" of wanting a certain kind of sneaker or ice cream.

I cannot agree with your covert pleading for the institution—as if the bread it baked were edible! I think there must be a third entity, next to voguish "religious sensation" and the homespun institutions that are in charge of such things. You are seeking something like that yourself, except that you call it spirituality.

FULBERT: When I speak of spirituality I always rule out the ideas of particularity and extraordinary experience. It's the name, more than anything else, that makes "spirituality" so alluring. What spirituality itself actually is has much to do with method, order, and repetition. It's a matter of constituting the self, in the midst of banality and everydayness. And everyone who is not utterly beaten down by life can work at it. Spirituality is not a *via regia,* an elevated pathway, but a *via laborosa,* a labor-intensive regimen for determining one's own vision and life options. And so I stick doggedly to the notion that something is important only when it's important for everyone.

But it's possible that in mysticism, what manifests itself in dramatically concentrated form and artistic expression, so to speak, is what constitutes the nature of piety and faith. This would mean that mysticism may in fact be neither the road of all nor of many. Rather, it may be that in poetic density the nature of a faith that is meant for all is revealed within mysticism.

DOROTHEE: My most important concern is to democratize mysticism. What I mean to do is to reopen the door to the mystic sensibility that's within all of us, to dig it out

from under the debris of trivia—from its self-trivial-
ization, if you like. An older woman in New York told
me about meeting a guru. When she told her black
minister about this, he asked only one question. It's a
question I too want to ask: "Didn't he tell you that
we're all mystics?"

FULBERT: " . . . that we're all mystics." That's no observation. It's
a demand placed on life! No human being ought mere-
ly to pass the time of day; no human being ought to be
exhausted in sheer survival. Everyone should be
allowed to come to the truth. For everyone there ought
to be places free of intentionality, places where vision
can happen, where the beauty of life is perceived and
fruitio occurs, where God is enjoyed.

"We're all mystics!" That sentence contains in itself
the right of every human being to beauty and vision. Is
there such a thing as a human right to behold God?

And this has led us by a circuitous route to your
second concept: resistance. Mysticism is the experience
of the oneness and wholeness of life. Therefore, mysticism's perception of life, its vision, is also the unrelenting perception of how fragmented life is. Suffering on
account of that fragmentation and finding it unbearable is part of mysticism. Finding God fragmented into
rich and poor, top and bottom, sick and well, weak
and mighty: that's the mystic's suffering. The resistance
of Saint Francis or Elisabeth of Thuringia or of Martin
Luther King grew out of the perception of beauty. And
the long lasting and most dangerous resistance is the
one that was born from beauty.

NOTES

Chapter One

1. Black Elk, *Black Elk Speaks: Being the Life Story of a Holy Man of the Oglala Sioux* (New York: Pocket Books, 1972), 15–16.
2. Joseph Epes Brown, ed., *The Gift of the Sacred Pipe: Based on Black Elk's Account of the Seven Rites of the Oglala Sioux as Originally Recorded and Edited by Joseph Epes Brown* (Norman, Okla.: Univ. of Oklahoma Press, 1982), 33.
3. Ibid.
4. Ibid., 37.
5. Ibid.
6. Ernst Bloch, *The Principle of Hope,* translated by Neville Plaice, Stephen Plaice, and Paul Knight (Cambridge, Mass.: MIT Press, 1986), 1376.
7. John Woolman, *The Journal and Major Essays of John Woolman,* edited by Phillips P. Moulton (New York: Oxford Univ. Press, 1971), 23.
8. F. C. Happold, *Mysticism: A Study and an Anthology* (Harmondsworth: Penguin, 1963), 129–30.
9. Possibility: Thomas Merton, *Raids on the Unspeakable: Prose and Verses* (New York: New Directions, 1966).
10. Aldous Huxley, *The Perennial Philosophy* (New York: Harper & Row, 1945), 297.
11. Martin Buber, *Ecstatic Confessions,* edited by Paul Mendes-Flohr, translated by Esther Cameron (San Francisco: Harper & Row, 1985), 19.
12. Huxley, *Perennial Philosophy,* 1.
13. Happold, *Mysticism,* 319.
14. Paul Mommaers, *Was ist Mystik?* (Frankfurt, 1979), 87.
15. William James, *The Letters of William James,* edited by Henry James, vol. 2 (London: Longmans, Green, 1920), 211.
16. Buber, *Ecstatic Confessions,* 53.
17. William James, *The Varieties of Religious Experience* (New York: Modern Library, 1929), 242ff.
18. Ibid., 245.
19. Rudolf Otto, *Mysticism East and West: A Comparative Analysis of the Nature of Mysticism,* translated by Bertha L. Bracey and Richenda C. Payne, 1932 (New York: Macmillan, 1962), 147.
20. Happold, *Mysticism,* 83.
21. C. S. Lewis, *Surprised by Joy* (London: Geoffrey Bles, 1955), 22.
22. Lewis, *Surprised by Joy,* 211–12.

Chapter Two

1. William James, *The Varieties of Religious Experience* (New York: Modern Library, 1929), 271–73.

2. Ibid., 388.

3. Martin Buber, *Ecstatic Confessions*, edited by Paul Mendes-Flohr, translated by Esther Cameron (San Francisco: Harper & Row, 1985), 1.

4. Ibid., 1–2.

5. Ibid., 2.

6. Annemarie Schimmel, *Mystische Dimensionen des Islam: Die Geschichte des Sufismus* (Munich, 1992), 53.

7. Georg Schmid, *Die Mystik der Weltreligionen: Eine Einführung* (Stuttgart, 1990), 132.

8. Annemarie Schimmel, *Rumi: Ich bin Wind und du bist Feuer: Leben und Werk des großen Mystikers,* 1978 (Munich, 1990), 132.

9. Schimmel, *Mystische Dimensionem*, 68.

10. Buber, *Ecstatic Confessions*, 31.

11. Schimmel, *Mystische Dimensionen*, 65–66.

12. Elmer O'Brien, S.J., *Varieties of Mystic Experience: An Anthology and Interpretation* (New York: Holt, Rinehart and Winston, 1964), 103.

13. Aldous Huxley, *The Perennial Philosophy* (New York: Harper & Row, 1945), 102.

14. Buber, *Ecstatic Confessions*, 31.

15. Schimmel, *Mystische Dimensionen*, 68.

16. Ibid., 111.

17. al-Husayn ibn Mansur Hallaj, *Märtyrer der Gottesliebe: Leben und Legende,* edited and translated by Annemarie Schimmel (Cologne, 1968), 37.

18. Schimmel, *Mystische Dimensionen*, 240–41.

19. Ibid., 112.

20. Buber, *Ecstatic Confessions*, 20.

21. Ibid., 21.

22. Ibid.

23. F. C. Happold, *Mysticism: A Study and an Anthology* (Harmondsworth: Penguin, 1963), 97.

24. Walter T. Stace, *The Teaching of the Mystics* (New York: Mentor, 1960), 214.

25. Schimmel, *Mystische Dimensionen*, 100.

26. Buber, *Ecstatic Confessions*, 21.

27. Hallaj, *Märtyer*, 10.

28. Martin Buber, *Tales of the Hasidim: Later Masters* (New York: Schocken, 1948), 249–50.

29. Happold, *Mysticism*, 97.

30. Johannes Thiele, *Perlen der Mystik* (Freiburg i. Br., 1989), 110.

31. Rudolf Otto, *Mysticism East and West: A Comparative Analysis of the Nature of Mysticism,* translated by Bertha L. Bracey and Richenda C. Payne, 1932 (New York: Macmillan, 1962), 117–18.

32. Buber, *Ecstatic Confessions*, 38.

33. Ibid.

34. Ibid., 53.

35. Ibid., 4.

Chapter Three

1. Somer Brodribb, *Nothing Mat(t)ers: A Feminist Critique of Postmodernism* (Toronto: Lorimer, 1992), 122.

2. Georg Schmid, *Die Mystik der Weltreligionen: Eine Einführung* (Stuttgart, 1990), 66.

3. See the two lectures on mysticism in William James, *The Varieties of Religious Experience* (New York: Modern Library, 1929).

3. Edwin Hatch (1835–1889), composer. *The Hymnary* (Toronto: United Church, 1930), no. 148.

Chapter Four

1. Frederick Franck, trans., *The Book of Angelus Silesius, with Observations by the Ancient Zen Masters* (New York: Vintage, 1976), 143.

2. Peter Dinzelbacher, *Christliche Mystik im Abendland: Ihre Geschichte von den Anfängen bis zum Ende des Mittelalters* (Paderborn, 1994), 246.

3. Martin Buber, *Ecstatic Confessions*, edited by Paul Mendes-Flohr, translated by Esther Cameron (San Francisco: Harper & Row, 1985), 8–9.

4. James Walsh, S.J., ed. *The Cloud of Unknowing* (New York: Paulist, 1981), 128.

5. Ibid., 140.

6. Ibid., chap. 9.

7. Ibid., 174–75.

8. Aldous Huxley, *The Perennial Philosophy* (New York: Harper & Row, 1945), 25.

9. Walsh, *Cloud of Unknowing*, 241.

10. J. Quint, ed., *Meister Eckhart: Deutsche Predigten und Traktate* (Munich, 1969), 227.

11. Ibid., 227.

12. Ibid., 299.

13. Angelus Silesius, *Sämtliche Poetische Werke*, vol. 3, edited by Hans Ludwig Held (Munich: Carl Hanser Verlag, 1949). See also Franck, *The Book of Angelus Silesius*, 66.

14. Quint, *Meister Eckhart*, 180.

15. Buber, *Ecstatic Confessions*, 52–53.

16. William James, *The Varieties of Religious Experience* (New York: Modern Library, 1929), 407.

17. Buber, *Ecstatic Confessions*, 28.

18. Kurt Ruh, *Meister Eckhart: Theologe, Prediger, Mystiker* (Munich, 1989), 58–59.

19. See also Bernard McGinn, *The Presence of God: A History of Western Christian Mysticism*, vol. 1: *The Foundations of Mysticism* (New York: Crossroad, 1991), 321–22.

20. Pseudo-Dionysius, *The Complete Works*, translated by Colm Luibheid (New York: Paulist, 1987), 141.

21. Dinzelbacher, *Christliche Mystik*, 192–93.

22. Cited in ibid., 19.

23. Buber, *Ecstatic Confessions*, 5.

24. Ibid.

25. See also the discussion of philosophical approaches to research in mysticism in McGinn, *Presence of God*, 456ff.

26. McGinn, *Presence of God*, 454.

27. Stephen Katz, ed., *Mysticism and Philosophical Analysis* (New York: Oxford Univ. Press, 1978), 166.

28. Kurt Ruh believes that it is by Eckhart himself, see Ruh, *Meister Eckhart*, 49.

29. Buber, *Ecstatic Confessions*, 43–44, transl. altered.

30. Ibid., 44.

31. Ibid.

32. Ingeborg Bachmann, *Songs in Flight: The Collected Poems*, translated by P. Filkins (New York: Marsilio, 1994), 303–4.

33. See the essay "Schweigen" in Christian Schütz, *Praktisches Lexikon der Spiritualität* (Freiburg i. Br., 1988).

34. Huxley, *Perennial Philosophy*, 216.

35. Schimmel, Annemarie. *Rumi: Ich bin Wind und du bist Feuer: Leben und Werk des großen Mystikers*, 1978 (Munich, 1990), 166–67.

36. Walter T. Stace, *The Teaching of the Mystics* (New York: Mentor, 1960), 220.

37. Buber, *Ecstatic Confessions*, 7.

38. Ibid.

Chapter Five

1. Martin Buber, *Ecstatic Confessions*, edited by Paul Mendes-Flohr, translated by Esther Cameron (San Francisco: Harper & Row, 1985), 17.

2. Ibid., 39.

3. Ibid., 17.

4. Annemarie Schimmel, *Mystische Dimensionen des Islam: Die Geschichte des Sufismus* (Munich, 1992), 434.

5. Buber, *Ecstatic Confessions*, 23.

6. Ibid.

7. Ibid.

8. Ibid., 25.

9. Ibid., 22.

10. Ibid., 27.

11. Gerhard Wehr, *Deutsche Mystik: Gestalten und Zeugnisse religiöser Erfahrung von Meister Eckhart bis zur Reformationszeit* (Gütersloh, Gütersloher Verlagshaus, 1980), 93.

12. F. C. Happold, *Mysticism: A Study and an Anthology* (Harmondsworth: Penguin, 1963), 51–52.

13. Peter Dinzelbacher, *Christliche Mystik im Abendland: Ihre Geschichte von den Anfängen bis zum Ende des Mittelalters* (Paderborn, 1994), 178–79.

14. Heinrich Seuse, *Deutsche Mystische Schriften*, ed. and trans. by Georg Hoffmann (Düsseldorf: Patmos, 1966), 174.

15. Kurt Ruh, *Meister Eckhart: Theologe, Prediger, Mystiker* (Munich, 1989), 124.

16. Dinzelbacher, *Christliche Mystik*, 114.

17. Buber, *Ecstatic Confessions*, 48.

18. Dinzelbacher, *Christliche Mystik*, 336–37.

19. Wilhelm Oehl, ed., *Deutsche Mystikerbriefe des Mittelalters: 100–1550* (Darmstadt, 1972), 634. See also Dorothee Soelle, *Death by Bread Alone*, translated by David L. Scheidt (Philadelphia: Fortress Press, 1978), 84.

20. Ernst Bloch, *Thomas Müntzer: Als Theologe der Revolution* (Frankfurt on Main, 1962), originally published in 1921.

21. Walter Nigg, *Heimliche Weisheit: Mystisches Leben in der Evangelischen Christenheit* (Zurich, 1959), 38–53.

22. Thomas Müntzer, *Die Fürstenpredigt: Theologisch-politische Schriften*, edited by G. Franz (Stuttgart, 1967), 59.

23. Ibid., 126.

24. Ibid., 59.

25. Ibid., 121.

26. Ibid., 100.

27. Ibid., 7.

28. Ibid., 24.

29. Ibid., 21.

30. Dorothee Soelle, *Suffering*, translated by Everett R. Kalin (Philadelphia: Fortress Press, 1975), 127ff.

31. Müntzer, *Die Fürstenpredigt*, 53.

32. Ibid., 181.

33. Ibid., 101.

34. Matthew Fox, *Wrestling with the Prophets: Essays on Creation, Spirituality, and Everyday Life* (San Francisco: HarperSanFrancisco, 1995), 20ff.

35. Abraham Heschel, *God in Search of Man: A Philosophy of Judaism* (New York: Harper & Row, 1955), 45–46.

36. Heschel, *God in Search of Man*, 46.

Chapter Six

1. J. Quint, ed., *Meister Eckhart: Deutsche Predigten und Traktate* (Munich, 1969), 197.

2. *Publik-Forum*, May 1995, 23.

3. Paul Mommaers has described Ionesco's experience and his subsequent disavowal of it in a small, tightly woven book, *Was ist Mystik?* (Frankfurt, 1979), 35–36.

4. See Traherne in Aldous Huxley, *The Perennial Philosophy* (New York: Harper & Row, 1945), 66.

5. Thomas Merton, *Raids on the Unspeakable* (New York: New Directions, 1966), 89.

6. Huxley, *Perennial Philosophy*, 69.

7. F. C. Happold, *Mysticism: A Study and an Anthology* (Harmondsworth: Penguin, 1963), 93.

8. William James, *The Varieties of Religious Experience* (New York: Modern Library, 1929), 402.

9. Ibid., 401–2.

10. Huxley, *Perennial Philosophy*, 67.

11. *The Hymnary* (Toronto: United Church, 1930), no. 539.

12. Ibid.

13. Peter Dinzelbacher, *Christliche Mystik im Abendland: Ihre Geschichte von den Anfängen bis zum Ende des Mittelalters* (Paderborn, 1994), 33.

14. Karl Barth, *Ethics,* translated by Geoffrey W. Bromily (New York: Seabury, 1981), 320.

15. Rudolf Otto, *Mysticism East and West: A Comparative Analysis of the Nature of Mysticism,* translated by Bertha L. Bracey and Richenda C. Payne, 1932 (New York: Macmillan, 1962), 92–95.

16. See also Karl Rahner, *Theological Investigations,* vol VII, translated by David Bourke (New York: Herder and Herder, 1971), 122.

17. Ibid., 15.

18. Matthew Fox, introd. and commentaries, *Breakthrough: Meister Eckhart's Creation Spirituality, in New Translation* (Garden City, N.J.: Doubleday, 1980), 96.

19. Anne Fremantle, ed., *The Protestant Mystics* (New York: Mentor, 1965), 198.

20. (Thoreau, 1958, 144–45).

21. Fremantle, *Protestant Mystics,* 14.

22. Wendell Berry, *The Wild Birds* (San Francisco: North Point, 1986), 136–37.

Chapter Seven

1. Peter Dinzelbacher, *Christliche Mystik im Abendland: Ihre Geschichte von den Anfängen bis zum Ende des Mittelalters* (Paderborn, 1994), 215, 259.

2. Gershom Scholem, *Von der mystischen Gestalt der Gottheit: Studien zu Grundbegriffen der Kabbala* (Frankfurt, 1995), 107.

3. *Zohar: The Book of Enlightenment,* translated by Daniel Chanan Matt (New York: Paulist, 1983), 55–56.

4. *Zohar,* 217.

5. Ibid., 236–37.

6. The Jewish tradition, such as in Abraham Heschel, *God in Search of Man: A Philosophy of Judaism* (New York: Harper & Row, 1955), for example, would provide very different and much more anthropomorphic clues for this topic.

7. Franz Rosenzweig, *The Star of Redemption,* translated by William W. Hallo (Boston: Beacon, 1964), 199; translation altered.

8. Dinzelbacher, *Christliche Mystik,* 110–11.

9. Ibid., 111.

10. Martin Buber, *Ecstatic Confessions,* edited by Paul Mendes-Flohr, translated by Esther Cameron (San Francisco: Harper & Row, 1985), 53.

11. Emilie Zum Brunn and Georgette Epiney-Brugard, eds., *Women Mystics in Medieval Europe,* translated by Sheila Hughes (New York: Paragon, 1989), 211.

12. Kurt Ruh, *Meister Eckhart: Theologe, Prediger, Mystiker* (Munich, 1989), 47ff.

13. Zum Brunn, *Women Mystics,* 150.

14. Ulrich Heid, "Studien zu Marguerite Porète und ihrem *Miroir des simples âmes,*" in *Religiöse Frauenbewegung und mystische Frömmigkeit im Mittelalter,* edited by Peter Dinzelbacher and Deiter R. Bauer (Cologne and Vienna, 1988), 207.

15. Marguerite Porète, *The Mirror of Simple Souls,* translated by Ellen L. Babinsky (New York: Paulist, 1993), 84–85.

16. Gerda Lerner, *Die Entstehung des feministischen Bewußtseins: Vom Mittelalter bis zur Ersten Frauenbewegung* (Frankfurt and New York, 1993), 106.

17. Porète, *Mirror,* 84.

18. Helga Unger, ed., *Der Berg der Liebe, Europäische Frauenmystik* (Freibug i. Br., 1991), 134.

19. Elisabeth Gössmann, "Die Geschichte und Lehre der Mystikerin Marguerite Porète," in *Gegenentwürfe: 24 Lebensläufe für eine andere Theologie*, edited by Hermann Häring and Karl-Josef Kuschel (Munich, 1988), 70.

20. Dinzelbacher, *Christliche Mystik*, 269.

21. Porète, *Mirror*, 193.

22. Gössmann, "Die Geschichte," 78.

23. D. H. Lawrence, *The Rainbow* (London: Heinemann, 1977), 481.

24. Ibid., 444.

25. Ibid., 447.

26. Ibid., 451.

27. Ibid., 547.

28. Ibid., 473.

29. Ingeborg Bachmann, *Werke*, vol. 1 (Munich, 1982), 318.

30. Ibid.

31. Annemarie Schimmel, *Mystische Dimensionen des Islam: Die Geschichte des Sufismus* (Munich, 1992), 236.

32. Paul Mommaers, *Was ist Mystik?* (Frankfurt, 1979), 129.

Chapter Eight

1. See also Dorothee Soelle, *Suffering*, translated by Everett R. Kalin (Philadelphia: Fortress Press, 1975), 109–19.

2. Gustavo Gutiérrez, *On Job: God-Talk and the Suffering of the Innocent*, translated by Matthew J. O'Connell (Maryknoll, N.Y.: Orbis Books, 1987), 4.

3. Leon Felipe, *Versos y orisones de caminante* (Madrid, 1981), 83–84.

4. Schimmel, Annemarie. *Rumi: Ich bin Wind und du bist Feuer: Leben und Werk des großen Mystikers*, 1978 (Munich, 1990), 152–53.

5. Peter Dinzelbacher, *Christliche Mystik im Abendland: Ihre Geschichte von den Anfängen bis zum Ende des Mittelalters* (Paderborn, 1994), 113.

6. Nisargadatta Maharaj.

7. Dinzelbacher, *Christliche Mystik*, 102.

8. Ibid., 171.

9. Ibid., 236.

10. See also Soelle, *Suffering*, 9–32, on the church's masochism.

11. Dinzelbacher, *Christliche Mystik*, 231.

12. Ibid., 302.

13. Johannes Boldt, ed. and trans., *Johannes vom Kreuz* (Olten, 1980), 204.

14. Margot Schmidt, "Frau Pein Ihr seid mein nächstes kleid: Zur Leidensmystik in Fliessenden Licht der Gottheit der Mechthild von Magdeburg" in G. Fuchs, editor, *Die dunkle Nacht der Sinne: Leiderfahrung und christliche Mystik* (Düsseldorf, 1989), 91.

15. Dinzelbacher, *Christliche Mystik*, 210.

16. Boldt, *Johannes vom Kreuz*, 121.

17. Ibid., 146–47.

18. Ibid., 143.

19. Ibid., 130.

20. Boldt, *Johannes vom Kreuz*, 130.

21. Alois M. Haas, "Die dunkle Nacht der Sinne und des Geistes: Mystische Leidenserfahrung nach Johannes vom Kreuz," in *Die dunkle Nacht der Sinne: Leidenserfahrung und christliche Mystik*, edited by G. Fuchs (Düsseldorf, 1989), 109–10.

22. Boldt, *Johannes vom Kreuz*, 25.

23. Ibid., 103.

24. Ibid., 49.

25. Ibid., 54.

26. Reinhold Schneider, *Winter in Wien: Aus meinen Notizbüchern*, 1957–58 (Freiburg i. Br., 1958), 251.

27. Waltraud Herbstrith, ed., *Edith Stein: Ein Lebensbild in Zeugnissen und Selbstzeugnissen* (Mainz, 1993), 64.

28. Elisabeth Otto, "Kreuzeswissenschsft als Anteilhaben am Leiden Christi: Die Mystik Edith Steins," in *Leiden und Weisheit in der Mystik*, edited by B. Jaspert (Paderborn, 1992), 238, 240.

29. Elisabeth Endres, *Edith Stein: Christliche Philosophin und jüdische Märtyrerin* (Munich, 1987), 249.

30. Ibid., 278.

31. Ibid., 9.

32. Ibid., 12.

33. Herbstrith, *Edith Stein*, 62.

34. Ibid.

35. See also Soelle, *Suffering*, 33–59.

36. Simone Weil, *Fabriktagebuch und andere Schriften zum Industriesystem* (Frankfurt, 1978), 106.

37. Simone Weil, *Das Unglück und die Gottesliebe* (Munich, 1953), 48.

38. Ibid., 75.

39. Simone Weil, *Schwerkraft und Gnade* (Munich, 1952), 79.

40. See also Dorothee Soelle, *Stations of the Cross: A Latin American Pilgrimage*, translated by Joyce L. Irwin (Minneapolis: Fortress Press, 1993), 220–21.

41. Dietrich Bonhoeffer, *Widerstand und Ergebung*, vol. 8 of *Dietrich Bonhoeffer Werke* (Gütersloh: Gütersloher Verlagshaus, 1998), 535, letter of July 18, 1944.

42. Schneider, *Winter in Wien*, 242.

43. Ibid., 178.

44. Ibid., 196.

45. Ibid., 22.

46. Ibid., 110.

47. Ibid., 172.

48. Ibid., 118.

49. Ibid.

50. Ibid., 195.

51. Ibid., 200.

52. Ibid., 188.

53. Ibid., 224.

54. Ibid., 233–34.

55. Ibid., 234.

56. Ibid., 57.

57. Ibid., 196.

Chapter Nine

1. Peter Dinzelbacher, *Christliche Mystik im Abendland: Ihre Geschichte von den Anfängen bis zum Ende des Mittelalters* (Paderborn, 1994), 316–17.

2. Gershom Scholem, *Von der mystischen Gestalt der Gottheit: Studien zu Grundbegriffen der Kabbala* (Frankfurt, 1995), 134.

3. Martin Buber, *Werke III: Schriften zum Chassidismus* (Heidelberg: Verlag Lambert Schneider, 1963), 54.

4. Ibid., 55.

5. Ibid., 170.

6. Martin Buber, *Buber für Atheisten: Ausgewählte Texte,* edited by Thomas Reichert (Gerlingen, 1996), 144.

7. Paul Mendes-Flohr, "Editor's Introduction" in *Ecstatic Confessions* by Martin Buber (New York: Harper & Row, 1985), xvii–xviii. Sects were of special interest to Troeltsch.

8. Martin Buber, *Buber für Atheisten: Ausgewählte Texte,* edited by Thomas Reichert (Gerlingen, 1996), 36–37.

9. Ibid.

10. Martin Buber, *Nachlese* (Heidelberg: Verlag Lambert Schneider, 1965), 121.

11. Martin Buber, *I and Thou,* trans. by Walter Kaufmann (New York: Scribner's, 1970), 134–35.

12. Ibid., 134.

13. Ibid.

14. Buber, *Buber für Atheisten,* 143.

15. Ibid., 277.

16. Buber, *Werke III,* 952.

17. Ibid.

18. Buber, *Werke III,* 952–53.

19. Buber, *Buber für Atheisten,* 140.

20. Ibid.

21. Ibid., 256.

22. Dinzelbacher, *Christliche Mystik,* 201.

23. See also Gerda Lerner, *Die Entstehung des feministischen Bewußtseins: Vom Mittelalter bis zur Ersten Frauenbewegung* (Frankfurt and New York, 1993), 101ff.

24. Dennis Devlin, "Feminine Lay Piety in the High Middle Ages: The Beguines," in *Medieval Religious Women,* edited by John A. Nichols and Lillian Thomas Shank, vol. 1: *Distant Echoes* (Kalamazoo, Mich.: Cistercian, 1984), 183–96.

25. Dinzelbacher, *Christliche Mystik,* 197.

26. Rainer Maria Rilke, *Neue Gedichte* (Leipzig, 1907), 79.

27. Martin Buber, *Ecstatic Confessions,* edited by Paul Mendes-Flohr, translated by Esther Cameron (San Francisco: Harper & Row, 1985), 155–56.

28. Rilke, *Neue Gedichte,* 79.

29. Howard H. Brinton, *Friends for 300 Years: The History and Beliefs of the Society of Friends since George Fox Started the Quaker Movement* (Wallingford, Pa.: Pendle Hill Quakerback, 1983), 29.

30. Walter Nigg, *Heimliche Weisheit: Mystisches Leben in der Evangelischen Christenheit* (Zurich, 1959), 274ff.

31. Ibid.

32. Ibid.

33. Anne Jensen, "Im Kampf um Freiheit in Kirche und Staat: Die 'Mutter des Quäkertums' Margaret Fell" in *Gegenentwürfe: 24 Lebensläufe für eine andere Theologie,* edited by Hermann Häring and K. J. Kuschel (Munich, 1988), 169–80.

Chapter Ten

1. Thich Nhat Hanh, *The Miracle of Mindfulness: A Manual on Mindfulness* (London: Rider, 1992), 4–5.

2. Ibid., 12.

3. Martin Buber, *Tales of the Hasidim: Early Masters* (New York: Schocken, 1947), 315–16.

4. Ibid.

5. Gershom Scholem, *Von der mystischen Gestalt der Gottheit: Studien zu Grundbegriffen der Kabbala* (Frankfurt, 1995), 123.

6. Abraham Heschel, *God in Search of Man: A Philosophy of Judaism* (New York: Harper & Row, 1955), 315.

7. Buber, *Tales of the Hasidim,* 248.

8. Ibid.

9. Peter Dinzelbacher, *Christliche Mystik im Abendland: Ihre Geschichte von den Anfängen bis zum Ende des Mittelalters* (Paderborn, 1994), 377.

10. Ibid.

11. Buber, *Tales of the Hasidim,* 43–44.

12. Annemarie Schimmel, *Rumi: Ich bin Wind und du bist Feuer: Leben und Werk des großen Mystikers,* 1978 (Munich, 1990), 33.

13. Ibid., 44–45.

14. Dinzelbacher, *Christliche Mystik,* 210.

15. Rudolf Otto, *Mysticism East and West: A Comparative Analysis of the Nature of Mysticism,* translated by Bertha L. Bracey and Richenda C. Payne, 1932 (New York: Macmillan, 1962), 190.

16. Dinzelbacher, *Christliche Mystik,* 321.

17. Ibid., 210.

18. Ibid., 172.

19. Johannes Boldt, ed. and trans., *Johannes vom Kreuz* (Olten, 1980), 63.

20. Francis of Assisi, Saint, *Legenden und Laude,* edited and translated by Otto Karrer (Zürich, 1975), 117–18.

Chapter Eleven

1. See also Bernard McGinn, *The Presence of God: A History of Western Christian Mysticism,* vol. 1: *The Foundations of Mysticism* (New York: Crossroad, 1991), 389–90.

2. Martin Buber, *Werke III: Schriften zum Chassidismus* (Heidelberg: Verlag Lambert Schneider, 1963), 803.

3. Gershom Scholem, *Von der mystischen Gestalt der Gottheit: Studien zu Grundbegriffen der Kabbala* (Frankfurt, 1995), 16.

4. Emmanuel Levinas, *Difficult Freedom: Essays on Judaism,* translated by Seán Hand (Baltimore, Md.: Johns Hopkins Univ. Press, 1990), 17.

5. Ibid., 17.

6. Peter Dinzelbacher, *Christliche Mystik im Abendland: Ihre Geschichte von den Anfängen bis zum Ende des Mittelalters* (Paderborn, 1994), 109.

7. See also Dorothee Soelle, *The Window of Vulnerability: A Political Spirituality,* translated by Linda M. Maloney (Minneapolis: Fortress Press, 1990).

8. J. Quint, ed., *Meister Eckhart: Deutsche Predigten und Traktate* (Munich, 1969), 286.

9. Ibid.

10. Ibid., 67.

11. Josef Sudbrack, *Erfahrung einer Liebe: Teresa von Avilas Mystik als begegnung mit Gott* (Freiburg i. Br., 1979), 78.

12. Ibid.

13. Rudolf Otto, *Mysticism East and West: A Comparative Analysis of the Nature of Mysticism,* translated by Bertha L. Bracey and Richenda C. Payne. 1932 (New York: Macmillan, 1962), 225.

14. Paul Mommaers, *Was ist Mystik?* (Frankfurt, 1979), 88–89.

15. McGinn, *Presence of God,* 271.

Chapter Twelve

1. Martin Buber, *Werke I: Schriften zur Philosophie* (Heidelberg: Verlag Lambert Schneider, 1962), 196–97.

2. Rudolf Otto, *Mysticism East and West: A Comparative Analysis of the Nature of Mysticism,* translated by Bertha L. Bracey and Richenda C. Payne, 1932 (New York: Macmillan, 1962), 60.

3. William James, *The Varieties of Religious Experience* (New York: Modern Library, 1929), 210.

4. J. Quint, ed., *Meister Eckhart: Deutsche Predigten und Traktate* (Munich, 1969), 154.

5. Ibid.

6. Quint, *Meister Eckhart,* 154–55.

7. Kurt Ruh, *Meister Eckhart: Theologe, Prediger, Mystiker* (Munich, 1989), 143–44.

8. Otto, *Mysticism East and West,* 226.

9. Ruh, *Meister Eckhart,* 54.

10. Johannes Boldt, ed. and trans., *Johannes vom Kreuz* (Olten, 1980).

11. Ibid., 86.

12. Ibid., 85–86.

13. James, *Varieties,* 151.

14. Ibid., 151.

15. Ibid., 182.

16. Dag Hammarskjöld, *Markings,* translated by Leif Sjöberg and W. H. Auden (London: Faber and Faber, 1964), 100.

17. Ibid., 108.

18. Ibid., 54–55.

19. Ibid., 64.

20. Ibid., 36.

21. Ibid., 34.

22. Ibid., 27.

23. Ibid., 37.

24. Ibid., 116.

25. Ibid., 120.

26. Ibid., 84.

27. Ibid., 86.

28. Ibid., 169.

29. Ibid., 130.

30. Martin Buber, *Ecstatic Confessions*, edited by Paul Mendes-Flohr, translated by Esther Cameron (San Francisco: Harper & Row, 1985), 19.

31. Hammarskjöld, *Markings*, 88.

32. Ibid., 135.

33. Ibid., 169.

34. Ibid., 88.

35. Simone Weil, *The Simone Weil Reader*, edited by George A. Panichas (New York: McKay, 1977), 45.

36. Ibid., 44.

37. Ibid., 46.

38. Ibid.

39. Ibid., 49.

40. Ibid., 50.

41. Peter Dinzelbacher, *Christliche Mystik im Abendland: Ihre Geschichte von den Anfängen bis zum Ende des Mittelalters* (Paderborn, 1994), 364.

42. Martin Buber, *Buber für Atheisten: Ausgewählte Texte*, edited by Thomas Reichert (Gerlingen, 1996), 286.

43. James H. Forest, "Thomas Merton's Struggle with Peacemaking," in *Thomas Merton: Prophet in the Belly of a Paradox*, edited by Gerald Twomey (New York: Paulist, 1978), 52.

44. Ibid., 53.

Chapter Thirteen

1. Annemarie Schimmel, *Mystische Dimensionen des Islam: Die Geschichte des Sufismus* (Munich, 1992), 32.

2. Annemarie Schimmel, *Rumi: Ich bin Wind und du bist Feuer: Leben und Werk des großen Mystikers* (Munich, 1990), 138–39.

3. William James, *The Varieties of Religious Experience* (New York: Modern Library, 1929), 313.

4. J. Quint, ed., *Meister Eckhart: Deutsche Predigten und Traktate* (Munich, 1969), 303ff.

5. James Walsh, S.J., ed. *The Cloud of Unknowing* (New York: Paulist, 1981), 251–52.

6. Erich Fromm, *To Have Or To Be?* (New York: Harper & Row), 69.

7. Francis of Assisi, Saint, *Legenden und Laude*, edited and translated by Otto Karrer (Zürich, 1975), 271.

8. Ibid., 168–69.

9. John Woolman. *The Journal and Major Essays of John Woolman*, edited by Phillips P. Moulton (New York: Oxford Univ. Press, 1971), 30.

10. Ibid., 33.
11. Ibid., 63.
12. Ibid., 59.
13. Ibid., 255.
14. Ibid., 61.
15. Ibid., 185–86.
16. Jim Forest, *Love Is the Measure: A Biography of Dorothy Day* (New York: Paulist, 1986), 38–39.
17. Ibid., 39.
18. Simone Weil, *The Simone Weil Reader,* edited by George A. Panichas (New York: McKay, 1977), 13.
19. Giorgio Tourn, *Geschichte der Waldenser-Kirche: Die einzigartige Geschichte einer Volkskirche von 1170 bis zur Gegenwart* (Erlangen, 1980), 17.

Chapter Fourteen

1. Thich Nhat Hanh, *Nenne mich bei meinem wahren Namen: Gesammelte Gedichte* (Berlin, 1997), 82.
2. Ibid., 83.
3. Perry Schmid-Leukel, "Das Problem von Gewalt und Krieg in der buddhistischen Ethik" in *Dialog der Religionen* 6, no. 2 (Gütersloh, 1996), 129.
4. See also Dorothee Soelle, *Gewalt: Ich soll mich nicht gewöhnen* (Düsseldorf, 1994), 88ff.
5. Henry David Thoreau, *Über die Pflicht zum Ungehorsam gegen den Staat und andere Essays,* edited by W. E. Richarz (Zurich, 1973), 69.
6. Henry David Thoreau, *Walden or, Life in the Woods, and On the Duty of Civil Disobedience* (New York: Harper & Row, 1958), 260.
7. Ibid., 254.
8. Ibid., 261.
9. Ibid., 255.
10. Ibid., 258.
11. Ibid.
12. Ibid.
13. Ibid., 261.
14. Ibid., 252.
15. Ibid., 259.
16. Mohandas K. Gandhi, *The Words of Gandhi,* selected by Richard Attenborough (New York: Newmarket, 1982), 25.
17. Ibid., 51.
18. Rosa Parks, *Rosa Parks: My Story* (New York: Dial, 1992), 116.
19. Stephen B. Oates, *Let the Trumpet Sound: A Life of Martin Luther King, Jr.* (New York: Harper Perennial, 1994), 88.
20. Ibid., 88–89.
21. Martin Luther King, Jr., *A Testament of Hope: The Essential Writings and Speeches of Martin Luther King, Jr.,* edited by James M. Washington (New York: HarperCollins, 1986), 323.
22. Oates, *Let the Trumpet Sound,* 78.

23. B. Howard Thurman, "Mysticism and Social Change" in *Eden Theological Seminary Bulletin* (spring 1938), 28.

24. King, *Testament of Hope*, 256–57.

Chapter Fifteen

1. João Cabral de Melo Neto, *Tod und Leben des Severino* (St. Gallen and Wuppertal, 1985), 85–86.

2. Dorothee Soelle, *Stations of the Cross: A Latin American Pilgrimage*, translated by Joyce L. Irwin (Minneapolis: Fortress Press, 1993), 3–5.

3. J. Quint, ed., *Meister Eckhart: Deutsche Predigten und Traktate* (Munich, 1969), 183.

4. Pedro Casaldáliga, "Mystik der Befreiung" in *Mystik der Befreiung: Ein Portrait des Bischofs Pedro Casaldáliga n Brasilien* by Teófilo Cabastrero (Wuppertal, 1981), 13.

5. Ibid., 81, 72.

6. Ibid., 66.

7. Ibid., 80.

8. Ibid., 83–84.

9. Ibid., 78–79.

10. Ibid., 78–79.

11. Ibid., 149.

12. Ibid.

13. Ibid., 150.

14. Ibid., 87.

15. José de Broucker, *Dom Helder Camara: Die Leidenschaft des Friedensstifters* (Graz and Vienna, Cologne, 1969), 40.

16. Ibid., 45.

17. Helder Camara, *Mach aus mir einen Regenbogen: Mitternächtliche Meditationen* (Zurich, 1981), 63.

18. Ibid., 9.

19. Ibid., 24.

20. Ibid., 9.

21. Broucker, *Dom Helder Camara*, 241.

22. Camara, *Mach*, 10.

23. Casaldáliga, "Mystik der Befreiung," 159.

24. Martin Buber, *Ecstatic Confessions*, edited by Paul Mendes-Flohr, translated by Esther Cameron (San Francisco: Harper & Row, 1985), 63.

25. Leonardo Boff, *Von der Würde der Erde: Ökologie, Politik, Mystik* (Düsseldorf, 1994), 141.

26. Angelus Silesius, *Cherubini: ScherWandersmann*, ed. L. Gnädinger (Stuttgart, 1984), 1:9.

27. Ernesto Cardenal, *Cosmic Canticle*, trans. Jonathan Lyons (Willimantic, Conn.: Curbstone, 1993).

BIBLIOGRAPHY

Angelus Silesius. *Sämtliche Poetische Werke.* Vol. 3. Edited by Hans Ludwig Held. Munich: Carl Hanser Verlag, 1949.
——. *Cherubinischer Wandersmann.* Edited by L. Gnädinger. Stuttgart, 1984.
Bachmann, Ingeborg. *Songs in Flight: The Collected Poems.* Translated by P. Filkins. New York: Marsilio, 1994.
——. *Werke,* 4 vols. Munich, 1982.
Barth, Karl. *Ethics.* Translated by Geoffrey W. Bromily. New York: Seabury, 1981.
Berry, Wendell. *The Wild Birds.* San Francisco: North Point, 1986.
Black Elk. *Black Elk Speaks: Being the Life Story of a Holy Man of the Oglala Sioux.* New York: Pocket Books, 1972.
Bloch, Ernst. *Thomas Müntzer: Als Theologe der Revolution.* Frankfurt on Main, 1962.
——. *The Principle of Hope.* Translated by Neville Plaice, Stephen Plaice, and Paul Knight. Cambridge, Mass.: MIT Press, 1986.
Boff, Leonardo. *Von der Würde der Erde: Ökologie, Politik, Mystik.* Düsseldorf, 1994.
Boldt, Johannes, ed. and trans. *Johannes vom Kreuz.* Olten, 1980.
Bonhoeffer, Dietrich. *Widerstand und Ergebung.* Vol. 8 of *Dietrich Bonhoeffer Werke.* Gütersloh: Gütersloher Verlagshaus, 1998.
Brinton, Howard H. *Friends for 300 Years: The History and Beliefs of the Society of Friends since George Fox Started the Quaker Movement.* Wallingford, Pa.: Pendle Hill Quakerback, 1983.
Brodribb, Somer. *Nothing Mat(t)ers: A Feminist Critique of Postmodernism.* Toronto: Lorimer, 1992.
Broucker, José de. *Dom Helder Camara: Die Leidenschaft des Friedensstifters.* Graz and Vienna, Cologne, 1969.
Brown, Joseph Epes, ed. *The Gift of the Sacred Pipe: Based on Black Elk's Account of the Seven Rites of the Oglala Sioux as Originally Recorded and Edited by Joseph Epes Brown.* Norman, Okla.: Univ. of Oklahoma Press, 1982.
Buber, Martin. *Tales of the Hasidim: Early Masters, Later Masters.* New York: Schocken, 1947 and 1948.
——. *Werke I: Schriften zur Philosophie.* Heidelberg: Verlag Lambert Schneider, 1962.
——. *Werke III: Schriften zum Chassidismus.* Heidelberg: Verlag Lambert Schneider, 1963.
——. *Nachlese.* Heidelberg: Verlag Lambert Schneider, 1965.
——. *I and Thou.* Translated by Walter Kaufmann. New York: Scribner's, 1970.

————. *Ecstatic Confessions*. Edited by Paul Mendes-Flohr. Translated by Esther Cameron. San Francisco: Harper & Row, 1985.

————. *Buber für Atheisten: Ausgewählte Texte*. Edited by Thomas Reichert. Gerlingen, 1996.

Cabastrero, Teófilo. *Mystik der Befreiung: Ein Portrait des Bischofs Pedro Casaldáliga in Brasilien*. Wuppertal, 1981.

Cabral de Melo Neto, João. *Tod und Leben des Severino*. St. Gallen and Wuppertal, 1985.

Camara, Helder. *Mach aus mir einen Regenbogen: Mitternächtliche Meditationen*. Zurich, 1981.

————. *Stimme der stummen Welt*. Zurich, 1989.

Cardenal, Ernesto. *Das Buch von der Liebe*. Wuppertal, 1985.

Casaldáliga, Pedro. "Mystik der Befreiung." In *Mystik der Befreiung: Ein Portrait des Bischofs Pedro Casaldáliga in Brasilien* by Teófilo Cabastrero. Wuppertal, 1981.

Devlin, Dennis. "Feminine Lay Piety in the High Middle Ages: The Beguines," in *Medieval Religious Women*, edited by John A. Nichols and Lillian Thomas Shank. Vol. 1: *Distant Echoes*. Kalamazoo, Mich.: Cistercian, 1984.

Dinzelbacher, Peter. *Christliche Mystik im Abendland: Ihre Geschichte von den Anfängen bis zum Ende des Mittelalters*. Paderborn, 1994.

————, ed. *Wörterbuch der Mystik*. Stuttgart, 1989.

Dinzelbacher, Peter, and Bauer, Dieter, eds. *Religiöse Frauenbewegung und mystische Frömmigkeit im Mittelalter*. Cologne, Vienna, 1988.

Dronke, Peter. *Women Writers of the Middle Ages. A Critical Study of Texts from Perpetua to Marguerite Porète*. Cambridge: Cambridge Univ. Press, 1984.

Eco, Umberto. *Der Name der Rose*. München, 1980.

————. *The Name of the Rose*. San Diego: Harcourt Brace Jovanovich, 1983.

Endres, Elisabeth. *Edith Stein: Christliche Philosophin und jüdische Märtyrerin*. Munich, 1987.

Felipe, Leon. *Versos y orisones de caminante*. Madrid, 1981.

Forest, James H. "Thomas Merton's Struggle with Peacemaking," in *Thomas Merton: Prophet in the Belly of a Paradox*, edited by Gerald Twomey. New York: Paulist, 1978.

Forest, Jim. *Love Is the Measure. A Biography of Dorothy Day*. New York: Paulist, 1986.

Fox, Matthew. *Vision vom Kosmischen Christus: Abufbruch ins dritte Jahrtausend*. Stuttgart, 1991.

————. *Wrestling with the Prophets: Essays on Creation, Spirituality, and Everyday Life*. San Francisco: HarperSanFrancisco, 1995.

————. *The Coming of the Cosmic Christ: The Healing of Mother Earth and the Birth of a Global Renaissance*. San Francisco: Harper and Row, 1988.

————, introd. and commentaries. *Breakthrough: Meister Eckhart's Creation Spirituality, in New Translation*. Garden City, N.J.: Doubleday, 1980.

Francis of Assisi, Saint. *Legenden und Laude*. Edited and translated by Otto Karrer. Zürich, 1975.

Franck, Frederick, trans. *The Book of Angelus Silesius, with Observations by the Ancient Zen Masters*. New York: Vintage, 1976.

Fremantle, Anne, ed. *The Protestant Mystics*. New York: Mentor, 1965.

Fromm, Erich. *To Have Or To Be?* New York: Harper & Row, 1976.

Fuchs, Gotthard, ed. *Die dunkle Nacht der Sinne: Leiderfahrung und christliche Mystik*. Düsseldorf, 1989.

Füssel, Kuno. "Brennende Liebe. Zu Schicksal und Werk der Begine Margareta Porète," in *Für Gerechtigkeit streiten: Theologie im Alltag einer bedrohten Welt*, edited by Dorothee Soelle. Gütersloh: Gütersloher Verlagshaus, 1994.

Gandhi, Mohandas K. *Non-Violent Resistance (Satyagraha)*. New York: Schocken Books, 1961.

———. *The Words of Gandhi*. Selected by Richard Attenborough. New York: Newmarket, 1982.

Goertz, Hans-Jürgen. *Thomas Müntzer: Mystiker, Apokalyptiker, Revolutionär*. Munich, 1989.

———. *Thomas Müntzer: Apocalyptic, Mystic, and Revolutionary*. Edinburgh: T&T Clark, 1993.

Gössmann, Elisabeth. "Die Geschichte und Lehre derMystikerin Marguerite Porète," in *Gegenentwürfe: 24 Lebensläufe für eine andere Theologie*, edited by Hermann Häring and Karl-Josef Kuschel. Munich, 1988.

Gutiérrez, Gustavo. *On Job: God-Talk and the Suffering of the Innocent*. Translated by Matthew J. O'Connell. Maryknoll, N.Y.: Orbis, 1987.

Haas, Alois M. "Die dunkle Nacht der Sinne und des Geistes: Mystische Leidenserfahrung nach Johannes vom Kreuz," in *Die dunkle Nacht der Sinne: Leidenserfahrung und christliche Mystik*, edited by G. Fuchs. Düsseldorf, 1989.

Hallaj, al-Husayn ibn Mansur. *Märtyrer der Gottesliebe: Leben und Legende*. Edited and translated by Annemarie Schimmel. Cologne, 1968.

Hammarskjöld, Dag. *Markings*. Translated by Leif Sjöberg and W. H. Auden. London: Faber and Faber, 1964.

Happold, F. C. *Mysticism: A Study and an Anthology*. Harmondsworth: Penguin, 1963.

Heid, Ulrich. "Studien zu Marguerite Porète und ihrem *Miroir des simples âmes*," in *Religiöse Frauenbewegung und mystische Frömmigkeit im Mittelalter*, edited by Peter Dinzelbacher and Dieter R. Bauer. Cologne and Vienna, 1988.

Herbstrith, Waltraud, ed. *Edith Stein: Ein Lebensbild in Zeugnissen und Selbstzeugnissen*. Mainz, 1993.

Heschel, Abraham. *God in Search of Man: A Philosophy of Judaism*. New York: Harper & Row, 1955.

Hildegard von Bingen. *Briefwechsel*. Translated by Adelgundis Führkötter. Salzburg, 1965.

Huxley, Aldous. *The Perennial Philosophy.* New York: Harper & Row, 1945.

James, William. *The Letters of William James.* Edited by Henry James. Vol. 2. London: Longmans, Green, 1920.

———. *The Varieties of Religious Experience.* New York: Modern Library, 1929.

Jaspert, B., ed. *Leiden und Weisheit in der Mystik.* Paderborn, 1992.

Jensen, Anne. "Im Kampf um Freiheit in Kirche und Staat: Die 'Mutter des Quäkertums' Margaret Fell" in *Gegenentwürfe: 24 Lebensläufe für eine andere Theologie,* edited by Hermann Häring and K. J. Kuschel. Munich, 1988.

Katz, Stephen, ed. *Mysticism and Philosophical Analysis.* New York: Oxford Univ. Press, 1978.

King, Martin Luther, Jr. *A Testament of Hope: The Essential Writings and Speeches of Martin Luther King, Jr.* Edited by James M. Washington. New York: HarperCollins, 1986.

———. *Mein Traum vom Ende des Hassens: Texte für heute.* Freiburg i. Br., 1994.

Lawrence, D. H. *The Rainbow.* London: Heinemann, 1977.

Lerner, Gerda. *Die Entstehung des feministischen Bewußtseins: Vom Mittelalter bis zur Ersten Frauenbewegung.* Frankfurt and New York, 1993.

Levinas, Emmanuel. *Difficult Freedom: Essays on Judaism.* Translated by Seán Hand. Baltimore, Md.: Johns Hopkins Univ. Press, 1990.

Lewis, C. S. *Surprised by Joy.* London: Geoffrey Bles, 1955.

McGinn, Bernard. *The Presence of God: A History of Western Christian Mysticism.* Vol. 1: *The Foundations of Mysticism.* New York: Crossroad, 1991.

Mendes-Flohr, Paul. "Editor's Introduction" in *Ecstatic Confessions* by Martin Buber. New York: Harper & Row, 1985.

Merton, Thomas. *Raids on the Unspeakable.* New York: New Directions, 1966.

Mommaers, Paul. *Was ist Mystik?* Frankfurt, 1979.

Müntzer, Thomas. *Die Fürstenpredigt: Theologisch-politische Schriften.* Edited by G. Franz. Stuttgart, 1967.

———. *Schriften und Briefe: Edited by Gerhard Wehr.* Frankfurt: Fischer Bücherei, 1973.

Navarre, Marguerite de. *Les Prisons.* Edited by Simone Glasson. Geneva, 1978. [Citations are derived from Emilie Zum Brunn and Georgette Epiney-Brugard, eds. *Women Mystics in Medieval Europe.* Translated by Sheila Hughes. New York: Paragon, 1989.]

Nhat Hanh, Thich. *The Miracle of Mindfulness: A Manual on Mindfulness.* London: Rider, 1992.

———. *Nenne mich bei meinem wahren Namen: Gesammelte Gedichte.* Berlin, 1997.

Nigg, Walter. *Heimliche Weisheit: Mystisches Leben in der Evangelischen Christenheit.* Zurich, 1959.

Oates, Stephen B. *Let the Trumpet Sound: A Life of Martin Luther King, Jr.* New York: Harper Perennial, 1994.

O'Brien, Elmer, S.J. *Varieties of Mystic Experience: An Anthology and Interpretation.* New York: Holt, Rinehart and Winston, 1964.

Oehl, Wilhelm, ed. *Deutsche Mystikerbriefe des Mittelalters: 100–1550.* Darmstadt, 1972.

Otto, Elisabeth. "Kreuzeswissenschsft als Anteilhaben am Leiden Christi. Die Mystik Edith Steins," in *Leiden und Weisheit in der Mystik,* edited by B. Jaspert. Paderborn, 1992.

Otto, Rudolf. *Mysticism East and West: A Comparative Analysis of the Nature of Mysticism.* Translated by Bertha L. Bracey and Richenda C. Payne. 1932. New York: Macmillan, 1962.

Parks, Rosa, with Jim Haskins. *Rosa Parks: My Story.* New York: Dial, 1992.

Porète, Marguerite. *The Mirror of Simple Souls.* Translated by Ellen L. Babinsky. New York: Paulist, 1993.

Pseudo-Dionysius. *The Complete Works.* Translated by Colm Luibheid. New York: Paulist, 1987.

Quint, J., ed. *Meister Eckhart: Deutsche Predigten und Traktate.* Munich, 1969.

Rahner, Karl. *Theological Investigations.* Vol VII. Translated by David Bourke. New York: Herder and Herder, 1971.

———. *Praxis des Glaubens: Geistliches Lesebuch.* Freiburg i. Br., 1982.

Rilke, Rainer Maria. *Neue Gedichte.* Leipzig, 1907.

Rosenzweig, Franz. *The Star of Redemption.* Translated by William W. Hallo. Boston: Beacon, 1964.

Ruh, Kurt. *Meister Eckhart: Theologe, Prediger, Mystiker.* Munich, 1989.

Ruhbach, Gerhard, and Josef Sudbrack, eds. *Große Mystiker: Leben und Wirken.* Munich, 1984.

Schimmel, Annemarie. *Rumi: Ich bin Wind und du bist Feuer: Leben und Werk des großen Mystikers.* 1978. Munich, 1990.

———. *Mystische Dimensionen des Islam: Die Geschichte des Sufismus.* Munich, 1992.

———. *Mystical Dimension of Islam.* Chapel Hill: Univ. of North Carolina Press, 1975.

Schmid, Georg. *Die Mystik der Weltreligionen: Eine Einführung.* Stuttgart, 1990.

Schmid-Leukel, Perry. "Das Problem von Gewalt und Krieg in der buddhistischen Ethik" in *Dialog der Religionen 6,* no. 2. Gütersloh, 1996.

Schmidt, Margot. "'Frau Pein Ihr seid mein nächstes Kleid': Zur Leidensmystik im Fließenden Licht der Gottheit der Mechthild von Magdeburg," in *Die dunkle Nacht der Sinne: Leiderfahrung und christliche Mystik,* edited Gotthard Fuchs. Düsseldorf, 1989.

Schneider, Reinhold. *Pfeiler im Strom: Essays.* Wiesbaden, 1958.

———. *Winter in Wien: Aus meinen Notizbüchern,* 1957–58. Freiburg i. Br., 1958.

Scholem, Gershom. *Von der mystischen Gestalt der Gottheit: Studien zu Grundbegriffen der Kabbala.* Frankfurt, 1995.

Schütz, Christian, ed. *Praktisches Lexikon der Spiritulität.* Freiburg i. Br., 1988.

Seuse, Heinrich. *Deutsche Mystische Schriften.* Edited and translated by Georg Hoffmann. Düsseldorf: Patmos, 1966.

Soelle, Dorothee. *Suffering.* Translated by Everett R. Kalin. Philadelphia: Fortress Press, 1975.

———. *Death by Bread Alone.* Translated by David L. Scheidt. Philadelphia: Fortress Press, 1978.

———. *The Window of Vulnerability: A Political Spirituality.* Translated by Linda M. Maloney. Minneapolis: Fortress Press, 1990.

———. *Stations of the Cross: A Latin American Pilgrimage.* Translated by Joyce L. Irwin. Minneapolis: Fortress Press, 1993.

———. *Mutanfälle: Texte zum Umdenken.* Hamburg: Hoffmann und Kampe, 1993.

———. *Gewalt: Ich soll mich nicht gewöhnen.* Düsseldorf, 1994.

Stace, Walter T. *The Teaching of the Mystics.* New York: Mentor, 1960.

Sudbrack, Josef. *Erfahrung einer Liebe: Teresa von Avilas Mystik als Begegnung mit Gott.* Freiburg i. Br., 1979.

Thiele, Johannes. *Perlen der Mystik.* Freiburg i. Br., 1989.

Thoreau, Henry David. *Walden or, Life in the Woods, and On the Duty of Civil Disobedience.* New York: Harper & Row, 1958.

———. *Über die Pflicht zum Ungehorsam gegen den Staat und andere Essays.* Edited by W. E. Richarz. Zurich, 1973.

Thurman, B. Howard. "Mysticism and Social Change" in *Eden Theological Seminary Bulletin,* spring 1938.

Tourn, Giorgio. *Geschichte der Waldenser-Kirche: Die einzigartige Geschichte einer Volkskirche von 1170 bis zur Gegenwart.* Erlangen, 1980.

Unger, Helga, ed. *Der Berg der Liebe. Europäische Frauenmystik.* Freibug i. Br., 1991.

Walsh, James, S.J., ed. *The Cloud of Unknowing.* New York: Paulist, 1981.

Wehr, Gerhard. *Deutsche Mystik: Gestalten und Zeugnisse religiöser Erfahrung von Meister Eckhart bis zur Reformationszeit.* Gütersloh, Gütersloher Verlagshaus, 1980.

Weil, Simone. *Schwerkraft und Gnade.* Munich, 1952.

———. *Das Unglück und die Gottesliebe.* Munich, 1953.

———. *The Simone Weil Reader.* Edited by George A. Panichas. New York: McKay, 1977.

———. *Fabriktagebuch und andere Schriften zum Industriesystem.* Frankfurt, 1978.

Woolman, John. *The Journal and Major Essays of John Woolman.* Edited by Phillips P. Moulton. New York: Oxford Univ. Press, 1971.

Zohar: The Book of Enlightenment. Translated by Daniel Chanan Matt. New York: Paulist, 1983.

Zum Brunn, Emilie and Georgette Epiney-Brugard, eds. *Women Mystics in Medieval Europe.* Translated by Sheila Hughes. New York: Paragon, 1989.

INDEX